REDEEMING PHILOSOPHY

REDEEMING PHILOSOPHY

From Metaphysics to Aesthetics

EDITED BY JOHN J. CONLEY, S.J.

AMERICAN MARITAIN ASSOCIATION

Distributed by

THE CATHOLIC UNIVERSITY
OF AMERICA PRESS

Washington, D.C.

Manufactured in the United States of America

Distributed by the Catholic Univesity of America Press
620 Michigan Avenue, N.E., 240 Leahy Hall
Washington, D.C. 20064

Library of Congress Cataloging-in-Publication Data
Redeeming philosophy from metaphysics to aesthetics /
edited by John J. Conley, SJ.
pages cm
Includes index.
1. Catholic Church and philosophy. 2. Philosophy.
3. Maritain, Jacques, 1882–1973. Ransoming the time.
I. Conley, John J., editor of compilation.
BX1795.P47R43 2014
149'.91—dc23
2013047638

ISBN 978-0-9827119-6-5

CONTENTS

Introduction: Disputed Questions of Redemption
John J. Conley, S.J. vii

I. METAPHYSICAL TURN

Being and the Twenty-First Century Thomist
John F. X. Knasas 3

Natural Mysticism—Gateway or Detour? Aquinas, Maritain, and the Core/Contextualist Debate *Heather M. Erb* 23

Simon and Maritain on the Vocation of *Species in Medio* *Daniel D. De Haan* 54

Incarnate Spirit: Proper Thomistic Definition of the Human Being or Merely a Description of the Human Soul? *James Capehart* 83

Maritain on the Void *Michael Novak* 99

II. THEOLOGICAL TURN

Christ's *Esse* and Filiation: Interpreting St. Thomas on the Metaphysical Status of Christ's Human Nature
Roger W. Nutt 115

The Proper Role of Credibility in the Work of Theology
James F. Keating 130

Jacques Maritain, Charles Journet, and *Humanae Vitae*
Bernard Doering 150

Sign, Symbol, Initiatory Sacrament *John J. Conley, S.J.* 163

Contents

III. HISTORICAL TURN

Hope and History *Randall B. Smith* 173

IV. AESTHETIC TURN

Spiritual Expressionism: Léon Bloy, the Maritains, and the Mystery of Israel *C. A. Tsakiridou* 203

Maritain's Influence on American Literature *John Marson Dunaway* 226

The Sound and the Fury, Symbolizing Something: Maritain and Percy on the Paradoxical Miracle at the Limits of Language *Joshua Hren* 235

V. SOCIAL TURN

Maritain on Education *Anne M. Wiles* 253

Aristotle's Gentleman: A Good and Noble Philosophy of Education *Samantha Bertrand* 263

Two False Theories of Human Equality Identified by Jacques Maritain: Applied to Feminist Issues *Bernadette E. O'Connor* 280

Philosophy and the Search for Peace *Nikolaj Zunic* 297

Moral Problems in Economic Organization in the Work of Yves R. Simon: Unequal Exchange and Man as the Principle of Integration *Thomas R. Rourke* 313

About the Authors 333

Index 337

JOHN J. CONLEY, S.J.

Introduction

Disputed Questions of Redemption

Jacques Maritain's *Redeeming the Time* is a collection of essays treating a wide diversity of philosophical subjects.[1] Topics covered include metaphysics, politics, religion, semiotics, mysticism, progress, love, skepticism, and anti-Semitism. Prominent philosophers treated range from Pascal to Bergson. In his foreword to the English translation of his work, Maritain himself recognized the disparate nature of the issues analyzed by the various essays. But he insisted that the work still possessed an underlying unity: the essays apply the perennial truths of Thomistic philosophy to the pressing social issues of his time, the tormented period of the Depression and the early years of World War II. "I believe ... that philosophy attains its aims, particularly in practical matters, only when vitally united with every source of light and experience in the human mind. Thus it becomes able, in its own intellectual domain, to ransom the time, and to redeem every human search after truth, however it wanders, in manifold, even opposite ways."[2] As the essays unfold, Maritain uses the philosophical realism of Aquinas to correct erroneous views on equality, justice, religious tolerance, progress, and the Jews that were current at the time. The originality of Maritain's version of Thomism appears in his sympathetic but critical analysis of Bergsonian intuition and in his use of the term *connaturality* to explore the phenomenon of mystical knowledge.

1. See Jacques Maritain, *Redeeming the Time,* translated by Harry Lorin Bisse (London: Geoffrey Bles: The Centenary Press, 1944). An earlier version of this translation was published as *Ransoming the Time* (New York: Charles Scribner's Sons, 1941).

2. Ibid., v.

Maritain's *Redeeming the Time* inspired the collection of philosophical essays we are presenting in our new anthology *Redeeming Philosophy: From Metaphysics to Aesthetics*. Maritain's book remains the prime reference and point of continuity for the authors in this volume, but not all provide a philosophical commentary on the actual text of Maritain. Each of the essays, however, follows Maritain's fundamental project in *Redeeming the Time*: the use of the resources of philosophical realism, as found in the works of Aristotle and Aquinas, to challenge and redeem a certain defect in contemporary social relations or in contemporary philosophy. Using the different analytical methods of philosophy, theology, history, literary criticism, and political science, the authors develop a realist critique of contemporary theories of human nature, Christology, equality, gender, and education. Walker Percy and contemporary American feminists now enjoy the critical realist analysis Maritain had once employed to interpret Pascal and Bergson.

I. From Metaphysics to Aesthetics

Despite their diversity, the five metaphysical papers all exhibit the "personalist" turn which characterized much of the Thomistic philosophy developed in the twentieth century. Analysis of being-in-itself is conjoined with analysis of the subject who comes to know being and of the various paths of cognition by which the noetic agent arrives at the recognition of being itself.

John F. X. Knasas studies the human person as an abstractor of being. Rather than passively gazing upon being or dispassionately analyzing its nature or implications, the dynamic subject abstracts being from the external world and forms an internal concept of being that incorporates the awe and other passions provoked by the recognition of being as such. In her study of contemplation, Heather M. Erb sides with Maritain and Aquinas in arguing for the link between mystical knowledge and dogma. Even natural mysticism, apparently spontaneous and free from dogmatic commitments, operates within a community marked by at least implicit religious doctrines. In his study of the metaphysics of Yves Simon, longtime friend of Maritain, Daniel De Haan argues that the transcendentals are already present in the act of sensation when the noetic agent grasps the *species in medio*. The agent is an intentional actor rather than a passive blank slate in the presence of the external material world. James Capehart's paper turns to questions of philosophical anthropology. In a defense of hylomorphism, he rejects the theory that the human person is an incarnate spirit; such an approach smacks of angelism and minimizes the properly corporeal dimension of humanity. Similarly, he rejects the claims of some Thomistic commentators that Aquinas himself had held the "incarnate spirit" view. In his commentary on the last essay in *Redeeming the Time,* "The Natural Mystical Experience and the Void," Michael Novak relates Maritain's theory of the void to the nihilism found in existentialists of the period, notably Sartre and Camus. He demonstrates how Maritain's combat against this nihilism through the path of mysticism can illuminate contemporary citizens who often experience a vertiginous void before the dazzling array of choices offered by a consumer society—choices which concern religious affiliation, moral commitments, family arrangements, and sexuality as much as they concern food, fashion, and recreation.

The theological essays similarly cover a wide spectrum of topics: Christology, moral controversies, the sacraments, and the practice of theology itself. They explore how Maritain's brand of Thomism might assist the church in understanding the theoretical and practical controversies which have roiled her since Vatican II.

Roger W. Nutt transfers the metaphysical question of essence to the field of Christology. He underlines that Aquinas insisted there was a single divine essence uniting and animating the two natures (divine/human) in Christ. He criticizes treatments of Christological essence which subtly downplay Christ's unity. James F. Keating's essay insists on the duty for Catholic theology to be credible in every generation. He criticizes the tendency of some contemporary theologians, appalled by the hostile anti-Christian nature of elite opinion, to form a Neo-Scholastic cocoon impervious to external intellectual trends and questions. He uses ecclesiastical history to argue that the quest to show that the faith is reasonable to its cultured despisers has always been one of the church's prime intellectual objectives. Bernard Doering studies Maritain's position on the most controversial moral issue in the church toward the end of Maritain's life: contraception. Analyzing the letters exchanged on the subject between Maritain and Cardinal Charles Journet, a prominent Swiss theologian, Doering explains why Maritain was not convinced by the natural lawyers' traditional arguments but also why Maritain attempted to provide convincing reasons for priests to support Paul VI's defense of the ban on contraception in *Humane Vitae* (1968). Turning to the practical life of worship, John J. Conley uses the semiotic theory of Maritain to probe the practice of the sacraments in their reformed version established in the wake of Vatican II.

History is the focus of Randall Smith's paper. He criticizes the gradual erosion of meaning in the ancient Judeo-Christian version of history. This linear version of history, which replaced the cyclical account of history more common among the pagan Greeks, was a history marked by hope, since it conceived history as a series of milestones pointing toward the coming of the Messiah, the return of Christ, the parousia, and the divinely-graced new heaven and new earth. But as faith in Christ declined, hope gradually vanished and the linear history now stumbled on under a veil of nihilism. The Victorian agnostic writer Matthew Arnold becomes the literary symbol of the educated person who can no longer find meaning in the claims of religion and finds disenchanted nature of little solace. According to Smith, only a revival of faith, focused on Christ and his grace, can bring authentic hope to contemporaries who now tend to choose the quiet nihilism of self-indulgence or the violent nihilism of political utopianism.

Aesthetic and literary concerns were always central in the philosophy of Jacques and Raïssa Maritain. The novelist Léon Bloy, the painter Georges Rouault, the dramatist Henri Ghéon, and the surrealist Jean Cocteau became close friends and correspondents with the couple. Their salon at Meudon became the center of many artists and writers associated with the *Renaissance catholique* of the interwar years.[3] The essays presented in our current anthology emphasize the literary influences on and of Jacques Maritain as his work became diffused throughout the francophone and Anglophone worlds.

Commenting on the essay "The Mystery of Israel" in *Redeeming the Time*, C. A. Tsakiridou questions the nature of the defense of the Jews and the critique of anti-Semitism developed by Maritain. In his portrait of Israel as a people doomed to endless exile and the sufferings of an elect nation, Tsakiridou detects the unbenign influence of the black mysticism of suffering championed by Maritain's early mentor, Léon Bloy, and his later colleagues, Georges Rouault and Jean Cocteau. In an exercise in literary history, John Marson Dunaway studies the specific influences of Maritain on two American writers: Caroline Gordon and Flannery O'Connor. Responding to "Sign and Symbol" in *Redeeming the Time*, Joshua Hren estab-

3. For a discussion of the large artistic circle of the Maritains, see Stephen Schloesser, *Jazz Age Catholicism: Mystical Modernism in Postwar Paris, 1919–1933*, 2nd ed. (Toronto: University of Toronto Press, 2005).

lishes a parallel between the semiotics of Maritain and that of the American novelist Walker Percy. In particular, he addresses the fascination of each author for the limits of language as a method of self-communication.

Throughout his life Maritain was involved as a public intellectual in various causes of social reform. His writings on education tried to heal the fissure between the Catholic Church and the anticlerical republic on the question of French education. He was a principal influence on the Declaration of Human Rights drawn up at the founding of the United Nations. Somewhat to the consternation of other Thomists, he attempted to provide philosophical justification for the parliamentary democracies which had survived the totalitarian nightmare of the middle of the twentieth century. Inspired by Maritain and more broadly by the Aristotelian-Thomistic tradition he represents, several essays in our collection develop a critique of contemporary social practices and theories from the perspective of philosophical realism. Education, equality, peacemaking, and economic justice pass in review.

Anne M. Wiles's study of education explains how Maritain places human personality at the center of his philosophy of education. Samantha Bertrand reaches further back to Aristotle to indicate how Aristotle properly prized formation to become a gentleman as the principal end of education. She champions this Aristotelian emphasis on character formation as a necessary, humanistic corrective to the more functionalist practices of education current today. Bernadette E. O'Connor uses Maritain's essay, "Human Inequality," in *Redeeming the Time* to correct several distorted theories of equality defended by some contemporary American feminists. On a more mystical note, Nikolaj Zunic argues that the quest for peace can only find fulfillment in the peace and harmony achieved within the individual mind. Purely political efforts to eradicate conflict will only disappoint. In his study of the Thomist philosopher Yves Simon's economic philosophy, Thomas R. Rourke argues that Simon focused the modern drive for economic equality on the struggle to remove institutionalized forms of unequal exchange.

II. Prospectus

The essays collected in this volume, all authored by members of the American Maritain Association, indicate the particular issues which will probably preoccupy Thomistic philosophers in the near future.

First, the question of the person recurs in many of these essays. The definition of the human person remains a political as well as a metaphysical controversy. How is personhood reconciled with the hylomorphic definition of human nature? How does human personhood differ from the angelic and divine? What are we to make of our close relationship to other simians, a closeness made ever more obvious through new genetic discoveries? The onset and cessation of human personhood remain philosophical questions which are currently ripping apart national and international society. Educating for virtuous personhood is a noble goal, but just what are the methods which advance or obstruct such a project?

Second, Thomism has a particular service to offer the church in her current theological reflection. In a time of vague spirituality which concedes much to idiosyncratic experience, Thomist authors stress objective precision as they discuss the natures of Christ and the visible marks of the true Church. In contradistinction to a purely internal mysticism, Thomists focus on the specific traits of the sacraments, right down to form and matter. During a time when moral reflection tends to emphasize intention and circumstance, Thomist ethics underlines the moral significance of the specific human act.

Third, the Maritainian variant of Thomism in particular refuses to limit philosophical analysis to the study of propositional phrases. In the world of human symbolic expression, poetry, music, and painting become the object of extensive philosophical exploration. The locus of truth cannot be reduced to scientific discourse alone. Beyond the artistic symbols created by humanity as expressions of the rational soul lies the silence of the mystic, much explored by Maritain and his disciples under the rubric of connaturality. Rather than being marginal, such silent knowing constitutes the highest knowledge of the human person, the moment at which the sublime simplicity of God begins to possess the human soul, otherwise so scattered.

Finally, the Thomist authors gathered in this collection indicate the various ways in which Thomism constitutes an exercise in being a public intellectual. The philosophical argument is never far from the medieval *disputatio*. Thomists will continue to use the resources of philosophical realism to contest the distorted theories of human nature which have sanctioned our ambient culture of death and reduced education to vo-tech drills. In this new age of *in vitro* fertilization and the iPad, the old Thomist quarrel with modernity's illusions of progress fights on.

≈ I ≈

METAPHYSICAL TURN

JOHN F. X. KNASAS

Being and the Twenty-First Century Thomist

While in the second grade my son had to do a report on the theme "What does my Daddy do?" So one evening I sat down with him and began to answer by saying, "Well, I study and teach philosophy." So far so good as I helped John write down "philosophy" by spelling it out. But John's next question was "And what is philosophy about?." If I did not know my son, I would have felt a trap being laid for me. On the one hand, I could answer boringly and prosaically by giving the usual litany of all the issues with which philosophy deals. On the other hand, I could cut to the chase and answer the question in its truest and most direct, but unfortunately esoteric, fashion. I went for the latter. "John, philosophy is about being." Instantly I could see the glaze form over his young eyes and I knew that I had just lost communication. Yes, there is something weird about the word "being" such that its mention invariably causes mental static to break out in one's hearers. Nevertheless, the topic of being witnessed a great revival in the twentieth century. I am thinking of the popularity of Heidegger and Sartre and the thinkers of the Thomistic revival. The greater popularity appears to have gone to the first two because both were able to combine discussion of being with the drama of human subjectivity. Undoubtedly this combination was because both Heidegger and Sartre, like so many others since Kant, had made the transcendental turn. In fact, among the twenthieth century Thomists it was the Transcendental Thomists Rahner and Lonergan who proved to have the greater staying power. Other Thomists (let us call them the "Neo-Thomists") discussed being as an abstraction from things and so missed the subject as subject. When they discussed the subject, they did it in terms of categories taken from things. Hence their treatment of the subject appeared to be too objective, too cool, too non-historical, to interest the current philosophical public. This criticism of Neo-Thomism can be discerned in Lonergan's remarks about the neglected and truncated subject in his 1968 Marquette Aquinas lecture entitled, *The Subject.*

I believe that there has understandably been some dropping of the ball by the Neo-Thomists. Because Kantian-style transcendental thinkers have lionized subjectivity in philosophy, Neo-Thomists have avoided a topic that they fear would cost them their metaphysics. And so I want to illustrate how one can exploit the Neo-Thomist understanding of the person as an abstractor of being to allow the entire spectrum of human subjectivity to parade before the philosopher's eyes.

I. Being as "the Bird that is a Flock"

What do I mean by "being?" I mean an intelligibility. By an intelligibility I mean a commonality, a sameness, grasped in the real things given in sensation, that is, in what you are aware of right now as you look this way and listen.[1] For example, my awareness of this right angle triangle, this isosceles triangle, and this equilateral triangle is more than an awareness of three figures. More accurately speaking, my awareness is of three figures *with something in common.* We mean to express this commonality by the word "triangle." The portion of our awareness that bears upon commonalities is called "intellection" or "conceptualization."

In his *Disputed Questions on Truth* q. 1, and q. 21, a. 1, Aquinas explains that there are two kinds of commonalities. On the one hand, we can intellect a commonality apart from the differences of the individual instances. "Triangle" is such a case. The proof lies in the reflection that its differences can be found in non-triangular figures. The right angle that is the difference of the first figure can be found in a rectangle; the two equal sides of the iscoceles triangle can be in a quadrilateral, and so on. In sum, if we intellected the commonality within the very differences, then the differences

1. Aquinas describes *ens* as a *ratio* and an *aliquid unum* (*In I Sent.*, Prol. q. 1, a. 2, ad 2m), as a *natura communis* (*In I Sent.*, d. 19, q. 5, a. 2, ad 1m), as *commune* (*In Meta*, proem) and as *universale* (*De veritate* [DV] I, q. 21, a. 1). These are all ways of speaking about the intellect's absolute consideration or first operation, conceptualization.

would carry the sameness wherever they appeared. But the differences do not. Commonalities of this type are called univocal commonalities.

On the other hand, we also intellect commonalities precisely within the very differences of the instances. This alternative might sound unbelievable. It seems to have been missed by Scotus who thought that if there was an intelligible unity between things, then *ipso facto* it must be univocal.[2] Consider the manner in which sanctity, or love of God, is applied to Teresa of Avila and to Francis Xavier. The first was a contemplative, the second a missionary. Yet different as these are, in the cases of Teresa and Francis they have a sameness that allows one to call each a saint. The very thing that makes Teresa different from Francis, namely, her contemplation, is the very thing that makes her the same as Francis, and vice versa. So to find what makes both the same, you have to go to the very things that differentiate both. The sameness lies in the differences. A double check lies in the realization that wherever you find contemplation like Teresa's, you find a great lover of God. Because the difference drags along the sameness, the sameness must be understood as within, not apart from, the difference.

Commonalities that behave in this manner are called analogical concepts. Scholastics also called them analogons. The instances that by their differences convey the analogon the Scholastics called analogates.[3] Hence, "saint" is the analogon, while Teresa and Francis are analogates of it. Because analogous concepts are samenesses perceived within differences, they lack the clarity and distinctness of univocal concepts that, as mentioned, we apprehend apart from the differences of the instances. Yet what analogons give up in clarity and distinctness, they make up for in richness of content. The analogates of Teresa and Francis enable us dimly to perceive the analogon of "great lover of God" that contains these analogates plus who knows how many more. We know that a Christian who lived in the fifth century would have been a fool to claim that he had seen all that there was to see of "great lover of God." Even though our Christian would have known Peter, Stephen, and Augustine, he would not yet have seen

2. In the Middle Ages, others, e.g., Thomas of Sutton and Hervaeus Natalis, denied a notion of being by claiming the notion was a disjunction. So what we meant by being was the understanding that things are either infinite or finite, substance or accident. But if there is not to be a complete arbitrariness here, one must insist "Why these alternatives?" Is not the disjunction dependent upon the recognition of a commonality in the disjuncts?

3. On the terminology, see George P. Klubertanz, *St. Thomas on Analogy* (Chicago: Loyola University Press, 1960), 6–7.

Benedict, Francis of Assisi, and Ignatius. This is why the parade of saints through the centuries is such an astonishing thing to watch. Each, through its differences, permits one to see a little more of the depths of love.

So, any analogon is an intrinsically fascinating object. An analogon possesses a richness of content that is only partially revealed through its analogates. In a surprising reversal of the situation with univocal commonalities, the background that is the analogon will always contain much more than is in the foreground. Now the impoverishment is in the data and the richness is in the commonality. This realization makes analgons fascinating objects of study. We want to plumb their depths, we want to know more of the richness. Unfortunately we cannot gaze on the analogon itself. Rather, we are condemned to increase our knowledge of the analogon only by increasing our knowledge of the analogates, which through new and unheard of differences reveal a little more of the analogon. The current inability to appreciate knowledge as intrinsically valuable makes sense if our intellectual life is fundamentally understood in terms of univocal concepts. As a sameness-apart-from difference, the univocal commonality is something more impoverished than the data from which it is abstracted. Hence, with univocal commonalities, it is impossible to provide any luster to the ideal of knowing just for the sake of knowing. The far richer sensible data will win every time. Understood in univocal terms, knowing can take on the appearance of value only extrinsically. This is the strategy that has been adopted since modern times, even for higher education. Knowing is related to some practical pursuit, for example, better engineering, better medicine, better entertainment. But an intrinsic value for knowing has been completely lost. Such is the result if knowing is fundamentally understood in terms of univocal commonalities.

But among analogons exists a special type. Scholastics called this type transcendental.[4] It is superior to the previous examples of analogons. Even though any analogon makes its way into a startling array of different analogates which our experience probably never exhausts, not all analogons are transcendentals. There are some differences into which some analogons cannot make their way. For example, Fido in his differences and the pine tree on the lawn with its differences will never manifest the analogon of

4. "[Being, *ens*] is what the Scholastics called a transcendental object of thought." Jacques Maritain, *The Degrees of Knowledge*, trans. by Gerald B. Phelan (New York: Charles Scribner's Sons, 1959), 210. Aquinas appears to call being a transcendental at ST I, q. 30, a. 3.

sanctity. Yet there are analgons that are illustrated by the differences of *all* things. And an example would be that of the notion or intelligibility of being, the *ratio entis*. Everything—for example, myself, the tree, Fido, Teresa, and Xavier—is a being or an actuality in a different way. At the very beginning of his *Disputed Questions on Truth* especially, but elsewhere[5] also, Aquinas indicates why we must regard being as an analogon that is transcendental. The reason simply is that if the differences of being were in anyway extrinsic to the analogous concept of being, then the differences would reduce themselves to non-being, and so actuality would take the form of one undifferentiated thing. In other words, the differences of things in order to differentiate have to be actual; but as actual they will be included within the *ratio entis*.

What I mean by the *ratio entis* is wider than, hence not identical to, *ens mobile*. Being includes cognition. Human awareness is never so focused on things that it loses an awareness of itself.[6] But, for Aquinas, sensory cognition *qua* cognition involves a spiritual change (*immutatio spiritualis*).[7] Hence, in that respect cognition resists categorization in the types of physical changes that comprise *ens mobile*. The phenomenon of cognition drives the intellect to frame the wider intelligibility of being.

To intellectually apprehend being is to experience an earthquake in one's intellectual life. Everything becomes of interest, because every thing in its uniqueness gives one another look at the *ratio entis*, whose treasure contains this difference and who knows what else. In my opinion, the analogous conceptualization of being provides the explanation from subjectivity of Aristotle's external observation in the first book of his *Metaphysics* that knowledge is intrinsically valuable because it is still sought after practical needs and necessities have been met.[8] Nevertheless, one would be wrong to think that intellectual pursuit demands an explicit philosophical presentation of the above. Aquinas understands being as such an automatic and

5. DV q. 21, a. 1; *Summa contra Gentiles* (SCG) I, q. 25, no. 6; ST I, q. 3, a. 5.

6. See Aquinas's *In XII Meta.*, lect. 11, no. 2608, on Aristotle's remark "But science, perception, opinion and thought always seem to be about something else and only indirectly about themselves."

7. See ST I, q. 78, a. 3. At. *In III De anima*, lect. 12 and in comparison to the change studied by the natural philosopher, this type of change, also found in understanding (*intelligere*) and willing (*velle*), is called change improperly speaking, for it does not involve the destruction of a previously existing contrary. In *In V de Trinitate* 4, ad 3m, and 2, ad 7m, this type of change is reserved for the study of the metaphysician..

8. Aristotle, *Metaphysics* 1.2, 982b22–27.

natural abstraction from self-manifestly real things provided by sensation that the *ratio entis* can lie unnoticed in the depths of our conscious life and nevertheless have conscious effects. Such thinking about being goes a long way to explain why the principle of non-contradiction ("Something cannot both be and not be at the same time and in the same respect"), which is about being, is self-evident to all, even to those who never thought about analogous conceptualization and transcendentals.

In the great Thomist revival of the previous century, the famous French Thomist Jacques Maritain wrote most passionately of the intellectual perception of being. Maritain calls it the intuition of being, *l'intuition de l'être.* Some classic texts from his greatest work, *The Degrees of Knowledge*, chapter 5, section 3, are as follows:

> Even in the perception of the generic or specific nature the intellect attains in the individual more than the individual itself. It attains a universal object of concept communicable to all the individuals of the same species or of the same genus. And this is called *univocal,* since presented to the mind by a plurality of transobjective subjects and restored to them in judgments, it is purely and simply one and the same in the mind. *Unum in multis,* it is an invariant without actual multiplicity, realized in several, and by that very fact positing among them a community of essence. But in the perception of the transcendentals, we attain in a nature more than itself, an object of concept not only transindividual, but trans-specific, trans-generic, transcategorical, as if in opening a blade of grass one started a bird greater than the world. Let us call such an object of concept *super-universal.* The scholastics call it *analogous,* ... It differs essentially, even as a concept, from the universals, not only because it has a greater amplitude, but also and primarily ... it is polyvalent, it envelops an actual multiplicity; the bird we spoke of a moment ago is at the same time a flock.

Maritain leaves the inimitable prose of "a bird that is at the same time a flock" for a more prosaic and philosophically garbed description:

> Everything which divides [electrons and angels] from one another is the same being which I find in each of them—varied. I simply have to fix my attention on it to see that it is at once one and multiple. It *would be* purely and simply one if its differentiations were not still itself, or to put it otherwise, if the analogue presented to the mind made complete abstraction from the analogates; if I could think being without thereby rendering present to my mind (whether I am *de facto* explicitly aware of this or not is quite accidental) in essentially different ways some of the others in which this object of concept is realizable outside the mind. It *would be* purely and simply multiple if it did not transcend its differentiations, or, to put

it otherwise, if the analogue presented to the mind made no abstraction from its analogates: in which case the word "being" would be purely equivocal and my thought would fly to pieces.

These texts reiterate the point that an analogous concept is not picked out apart from the differences of its instances, but within those very differences.

II. Being and Its Epiphanies

Yet if the abstraction of the *ratio entis* is important for understanding the generation of the pure, disinterested, desire to know, it is also the basis for our practical lives. I want to continue Aquinas's phenomenology of the human intellector of being for purposes of understanding both the basis of a moral life that is heroic and the fact that so few are faithful to it. To do this I want to begin speaking about the first principle of practical reason, or of Aquinas's natural law. At ST I-II, q. 94, a. 2, Aquinas presents "The good ought to be done and pursued, and evil avoided" as a *per se notum*, or self-evident, proposition. By a *per se notum* proposition Aquinas says that he means a proposition in which the meaning of the predicate is contained in the meaning of the subject. How is Aquinas understanding "the good," the *ratio boni*, so that the notion includes "oughtness"? By the good Aquinas also means the notion of being, the *ratio entis*, which he also mentions as the basis of the first principle of speculative reason—the principle of non-contradiction. It makes sense to call being the good because of the previously mentioned intelligible richness of a transcendental analogon. Aquinas remarks that the last end moves the will automatically because it is the perfect good.[9] Aquinas also remarks that "goodness expresses perfection, which is something desirable, and hence it expresses something final."[10] The good is the perfect and the perfect is the attractive. That proposition certainly applies to the transcendental of being. Being should then command attraction from the will.

From his linking of being with the good, Aquinas elsewhere deduces two things. The first is a necessary and automatic volition consequent upon the intellect's presentation of the *ratio boni* to the will. There is no moral necessity here because there is no freedom. The will acts automati-

9. ST I-II, q. 10, a. 2, ad 3.
10. ST I, q. 5, a. 1.

cally. Earlier at ST I-II, q. 10, a. 1, Aquinas said that the will tends naturally to the good in common (*bonum in communi*), just as the intellect knows naturally the first principles of demonstration.[11] The second implication of linking being with the good is the indeterminate disposing of the will before any individual thing that is only "a" good, not the good itself. Now the will is free but moral constraint, or oughtness, still seems absent. Rather, what is present is an awareness of being equally and indifferently disposed to all finite goods.[12] These two points are significant additions to Aquinas's phenomenology of subjectivity. Yet the issue remains of how we are to configure properly being as the good so that precisely moral obligation, not necessary volition nor raw freedom, follows. In that way one would understand "Good ought to be done" as self-evident.

My resolution of the issue is the realization that Aquinas is not speaking of being as the good pure and simple, but of being as the good when present in the human through the human's intellection.[13] Among all the instances of being as the good, the human, through his intellection, has the good in an especially intense manner. Does not that fact issue to our freedom a command of respect and solicitude? Before such an instance we are free undoubtedly, but we are also morally constrained. In sum, the subject of the first practical principle should not be understood simply as the good but as the good intellected by the human.

So the first rule of a moral life is to be respectful and solicitous of the human person. The human person is the lighthouse from which shines the good and to which we should direct our moral vessel. For example, the immorality of murder, theft, and lying is patent. In striking at the person, each of these actions strikes unseemly at the good. Also, our awareness of ourselves as intellectors of being creates the injunctions to do what respects our existence and to avoid what disrespects it, for example, abuse and suicide. Moreover, by its essentially unitive and procreative character the sexual embrace is unique among human activities. In one's sexual partner and also in

11. Also, at ST I, q. 82, a. 1, Aquinas says that just as the intellect necessarily adheres to the first principles, so too the will necessarily adheres to the last end which is happiness (*ultimo fini, qui est beatitude*). But "happiness" here is the *ratio boni* for elsewhere the last end is the object of the will (ST I-II, q. 10, a. 1) and the object of the will is said to be the *ratio boni* (ST I-II, q. 8, a. 2). Also, at ST I-II, q. 10, a. 2, ad 3, "The last end moves the will necessarily, because it is the perfect good [*bonum perfectum*]."

12. ST I-II, q. 10, a. 2.

13. See John F. X. Knasas, *Being and Some Twentieth-Century Thomists* (New York: Fordham University Press, 2003), 261–72.

the procreative teleology of the sexual embrace, one is handling the good and so sexual activity ought to be exercised in the context of a committed monogamous relation, that is, of marriage. The fornicator and adulterer unseemingly discard the *ratio boni* given in the sexual embrace.

The evil of contraception is likewise evident. By striking at the procreative powers, contraceptors strike at the *ratio boni* in the offspring who is at least essentially, if not actually, present. Great lovers take this norm of respect and solicitude of the human person with deep seriousness. Their most important thing is other people, or life in society. Nothing should be substituted for people and their well-being, not hobbies, studies, pleasure, money, fame, and so forth. Pursuit of these things must always defer to the needs of persons. Aquinas's conception of the human as an intellector of being also makes understandable the self-sacrifice involved in friendship. Following Aristotle Aquinas roots friendship in self-love.[14] What I find loveable in myself, namely, the notion of being, is found in others. Hence, my fellow is another self. In this context, my loss should not be looked at simply as another's gain. To see the other as a friend is to see my loss for his sake as *our* gain. Love for self extended to others makes it possible to genuinely rejoice in their good fortune, even when that good fortune demands a sacrifice from us. Jealousy should have no place among people if they relate to each other as friends. And people should relate to others as friends if they view themselves as intellectors of being. The deep truth here is indicated by its contrary, namely, rejection and its lacerating effect of isolation. Since being is so intensely present in our fellows, then their rejection of us can appear as being's rejection of us. And since being includes all, rejection can be experienced as total isolation. That is why though we may disagree, we should always remain friends.

III. Being as Hiding and Revealing Itself

In sum, the above shows that for Aquinas reality itself prompts us to love. His epistemology of intellectual abstraction from the real things given to us in sensation establishes confidence in the notion of being. Being is not a pipe dream but a deep plunge into reality. In Thomistic psychology

14. See James McEvoy, "The Other as Oneself: Friendship and Love in the Thought of St. Thomas Aquinas," in *Thomas Aquinas: Approaches to Truth*, edited by James McEvoy and Michael Dunne (Dublin: Four Courts Press, 2002).

love is not to suffer a delusion. Reality itself provides the motivation. But as so relentlessly developed from the real, Aquinas's ethics prompts another question. If we are structured as Aquinas says, why is human experience marked by so much disagreement about how to behave? For example, how do proponents of euthanasia respect their own existence; how do proponents of recreational sex acknowledge its procreative and unitive nature; how do institutions of higher learning continue to acknowledge the intrinsic value of knowing, never mind Aquinas's mentioned obligation to know the truth about God? In fact, Aquinas seems to force the issue. At ST I-II, q. 94, a. 6, he claims that "as to the common principles, natural law, in its universal meaning, cannot in any way be blotted out from men's hearts."[15] Earlier in article 4, Aquinas describes these principles as equally known to all and as self-evident to us. Now it is possible that opponents of Aquinas clearly understand these common principles but are driven by passions and bad habits to live otherwise. Aquinas does assign to the passions a large role in engendering immorality. But on the other hand, among ordinary people, how many, if any, have cognizance of the connection between "oughtness" and the human as an intellector of being? In short, the drama of real human life still appears to escape Aquinas's analyses. Better to turn to an existentialist like Heidegger or Marcel or Kierkegaard to supplement a naivety in Aquinas. A treatment of this disconnect from the side of subjectivity would be invaluable for any Thomist who ponders going forth into his cultural milieu.

The intellectual character of Aquinas's position should not be held against it, for Aquinas does not equate a proposition being self-evident to us with our explicit acknowledgement of the proposition. Like the human heart that functions automatically but with conscious effects, so too the intellect can automatically abstract the notion of being and grasp it as the good. Such an automatic abstraction can go a long way to explain why people try to avoid contradiction, yearn for something that life cannot give, and experience freedom and also obligation. Evidently we know more than we are aware, as I would like now to explain.

Despite the *quoad nos* self-evident character of the primary practical precepts, Aquinas holds a dim view of the workings of the intellect. For ex-

15. *The Basic Writings of St. Thomas Aquinas,* translated by Anton C. Pegis (New York: Random House, 1945), 2:781. All English quotations from the *Summa theologiae* are from this translation.

ample, in the *Summa Contra Gentiles* (SCG) III, chap. 26, he explains that it is not strange that humans act for sensual pleasures rather than intellectual ones because most humans lack intellectual experience. For this lack Aquinas appeals to his abstractionist epistemology. He says that external things are better known because human cognition begins from sensible things.[16] Later in the same work at IV, chap. 52, he speaks of the "frailty of reason: *debilitas rationis*" and of the predominance of the phantasms. But instead of contradicting Aquinas's position that the primary precepts are known to all, these remarks produce a better understanding of Aquinas's position. For one would be wrong to interpret these remarks to mean that the workings of the intellect are totally absent or that these workings have no experienced effects. Even though our attention is focused on sensible things, our intellection has gone on to grasp commonalities of which we are still unaware. How else does one explain that we abide by the non-contradiction principle, are inevitably dissatisfied by finite goods, and know that we are free in respect to anything in our experience? These phenomena show that the notion of being haunts the human mind. A clever Thomist would seize upon each phenomenon to lead the person to realize something that the person in fact already knows, namely, the notion of being and the understanding of being as the good. So much of Thomism is making the implicit explicit, to rob some language from Transcendental Thomism.

Furthermore, as mentioned earlier, our awareness of things and the intelligibilities that things contain is never so focused that all self-awareness is lost. Hence, we cannot but have some awareness of ourselves as intellectors of being. So, with avoidance of contradiction, yearning, and freedom, the phenomenon of obligation is another outcropping indicating the presence of the *abstractum* of being in the depths of human consciousness. Again, we know more than we are aware. While our attention is on sensible things, or phantasms, the intellect can be doing its own work with the mentioned results.

So, a Thomist is not upset that most people appear to be living with no

16. "Nor do more persons seek the pleasure that is associated with knowing rather than the knowledge. Rather, there are more people who seek sensual pleasures than intellectual knowledge and its accompanying pleasure, because things that are external stand out as better known, since human knowledge starts from sensible objects." As translated by Vernon J. Bourke, *Summa contra Gentiles* (Notre Dame, Indiana: University of Notre Dame Press, 1975) 3:109–110. All English quotations from book 3 (parts 1 and 2, indicated below as I-III and II-III, following the convention used for the *Secunda pars* of the *Summa theologiae*) of the SCG are from this translation.

awareness of themselves as intellectors of being. In the Thomist's contemplation of his fellows, the knowledge of themselves as intellectors of being is present and is explaining their inchoate sense of their own dignity. This inchoate sense of dignity appears in proponents of euthanasia who point out the indignity of a long, lingering, painful death. Even proponents of recreational sex acknowledge it when they insist that recreational sex is morally acceptable because "no one is getting hurt" and it involves only "consenting adults." A Thomist will continue to regard euthanasia and recreational sex as morally abhorrent, but that dislike should not cause him to miss a concession to his understanding of the value of the human person. Furthermore, the Thomist's understanding of human epistemology allows the Thomist to understand the genesis of the moral confusion. His opponent knows that he ought to respect himself and others but does not know why. And the opponent does not know why because the opponent still lacks an awareness of his apprehension of being as the good. The awareness is lacking because even though intellection has already discerned in external sensible things the notion of being, attention is focused on the sensible things. With only a superficial grasp of themselves, people can honestly believe that they are respecting their dignity when, tragically, they are not.

So even though the primary precepts are self-evident to all, it does not follow that all are equally aware of the meaning of the subjects. In the case of the primary precept, "The human ought to be treated with respect and solicitude," the subject is the human person. In light of Aquinas's abstractionist epistemology, is it not possible to have varying depths of understanding of this subject? Can it not be the case that we are intellectors of being long before we become aware of that fact? An affirmative reply would explain why most people experience obligation both to themselves and their fellows yet can be so confused in what this obligation consists. That confusion would also explain why these people go on to miss knowledge of the secondary precepts of natural law. Hence, at ST I-II, q. 94, a. 4, Aquinas mentions Caesar's observation of the approval of theft among the Germans. The Germans permitted armed robbery of others outside the tribe. The basic reason appears to have been their paranoid opinion that outsiders were potential enemies. This opinion is indicative of a shallow understanding of what lies in the depths of the human person.

IV. Being and "Fauxizing"

Aquinas's distinction between what we know about ourselves vs. what we realize about ourselves helps to understand another primary precept mentioned by Aquinas at ST I-II, q. 94, a. 2: "Divine truth ought to be sought." Along with other primary precepts, Aquinas says that this one has universal truth and is *per se notum quoad nos*. But is it clear that God exists and, even if it is clear, is it clear that we ought to concern ourselves with knowing God? How does a primary precept about God arise in Aquinas's natural law?

Earlier at SCG III, chap. 38, Aquinas describes an ordinary knowledge of God possessed by all mature human beings.[17] Perhaps it will answer my questions. This ordinary knowledge of God is *a posteriori* and appears to recount a primitive version of the teleological argument. Aquinas concedes that the argument has many shortcomings. For example, he notes that one does not yet grasp who or what is this orderer or whether the orderer is one or many. On the strength of this argument, some identify the orderer with the heavenly bodies, the elements, or other human beings. But does not Aquinas's concession contradict his thesis that men are knowing God? None of the characterizations of the orderer are remotely similar to the God of Aquinas's religious belief who is spiritual, unique, and non-human. Would it not have been clearer for Aquinas to say that men fail to attain a knowledge of God? In other words, when a physicist discovers a new particle, he does not exclaim "God!" And if he did, we would think him strange. Hence, is not Aquinas odd to attribute man's knowledge of God to man's knowledge of the elements? In fact, on another occasion Aquinas is uncompromising, if not uncharacteristically cruel, in his dismissal of David

17. "[W]hat seems indeed to be true, that man can immediately reach some sort of knowledge of God by natural reason. For, when men see that things in nature run according to a definite order, and that ordering does not occur without an orderer, they perceive in most cases that there is some orderer of the things that we see. But who or what kind of being, or whether there is but one orderer of nature, is not yet grasped immediately in this general consideration.... But this knowledge admits of a mixture of many errors. Some people have believed that there is no other orderer of worldly things than the celestial bodies, and so they said that the celestial bodies are gods. Other people pushed it further, to the very elements and the things generated from them, thinking that motion and the natural functions which these elements have are not present in them as the effect of some other orderer, but that other things are ordered by them. Still other people, believing that human acts are not subject to any ordering, other than human, have said that men who order others are gods. And so, this knowledge of God is not enough for felicity." SCG I-III, chap. 38, no. 3.

of Dinant's identification of God with matter.[18] Returning to the *Summa Contra Gentiles,* it is important to realize that Aquinas does not say that men reach something "like" God. Aquinas's assertion is unqualified. Men reach God, even though they take what they reach and identify it with the mentioned non-divine instances. Consequently, when in the next chapter (chap. 39) Aquinas introduces philosophical demonstrations to remove the errors, the removal does not consist in moving on to a higher being than those mentioned. Rather, the corrections consist in purifying through removal what the general reasoning had reached.[19] So, before this text on an ordinary knowledge of God can be used to support a universal knowledge of the primary precept obliging us to know divine truth, some explanation of how the conclusion of the reasoning can be so wrong and still be right is required. Here a return to Aquinas's abstractionist epistemology can be helpful.

According to Aquinas, the errors in man's ordinary knowledge of God are set aside by demonstration. The backward reference is important. Early in book one of the *Summa Contra Gentiles,* Aquinas reserves these points of demonstration to the last part of philosophy to be learned, namely, metaphysics.[20] This assignment should mean that the ordinary knowledge of God is in some way metaphysical. Only as metaphysical could it successfully reach God, albeit imperfectly, as Aquinas claims. But can one possibly regard ordinary individuals to be in possession of Aquinas's metaphysics?[21]

The key note in Aquinas's metaphysics is his understanding of the ex-

18. "The third error is that of David of Dinant, who most stupidly taught that God was primary matter." ST I, q. 3, a. 8.

19. "On the other hand, there is another sort of knowledge of God, higher than the foregoing, and we may acquire it through demonstration. A closer approach to a proper knowledge of Him is effected through this kind, for many things are set apart from Him, through demonstration, whose removal enables Him to be understood in distinction from other beings. In fact, demonstrations shows that God is immutable, eternal, incorporeal, altogether simple, one, and other such things which we have shown about God in Book One." SCG III, chap. 39, no. 1.

20. "In order to know the things that the reason can investigate concerning God, a knowledge of many things must already be possessed. For almost all of philosophy is directed towards the knowledge of God, and that is why metaphysics which deals with divine things, is the last part of philosophy to be learned." SCG I, chap. 4, no. 3. In the just previous chapter naturally knowable truth about God includes the knowledge of his existence: "But there are some truths which the natural reason also is able to reach. Such that God exists, that He is one, and the like." SCG I, chap. 3, no. 2, from Anton C. Pegis's translation (South Bend, Indiana: University of Notre Dame Press, 1991). All quotations from SCG I are from this translation.

21. For the Thomistic texts behind the many points in my summary description of Aquinas' metaphysics, see chapters 6 and 7 of my *Being and Some Twentieth-Century Thomists.*

istence of the thing. Unlike in our common usage, in Aquinas's metaphysics "the existence of the thing" does not mean simply the fact of the thing. Aquinas regards existence as a distinct principle or act composed with the individual substance to render the substance a being (*ens*), an existent. Aquinas employs the phrase "actus essendi" and the Latin infinitive *esse* to express his unique act-sense of the thing's existence. A being or an existent *qua* a being or an existent is a *habens esse*, a possessor of the act of being.

The relation of this act to the substance with which it is composed also bears mentioning. In respect to the substance rendered a being by composition with *esse*, *esse* is prior (*prius*), first (*primus*), most profound (*profundius*), and most intimate (*magis intimum*). We are so accustomed to conceiving acts of a thing as items subsequent and posterior to the thing that the notion of an act basic and fundamental to a thing is strange. But if one is to correctly appreciate *esse*, usual ways of thinking must be suspended.

As an act *esse* is an *ipso facto* dependent item. Every act as an act, even the *sui generis* act that is *esse*, is found in, and is of, a subject. However, no chance exists to explain *esse* completely by the substance that is its subject. Substances that are complete explainers of an act are in some respect already in act. As a potency for its existential act, substance cannot position itself to explain completely its *esse*. The need for complete explanation in the case of *esse* drives the mind to conclude to a further being in which *esse* is not found as an act of the substance but as the very substance itself. Aquinas calls this further cause *esse subsistens* (subsistent existence), *esse tantum* (existence alone) and *esse purum* (pure existence). He also refers to it as *Deus* (God). Aquinas's stated reason is God's revelation to Moses in the Book of Exodus that God's name is *Ego sum qui sum*: I am who am.[22] As subsistent *esse*, the first cause of every creaturely *esse* embodies the key component in Aquinas's understanding of the notion of being, the *ratio entis*. Since the *ratio entis* is also the *ratio boni*, then the first cause is the pre-eminent epiphany of the good among all such epiphanies. If the human commands respect and solicitude because the human as an intellector of being is an epiphany of the good, then *a fortiori* the first cause

22. "This sublime truth Moses was taught by our Lord. When Moses asked our Lord: 'If the children of Israel say to me: what is His name? What shall I say to them?' The Lord replies: '*I am who am*. . . . Thou shalt say to the children of Israel: *He who is* hath sent me to you.' (Exod. 3:13, 14). By this our Lord showed that His own proper name is He who is. Now, names have been devised to signify the natures or essences of things. It remains, then, that the divine being is God's essence or nature." SCG I, chap. 22, no. 10.

does likewise. In the light of Aquinas's metaphysics, the obligation to orient ourselves to the divine instance is an obvious *per se notum* truth. This analysis also illustrates a profound opening in human subjectivity for the life of grace and its culmination in beatitude.

But again, is it plausible to regard Aquinas's metaphysics as a natural and automatic achievement that exists below the level of conscious articulation so that most will have a knowledge of God, imperfect as it is? The answer depends upon our access to the data in which are Aquinas's key metaphysical notions. The setting up of things in various multiplicities is the standard procedure for the discernment of the thing's acts.[23] For example, because I find the water both hot and cold, I come to discern the various temperatures as acts of the water that in itself is temperature neutral. Moreover, I come to understand each of the instances as a composition of the water plus some temperature. Likewise, because I can find Tom both pale and ruddy, I come to discern the complexions as acts of Tom who in himself is complexion neutral. But for Aquinas things are found not only in temperature and complexion multiplicities but also in existential multiplicities. Aquinas is an immediate realist in his understanding of sensation. Sensation provides not an image, a representation, a picture of the real thing but the real thing itself. Consequently, the hot water or the pale Tom does not just really exist, in my sensation, it also cognitionally exists. The presentation of some thing in an existential multiplicity should drive the mind to understand the thing to be in itself existence-neutral and to understand each instance as a composition of the said thing plus a real or cognitional existence in the sense of an act.

The answer to the above question reduces to an answer to this question. Is the mentioned existential multiplicity available to the ordinary person? Certainly. No ordinary person doubts a real world in his sensation. No ordinary person questions the distinction between remembering their beloved in a memory versus being in the beloved's presence when in her arms. Even though modern philosophy has run away from the immediate presence of the real in sensation, ordinary people continue to live according to that marvelous truth. Furthermore, ordinary people have sufficient presence of mind that none lack an awareness of their own sensation. Hence, they not

23. The following is a non-technical paraphrase of Aquinas's approach to the *actus essendi* of a thing by the twofold operation of the intellect, viz., conceptualization and judgment. For the twofold operation of the intellect presentation, see Knasas, *Being and Some Twentieth-Century Thomists*, 182–96.

only know real things, they know that they know real things. In other words, ordinary people not only sense real things, they also are aware that they sense real things. In short, there is every reason to think that the intellect not only discerns the notion of being, as I have claimed above, but that it also apprehends being in the sense is of *habens esse*. The data is sufficiently available for the intellect to be led to the metaphysical distinction between a thing and its *esse*, even if our awareness is elsewhere.

But upon a grasp of the composition, cannot the intellect go on to grasp the conclusion that the *esse* is caused? One conscious outcrop of this activity is Leibniz's question, "Why is there something rather than nothing?" As Heidegger points out at the very start of his *An Introduction to Metaphysics*, the question steals upon us in moments of despair, rejoicing, and boredom. Looked at Thomistically, Heidegger's remark makes sense. Common to these moods is the shutting down of our plans and designs so that we are left simply in the presence of things. But that hovering of things in our awareness bespeaks, as explained, an instability in existents that prompts Leibniz's question. Aquinas's metaphysics is as near as the sense realism of ordinary experience.

In my opinion, another indication of Aquinas's metaphysics is Aquinas's listing of identities for the orderers in this ordinary knowledge of God. All of these orderers are intensely related to the notion of being. I have spoken about the relation of the person to the notion of being. But even the heavens would impress being upon us. Because of their gargantuan dimensions, only the notion of being would allow us to profile the heavens in our mind. But such an intense presence of the notion of being might lead one to confuse the heavens with the cause of being. As mentioned, the notion of being harbors causal implications. Causality goes with the notion of being. In an ordinary person these implications may not be sufficiently distinguished from the instance whose objectification makes the notion of being so necessary.

But if the physically great prompts the notion of being, so too does the physically small. Hence, Aquinas also mentions the elements as the identity of the orderer. To contemplate the physically small, everything else must be removed from our awareness. That move leaves the physically small alone with the notion of being. The heightened presence of being in the contemplation of minutiae could lead one to confuse the causal implications with the minutiae themselves.

In sum, God can be confused with both the great and the small because the presence of the notion of being, in which there are causal implications, is so natural for our contemplation both of the great and the small. It is no surprise that people basically divide into those who like the mountains and those who like the shore. One looks at the expanse of the sky, the other at vessels on the vast ocean. As the Thomist considers both observers, he believes that the genuine object of the contemplation is being and that their relaxation is some approximation of the happiness that would be achieved in knowing being itself.

V. Being and Human Subjectivity

So, the primary precepts of Aquinas's natural law are both known to all and possess a universal truth. Yet understanding this position correctly requires some precisions that are related to two tricks that the notion of being can play upon its intellector. The first precision concerns the unequal knowledge of the subject of the precepts. For example, all have a sense of obligatory respect and solicitude towards themselves and others. That sense of obligation is what cannot be eliminated from the human heart. But few grasp that that respect stems from the human's status as an intellector of being. The disparity reduces to the fact that not all appreciate their own intellection. That failure, in its turn, is traced to the abstractive nature of human intellection. What the intellect abstracts can be hidden from awareness by the data which is more out front in our awareness. This is the first trick of being. It can hide itself in the process of revealing itself. Hence, some people can be honestly ignorant and confused about even the primary precepts of natural law. Their explicit knowledge of themselves can be so superficial that it will allow confusions about what is congruent or incongruent with human dignity. We need not ascribe to them an ill will nor bad habits, though Aquinas is fully cognizant of these factors. Weakness of reason suffices.[24]

24. In his commentary on the third book of Aristotle's *Nicomachean Ethics* at lect. 3, no. 412, Aquinas agrees with Aristotle that universal ignorance does not excuse. As an example of universal ignorance, Aquinas cites being ignorant of the norm that fornication is always wrong. Does Aquinas mean that everyone should know that fornication is wrong so that if they do not, then they are blameworthy? I do not think so. In the just preceding paragraph, no. 411, Aquinas makes the context clear. The ignorance that does not excuse belongs to a man "having the use of reason" (*homini habenti usum rationis*). But in my text above in section III, I thought that I showed that,

The second precision concerns the misidentification of the subject of the precepts. Here the founding ethical role of the human as intellector of being is missed and other things, namely, the gargantuan or the minute, take its place. In sum, being's second trick is to create faux epiphanies of itself. Again the abstractive epistemology is operative. What is unwittingly abstracted can be unwittingly associated with items whose features call for being. The item can come to possess a value out of all proportion to the truth. In a recent monograph, *Thomism and Tolerance,* I have tried to exploit this second trick to understand the vagaries of cultural pluralism as described in Christopher Dawson's magisterial *Progress and Religion.* But the second trick has many other applications, for instance, in discussions of the problem of evil.[25]

In conclusion, the Neo-Thomist understanding of the human as an intellector of being need plead no excuse about handling subjectivity. From their understanding of Aquinas, these Thomists can locate enough material to show that the notion of being controls, and has always controlled, human psychology. Though not the entire story, the intellection of being is the central theme about the human. It is there when we are moral, it is there when we are immoral. It is there when we understand, it is there when we do not understand. Fundamentally and always, even if we do not realize

---

for Aquinas, few men fit that description. Rather, among men there is a *debilitas rationis* (SCG IV, chap. 52) reflected in the fact that men abstractively draw their knowledge from phantasms. Hence, earlier (SCG III, chap. 26) phantasms, because they are more obvious, are described as occluding an awareness of intelligibilities. That is why most men lack intellectual experience and satisfaction so that sense pleasure is predominantly pursued. So I do not think that an analogy exists between ordinary people and a third grade student who is incorrectly doing simple addition. In the latter case you can presume enough reason to hold the student responsible for his errors. But grasping the natural law precepts correctly is not as simple as that. Some intellectual sophistication is required and few have that. The rest of men bumble around and only vaguely understand their dignity with the result that they tragically judge some actually bad behaviors to be congruent with that dignity. In the context of all that, I interpret the fact that Aquinas addresses their confusion intellectually indicates that the confusion is not a moral one, as he does the proponent of fornication at SCG III, chap. 124, and the person in "universal ignorance" at DV q. 24, a. 10. Aquinas also compares the "malas persuasiones" by which some can be ignorant of the secondary precepts to errors in speculative matters (ST I-II, q. 94, a. 6). But surely not all speculative errors are blameworthy. "Malas" does not have to mean "morally evil." For example, there can be natural evil, "malum naturalis defectus" at ST I, q. 19, a. 9. Sometimes the intellect leads the will astray instead of the will leading the intellect.

25. John F. X. Knasas, *Thomism and Tolerance* (Scranton, Pennsylvania: University of Scranton Press, 2011), 115–26. My *Aquinas and the Cry of Rachel: Thomistic Reflections on the Problem of Evil* (Washington, D.C.: The Catholic University of America Press, 2013) contains integrations of the second trick with the discussion of evil.

it, we face each other as fellow intellectors of being; that is the stage upon which human existence is played. In the light of this philosophical psychology, as well as the good news of his faith which is a marvelous completion of this psychology, our twenty-first century Thomist goes out to meet his fellows. He will find thick walls of cultures or philosophies, but the walls will not be impenetrable. Aquinas's psychology provides a commensurating discourse. Being cannot be eliminated from the heart of the human.

HEATHER M. ERB

Natural Mysticism—Gateway or Detour?

Aquinas, Maritain, and the Core/Contextualist Debate

I. Introduction

Spiritual progress is marked by a mystical knowledge in which dogmas shine like stars in the midday sun and is a result of persevering in grace through the dim awareness of faith.[1] Through the byways of sensible realities and the fragilities of human existence, theological speculation helps us penetrate the knowledge of simple faith, bathing our early certitudes in a "second clarity."[2] Maritain echoed Garrigou-Lagrange's focus on the close association of metaphysics, theology, and mysticism, and his zeal for climbing the "luminous summits which must illuminate all the rest."[3] For

1. Charles Cardinal Journet, *What is Dogma?* (San Francisco: Ignatius Press, 2011), 121, speaks of mystical knowledge thus: "[C]onceptual knowledge of revealed truths is not in any way *laid aside*, or in any way got rid of, it is merely for the moment covered over, *transcended*. All the dogmas thus subsist in the faith of the contemplative, but like the stars in the midday sunlight.... The passing light which throws them into the shade strengthens them to a wonderful degree." Emphasis in original.

2. The notion of "first" and "second" clarities is developed by Baron Friedrich Von Hügel and Andrew Louth. In von Hügel's words, only in the saint is thought about God transformed into a religious act, and the "dim apprehension" of nascent faith becomes the "clear perception" of true knowledge of God. See Andrew Louth, *Discerning the Mystery: An Essay on the Nature of Theology* (Wichita, Kansas: Eighth Day Books, 2007), 135.

3. Garrigou-Lagrange, *Christian Perfection and Contemplation According to St. Thomas Aquinas and St. John of the Cross,* translated by Mary Timothea Doyle (St. Louis, Missouri: Herder, 1949), 50–51.

Maritain, realist metaphysics is shot through with a mystical aspiration for union with the first principle of being.[4] In their syntheses of the fundamental doctrines of Aquinas with the fruits of mystical theology, Garrigou and Maritain echo the integral approach of the commentatorial tradition and together constitute what has rightly been called the "Thomistic-mystical movement."[5]

The binary structures that permeate mystical theology (eternity/time; transcendent/immanent; etc.) also appear in the contrast of interpretation and religious experience, in the "core/contextualist" debate among late twentieth-century scholars of mysticism. Whether there is an initial core of mystical experience that is subsequently interpreted by reference to texts and traditions, or whether an experiential and conceptual matrix precedes and informs mystical experience, is also relevant to Garrigou's and Maritain's considerations of mystical experience "outside the Church."[6] Terms such as natural or pre-mysticism, implicit faith, pan-supernaturalism and pseudo-supernaturalism, emerge in the attempt to reconcile the authentic

4. "The natural desire to see the Cause of being derives from the natural desire of knowing being.... [E]very great metaphysic is indeed pierced by a mystical aspiration." Jacques Maritain, "The Natural Mystical Experience and the Void," in *Ransoming the Time*, translated by Harry Lorin Binsse (New York: Charles Scribner's Sons, 1941), 260–61. The article was based on a talk Maritain gave to the Fourth Congress of Religious Psychology in 1938. For a good summary, see Henry Bars, "Maritain's Contributions to an Understanding of Mystical Experience," in *Jacques Maritain: The Man and His Achievement*, edited by Joseph Evans (New York: Sheed and Ward, 1963), 119–120. Compare this with what Evelyn Underhill says in "What is Mysticism?" in *Collected Papers of Evelyn Underhill* (London: Longmans, Green and Company, 1946), 107: "[A] mystic is not a person who practices unusual forms of prayer, but a person whose life is ruled by this thirst," echoing St. Augustine's saying that "Thou hast made us for Thyself, and our hearts are restless until they find rest in Thee." This thirst seeks nourishment from God's hand, not by snatching at spiritual satisfactions "like greedy greyhounds" (Julian of Norwich, *Revelations of Divine Love*, chap. 46) in the pursuit of rarified, abstract mental states, but through the course of daily circumstance and struggle. Progress in the Christian spiritual life is won, in part, by wrestling with the paradox of eternity entering into and transforming time.

5. Aidan Nichols indicates that this trend at unification anticipates readings of Aquinas such as are found in Jean-Pierre Torrell. See Aidan Nichols, *Reason with Piety: Garrigou-Lagrange in the Service of Catholic Thought* (Naples, Florida: Sapientia Press, 2008), 117.

6. Garrigou-Lagrange, "The Grace of Christ and the Mystics Outside the Church," in *Our Savior and His Love for Us*, translated by Bouchard (Rockford, Illinois: Tan Books, 1998), 355–84. Maritain deals with the topic of natural mysticism and mystical experience outside the Church in several works, such as: "The Natural Mystical Experience and the Void," 255–89; "Mystical Experience and Philosophy," in *Distinguish to Unite, or The Degrees of Knowledge*, fourth edition, translated by Gerard Phelan (New York: Charles Scribner's Sons, 1959), 247–90; *On the Church of Christ: The Person of the Church and Her Personnel*, translated by Joseph Evans (Notre Dame, Indiana: University of Notre Dame Press, 1973), 93–134, for instance.

ecclesial experience of God in Catholicism with the universal call to grace and divine omnipotence.

For Aquinas and Garrigou, authentic supernatural mystical experience is possible outside the visible Church, but only as accompanied by an "implicit faith" which grounds the experience on a minimal set of explicitly held truths about God concerning His existence and providence.[7] Given this demand, what are the chances that a core cross-religious mystical experience exists, let alone one prior to interpretation? The question of "natural" mystical experience outside Christianity is, nonetheless, of importance for inter-faith dialogue, spiritual pedagogy, and cross-disciplinary topics such as the role of the subconscious. For Maritain, natural mystical experience involves both a turning of intelligence from its metaphysical outward course towards a lived nescience and self-denial, and a metaphysical and ascetic discipline which accesses the immensity of God through a return on the self's own act of existence. I will argue that Garrigou maintains a closer affinity to Aquinas on the parameters of the spiritual life, and that he does so by consistently and sharply subordinating mystical experience to the life of theological virtue, understood as a process of conformity, through charity, to Christ.

There are several factors at work in discerning the positions of Aquinas, Maritain, and Garrigou with respect to the contemporary core/contextualist debate. First, there is the seventeenth-century rupture of ascetic and mystical theology which ironically laid the groundwork for the nineteenth-century cultural shift to a personal, experiential approach to religion.[8] Second, Aquinas's sacramental, ecclesial approach is invariably absent in treatments of

7. "However, we can inquire whether the Gospel is to be considered as promulgated in places where it has not yet been preached or where it has been completely forgotten. In any event, true mysticism presupposes at least an implicit faith in the Redeemer." Garrigou-Lagrange, *Our Savior and His Love for Us*, 362 n. 13. He develops the notion of implicit faith in this chapter, resting his view on Aquinas's use of Hebrews 11.6 ("But without faith it is impossible to please God. For he that cometh to God must believe that he is: and is a rewarded to them that seek him" [Douay-Rheims]), where belief in God's existence and providence conditions true faith. Implicit faith in the Redeemer is virtually contained in explicit faith in these two *credibilia*. Aquinas develops the notion of implicit faith in his outline of the categories of unbelief, in ST II-II, q. 2, aa. 7–8 and ST II-II, q. 10, for instance.

8. On the contribution of William James to the modern "episodic" notion of mysticism as a set of discrete paranormal phenomena, see John Peter Kenny, *The Mysticism of St. Augustine* (New York: Routledge, 2005), 147: "[I]n the nineteenth and twentieth centuries … mystical experience became an unusual but highly prized phenomenon, conferring upon its subject the sensation of transcendence and the feeling of certainty."

core mysticism, since his spirituality is resistant to the psychological analysis favored by them. In addition to the distinction of explicit and implicit faith and the various types of union with the divine (differentiated vs. undifferentiated), there are other intersecting questions, such as the role of apophatic or "dark" metaphysical contemplation and the treatment of paradoxes in scriptural texts.

Amidst this web of issues lie three tasks. First, I will note the terms and assumptions of the core/contextualist debate. Second, I will examine Maritain's and Garrigou's ideas of natural or pre-mysticism and implicit faith in light of relevant texts of Aquinas as these Thomists become our imaginary interlocutors in the debate. Third, I will ask whether Aquinas's use of paradox in his texts on natural contemplation and in his Christology as developed in two biblical commentaries provides any evidence for elements of the core view in his thought.

II. The Core/Contextualist Debate

Two opposed approaches to religion have helped set the terminology and parameters of the twentieth-century debate about the nature and possibility of union with the divine. These are the secular philosophy and religious studies camp, which flourished at the turn of the twentieth century and set the terms of the core/contextualist debate, and the French Catholic camp, consisting of a medley of scholastic and transcendental Thomists, *nouvelle théologie* adherents, and interreligious scholars. The secular camp combines a post-Enlightenment divorce of thought and being with the notion that the study of mysticism is at root an endeavor to assess epistemic and psychological claims about religious experience. The French Catholic camp develops various views on religious experience in relation to a Thomist, ecclesial, sacramental spirituality.[9]

9. An overview of modern mysticism scholarship approaches can be found in: Bernard McGinn, *The Foundations of Mysticism*, vol. 1 of *The Presence of God: A History of Western Christian Mysticism* (New York: Crossroad Publishing, 1991), 265–343. Closer than many of these to Garrigou's account is the German Benedictine Anselm Stolz, who retrieves a Scriptural and Patristic basis for a Eucharistic mysticism. See McGinn, *Foundations of Mysticism*, 281. On Garrigou-Lagrange, see ibid., 279–80. McGinn also treats Maritain, but does not analyze his views on natural mysticism in any detail; see ibid., 305–310. Both the secular and French religious camps boast adherents of both the core and contextualist views on mysticism, which points to the pervasive desire for both universality and historical context.

1. *The "Core" View*

First is the core or "essentialist" position, an interesting term hinting at a kind of "abstraction with precision" from lived religious traditions. Here, mystical experience or consciousness is pre-linguistic and has a cross-religious set of key characteristics. Divisions and distinctions among objects, and later, religious dogmas, are said to emerge through the filters of language, tradition, and cult. Christian, Buddhist, Hindu, and Sufi mystics are said to experience the same absolute, expressed variably in terms of God, Brahman, Atman, or Allah, or Emptiness.[10] A core of mystical experience is said to precede interpretation and tradition, such that three elements in mysticism are cemented and seen as invulnerable to skeptical critique or dismantling. These elements are a comprehensive phenomenology of mysticism, a nonsectarian "spirituality," and a robust ecumenism.

The core view on the inner unity or fundamental sameness of all mystical experience was popularized by Stace and Smart, and by William James, who extracted four "marks" of mystical experience—ineffability, noetic quality, transiency, and passivity (some core adherents add Evelyn Underhill's phenomenology of mysticism to the list).[11] Core adherents are fond of lists and charts wherein typologies and traits are compared and distilled into universal categories of experience.[12] Cross-religious access to a core of pure consciousness, accessed by a non-conceptual unity with the universality of being, is sometimes claimed,[13] suggesting a confusion of mystical and metaphysical contemplation, and of absolute and universal being.

10. On this view, see Larry Short, "Mysticism, Mediation, and the Non-Linguistic," *Journal of the American Academy of Religion* 63, no.4 (1995): 659. Short defends the view that there is, in fact, no dichotomy of the core and contextualist positions, and that both are true, since there can be a nonlinguistic basis of mediated experiences.

11. William James, *The Varieties of Religious Experience* (London: Longmans, Green and Company, 1902), 380–82. For a list of authors on either side of the core/contextualist debate, see, for example Edward Howells, "Mysticism and the Mystical: The Current Debate," supplement, *The Way Supplement* 102 (2001): 15–27. In 1960, Stace made an unsuccessful attempt to overcome the problems of the experience/interpretation dichotomy by distinguishing introvertive and extrovertive species of mystical experience, which still share seven common characteristics. See: Walter Stace, *Mysticism and Philosophy* (Philadelphia: J.B. Lippincott, 1960).

12. Jose Nieto, for example, gives an appendix with various charts on the essentials of "universal mysticism." See his *Religious Experience and Mysticism: Otherness as Experience of Transcendence* (Lanham, Maryland: University Press of America, 1997).

13. *The Problem of Pure Consciousness: Mysticism and Philosophy*, edited by Robert K. Forman (Oxford: Oxford University Press, 1990), and *The Innate Capacity: Mysticism, Psychology and Philosophy*, edited by Robert K. Forman (Oxford: Oxford University Press, 1998).

The core thesis is flawed in many ways. First, it errs in its circularity,[14] in that mystical experience of objective, transcendent being is purportedly based on a subjective state of content-less pure consciousness, which claims universality while failing to escape the privacy of an inner psychological state. Second, it errs in its ahistorical artificiality and withdrawing of texts from their religious contexts in order to attain a level of "pure experience." The monistic tendency among core adherents often assumes a hiatus between religion and spirituality in the critique of the divisive effects of theistic revelation.[15] Third, it errs in claiming that traditional religious claims about divine union are extraneous and secondary to the real nature of mysticism.[16] Fourth, the core view fails to recognize the ways in which language and belief systems influence and shape experience, such that a defense of the thorny claim of 'pure experience' is again sidestepped. "Pure experience", a rebellious stepchild of the Cartesian and Kantian self/world divide, is a notion that situates the core/contextual debate in a nest of modern approaches to religion. George Lindbeck's "post-liberal" theology represents an objection to the kind of direct, universal intuition of the divine which the core view assumes.

Robert Bellah situates the core theory within George Lindbeck's pantheon of religious typologies as outlined in the latter's *The Nature of Doctrine*.[17] Lindbeck's own "cultural-linguistic" approach makes doctrines "commonly authoritative rules of discourse, attitude, and action" and interprets inner religious experiences as formed by and derived from outer influences such as language and community. Opposed to this view are two views: the traditional "cognitive" or "propositional" approach, which sees religious doctrines as truth claims about objective realities, and the "experientialist-expressivist" approach, which views religious doctrines as expres-

14. On this critique, see Bernard McGinn, "*Quo Vadis*? Reflections on the Current Study of Mysticism," *Christian Spirituality Bulletin* 6, no. 1 (1998): 15.

15. The familiar narrative of the Church incorporating alien mystical strands for the stated purpose of determining which strands are orthodox or heretical, but with the actual motive of suppressing it under institutional, hierarchical control, is stated explicitly, or implied, by many core adherents. See, for example, Jose Nieto, *Religious Experience and* Mysticism, 165. Core's monism is not only antireligious and a confusion of mystical and metaphysical contemplation; it is a Platonic rejection of individuality. Personhood, Nieto thinks, belongs to the realm of matter, and so pure mystical consciousness must be monistic to be properly metaphysical.

16. See McGinn, "*Quo Vadis?*" 15, for some of these critiques.

17. See Robert Bellah, *Religion in Human Evolution: From the Paleolithic to the Axial Age* (Cambridge, Massachusetts: Belknap Press, 2011), 11, where he discusses George Lindbeck's *The Nature of Doctrine* (Philadelphia: Westminster, 1984).

sions of non-discursive inner states,[18] a view Lindbeck associates with the liberal theologies of Schleiermacher and Tillich.

The "experientialist-expressivist" version of the core theory assumes internally common states or intuitions of the divine among mystics, which language and culture then diversify into outer formulae (creeds), rituals, and doctrines. Lindbeck rejects this model of religious typology, viewing it as a denial of what religious traditions have understood as radically distinct ways of experiencing and being oriented toward self, neighbor, and cosmos. Finally, the core view errs by introducing pantheistic monism, which is entailed by the suggestion that a universal intuitive grasp of the unity of being that excludes the God/creature distinction.[19]

There is a knot of assumptions at work in the core view, starting with the assertion that authentic and "pure" mystical experience transcends creed as well as the Western God/creature distinction. Bellah notes the problems with the notion that the "unitive event" is a kind of "ground zero" with respect to interpretation. A core experience requires conceptual representation if it is to be communicable.[20] The reality/interpretation duality (as well as the particularities of symbol and tradition) is said to be transcended by a nugget of pure experience. This fundamental event is said to then issue in paradox and apophatic language (*sunyata*/emptiness, void, silence, incomprehensible *lux inaccessa,* etc.), which highlights the inadequacies of the rational discourse in interpretation. The core view also assumes that non-religious mystics (including those who have "transcended" or ignored their religious heritage) embody the vocation of mystic more properly than do religious ones; and third, that religion is a step along the way to a fuller, more metaphysically developed, spirituality.

The pitting of spirituality against religion and the confusions about the types of contemplation and of concepts such as personhood[21] are symptomatic of pseudo-scientific approaches to mysticism. In addition to distinguishing the levels of contemplation with clarity and precision, Aquinas *rejected* monism on the grounds that God is not the "formal being" of all

18. Core theorists often view religious experience as "existing generically in the human psyche," with particular religions as "surface manifestations" of a "panhuman" experiential potentiality, and other such vagaries. See Bellah, *Religion in Human Evolution,* 11.

19. On some of these errors, see McGinn, *Foundations of Mysticism,* 315–16, where he focuses on the problems with Walter Stace's views in *Mysticism and Philosophy.*

20. Bellah, *Religion in Human Evolution,* 12.

21. See note 15 above.

things. Rather, God is separate and transcendent, yet omnipresent causally through His essence, presence, and power.[22] Thus, the intellectual basis of a core mystical experience is mistaken, inasmuch as the undifferentiated unity of absorption it entails is, in fact, impossible. Maritain himself viewed the divine immensity supposedly experienced by the Hindu mystics' contact with the substantial *esse* of the soul as distinct from the mystical depths of God accessed by Christian supernatural charity.[23]

2. *The "Contextualist" View*

In 1983, the core view came under attack by Steven Katz, whose contextualist or "constructivist" view complemented the historical research of Bernard McGinn. Katz's work of retrieval is a curio cabinet of religious phenomena (autobiographical, doctrinal, and literary narratives), produced to prove the dependence of mystical experience on particular cultures, traditions, and belief systems. Bridal mysticism, as well as Jewish Kabbalistic literature, for instance, presupposes a personal, differentiated union of love, based on *The Song of Songs*. As removed from Scripture as Zoharic Kabbalah may seem, with its doctrine of the divine *Sefiroth* reunited through human action, it is nonetheless true that biblical education is thought to provide the context of divine encounter, and biblical texts anchor and enrich Rabbinic literature. As Katz puts it, "what the rabbinic mystic 'saw' was not independent of what he had studied in order to 'see.'"[24] Interpretation not only follows, but precedes and permeates, mystical experience, and these accounts draw on cosmologies telling us about origins and ourselves and of ascending paths towards perfection.[25]

Metaphysical frames-of-reference are neither accidental conditions nor biased reprises of content-less, ineffable "experiences." If dogmas are like the stars that shine in the midday sun of mystical experience, then ontic sche-

22. See SCG I, chap. 26, "Is God the formal being of things?" Steven A. Long details the metaphysical path of Aquinas's rejection of Parmenidean monism, from his adoption of Aristotelian notion of potency and the hierarchy of being, to the implications of an infinite act which is not self-limiting, in his recent book *Analogia Entis: On the Metaphysics of Analogy, Being, and the Act of Faith* (South Bend, Indiana: University of Notre Dame Press, 2011), 13–38.

23. See Maritain, "The Natural Mystical Experience and the Void," 279–80 n. 18.

24. *Mysticism and Religious Traditions*, edited by Steven T. Katz (Oxford: Oxford University Press, 1983), 9. McGinn denies the relativism and truth-denying character of the contextualism, but does agree that there are no "mysticisms" but only mystics adhering to various traditions and beliefs.

25. See ibid., 33.

mas are the like the light-transmitting atmosphere itself, which make them possible. So, a Buddhist undifferentiated absorptive state, which makes no room for individual souls, is *not* a Western relational union of charity; grace as exercised by an omnipotent benevolent divine will is *not* necessitarian *karma;* Buddhist release from *samsara* (cycle of rebirth) is *not* the perfection of Christian resurrection, and so on, *contra* the "one summit" view of spirituality.

Despite its nuances, the contextualist view is also flawed. Katz not only affirms mystical contexts, but also denies any direct contact with ultimate reality, and denies the truth value of any proposition about mystical experience. Katz thus accepts the dichotomy that *either* mystical experience is unmediated and direct (the core view), *or* it is generated and limited by context and tradition, precluding access to objective truth—in short, a religious relativism.

To bracket out religious texts, doctrines, and even sacraments as either mere triggers, or as secondary reflections on primary ineffable and certain "experience" also reduces mysticism to a transitory alteration of consciousness, instead of the complete appetitive and personal transformation called for by Maritain in his distinction of mystical from mere philosophical contemplation. The post-Enlightenment "contents-of-consciousness" ersatz[26] mysticism also ignores the influence of language on experience, yet the power of language effects personal transformation in the mystic, especially considering the incommensurability between the finite and infinite subjects.[27] The paradox of presence and absence is a verbal strategy in the *via negativa,* for example.

Bernard McGinn hits on the Achilles heel of the core view in noting that the fundamental error involved "lies in thinking that there is a real division between the experiential and the theological in … the mystical tradition. The mystics themselves never thought that this was the case."[28] James's contribution to the erroneous split in his *Varieties of Religious Experience* (1902) set the tone for a three-pronged approach to mysticism as:

26. As Howells puts it: "In the modern period, this Christian framework broke down under the influence of the new science, and was replaced by an ersatz 'scientific' field of 'mysticism' focusing on extraordinary phenomena, now divorced from the system of thought which gave it meaning." Howells, "Mysticism and the Mystical: The Current Debate," 22.

27. Cf. McGinn, *Foundations of Mysticism,* xviii.

28. Bernard McGinn, "The Changing Shape of Late Medieval Mysticism," *Church History* 65, no. 2 (1996): 214.

i. experiential and autobiographical; ii. focused on the paranormal and extraordinary; and: iii. involving an exchange of the properly theological for an empirical, inductive, psychological approach—a fundamental failure of methodology, according to Garrigou, which further separated ascetical and mystical theology.[29] Anglicans such as Dean Inge and Evelyn Underhill rightly rejected this artificial division, as well as the pseudo-spirituality of the paranormal promoted since the seventeenth century, but it was Garrigou who reintegrated the elements of the spiritual life by positing a continuity of natural, acquired, and infused levels of contemplation, to make mysticism a normal, if rare, culmination of the universal call to holiness.[30]

III. Garrigou, Aquinas, and Maritain on Implicit Faith and the "Mysticism of Self"

1. Garrigou and Aquinas

Despite the universal call to holiness and the possibility of grace being dispensed outside the visible Church, however, Garrigou does not accept the core thesis. Why not? First, his limitation of authentic mysticism to the supernatural life of grace precludes Pelagian-style generated states of consciousness as an index of spiritual progress. Second, his goal of reunifying ascetical and mystical theology (in *Christian Perfection and Contemplation,*

29. On Garrigou-Lagrange's rejection of modern approaches to mysticism, both within and outside the Church, see the excellent review by Aidan Nichols, O.P., *Reason with Piety: Garrigou-Lagrange in the Service of Catholic Thought* (Ave Maria, Florida: Sapientia Press, 2008).

30. Garrigou's articles in *La vie spirituelle* were taken up in his 1923 book *Perfection chrétienne et contemplation selon S. Thomas d'Aquin et S. Jean de la Croix* (*Christian Perfection and Contemplation According to St. Thomas Aquinas and St. John of the Cross*), where the universal call to contemplation and holiness as the normal outcome of the development of the life of grace, is asserted. In the same stroke, the artificial division of the ascetic and mystical, and the confusion of contemplation with paranormal phenomena was dispelled. Inspired by Aquinas, for whom mysticism is not a discrete set of experiences, but a *life* whose principle and end is charity, Garrigou detailed the stages of spiritual growth in which the giving and uniting of ourselves to God is made possible. Mystical union for the *viator* shares in the secret wisdom of God, the loving knowledge proceeding from the gift of wisdom. For the theologian, the Gifts open an inward vision of the mysteries of faith in a joining of the practical (end-directedness) and theoretical loving contemplation. See Reginald Garrigou-Lagrange, *The Three Ages of the Interior Life,* translated by Mary Timothea Doyle, 2 vols. (Herder: St. Louis, 1946). On the various components of the mystical life in terms of the definition of contemplation in Aquinas, see ST II-II, q. 24, a. 9. On the degrees of charity, where Aquinas distinguishes between the charity of the *incipientes, proficientes,* and *perfecti,* see ST II-II, q. 24, a. 9. Cf. David Knowles, "Contemplation in Saint Thomas Aquinas, Part 2," *Clergy Review* 8 (July, 1934): 85–103.

for example[31]) involved a hinging together, in a broad continuum, of active discipline—acquired and infused—and passive contemplation, both animated by charity. In his view, mystical contemplation is a rare but normal flowering of the ordinary life of grace, involving the supernatural initiative of God, the passivity of the Gifts of the Spirit, the presence of charity, and the goal of differentiated, personal union with Christ. Third, natural or pre-mysticism involves the potential confusion of levels of contemplation, and is open to error. How so?

Garrigou develops a view midway between naturalism (the modern core version of Pelagianism) and pseudo-supernaturalism (the Jansenist view that makes grace and infused faith the condition for all good works, and denies the dispensation of grace to pagans).[32] Naturalism denies the necessity of sacraments and Christ for salvation, and leads to false mysticisms which confuse the realms of nature and grace, God and self. It is open to inspirations from lower spirits in the inevitable confusion of "darkness from above" (God) and "darkness from below" (the self). Supernaturalism denies divine omnipotence and the role of implicit faith in those advancing towards salvation.

Little allowance is made for natural mysticism as an ascetically prepared meditation on the self. Neoplatonism stands alone as a natural mysticism that can exist in souls in a state of grace, over and against Buddhism, Hinduism, and theosophy. *De jure*, major mystical graces can occur outside the visible Church, in some Protestants and Muslims, but *de facto*, even minor mystical graces occur only very rarely outside the visible Church, and occur within the Church, only as compensation for defects in environment.[33] This 1951 position parallels the early edition of Maritain's *The Degrees of Knowledge* (1926), which, unlike his treatment of mysticism in *Ransoming*

31. See Garrigou-Lagrange, *Christian Perfection and* Contemplation, 23, 27, 29. He also emphases the distinction of the "traditional thesis" (the unity of mystical and ascetical theology), the "modern" thesis (their rupture after the seventeenth century) and his "return to the traditional thesis" in his other works. Cf. Robert Eiten, "Recent Theological Opinion on Infused Contemplation," *Theological Studies* 2, no. 1 (1941): 95–98.

32. See Garrigou-Lagrange, *Our Savior and His Love for Us*, 355–84.

33. See ibid., 379. In note 50 on page 379, Garrigou quotes Lemonnyer: "The minor mystical graces are properly supplementary graces. When God grants them, He takes into consideration need rather than merit. He holds them in reserve as help mercifully granted to weakness rather than as direct means of accelerating progress in perfection. If there are born-candidates for the minor mystical graces, they are those unknown Catholics, members of the one spiritual Church.... They lack so many things." See Antoine Lemonnyer, "L'Existence des phénomènes mystiques, est-elle concevable en dehors de l'Eglise?" *La vie spirituelle* (May 1, 1932): 73ff.

the Time (1938), downplays the possibility of natural or pre-mysticism by reducing it to asceticism and natural contemplation.

The quest for a universal core mystical experience resembles a search for prayer shorn of doctrine. For Garrigou, an inductive, empirical approach to religious phenomena (found in the core view) removes mysticism from its theological moorings, reducing it to an experientialist caricature while destroying the unity of the spiritual life. Any experience of God outside the boundaries of the visible Church must also involve divinely instituted graces, and must rest on explicit faith in God's existence and providence. Aquinas's view on the implicit faith of non-Christians, and the content and direction of the first act of freedom, is relevant here. Three cases warrant analysis: i. the uncatechised savage; ii. the child's first act of freedom; and: iii. the pagan mystic.

In *De veritate* q. 14, a. 11, Aquinas raises the question of the salvation of a savage brought up among wolves, or, as Garrigou would add, the case of one who has forgotten or rejected a caricature of the faith.[34] Such a person is not automatically damned, Aquinas argues, for providence fittingly provides all with what is necessary for salvation. This early view is replaced in later texts by a more Augustinian pessimism, as some have noted.[35] In *De veritate,* the savage can possess "implicit" faith by following natural reason, by seeking good and shunning evil, God providing either internal inspiration or external guidance to make this faith explicit, as the case of Cornelius and Peter (Acts 10) illustrates. Explicit faith in the two truths of Hebrews 11.6 (God's existence and providence) implicitly contains truths necessary for salvation.

Every truth of faith cannot reasonably be believed with clarity in every age by every person, Aquinas reasons. The case of the pagan of good will resembles that of ordinary folk between the fall and the age of grace—both can possess the two necessary *credibilia*. After the coming of Christ, however, the evangelized must *also* have explicit faith in the Trinity, the Redeemer, and the general articles of faith.

34. Interestingly, Garrigou aligns two scenarios—one, where the Gospel has not been preached, and the other, where it has been "completely forgotten." Garrigou-Lagrange, *Our Savior and His Love for Us*, 362 n. 13.

35. F. A. Sullivan, *Salvation Outside the Church? Tracing the History of the Catholic Response* (New York: Paulist Press, 1992), 53–55. Sullivan believes that Aquinas's silence in later texts on the inevitability of a preacher or inspiration being provided to make implicit faith explicit (and so salvific), led him to adopt an Augustinian view on the possibility of salvation for pagans.

Does Aquinas's early optimism about the uncatechised man of good will (who possesses implicit faith) bear any relation to the situation of the pagan who practices a natural or pre-mysticism? Such a pagan must also possess implicit faith for the comparison to be apt.

The second case Aquinas considers is that of an unbaptized child, who chooses between himself and God, or goodness in itself as a "due end" in his first act of freedom. Does this second case bear any relation to the mystical experience of an unbeliever? At ST I-II, q. 89, a.6, Aquinas takes up the issue of grace and the types of sin in a discussion of the child's first act of freedom in relation to his final end:[36]

> Now the first thing that occurs to man to think about then, is to deliberate about himself. And if he then direct himself to the due end, he will, by means of grace, receive the remission of original sin; whereas if he does not . . . as far as he is capable of discretion at that particular age, he will sin mortally, for through not doing that which is his power to do.[37]

A person of the age of reason, upon directing himself by deliberation to his due end, can avoid mortal sin and receive grace,[38] but will never have original and venial sin together without mortal sin, should he turn from God. Rather, he will either have grace together with later venial sin (if he turns to God immediately prior to reaching the age of reason, "insofar as he is capable of discretion"), or, he will have mortal and venial sin (if he fails to turn to God immediately). There is no hiatus period once reason dawns, where sinners simply have original sin with venial sin in the absence of any choice either for or against God.

So, an unbaptized child can have implicit faith by turning to God through his natural reason. Could this also be true for a pagan who has reached the age of reason, who decides about his end without the benefit of the sacraments? Can he also receive grace and the remission of original sin before explicit membership in the Church? If so, this might be used as evidence for the veracity of his mystical experiences.

If the pagan possesses implicit faith, however, it would *not* be because he has yet to turn to God through his natural reason, as in the case of the

36. See ST I-II, q. 89, a. 6: "Whether venial sin can be in anyone with original sin alone?"

37. ST I-II, q. 89, a. 6 in *Basic Writings of Saint Thomas Aquinas,* edited and translated by Anton C. Pegis (Random House: New York, 1945). All quotations from the *Summa theologiae* are from this translation.

38. See ST I-II, q. 89, a. 6, ad 3.

child prior to reaching the age of reason. The pagan mystic will *already have made the original choice* with respect to his end at the point of reaching the age of reason. So, the pagan is already either in a state of implicit faith, and is open to further grace, or he is in a state of mortal plus venial sin. His continuance in a state of grace would depend on his response to God's providential invitation to explicit faith, or he would fall into mortal sin and be guilty of the sin of rebellious unbelief. At ST II-II, q. 10, a. 4, ad 3, Aquinas argues that the pagan centurion Cornelius had implicit faith: the truth of the Gospel was not yet made manifest to him, but Peter was sent to give him fuller instruction, to make that faith explicit. Aquinas's texts concerning implicit faith cannot be used to bolster the case for an authentic natural mysticism, unless the pagan is like the savage who is already *on the way* to faith. The case of the individual's first moral act is not analogous to that of the pagan or unbeliever's every act, despite some scholars' views to the contrary.[39]

This conclusion is confirmed by a glance at the three categories of unbelief listed at ST II-II, q. 2, aa. 7–8.[40] There are those who i. deliberately reject faith, ii. those who lack faith without explicitly rejecting it, and iii. those with implicit faith before the time of Christ. Those who have involuntary or sinless disbelief, in the second category, will nonetheless be damned if they fail to repent, according to Aquinas, for they have received the punishment of sin, even if they have committed no sin.[41] "Without faith," he states, "they are unable to be forgiven: but they are not damned on account of the sin of unbelief."[42] There is no middle ground or state of "pure nature" in which the human will could be suspended between a state of grace and mortal sin, and there is no indifference or neutrality with respect to our

39. Both Thomas F. O'Meara (*Thomas Aquinas: Theologian* [Notre Dame, Indiana: University of Notre Dame Press, 1997], 239) and Joseph A. DiNoia (*The Diversity of Religions: A Christian Perspective* [Washington, D.C.: The Catholic University of America Press, 1992], 97) collapse these cases, as is noted by Thomas M. Osborne, Jr. in "Unbelief and Sin in Thomas Aquinas and the Thomistic Tradition," *Nova et Vetera* [English edition] 8, no. 3 (2010): 625. Osborne notes that unbelievers' morally good acts, which are indifferent to merit by lacking charity, are not salvific according to Aquinas.

40. On this text, and its various interpretations, see Osborne, "Unbelief and Sin in Thomas Aquinas," 614–16.

41. See ST II-II, q. 34, a. 3 ad 2. Sinless unbelief stands outside the economy of salvation because the unbeliever, while not guilty of sinning against faith, still reaps under the effects of original sin. In contrast with his optimism in the *De Veritate* text, Augustinian pessimism about the role of original sin increased in Aquinas, by the time of the *Summa.*

42. ST II-II, q. 10, a. 1, as cited in Osborne, "Unbelief and Sin in Thomas Aquinas," 615.

ultimate end. To make this error involves confusing moral goodness and merit, and overlooking the superadded charity by which we are ordered to God and eternal life.[43]

Neutral or negative unbelief must be overcome by faith and charity for salvation to occur. So it seems that mystical experiences must occur either in a state of grace, on the way to salvation, or in a state of mortal sin, on the way to damnation. Unbelievers *can* perform good acts without grace, if their unbelief is non-voluntary, and non-hostile to Christianity, but they lack the developed faith, and thus charity, of authentic mystical union. Natural mysticism in one who has implicit faith is thus not a neutral, independent, trans-religious state, as core adherents would have it, but a vestibule to the feast of charity.

From the *De veritate* and *Summa* texts, we see that explicit faith regarding God's existence and providence is necessary for salvation, but not to attain an initial state of grace. It seems possible for a child or a pagan of good will to attain and maintain sanctifying grace by following natural reason. Their implicit faith involves a state of readiness for the Gospel, or even a neutral sort of unbelief, if it falls short of a positive, or rebellious, unbelief. How does this state of affairs relate to the status of mystics outside the Church? Is there a parallel between the implicit faith of a pagan and his natural mystical experience?

According to Garrigou, those who have natural or pre-mystical experiences are in the same category as the unbaptized savage, those with implicit faith who preceded Christ, and as those who have "forgotten" Him through no fault of their own.[44] But implicit faith requires a conviction that God, in His mercy, has provided some undefined means of salvation.[45] Charity, and thus faith, are required for salvation and for supernatural union with God. And the pagan mystics' state of grace would depend on their response to a divine offer of explicit faith. Their natural love of God is no more efficacious for salvation than the angels' natural desire, which does not raise them to union with God. Because men did not remain in the state of pure nature, their natural drives are fallen and cannot result

43. ST I-II, q. 21, a. 1; q. 18, a. 5; q. 23, a. 3; *In III Sent.*, d. 18, a. 2. By condign merit, the moral agent is made a sharer of God's nature, by charity; see ST I-II, q. 114, a. 3.

44. Garrigou-Lagrange, *Our Savior and His Love for Us*, 363.

45. Ibid., quoting Father Eliseus of the Nativity. On the text of Hebrews 11.6 on explicit faith, see ibid., 375.

in divine union.[46] Pagans' deliberations about the end, and by extension, their mystical experiences, are *not* in the same situation as a child's initial reception or rejection of grace;[47] they await, it would seem, formation by Christian inspiration, which God would infallibly provide, as long as they put no obstacle in the way.[48]

Unlike the situation of the child, pagan mystics dwell in a spiritual hiatus between the explicit *natural* desire for reunion with the cause of their being and *supernatural* faith. The only place for non-Christian natural mysticism in this schema is the case of mystics with implicit faith, moving *towards* the Faith, mystics in whom the grace of Christ is working through the invisible Church. Such a situation excludes the core view inasmuch as non-theists cannot possess implicit faith.

To sum up, contrary to "anonymous Christian" interpretations of grace, Aquinas thinks that even neutral unbelief incurs damnation, and implicit faith requires explicit faith in the two Pauline *credibilia.* For Garrigou, natural mysticism can co-exist with Christian mysticism in the Christian Neoplatonist,[49] or in the pagan mystic, only through the grace of Christ working in the invisible Church. However, original sin, combined with the danger of confusing mystical and natural forms of contemplation, and the angelic sin which pulls the intellect towards union with evil spirits,[50] makes pre-mysticism the exception to, rather than a condition of, spiritual progress. While Garrigou examines mysticism from the side of the rule rather than from the side of the exception, Maritain, inspired by French scholars of Hinduism and Islam,[51] also embraces the exception as a spiritual guide in his interpretation of natural mysticism. However, he moderates his enthusiasm for the invisible workings of grace outside the visible Church

46. Ibid., 373. The text of Aquinas is ST I, q. 62, a. 2.

47. See Osborne, "Unbelief and Sin in Thomas Aquinas," 625. He notes that both O'Meara and DiNoia make a false parallel between the case of an individual's first moral act and an unbeliever's every act.

48. See DV q. 14, a. 11.

49. Osborne "Unbelief and Sin in Thomas Aquinas," 380.

50. On this point, see Garrigou-Lagrange, *Our Savior and His Love for Us*, 374, where he cites Maritain, who cites Aquinas, on the temptation of the Arabic philosophers; see SCG III, chaps 41–45.

51. See Louis Gardet, *Expériences mystiques en terre non chretiennes* (Alsatia, 1953); *Mystique musulmane—Aspects et tendances, éxperiences et techniques* (Paris: Vrin, 1961). Cf. Olivier Lacombe, *L'Absolu selon le Vedanta* (Paris: Geuther, 1937). Cf. Maritain, "Appendix V: On a Work of Father Gardiel," in *Distinguish to Unite, or The Degrees of Knowledge*, translated by Gerald B. Phelan, 4th edition (New York: Charles Scribner's Sons, 1959), 445–50.

with his last word on the subject, in *On the Church of Christ* (1973), in a view closer to that of his Dominican mentor.

2. *Maritain on Natural Mysticism*

Every great metaphysic is pierced by a mystical aspiration which a purely conceptual exercise cannot satisfy.[52] Metaphysics tends towards mysticism in what Maritain calls our "hyper-finality," or rational mode, of reunification with the Cause of our being. Mysticism, he says, is "an experimental knowledge of the deep things of God," or, with Dionysius, a "suffering of divine things."[53] Maritain's differences with Garrigou in "Natural Mystical Experience and the Void" over the validity and nature of natural mysticism stem from three sources: i. his contact with French religion scholars (particularly those of Hinduism and Islam);[54] ii. his pioneering work on the "spiritual supra-conscious" (an inversion of Freud), in which he exchanges the implicit/explicit faith distinction for the terminology of connaturality and levels of consciousness; and, iii. his efforts to explain the thirst for the absolute which he finds in modern atheism across various religious families.

Abandoning his earlier agreement with his mentor on the inauthentic nature of natural mysticism in *The Degrees of Knowledge,* in "Natural Mystical Experience" Maritain describes a natural, pre-conscious mysticism as a preparation and even tutor for Christian spirituality. In *On the Church of Christ,* he reaffirms the virtual and invisible presence of the Church in her entirety in those with implicit faith, such as the savage, or one "born in the forests."[55]

In *On the Church of Christ,*[56] Maritain distinguishes the person and elements of the Church, noting that while personality presupposes a nature that is "whole in its proper order," where there is nothing lacking that is essential (Roman Catholicism), "elements" properly so-called (*vestigia*) of supernatural faith can exist in Christian groups formally separated from

52. Maritain, "The Natural Mystical Experience and the Void," 261.

53. Maritain, *The Degrees of Knowledge,* 247. Cf. Henry Bars, "Maritain's Contributions to an Understanding of Mystical Experience," 111–27.

54. Olivier Lacombe's work on the *Vedantas,* and Gardiel's work on the soul's self-knowledge are discussed by Maritain in "Natural Mysticism and the Void." Cf. note 51 above.

55. Maritain, *On the Church of Christ,* 31. Cf. DV q. 14, a. 11. The topics of natural mysticism and the child's first act of freedom are closely related for Maritain, as we shall see.

56. Maritain, *On the Church of Christ,* 93–134.

Rome (dissident Christian communions). The "elements" *improperly* so-called also exist in all monotheisms (Judaism and Islam), whereas mere "pre-elements" of the Church may exist in non-supernatural, non-salvific, spiritual families (Eastern religions). There is thus a descending participation in truth, ending in "traces" of the supernatural, in the natural preparations and recognition of a "call" present even among atheists. Hinduism and Buddhism are merely natural forms of deliverance, and Buddhism crushes idolatry in a metaphysical suicide that withdraws the delivered one from both suffering, the human condition, and even from existence itself. Judaism "truncates" the means of salvation by denying the New Covenant, and Islam denies intimacy with God.[57]

The contribution that natural mysticism might make to inter-religious dialogue, which is discussed in "Natural Mystical Experience and the Void," is muted in *On the Church of Christ*, Maritain's late masterwork on ecclesiology.[58] In this sense, *On the Church of Christ* (1973) retrieves the early perspective of *The Degrees of Knowledge* (1926), in which Maritain echoes Garrigou: there is no authentic mysticism outside the visible Church, although the intervention of grace in rare individuals could result in mystical graces. Natural mysticism lacks grace and charity, and thus does not qualify as *pati divina*. Plotinus' mysticism is a combination of asceticism and natural contemplation, and the *Upanishads* is an anticipation of mysticism. The dangers of confusion of absolutes and of contact with spirits, also illumine the dubious status of natural mysticism. The shift away from Garrigou's synthesis came with a 1931 Appendix to *The Degrees of Knowledge*, where Maritain describes an intuitive, experimental, and indirect knowledge of the soul's existence through its own acts—the nucleus of his own view of natural mysticism defended in his 1938 "Natural Mystical Experience and the Void."

57. In *Peasant of the Garonne*, however, he had expressed approval of Massignon's desire to canonize al-Hallaj. Maritain, *Peasant of the Garonne* (New York: Macmillan, 1969), 320. The original was published in 1968.

58. Maritain lists four factors which prevent the natural mysticism of Hinduism and Buddhism from being a sign of the invisible presence of the Church. First, the vocabulary of grace and salvation is a verbal facsimile of Christianity, and nothing more—nonhistorical revelation claimed by Hindus, for example, results in an apophatic world-denying experience. Second, the Pelagian tenor of Eastern asceticism differs from the ascent of faith required for Christian mysticism—this spiritual technology is an ecstasy of natural spirituality which is confused with an obscure metaphysical imagination. Third, the "grace" issuing from the Hindu pantheon is benevolence, favor, or protection, he states, but is not the divine gift which elevates the soul to the interior life of God; and fourth, the Hindu Absolute, Brahman, is mingled with cosmic energy so as to deny the pure transcendence of the first principle. See Maritain, *On the Church of Christ*, 122.

In "Natural Mystical Experience and the Void," mystical experience is treated as one of four types of knowledge by connaturality, also known as knowledge by way of inclination.[59] The fourth type is mystical knowledge, which is neither a knowledge for action or for creation, nor pure speculative knowledge. It can be affective, as in supernatural contemplation and the union of love—here, the gift of wisdom, under God's action, frees the human mind from the mode of concepts and analogy as the means of knowing, and suppresses, by way of love, the distance between subject and object.[60] Or, mystical knowledge can be intellectual, by which he means a natural but non-conceptual contemplation that attains three things at once: i. the "ultimate goal of the act of knowing in its perfect immanence"; ii. the "absolute" as the very *esse* of the soul, known obliquely as the source of its acts; and, iii. a brushing contact with divine immensity, or the presence of *Ipsum Esse* as the source of all existence.[61]

In an ebullience of spiritual energy, Maritain describes the "mysticism of the self" as a retorsion of our minds' drive to know universal being which yet reflects our desire to be united practically and entirely with the *cause* of our being. The mind "voids" itself of all concepts, images, and distinctions in a "lived *via negationis*"[62] and an "act of abolition of all act."[63] The term of this experience of negation is not the essence, but the existence, of the soul.

When united with the body, the soul cannot know its own essence directly, but it nevertheless experiences the act of existence at the root of its own powers. Through the medium of the void (the act of abolition of all acts or operations), the soul is said to have contact with divine immensity: "existence in its metaphysical amplitude, and the sources of existence … is something emanating from … an influx wherefrom it obtains its all."[64] The effort to gain this contact is one against the grain of nature, "an art," he says, "of entering while living into death … which is not evangelic death, intended to give place to the life of Another, but a metaphysical death, intended

59. Maritain, "The Natural Mystical Experience and the Void," 255–90. The first type is knowledge for *right action*, by way of practical inclination, in moral judgment (Aquinas used this type as an analogy to explain the "suffering of divine things"). The second type is *intellectual connaturality*, which is a natural contemplation by the wise man of divine things. Third, there is *poetic connatural knowledge*, which tends not to silent contemplation but to the creative word. The fourth type is *mystical connaturality* (affective or intellectual).

60. See Maritain, "The Natural Mystical Experience and the Void," 264.

61. See ibid., 263–65.

62. Ibid., 275.

63. Ibid., 276.

64. Ibid., 279.

to winnow spiritual activities away from the body."[65] Natural mysticism thus involves a perilous denial of the human condition and an indifference to the demands of charity,[66] and requires cautious awareness of the dark ends of spiritual manipulation. Yet it also parallels Maritain's later development of the theme of subjectivity and nonintellectual pathways to God found in his 1945 essay on the first act of freedom.[67]

Maritain develops four basic claims in his natural mysticism of the self. First, through nescience, the soul can attain an intellectual experience of its own *esse* through the medium of the void (this medium takes the place of love, as found in supernatural mysticism). Second, through contact with this *esse* (the first absolute), the soul is said to contact divine immensity (the second absolute), not through a judgment of existence, or of metaphysical *separatio*, but through an experiential "touching" that culminates in an intellectual apophasis. Hindu mysticism is seen as propadeutic to Christian mysticism, even though it ends in Buddhism's metaphysical suicide of sorts, and involves a potential confusion of absolutes (atman/Brahman; self/God). While Maritain does not detail the nature of natural mysticism's relationship to Christian mysticism in "Natural Mysticism and the Void," it is clear that its priority is temporal and sometimes in the order of discovery; it is also clear that natural mysticism is not in any way ontologically prior to Christian mysticism in the order of perfection.[68]

65. Ibid., 278.

66. And yet even Georges Cardinal Cottier, O.P., theologian of the Pontifical Household under Pope John Paul II, said that natural mysticism of the self even if fraught with dangers, "does not in principle raise any objection." Georges Cardinal Cottier, "Metaphysics and Mysticism," *Nova et Vetera* (English edition) 1, no. 2 (2003): 281.

67. The 1945 essay appeared in English as "The Immanent Dialectic of the First Act of Freedom" in Jacques Maritain, *The Range of Reason* (New York: Charles Scribner's Sons, 1948), 66–85.

68. And even here, we can point to instances of cross-religious mystical experiences that are indicative of confusion, error, and psychic darkness, more than of a straight path towards the fullness of truth. One thinks immediately of the Christian/Hindu hybrid Bede Griffiths, explaining his experiences of "nondual wholeness, an experience of *advaita* or oneness"—which he calls, in line with Sankara, an "awareness of being which is nothing but being's reflection on itself"—in other words, the self's identification with the divine Self in a state of nonduality: "In meditation (*beyond the conscious mind—viz.*) I become aware of the ground of my being in matter, in life, in human consciousness. I can experience my solidarity with the universe.... I can get beyond all these outer forms of things in time and space and discover the Ground from which they all spring. I can know the Father, the Origin, the Source, beyond being and not being, the One." Bede Griffiths as quoted in Judson P. Trapnell, *Bede Griffiths: A Life in Dialogue* (Albany, New York: State University of New York Press, 2001), 129–30; emphasis in original. Bede Griffiths is a fine example of the dangers of natural mysticism and is proof of the fact that natural mysticism can furnish its own term of awareness and need not ever lead towards the affective union of Christian mysticism.

How one is to transcend a flawed monism to enter a Christian differentiated union is unclear. Only a union *secundum intentionem*, not *secundum esse*, prevents the soul's being dissolved into the divine, and the levels of consciousness at play in Maritain's account do not give way to deification in the Plotinian sense, as the union of love always involves a duality.[69] This is the mystery of the spiritual marriage between the created will and Uncreated Love, a marriage in which, Maritain says, God "becomes her [namely, the soul] more than she herself, and is the principle and agent of all her operations."[70] Stratford Caldecott has argued for a Christian non-dualism in contrast to a Hindu "monistic" non-dualism, by stressing the nonreciprocal relation of dependence of creatures on their cause, which means their nothingness outside God.[71]

As we have seen, Maritain, unlike Garrigou, exchanged Aquinas's language of implicit vs. explicit knowledge for the more inclusive language of connaturality and a spiritual "supra-conscious." Placing his views on natural mysticism alongside his interpretation of the first act of freedom reveals his optimism regarding the capacity of the will to influence the intellect in our moral and spiritual lives.[72] Maritain links his essay on the first act of freedom to ST I-II, q. 89, a. 6, where Aquinas considers the possibility of the coexistence of original and venial sin.[73]

The problem with Maritain's account, Lawrence Dewan shows,[74] is his relegation of cognition to the sidelines in the dawn of our moral life, and its replacement with appetite as assigning our ultimate end. As Dewan notes, the rectitude of appetite which influences the intellect concerns the practi-

69. See Maritain, *The Degrees of Knowledge* (p. 368, for example) on the distinction between types of union. Cf. Curtis Hancock, "Maritain on Mystical Contemplation," in *Understanding Maritain: Philosopher and Friend*, edited by Deal Hudson and Matthew Mancini (Macon, Georgia: Mercer University Press, 1987), 265.

70. Maritain, *The Degrees of Knowledge*, 369. Cf. Hancock, "Maritain on Mystical Contemplation," 265 on Maritain's avoidance of monism.

71. See Stratford Caldecott, "'Face to Face': The Difference between Hindu and Christian Non-Dualism," *Communio* 34, no. 4 (2007): 616–39. Cf. Sara Grant, *Towards an Alternative Theology: Confessions of a Non-Dualist Christian* (South Bend, Indiana: University of Notre Dame Press, 2002), which draws lines of similarity between the Hindu Sankara and Aquinas, on the basis of nonreciprocal dependence. Caldecott claims his view is similar to Grant's. See Caldecott, "'Face to Face,'" 627 n. 21.

72. See Maritain, "The Immanent Dialectic of the First Act of Freedom," in *The Range of Reason*, 66–85.

73. See Maritain, "The Immanent Dialectic," 85 n.

74. See Lawrence Dewan, "Natural Law and the First Act of Freedom: Maritain Revisited," in *Wisdom, Law, and Virtue: Essays in Thomistic Ethics* (New York: Fordham University Press, 2007), 221–41.

cal judgment of means, not of final ends (since we cannot *but* will our final natural end). The practical syllogism involved in the first act of freedom involves an acknowledgement or declaration of an ultimate end. It is this conscious, albeit imperfect, cognition which is our gateway into the moral universe, reasons Dewan.[75] In contrast, for Maritain, just as natural mysticism stresses the power of the non-conceptual, so the first act of freedom is said to be directed God-wards by a pre-conceptual appetite for the good as the ultimate end of our existence, such that,

> God is thus naturally known, without any conscious judgment, in and by the impulse of the will ... [in a] purely practical, non-conceptual and non-conscious knowledge of God, which can co-exist with a theoretical ignorance of God.[76]

Both pre-conceptual cognition and appetite are seen as capable of directing the soul to God, where conceptual knowledge is posterior and accidental.[77] The priority given to the impulse of the will unwittingly leans Maritain towards the core view's emphasis on the pre-conceptual experiential matrix. His view of the "void" as the term of an act of abolition of all acts in natural mysticism also reveals the light work he assigns to discursive reason in the spiritual life.[78]

Two facts mitigate against a clear trajectory from natural mysticism to the culmination of holiness, namely, the centrality of love in Christian spirituality and the nonappetitive nature of much of natural mysticism. Further, there is the question of the soul's use of signs in mystical ascent. "Philosophical inquiry," de Lubac reminds us,

> rises analytically from effect to cause, in virtue of a rational necessity. The mystical impulse rises from effect, perceived as a sign, to that same cause, by a movement

75. "In the very moment of entering into the moral universe, one must be declaring an ultimate end." And even the "moral debutant", he shows "must have a natural knowledge of God, though a confused knowledge." Ibid., 236. Cf. "Thomas's primary doctrine concerning inclination is that it presupposes cognition." Natural inclinations form the basis of the natural law (ST I-II, q. 94, a. 2). The child not only has the chosen object before its mind, but the process of deliberation itself is an object of reflection.

76. Maritain, "The Immanent Dialectic," 70.

77. Cf.: "The extent to which we are asked to set aside conceptual knowledge of God here is remarkable. If it is not 'in the way,' an impediment, it is certainly not appropriate as a help or as furthering the process of which Maritain wishes to speak." Dewan, "Natural Law and the First Act of Freedom," 230.

78. The experience of the self could be argued to negate (or compete with) the influx of love that is the remote call to mystical union, and to holiness, in the Platonic attempt to separate the spirit from its material conditions.

which cannot be wholly justified by pure reason … [and] the mystic, in the end, will reject all signs … in order to rest in the contemplation of God alone. [79]

In Christian mysticism, the effect of charity in the soul serves as a starting point or sign; in the natural mysticism of the self, the soul's contingent existence is the sign by which divine immensity is imperfectly experienced.[80] In natural mysticism, contrary to Christian mysticism (which involves the act of faith and the theological virtues), there is a gradual short-circuiting of intellectual ascent, culminating in Buddhist emptiness/*sunyata*. In its final stages, natural mysticism refines the soul by destroying it, through removing the condition of its true progress—the purifying force of love.

III. Aquinas on Christ and Paradox in Biblical Commentaries

Paradox, the holding together in tension of intelligible opposites, is often linked to the core position, as a sign that mystical experience eludes the net of syllogistic reasoning. Whether ultimate reality is expressed as the nameless Tao, as *Advaita* (non-dualist) by Vedanta philosophers such as Sankara, as Zen's impersonal "suchness," as the hidden essence of Allah, or as the ultimate reality of which we know more what it is *not* than what it *is*,[81] (Maimonides and Aquinas), the trans-discursive quality of paradox serves the core approach's suppression of particularity and the discursive approach to theology. Since the truths of faith are in no wise known or comprehended in this life,[82] no demonstrative proofs of reason are possible.[83] Paradox often plays a role in the exhortative and pastoral character of Christian theology in meditations on the fittingness of the mysteries of faith.[84]

In Aquinas, there are metaphysical paradoxes involved in the "dark

79. Henri de Lubac, *The Discovery of God*, translated by Alexander Dru (New York: Darton, Longman, and Todd, 1960), 146–47.

80. Maritain's notion of divine immensity here recalls his "sixth way" of attaining God through a realization of the contingent existence of the self.

81. See Aquinas, *De potentia*, q. 7, a. 5, ad 14. Cf. Denis Janz, "Syllogism or Paradox: Aquinas and Luther on Theological Method," *Theological Studies* 59, no. 1 (1998): 16.

82. See Aquinas, *In de Trinitate*, q. 3, a. 1c.

83. See Aquinas, *In de Trinitate*, q. 1, a. 4c and ad 7.

84. Chenu pointed to the many theological syllogisms that are "purely expository in character" (providing arguments of fittingness, not logically necessary proofs). See Chenu, *Toward Understanding Saint Thomas*, translated by Albert Landry and Dominic Hughes (Chicago: Henry Regnery Company, 1964), 80. Torrell agrees that demonstrative syllogisms are rare in Aquinas's

knowledge" of God, where the higher mode of divine perfections is found to exist preeminently.[85] God is said to be good and not-good, wise and not-wise, and so on. Often, these paradoxes are dissolved through appeal to analogy, which explains the apparent equivocity through causal perfection or *pros hen* (causal one-to-many) predication; the affirmation of supereminence to some degree, removes the negation.[86]

While metaphysical paradoxes can be unraveled by showing their internal coherence, paradox resists dissolution in its native home of scriptural exegesis. And it is here that Aquinas's use of paradox is particularly inhospitable to the core interpretation.[87] True, he does dissolve many biblical paradoxes through introducing levels of meaning that illumine the trajectory of spiritual development. For example, that "the first are last, and the last first" points to the difference between pride and humility,[88] as does the

---

theology. See Jean-Pierre Torrell, *Saint Thomas Aquinas: His Person and His Work*, translated by Robert Royal (Washington, D.C.: Catholic University of America Press, 1996), 266. Torrell also emphasizes the pastoral role of Aquinas's arguments.

85. See, for example, ST I, q. 13, a. 2.

86. "It cannot be said that whatever is predicated of God and creatures is an equivocal predication; for, unless there were at least some real agreement [*convenientia*] between creatures and God, His essence would not be the likeness of creatures, and so He could not know them by knowing His essence. Similarly, we would not be able to attain any knowledge of God from creatures, nor from among the names devised for creatures could we apply one to Him more than another." DV q. 2, a. 11, in *St. Thomas Aquinas: The Disputed Questions on Truth*, vol. 1, translated and edited by Robert M. Mulligan (Chicago: Henry Regnery Company, 1952), 112. On Aquinas's avoidance of the irrationalities implied by pure equivocity, see Gregory Rocca, "The 'Dark Knowledge of God' and Our Worship of the Divine Mystery," *Nova et Vetera* (English edition) 3, no. 1 (2005): 818–19. Joseph Owens argued that Aquinas imposed a metaphysical interpretation on Dionysius' mystical "darkness of ignorance," such that the metaphysician holds three propositions in logical tension: first, that the primary efficient cause is subsistent existence; second, that it contains all perfections in the highest degree; and third, that we cannot conceive of its nature or any of its perfections, nor intuit its existence, yet knowledge *si est* of this cause contains the riches and starting point of metaphysics. See "Aquinas: 'Darkness of Ignorance' in the Most Refined Notion of God," in *Bonaventure and Aquinas: Enduring Philosophers*, edited by Robert W. Shahan and Francis J. Kovach (Norman, Oklahoma: University of Oklahoma Press, 1976), 69–86.

87. Chenu notes that reason operates with "great mobility" in Aquinas's theology. See, *Toward Understanding Saint Thomas*, 177. Theology's need for a variety of uses of language and reason is also due to the pastoral exigencies of the trade, and partly to the nature of theological truths, which refer to contingent realities dependent solely on the will of God, not to any predictable natural causes. Theology, says Torrell, is an "organization of contingent data received from revelation upon which the theologian labors to find the arrangement of God's design." Torrell, *Thomas Aquinas: His Person and His* Work, 266. Cf. Janz, "Syllogism or Paradox," 14.

88. Aquinas, *Super 19 Mattheum*, lectio 2, in *Super Evangelium S. Matthaei Lectura*, 5th ed., edited by Raphaelis Cai (Rome: Marietti, 1951).

saying "these things are hidden from the wise and prudent, and revealed to the little ones" (Matthew 11.25).[89] The loss of one's soul being "gain" is taken to refer to the willingness to expose oneself to physical danger for Christ's sake,[90] for example. But in St. Paul's paradox of the Cross, Aquinas saw the brilliant star of Christian doctrine against his own midday sun. Here, Aquinas did not find a content-less "core" or bedrock of spiritual experience, but rather the persistent demands of a Christocentric soteriology.

Chenu notes the fact that many theological syllogisms are "purely expository" and exhortative in character," drawing out the intelligibility of faith—the wide sense of proof/*probare* not as logical demonstration, but as "fittingness"/*convenire* based on an accepted proposition—for instance, the Incarnation.[91] The mysteries of the faith also require non-discursive uses of language to reveal scriptural truths to the initiated, and to communicate truths that are not only beyond reason but also contrary to the senses.[92]

The intractability of mystery in which theological reason moves permeates Aquinas's commentaries on the paradox of the Cross, a favorite meditation in his mystical theology. Once he has established the counterintuitive "fittingness" of the Incarnation, Aquinas defends the counterintuitive "fittingness" of the Passion itself. The various texts contain many paradoxes: the essential hiddenness by which all things are re-established in Christ; the mystery of God's self-sacrifice; the folly of the Cross, which juxtaposes the strength of God in weakness with the power of the empty wisdom of words which would empty the Cross of Christ of its power, and so on.[93]

Here, I note two texts which show the distance between the core interpretation and Aquinas's scriptural meditations on God.[94] First, there is Aquinas's *Commentary on Ephesians* 3.18–20, on the dimensions of Christian charity. Second, there is his *Commentary on Philippians* 2.5–8, where

89. Aquinas, *Super 11 Mattheum*, lectio 3.

90. Aquinas, *Super 10 Mattheum*, lectio 3.

91. On this, see Chenu, *Toward Understanding Saint Thomas*, 180; Torrell, *Thomas Aquinas: His Person and His Work*, 266. Cf. Janz, "Syllogism or Paradox," 14.

92. See Aquinas, *In IV Sent.*, d. 10, q. 1, a. 1. Cf. Chenu, who said that reason operates with "great mobility" in Aquinas's theology, pointing to the pastoral exigencies of the trade, and to the nature of theological truths as referring to contingent realities dependent solely on the will of God, not to any predictable natural causes. In theology, reason functions "within the mystery." Chenu, *Toward Understanding Saint Thomas*, 180 n.

93. Many of these texts of Aquinas are noted in Janz, "Syllogism or Paradox," 20.

94. Although there is no autobiographical mystical account in either of these texts (as we find with Augustine, for example), the interpenetration of doctrine, exegesis, and devotion is at work, and to this extent, we can call them "mystical meditations."

we see him discussing St. Paul's notion of the *kenosis* of Christ. Paul's text introduces a famous theme often used to argue the core view, through a parallel of Christ's self-emptying to Buddhist *sunyata*.[95]

1. *Commentary on Ephesians 3.18–20*

Aquinas applies an Augustinian definition of wisdom as knowledge of divine realities,[96] to contrast human flawed human knowledge (*scientia*) with transcendent divine wisdom, the origin of charity. The text of the *Commentary on Ephesians* 3.18–20 is a meditation on that charity and power of Christ which works in the elect through the Church:

> 18 I pray that you may have the power to comprehend, with all the saints, what is
> the breadth and length and height and depth, 19 and to know the love of Christ
> that surpasses knowledge, so that you may be filled with all the fullness of God. 20
> Now to him who by the power at work within us is able to accomplish abundantly
> far more than we can ask or imagine, 21 to him be glory in the church and in Christ
> Jesus, to all generations, forever and ever.[97]

Aquinas ponders the wisdom given to us through faith and charity, and the transforming power of this wisdom, through the power of the Cross.[98] The four dimensions are applied to three objects in the text: to God's nature, to Christ's love expressed through the Incarnation and Redemption, and to the four parts of the Cross.

Regarding God's nature, God's depth is His incomprehensible wisdom, His breadth is His power over all creation, His length is His eternal duration, and His height, the nobility of His nature. Christ's charity manifests what God the Father has accomplished through reconciling the world to Himself. "Depth" here signifies the origin of charity in the Spirit; "breadth"

95. Masao Abe, for instance, makes this leap. See Masao Abe, "Kenotic God and Dynamic *Sunyata*," in *The Emptying God: A Buddhist-Jewish-Christian Conversation*, edited by John B. Cobb and Christopher Ives (Maryknoll, New York: Orbis, 1990), 3–65.

96. See Aquinas, *In Eph.*, c. 5, lectio 6, no. 305. Cf. Mark Edwards, "Aquinas on Ephesians and Colossians," in *Aquinas on Scripture: An Introduction to his Biblical Commentaries*, edited by Thomas Weinandy, Daniel Keating, and John Yocum (New York: Continuum, 2005), 155.

97. Ephesians 3.18–20, New Revised Standard Version. All Bible references are from this translation.

98. *Commentary on the Letter of Saint Paul to the Ephesians* cap. 3, lectio 5, in *Saint Thomas Aquinas: Commentary on the Letters of Saint Paul to the Galatians and Ephesians*, Biblical Commentaries Series, vol. 39, translated by Fabian Larcher and Matthew Lamb, edited by John Mortensen and Enrique Alarcón (Lander, Wyoming: The Aquinas Institute for the Study of Sacred Doctrine, 2012).

signifies the extension of charity even to our enemies; the "length" of charity is its eternal duration; its "height" is its heavenly motivation. Christ's obedience unto death was motivated by charity, and the Cross also exhibits these dimensions. He states that the breadth of the cross-beam signifies charity stretched out to our enemies; the length of the trunk of the cross against which Christ leans, signifies the enduring, sustaining nature of charity; the top part of the cross on which Christ's head has a height, which signifies our hope of eternity; and the base of the cross driven into the earth signifies the depth of divine love, which sustains us yet is not visible insofar as the mystery of predestination eludes our comprehension.

This meditation flows from Aquinas's own devotions to the Crucifix, in which charity stimulates knowledge, and knowledge influences one's life and conduct. God's elevation of man to the status of sharer in the divine nature, he says, is accomplished in the Incarnation of His Son. Here, mysticism is less a transient Platonic detachment from material particulars than it is conformity to Christ, the spiritual exemplar, in a charity which is "lasting, extensive, sublime and deep." Christ is the door to mystical union, in which the soul "finds pasture" (cf. John 10.9) in the contemplation of His divinity and humanity.[99]

2. *Commentary on* Philippians 2.5–9

The famous *kenosis* text is Paul's hymn to Christ, who emptied himself for the sake of the world:

> 5 Let the same mind be in you that was in Christ Jesus, 6 who, though he was in the form of God, did not regard equality with God as something to be exploited, 7 but emptied himself, taking the form of a slave, being born in human likeness, and being found in human form, 8 he humbled himself, and became obedient to the point of death - even death on a cross. 9 Therefore, God also highly exalted him and gave him the name that is above every name.

Here, we see the double paradox of a self-emptying God who, through His humility, is exalted. The Japanese religion scholar Masao Abe gives a Buddhist reading of Paul's hymn to Christ,[100] interpreting it as a total renunciation of Christ's divinity, by which God establishes solidarity with man, who can then respond in loving witness.

99. Aquinas, *Comm. in Eph.*, cap. 3 lect. 5, no. 179.
100. See Masao Abe, "Kenotic God and Dynamic *Sunyata*," 3–65.

Abe uses the text to show the ways in which Buddhist forms of emptiness or *sunyata* could be used to tease out the basis of Paul's Christology and provide evidence for an interfaith interpretation of mystical experience. Using the paradoxical language of "emptiness" in the school of Nagarjuna and his predecessors, Abe argues that Christ embodies Buddhist *sunyata*, reaching enlightenment and reclaiming His sonship by "not clinging" to His own divinity.[101] By means of this paradoxical exaltation through humiliation, Christ is said to become an icon of the living God instead of a distant unattainable idol. As a parallel to the paradoxical Buddhist "emptiness of emptiness," Jesus is said to *be* the Son of God precisely because is he *not* the Son of God. Upon analysis, Abe's paradoxical transcendence and immanence through *kenosis* or self-emptying, as an application of Nagarjuna's "emptiness" is less an affirmation of the core view of mystical experience than it is a powerful negation of the Christian God through Arianism.[102]

The text from Philippians is not evidence of the core view, since Buddhism and Christianity have opposed ontic schema, and thus possess different goals and strategies of negation or self-emptying. While both Buddhist *sunyata* and Aquinas's *via negativa*, for example, engage the self in exercises of detachment, Buddhists are not directed towards a transcendent realm, but merely towards the relief of suffering through the denial of *all* forms of existence. Christian asceticism and Aquinas's way of denial, on the other hand, inhabit what has been described as a "fulfilment theology,"[103] a term which expresses Aquinas's final affirmation of deepening levels of desire, and the reality of their term in a fruitful but non-comprehensive, personal contact with divine excess of being.

If we go on to compare the experience of divine incomprehensibility in earthly mystical union in Aquinas with the Eastern concept of *nirvana* in Buddhist *sunyata*, we find no core experience to speak of. Aquinas's self-subsistent, transcendent Creator is a personal plenitude acting through grace to elevate human faculties, while Buddhist emptiness or *sunyata* is

101. Cf. James L. Fredericks, *Buddhists and Christians: Through Comparative Theology to Solidarity* (Maryknoll, New York: Orbis, 2004), 72–95.

102. The Council of Chalcedon (451 ad) clarified belief about Christ by proclaiming him fully divine and fully human. The view that Jesus was human but not fully divine (Arianism) is heterodox. This is detailed in Fredericks, *Buddhists and Christians*, 93–94.

103. Fredericks refers to "fulfillment" theologies as ones which acknowledge the goal of theology as the term of human desire. Ibid., 97.

a strategy of negation by which false attachments, even the pull towards emptiness itself, are discarded. Catholic mystical ascent is not a metaphysical contemplation of immanence, or a supreme deliverance by final renunciation, in the way that Buddhist spirituality envisions. Rather, it is a lifting of the mind and heart through a purgative way to the *excessus* of divine being by which vision and ontological desire are ultimately transformed.

In his commentary on Paul's hymn to the Philippians,[104] Aquinas labors to balance the humility of Christ in self-emptying with the truth of his divine nature, expressed as Christ's majesty. Christ's equality with the Father is expressed by Paul's saying he was "in the form of God." The proper names of Jesus as the Son, Word, and Image of God denote the perfection of form, and underscore His equality with the Father. Jesus is the Son as "one begotten," and the end or perfection of begetting is the form. Jesus is the Word in the sense that a perfect word leads to the knowledge of a thing's nature; in having the "entire nature" of the Father, Jesus is the perfect "word" leading to knowledge of God. Finally, Jesus is the perfect Image of the Father, since a perfect image has the form of its original.

The emptying of Christ does not refer, *contra* Rabanus the heretic (who made it a function of Christ's divine nature), to Christ's forfeiting His divinity for his humanity, but to his assuming a human nature, itself only capable of fullness. Christ's true self-emptying is known first, in the Incarnation itself, and second, in the Passion. Christ took the form of a servant by assuming weak human nature. By becoming man, God was born into our species, and so assumed all non-sinful defects and properties of our human nature. In "being found in human form," Christ's divinity is not changed by way of addition, as a fool is changed by gaining wisdom. Just the reverse is the case, says Aquinas. By becoming man, our human nature itself is changed for the better "because it was full of grace and truth" (cf. John 1.14).

Christ's *kenosis* is also apparent in His Passion. The fittingness of Christ's suffering and death stems from the sapiential plan of the reversal of Adam's sin through the obedient sacrifice of Christ. Sacrifice is perfect in the offering of one's own self, and by slaying one's own will in obedience

104. Aquinas, *In Philipp.*, cap. 2, lect. 2–3, in *Saint Thomas Aquinas: Commentary on the Letters of Saint Paul to the Philippians, Colossians, Thessalonians, Timothy, Titus, and Philemon*, Biblical Commentaries, vol. 40, translated by Fabian Larcher, edited by John Mortensen and Enrique Alarcón (Lander, Wyoming: The Aquinas Institute for the Study of Sacred Doctrine, 2012).

to another, Aquinas says, perfect charity is made known. Even as the human will tends towards life and honor, so in his perfect subjection to the Father's will, Christ fled neither death nor ignominy (death on a cross). He was thus exalted by God[105] not by earning his divinity (Arianism, and Masao Abe), nor by gaining a kind of pre-eminence over creatures (Photius). Rather, Christ's Lordship is a reward for humility given eternally in a grace of union, not of adoption, by which Christ is both God and man.

In his commentaries on the Ephesians and Philippians texts, Aquinas develops a spirituality of conformity to Christ, the moral and mystical exemplar. He is not engaging in a series of techniques by which an introvertive monist comes to experience inner harmony and the falling away of all distinctions. Aquinas's differentiated union is at once personal, incarnational, ecclesial, doctrinally rich, and demanding of an ethical response of love to the divine personality of Christ. The Christocentric mutual indwelling of God and the soul developed here and elsewhere in Aquinas is far from the core view, which suppresses intellectual, moral, and transformative considerations. The key loci of paradox in Aquinas, namely, the Incarnation and Passion, cannot be used to support the core view.

IV. Conclusion

The core/contextualist debate reveals a set of motives, arguments, and problems which displace the integral unity of ascetical and mystical theology in Thomist circles. Through an examination of various texts and Thomist interpretations of the levels of contemplation, faith, freedom, and paradox, I identified points of intersection between Aquinas's mystical theology as developed by Garrigou, Maritain's natural mysticism, and modern theories of religious experience. In contrast to the core/contextualist template which juxtaposes experience and tradition stands the robust synthesis developed by Aquinas and the Thomist-mystical movement.

The core view, which assumes a cross-religious experiential ground for mysticism, was argued to be impossible for Aquinas and Garrigou. Even natural mysticism cannot provide the necessary content, for the core view lacks the key component of implicit faith, and religious experience is neither neutral nor static.

105. Aquinas develops the theme of "exaltation" in *In Philipp.*, cap. 2, lect. 3.

Motivated by interfaith concerns and the link between contemplation and levels of consciousness, Maritain developed his mysticism of the self, echoing some aims of the core view. Here, practitioners of natural mysticism served as porters at the door of the supernatural life, in an interiority provided by the invisible power of God. But the sparks of the invisible Church seemed more sparsely scattered, if not less dimmed, in Maritain's narrative of God's activity in non-Christian spiritual families, in his final work, *On the Church of Christ.*

Finally, Aquinas's texts on implicit faith, and those employing metaphysical and theological paradox (particularly the *kenosis* and Cross of Christ) distinguish his approach from the core view for several reasons. First, implicit faith is impossible for nontheistic religions, for it propels the soul towards an affective indwelling of God in the soul. Second, metaphysical paradoxes are usually dissolved into affirmations about being, and involve natural, not mystical, contemplation. Third, his mystical meditations are Christocentric and resistant to the diluted abstractions required by the core view. Thus, while natural mysticism and paradox may serve as fruitful ground for comparisons with unbelievers, they cannot serve as signposts for a universal core of mystical experience.

DANIEL D. DE HAAN

Simon and Maritain on the Vocation of *Species in Medio*

Jacques Maritain and Yves Simon contributed a wealth of philosophical insights to the problems of cognition, noetics, and epistemology. Their developments of Thomism and the *philosophia perennis* were achieved through their erudite dialogue with ancient, medieval, and contemporary approaches to the nature of being. Maritain and Simon both defended sophisticated Thomist accounts of critical realism. Simon, in particular, dedicated a number of studies to the Thomist doctrine of sensation, and it is within these detailed studies that he took up the problem of intentions in the medium.[1] This paper aims to develop further Maritain's and Simon's accounts of Thomist realism by placing their treatments of sensation and intentional beings in the medium, i.e., *species in medio*, within Aquinas's robust metaphysical account of the transcendentals thing and truth.

I shall begin with a brief introduction to the problem of sensation and the medium.[2] Next, I turn to Thomas Aquinas's approach to the nature of

1. See Yves Simon, *Introduction to Metaphysics of Knowledge*, translated by Vukan Kuic and Richard J. Thompson (New York: Fordham University Press, 1934), chap. 3; Yves Simon and Julien Peghaire, "The Philosophical Study of Sensation," *The Modern Schoolman* 23, no. 3 (1946): 111–19; Yves Simon, "An Essay on Sensation," in *The Philosophy of Knowledge*, edited by Roland Hude and Joseph P. Mullally (Chicago: Lippincott, 1960), 55–95; reprinted in *Philosopher at Work: Essays by Yves Simon*, edited by Anthony O. Simon (Lanhama, Maryland: Rowman and Littlefield, 1999), 57–111. All citations are from the original. Jacques Maritain, *Distinguish to Unite or The Degrees of Knowledge*, translated by Gerald Phelan and Ralph McInerny, Collected Works of Jacques Maritain, vol. 7 (Notre Dame, Indiana: University of Notre Dame Press, 1995).

2. Sensation and the problem of intentions in the medium in Thomas Aquinas and other related issues are treated in the following recent studies. George Klubertanz, "*De Potentia* 5.8: A Note on the Thomist Theory of Sensation," *The Modern Schoolman* 26, no. 4 (1948): 323–31;

intentional beings in the medium and the distinction between natural being and intentional being. I will then summarize Yves Simon's development of Aquinas's theory of sensation before addressing the central problem of *species* in the medium. Simon will be our guide through various medieval attempts to understand the peculiar kind of participated causality exhibited in the medium's capacity to communicate intentional beings apsychically from the sensible reality to the sense powers of the animal. Simon's treatment of the *transitive intentional acts* of sensible things will uncover for us the vocation of *species in medio*. As we will see, the doctrine of transitive intentional acts elucidates the manner in which all sensible things communicate *species* into the medium, not for the sake of themselves, but for the sake of potential knowers. Finally, in the last section we will address the unusual sort of participation in separate substances that Aquinas attributes to *species* in the medium. But instead of supporting this doctrine's more mysterious elements by appealing to the empirical physics of medieval cosmology, we will avail ourselves of Aquinas's doctrine of the transcendentals thing and truth to explain the intentional vocation of *species in medio*. This paper does not promise to offer a complete solution to this recondite difficulty, but instead aims to set the contours of the problem in relief, to take note of the theoretical advances of Aquinas and Simon, and finally,

David W. Hamlyn, *Sensation and Perception* (London: Routledge and Kegan Paul, 1961), 46–51; Sheldon M. Cohen, "St. Thomas Aquinas on the Immaterial Reception of Sensible Forms," *The Philosophical Review* 91, no. 2 (1982): 193–209; John Haldane, "Aquinas on Sense-Perception," *The Philosophical Review* 92, no. 2 (1983): 233–39; Paul Hoffman. "St. Thomas Aquinas on the Halfway State of Sensible Being," *The Philosophical Review* 99, no. 1 (1990): 73–92; Martin Tweedale, "Origins of the Medieval Theory That Sensation Is an Immaterial Reception of a Form," *Philosophical Topics* 20, no. 2 (1992): 215–31; Robert Pasnau, *Theories of Cognition in the Later Middle Ages* (Cambridge: Cambridge University Press, 1997), introduction to chap. 3; Gabriele De Anna, "Aquinas on Sensible Forms and Semimaterialism," *Review of Metaphysics* 54, no. 1 (2000): 43–63; Myles Burnyeat, "Aquinas on 'Spiritual Change' in Perception," in *Ancient and Medieval Theories of Intentionality*, edited by Dominik Perler (Leiden: Brill, 2001), 129–53; John O'Callaghan, "Aquinas, Cognitive Theory, and Analogy: A Propos of Robert Pasnau's *Theories of Cognition in the Later Middle Ages*," *American Catholic Philosophical Quarterly* 76, no. 3 (2002): 451–82; Robert Pasnau, "What is Cognition? A Reply to Some Critics," *American Catholic Philosophical Quarterly* 76, no. 3 (2002): 483–90; Paul MacDonald Jr., "Direct Realism and Aquinas's Account of Sensory Cognition," *The Thomist* 71, no. 3 (2007): 348–78; Jörg Alejandro Tellkamp, "Aquinas on Intentions in the Medium and in the Mind," *Proceedings of the American Catholic Philosophical Association* 80 (2007): 275–89. With the sole exception of Klubertanz, none of these studies even cites, let alone discusses, Yves Simon's perspicuous treatment of these problems. What is also astonishing is that, aside from Klubertanz, none of these studies on Aquinas addresses the *locus classicus* treatment of intentions in the medium in *De potentia* q. 5, a. 8, which plays a central role in Simon's explication of Aquinas.

to propose that a robust metaphysics of the transcendentals provides an insightful way to understand the vocation of *species in medio*.

I. The Problem of Sensation in the Medium

Let us begin with the problem of the medium. In acts of sensation we cognize the real as sensible. To be sure, sensory cognition of reality is not equivalent to the cognition of reality in the full sense of human knowledge of reality. For human knowledge of reality requires the additional complementary acts of cogitative perception and intellectual insight and judgment. Nonetheless, given the proper qualifications, acts of sensation do make consciously present a sensory awareness of reality as sensible. What is involved in such acts of sensation? Quite a lot as it turns out. In this study we restrict ourselves to questions about the exigencies of the medium in all acts of external sensation. Prior to investigating *what* these exigencies are, we must first affirm *that* a philosophical analysis of the medium is required for a philosophical account of sensation and perception. For both questions we must begin with what is more known with respect to us, prior to plunging into an explanation of what it is in itself.

That there is some sort of medium between the sensor and the sensible is abundantly clear in the case of vision, audition, and olfaction. The source of visibles, audibles, and olfactibles within the world need not come into corporeal contact with our eyes, ears, and nose in order for us to see, hear, and smell such realities. In fact, our acts of vision are often impeded if not thwarted whenever visible realities do come into corporeal contact with our eyes. Clearly enough the sensible reality one sees, hears, and smells can be a distant corporeal thing, and despite such distance this reality's *per se* sensible qualities and *per accidens* sensible features can act on one's sense faculties, making consciously present these cognoscible features of reality.[3] The distance between the sensible sensed and the sensory power that is sensing is what we call the "medium," whether it is a gaseous, liquid or solid medium. The medium is whatever is "in the middle" between the sensory observer and the distant sensible reality. The distant sensible reality is itself

3. See Aristotle, *De anima* 2.6; Thomas Aquinas, *In De anima* 2.13 (Leonine vol. 45.1). All quotations of Thomas's commentary on the *De anima* will be from the Leonine edition. I have also included in brackets references to the earlier Marietti edition; see Thomas Aquinas, *Sententia libri de anima*, edited by A. M. Pierotta (Rome: Marietti, 1959).

sensed as a distal corporeal thing; indeed, "distance" itself falls under the *per se* common sensible qualities.

Often enough the medium itself is not sensed when the sensible realities are sensed; rather, the medium seems to be absent relative to the sensibles that we attend to consciously. Within most acts of sensation the medium remains unnoticed, if not entirely unnoticeable, without additional instrumentation. Hence, the medium's function, one might suggest, is to be absent so that it can make sensibles present. Yet we also know that the medium can influence or affect the presentations of the sensibles. Listening to an audible reality when submerged under water is not the same as hearing the same audible reality when not submerged. Seeing a visible thing under different shades of light, or through a transparent or translucent liquid, gas, or solid alters the visible presentations of the thing. It seems that at the level of description of what is more known to us, we can affirm that the medium allows sensible realities to be communicated across distances, while also shading and influencing whatever sensibles are communicated through it. How is this possible?

One is tempted to say that the sensible reality itself must be able to travel across a great distance to one's sensory organs, and yet without us noticing the sensible reality making this journey. Such an explanation, however, confuses natural corporeal activities with what we will call "intentional" activities. While it is certainly true that sensible bodies do not transverse spatial distances without physically negotiating through a physical medium—which is true at the orders of both description and explanation—we cannot affirm that such explanations apply to our sensations of sensible realities through the medium in the same way. The first problem is that our sensory observations and descriptions of the sensible realities communicated through the medium to sensory faculties do not consist in also observing and describing sensible bodies moving across a medium towards us. If they did, then we would always see and hear dynamic visible and audible realties with the ordinary trajectories they have with respect to other realities *and* their additional visible and audible movements of converging upon our eyes and ears. But this is not what we find at the order of sensory observations and descriptions of sensible things. I see the visible thing moving at a distance with respect to other dynamic visible things interacting at a distance. What I do not see are the exact same distal visible realties shooting at my eyes. I can judge that there are dynamic visible bodies in motion, that visible things communicate their visibility to me, and that this visibility is communicated through a medium, but as for there being an additional kind of bodily movement on the part of visible realities—such as a motion that is ubiquitously and continuously flying towards my visual standpoint—this is something I do not observe and cannot affirm on the basis of a description of visual-perceptual experience alone.[4] Moreover, the same visible reality can be seen at the same time by another observer, albeit, with a distinct profile or perspective. Nonetheless, the same invariant identity within the manifold is observed, described, and affirmed as seen by others. In short, the same visible body is not seen to be moving around on its own behalf as well as simultaneously shooting in two other directions at two different sensory observers.[5]

This account might seem to fly in the face of everything we now know today about optics and the visual system of human beings. However, we must be clear about what order of description and explanation we are concerned with. That there is a continuous onslaught of quanta barraging my retina is a probable empirical account of what physical entities do to parts of my body when I see, but photons and other items identified through scientific experimentation are not visible to any ordinary human power of vision, and to call such items visible without qualification is to lapse into the worst kind of equivocation. Our knowledge of such items and their nomological characteristics regularly requires vision in the ordinary sense (we must be able to *see* the evidence presented through various experi-

4. "How are we to take talk of sounds being heard to 'come from' a location? It might be that sounds are heard to come from a particular place by being heard first to be at that place, and then to be at successively closer intermediate locations. But this is not the case with ordinary hearing. Sounds are not heard to travel through the air as scientists have taught us that waves do. Imagine a scenario in which engineers have rigged a surround-sound speaker system to produce a sound that seems to be generated by a bell across the room. This sound subsequently seems to speed through the air toward you and to enter your head like an auditory missile.... This would indeed be a strange experience unlike our ordinary experiences of sounds, which present them as stationary relative to the objects and events that are their sources." Casey O'Callaghan, *Sounds: A Philosophical Theory* (Oxford: Oxford University Press, 2007), 35.

5. Many of these kinds of objections to eliminativist and reductionist accounts of sensible qualities have been raised and developed at length by James Gibson, Alva Noë, and Casey O'Callaghan. See James J. Gibson, *The Senses Considered as Perceptual Systems* (Boston: Houghton Mifflin, 1966); *The Ecological Approach to Visual Perception* (Boston: Houghton Mifflin, 1979); Max R. Bennett, and Peter M.S. Hacker, *Philosophical Foundations of Neuroscience* (Oxford: Blackwell Publishing, 2003), chap. 4; Robert Sokolowski *The Phenomenology of the Human Person* (New York: Cambridge University Press, 2008), chaps. 12–13; Alva Noë, *Perception in Action* (Cambridge: MIT Press, 2004); O'Callaghan, *Sounds: A Philosophical Theory.*

mental apparatuses), but the sophisticated experimental instrumentation required to examine them shifts our sensory-perceptual orientation to a different order of description and explanation. The conclusions empirical scientists arrive at concerning the dynamics of the medium or our nervous system are obtained through various experimental techniques, which will always presuppose the ordinary use of sensory-perceptual systems and could not undermine the veridicality of the latter without undercutting the scientific conclusions achieved through the former. It is self-defeating to affirm both that photons are real, and that visible bodies are only phenomenal and consequently not real. We can only scrutinize and assess the empirical evidence for the reality of photons by first affirming the reality of visible bodies, such as, for example, the computer monitors we must be able to see to acquire the data our instruments register and display with respect to the activities of photons.[6] If we wish to avoid such embarrassing consequences as denying the reality of visible qualities like color, because we empirically affirm the reality of the colorless photons we cannot see, then we must carefully distinguish philosophical from empirico-logical questions, as Maritain and Simon so often sought to do. While empirical scientists should conduct experiments on and provide explanations of the physical and chemical properties that travel through the medium, such accounts cannot of themselves provide a philosophical solution to the cognitional, epistemological, and ontological problems of how sensible realities are communicated through the medium. The particular philosophical problem at hand requires that we explain the following peculiarity: acts of sensation require a medium that is somehow able to communicate sensible

6. "[T]hat photons reflected off the illuminated object cause changes to protein molecules in the retina, which in turn transmits electrical impulses to the fibres of the optic nerve, does not show that what we see is not really coloured, any more than it shows that we do not see what we see directly. *What* we see is not the *effect* of an object on us. The effect of an object on our nervous system is the stimulation of the cells of the retina, the effect of this on the optic nerve, the consequent excitation of the cells in the hypercolumns of the 'visual' striate cortex—but none of this is perceived either by the brain (which can perceive nothing) or by the person whose brain it is. Rather, *that* we see is a consequence of the action of illuminated or luminous objects on our visual system, and *what* we see are those objects, colour and all.... So too, it is confused to suppose that because it is senseless to attribute colour to light waves or sound to sound waves, therefore *what* we see is not coloured and *what* we hear is not noisy—but rather the colour and sound *in us*, being 'mental constructions created in the brain.' ... This misconception stems, among other things, from a miscegenous crossing of the scientist's causal explanation of the neurophysiology of perception with the normal description of a creature's perceiving an object." Hacker, *Philosophical Foundations of Neuroscience*, 131–32. Emphasis in original.

realities to multiple sensory observers without the medium itself becoming the reality that is sensed. This is ubiquitous to all acts of sensation, for all acts of sensation quite obviously minimally require the medium of our neurophysiology. Vision, audition, olfaction, gustation, and tactility all require the proper dispositions and some degree of optimum functioning of our bodily organs. Let us begin with the medieval approach to the philosophical problem of sensing through the medium.

II. Aquinas on Natural and Intentional Being

Medieval Aristotelians like Thomas Aquinas accounted for the phenomenon of sensation through a medium by distinguishing two distinct *ways of being*. Any sensible reality is able to be present and act according to the manner of natural being (*esse naturale*) and intentional being (*esse intentionale*) or spiritual being (*esse spirituale*).[7] Such realities, on the basis of their essence specified powers, i.e., first acts (*actus primus*), and ordered activities, i.e., second acts (*actus secundus*), are able to determine the surrounding environment according to these two modes of being. When a physical being acts according to the mode of natural immutation, the result is a formal displacement of contraries. The heat of the agent displaces its contrary in the patient, making the non-hot patient actually hot, but the same physical being is also simultaneously acting according to the mode of intentional being in virtue of which no such displacement occurs. Rather, the same formal determination of the essence-structured acts can be inten-

7. The *locus classicus* for the problem of intentional beings in the medium in Thomas Aquinas is *De potential*, q. 5, a. 8. For the distinction between natural being and intentional or spiritual being, see Aquinas, *In De anima* 2.14 (Leonine vol. 45.1:128.268–71): "Immutatio uero spiritualis est secundum quod species recipitur in organo sensus aut in medio per modum intentionis." ST I, q. 78, a. 3: "Ad operationem autem sensus requiritur immutatio spiritualis, per quam intentio formae sensibilis fiat in organo sensus. Alioquin, si sola immutatio naturalis sufficeret ad sentiendum, omnia corpora naturalia sentirent dum alterantur." ST I–II, q. 22, a. 2, ad 3: "Dupliciter organum animae potest transmutari. Uno modo, transmutatione spirituali, secundum quod recipit intentionem rei. Et hoc per se invenitur in actu apprehensivae virtutis sensitivae, sicut oculus immutatur a visibili, non ita quod coloretur, sed ita quod recipiat intentionem coloris. Est autem alia naturalis transmutatio organi, prout organum transmutatur quantum ad suam naturalem dispositionem, puta quod calefit aut infrigidatur, vel alio simili modo transmutatur." See also Thomas Aquinas, *In IV Sent.*, d. 44, 3.1.3; *In I De anima*, 10; II, c. 24; *In De sensu*, 4; ST I, q. 56, a. 2, ad 3; q. 75, a. 1, ad 2; *Quaestio disputata de spiritualibus creatures* 1, ad 11; Simon, *Metaphysics of Knowledge*, chaps 1 and 3; Maritain, *The Degrees of Knowledge*, "Critical Realism" §III. 22. [V]-[VII], 121–25ff.

tionally impressed into a medium, sensory organ, or sensory faculty without any displacement of the patient's formal constitution. This intentional presence, when received by a cognitive faculty, makes the thing cognitionally present to the cognitive subject by displaying the object itself to our conscious awareness. The red thing can act on the eye and the faculty of sight—thereby causing vision—without the eye becoming red.[8] In vision, the form of both the agent and receptive faculty are maintained, the former according to intentional being, the latter according to natural being. Aquinas employs the same distinctions in his commentary on Aristotle's famous analogy of the signet ring that impresses its form into the wax without impressing the matter of the ring.[9] In the case of natural immutations, the patient becomes hylomorphically like the agent, that is, the resultant formal change terminates in the material patient accidentally becoming a red thing. With intentional immutations, the patient only becomes like the agent in form, while the material substrate of the patient does not alter with respect to its own form.

In vision, audition, olfaction, gustation, and tactility, the same intentional form must first be transferred through a medium before it is impressed on a sense faculty. According to Aquinas, the sensible reality communicates a likeness (*similitudo*) of its form into the medium, which does not displace the formal constitution of the medium itself. The red sensible object does not cause the air to become red before I actually see the red object; the medium is able to transmit the sensible reality in an apsychic intentional way prior to my intentional psychic reception of the sensible object. How the medium is able to intentionally transfer the forms of material substances will be briefly taken up later on. Before we address this thorny problem, we must examine a few more details of this Thomist account of natural and intentional immutation, especially with respect to sensation. Yves Simon's various treatments of the problem of sensation will guide us through this perennial problem.[10]

8. See Thomas Aquinas, *In De anima*, 3.26 (Leonine vol. 45.1:179.98–180.145), (Marietti, III.2, nos. 589–590).

9. See Aristotle, *De anima*, 2.12, 424a17–24; Thomas Aquinas, *In De anima*, 2.24 (Leonine vol. 45.1:168.13–169.17) (Marietti, nn. 551–554).

10. See Simon, *Metaphysics of Knowledge*, chap. 3; *Essay on Sensation*.

III. Simon on Sensation: Passions, Actions, and Unions

Simon distinguishes three prominent features of change: passion, action, and union. He applies these three features of immutation to the case of sensation to place in relief what is distinctive about sensation in contrast to physical change. These distinctions help us to elucidate the differences between the natural mode of being and intentional being. In natural being, the displacement of one form by another in the subject involves a *heteronomic passion* and a *subjective union* of the form and the subject. But in intentional being we find an *autonomic passion* whereby the subject is able to maintain the form received without any subjective alteration occurring through the union. Simon notes that in the first case, "the patient undergoes a law that is not its own, but that of the agent: it would be quite fitting to designate such a passion as *heteronomic passion*." But in the second case, "[t]he sense receives its own perfection from the object, which acts as a friendly principle. This is what St. Thomas calls a *passio improprie dicta*; let us say, an *autonomic passion*."[11] With the reception of intentional being into a subject, i.e., the form without the matter, there is an *objective union* of the form and the subject. Finally the act that brings about the subjective union of heteronomic passions is a *transitive action*, whereas the objective union of autonomic passions occurs through an *immanent action*.[12]

Salient to sensation as a distinct kind of cognition from intellection is its essential involvement with heteronomic passions, transitive actions, and subjective unions. Any act of sensation involves the alteration of some aspect of our physiology. Sensory powers are the formal organization of a material substrate that involves an integrated complex of diverse organs, and in particular, our peripheral and central nervous systems. The action potential of any neuron involves a heteronomic passion stimulated by a

11. Yves Simon and J. L. Péghaire, "The Philosophical Study of Sensation," 113. For Aquinas, see ST I-II, q. 22, a. 1. Emphasis in original.

12. The salient difference between transitive and immanent action, Simon insists, is not whether the act produces an effect or whether the act remains in the subject, but whether the act is an end in itself or for the sake of an end. Intellectual apprehension is a paradigmatic instance of immanent action, but this immanent action produces a concept or *verbum mentis*. Nevertheless, intellectual apprehension does not *consist in* producing a concept, but in understanding, which involves a conceptual expression of a mental word. See Aquinas, *Summa contra Gentiles* I, chap. 53; *De potentia* q. 8, a. 1; ST I, q. 85, a. 2, ad 3. For Simon's own erudite and comprehensive treatment of transitive and immanent action, see Simon, *Metaphysics of Knowledge*, chap. 2.

transitive action brought about through the reception by various dendrites of neurotransmitters from the axons of other pre-synaptic neurons; the result is a subjective union of the neuron with its altered state as being momentarily either negatively or positively charged.

Simon cautions us to avoid taking these two modes of being, the physical and the psychical, as two reified atomic units of being with entirely independent lives of their own, as theories like property dualism and epiphenomenalism often do. For example, if I place my cold hands near a fire, it will warm them up, which is also true of my garments, but my garments do not also have a concomitant act of sensation. My hands are indeed heated through a heteronomic passion, but I also *feel* heat, that is, heat is intentionally present to my tactile powers through a concurrent autonomic passion and immanent action. In sensation, the physical and psychical are distinct yet inextricable aspects of the same hylomorphic reality, even in vision and audition. For Simon, this latter contention is a development of Thomas Aquinas's and other medievalist's views on the entirely *spiritual* immutation proper to sight.[13] The confluence of immutations by way of natural and intentional being belongs to the essence of sensibles communicated through a medium to a sense organ and sense faculty. Not even God can cause an act of sensation without physical sensible objects acting on our organs by a natural immutation, and our sensory faculties by an intentional immutation.[14]

Thus far we have articulated the essential differences between *things* and *intentions*, what the scholastics often called *species*.[15] Natural things are primarily what they are, a white thing's self-identify as white is primary, it is only secondarily that its whiteness might *represent* something else, like purity. But *species* are primarily representative. *Species* are first the identity of *the other*, i.e., they are intentional entities, and it is only on reflection that we directly address them as real entities in themselves that are intentional. With these distinctions in mind we can now turn to the central problem of sensible *species* in the medium.

13. Simon, *Essay on Sensation*, 76; *Metaphysics of Knowledge*, 96–99 n. 17; Thomas Aquinas, *In De anima*, 2.23 (Leonine v. 45.1:166.205–217) (Marietti, no. 544); ST I, q. 78, a. 3.

14. See Simon, *Essay on Sensation*, 65 n. 13; Aquinas, ST I, q. 84, a. 6; II-II, q. 173, aa. 2–3; Tellkamp, "Aquinas on Intentions in the Medium and in the Mind," 282–83.

15. See Simon, *Essay on Sensation*, 75ff.; Maritain, *The Degrees of Knowledge*, "Critical Realism," § III. 22. [VI]-[VII], 122–25ff.

IV. The Origins of Sensible *Species* in the Medium

We want to understand the nature of how sensation is able to apprehend its objects, and in particular, how *species* and the medium are so disposed that they can be principles of sensation. The central question for Simon concerns the initial act of sensation: *How did sense impressions get there?*[16] Simon insists that there could not be a more pressing philosophical problem than the genesis of sensation and its apprehension of a sensible reality. Since all scientific knowledge has its origins in the humble acts of our external senses, the absence of any sophisticated account of the genesis of sensation leaves the foundations of our philosophical noetic in an embarrassing state. Sensation is epistemically fundamental.[17] Unfortunately, most philosophers just assume we have sensations and on the basis of this assumption they proceed to build up their own cognitive theory without any account of how we are able to have sensations at all. We, like Simon, want to know: *How do sensible species even come to act and be present in our faculties?*

The Thomist doctrine brings into relief two distinct modes of immutation, and "this double effect calls for a double system of influence."[18] The sensible quality of some reality acts both as a *thing* and as a *species*. When the heat causes the garment and my hands to warm up we have a physical change that involves a heteronomic passion, transitive action, and subjective union, but concurrently the same heat is also *sensed* by my tactile faculties as warm. How is this phenomenon to be explained causally? Certainly by some *species*, but where did it come from? Are *species* caused by things in reality or are they a construction of the sense faculty?

Simon warns us not to make the mistake of burdening *species* with what is proper to *things*, and *things* with what is proper to *species*. We should not sell short the activities that are the privilege of *species*, which is to represent, by attributing them to things, which do not represent.[19] The difficulty for us today is that the majority of philosophers and scientists believe that the battle over the realism of secondary qualities was lost long ago.[20]

16. See Simon, *Essay on Sensation*, 70–71 and 73.

17. Ibid., 75.

18. Ibid., 76.

19. Ibid.

20. For recent arguments to the contrary, see Christopher Decaen, "The Viability of Aristo-

In other words, the predominant assumption is that colors and sounds can be entirely explained through electromagnetic radiation and mechanical percussions of various things in motion. But this view, despite the sophistication of its contemporary presentations, makes glaring category mistakes and incredulous causal inferences. Any view that contends that intentions emerge from entirely non-intentional bodies, i.e., from brute matter there arise *species*, will ultimately eliminate all sensible phenomena in favor of physical mechanisms, i.e., non-sensible phenomena. After giving up reality as intrinsically knowable, what often follows is the reduction of all our epistemological theories to anti-realism and skepticism.

Indeed this is precisely the well-known historical path taken from Galileo to Kant. The mysterious problem of how information is communicated through a medium is not made any less mysterious by reducing all acts of sensation to the stimulation of what is philosophically assumed to be the really real—such as the non-informative radiant or chemical energy—simply because it admits of quantifiable measurements and satisfies the *petitio principii* of various dogmas of empiricism. A reductionist mechanical account of reality and sensation is not only mysterious, it also asks us to assent to the impossible. It leaves entirely unexplained a fundamental feature of human cognition, namely, veridical sensations across a medium, which is the putative initial data from which all empirical investigations begin.[21] Such an account leaves inexplicable how intentional sensorial acts could result from non-intentional mechanical stimulation.[22] Scientists should either accept anti-realism and the sensory skepticism, which rationally

telian-Thomistic Color Realism," *The Thomist* 65, no. 2 (2001): 179–222; Gabriele De Anna, "The Simple View of Colours and the Reference of Perceptual Terms," *Philosophy* 77, no. 299 (2002): 87–108; William Wallace, "The Measurement and Definition of Sensible Qualities," *The New Scholasticism* 39, no. 1 (1965): 1–25; Bernard Lonergan, *Insight: A Study of Human* Understanding, edited by Frederick E. Crowe and Robert M. Doran, Collected Works, vol. 3 (Toronto: University of Toronto Press, 1992); Gibson, *Senses Considered as Perceptual Systems*; *Ecological Approach to Visual Perception*; Alva Noë, *Perception in Action*; Casey O'Callaghan, *Sounds*. For a recent collection of essays on the debate, see *Primary and Secondary Qualities: The Historical and Ongoing Debate*, edited by Lawrence Nolan (Oxford: Oxford University Press, 2011).

21. See Wallace, "The Measurement and Definition of Sensible Qualities," 4–5ff.

22. "It is sometimes said that mechanical philosophers like Hobbes reduce all perception to the tactile, but this is not true; they reduce it to mere impulse and striking, and then they cannot explain how the impact can become an appearance. They have to say that the brain constructs the seeming. The problem would be less intractable if they did reduce the other senses to touch, because touch does involve appearances." Sokolowski, *The Phenomenology of the Human Person*, 201 n. 9.

follows from their conceptions of primary and secondary qualities, or reject the category mistakes and confused conceptions of sensible qualities found in Galileo, Hobbes, Locke, *et al.*, and begin afresh.

It is not the purpose of this paper to refute the paths that lead to skepticism, but to suggest an alternative approach to the nature of sensible qualities in reality and how they are able to incept acts of sensation by their intentional presence and communication through a medium. Simon provides us with a fine summation of the alternative approach taken by medieval Aristotelians.

> Few philosophers went deeply into this problem of causality. Among these few, some maintain that the things of nature, over and above causal ways proportionate to their own mode of being, enjoy a participation in the causal ways proper to spiritual substance. In the present state of the question, the most urgent task is to understand precisely why such a daring theory was ever needed.[23]

Simon is referring to the philosophical accounts of Averroes, Aquinas, and Cajetan. Averroes seems to find this problem as perplexing and as important as Simon. Following his own brief treatment Averroes admonishes us: "You ought to give this consideration, since it requires investigation."[24] What is the problem?

Within Aristotelian natural philosophy it would seem that a pure physical alteration by a sensible quality is not sufficient to cause an act of sensation; it can only stimulate our organs. Some higher power is required to bring about such proto-immaterial intentional immutations in the sensible environment. What needed to be clarified was the twofold action of natural and intentional immutations.[25] Specifically, how is the sensible object capable of acting on the medium or other bodies through a mode of immutation that is proper to separate substances?

According to Aquinas the *species* are introduced into the medium by things that participate in an activity proper to the separate substances, namely, the activity of intentional immutation. It is often found that low-

23. Simon, *Essay on Sensation*, 77.

24. Averroes, *Averroes (Ibn Rushd) of Cordoba. Long Commentary on the De Anima of Aristotle*, translated with introduction and notes by Richard C. Taylor with Thérèse-Anne Druart, subeditor (New Haven: Yale University Press, 2009), II. sec. 60 (commenting on Aristotle, *De anima* 2.5, 418b22).

25. On the history and use of the term *intention* in this context, see also Tellkamp, "Aquinas on Intentions in the Medium and in the Mind" and Klubertanz, "*De Potentia* 5.8: A Note on the Thomist Theory of Sensation."

er natures participate in something of higher natures, as some nonhuman animals are said to partake in activities akin to prudence in humans. This mode of immutation allows bodies to diffuse similitudes of their form into the medium; such forms are the spiritual intentions that act on our sense powers and intellect. In perhaps his longest treatment of the problem, Aquinas writes,

> We must remember that a body has a two-fold action. It has one action according to the property of a body, namely, its action through motion (for it is proper to a body to move and act after it has been moved). It has another action, according as it approaches the order of separate substances and participates somewhat of their way. Thus, lower natures usually participate in something of the proper character of higher natures, as we see in some animals which share in a kind of likeness to prudence which is proper to men. This second action is the action of a body, which is not directed to the transformation of matter, but to a certain spreading of the likeness of a form in medium. This latter is like the spiritual intention which is received from a thing in sense or intellect [*diffusionem similitudinis formae in medio secundum similitudinem spiritualis intentionis quae recipitur de re in sensu vel intellectu*]. This is the way in which the sun illuminates the air, and color multiplies its likeness [*species*] in the medium.
>
> But both these ways of action in sublunary bodies are caused by the heavenly bodies. For fire by its heat changes matter, through the power of the heavenly body; and visible bodies multiply their likenesses in the medium through the power of light, whose source is in the heavenly body.[26]

Aquinas's account of the medium is not entirely transparent.[27] It is not clear whether there is simply a sort of resemblance involved in such participations, as we find in other animals, like dolphins, which engage in rather elaborate calculations and stratagems akin to the activities of humans, or is it the participation based on the extra causal influence of the higher on the lower? Are sensible qualities able to impose intentional forms into the medium, or can they only do this through the influx of a superior order of causality not native to their essence? We will return to Aquinas's account, but before we address this problem we should first listen to what Cajetan has to say on such matters.

Cajetan emphasizes that the distinction between *esse naturale* and *esse intentionale* constitutes a diversity in modes of *being*, and not in a diversi-

26. Thomas Aquinas, *De potentia*, q. 5, a. 8, translation from Klubertanz, "*De Potentia* 5.8: A Note on the Thomist Theory of Sensation," 323.

27. See Simon, *Essay on Sensation*, 77–79 n. 31; *Metaphysics of Knowledge*, 104–106 n. 25.

ty of essences, like that between whiteness and sweetness. This is crucial because *like causes like,* and diverse natures cannot produce something essentially other than themselves. Color, which we take for granted as being *real,* is the cause of its intentional forms.[28] But even this distinction is not sufficient to resolve the medieval difficulty. The problem remains because intentional forms, as at least *quasi-immaterial,* seem to be nobler than the physical forms, and the less noble physical form cannot produce the more noble intentional form.[29] So what is the cause of the intentional form in the physical reality? Is the *thing* itself the cause of its intentional presence in the medium?

Cajetan contends we must hold that the cause is the sensible object itself, because the sensible object is able to cause a *per se* act of sensation by communicating an intentional form into the power; its ability to communicate such intentional forms is manifest in such phenomenon as the production of a color's intentional form in a mirror. The proximate efficient cause of a sensible form as an intentional being must be the form of the thing itself. Nevertheless, the primary and principal cause—which the sensible thing participates in—is a separate agent.[30] Notwithstanding any advances Cajetan might have gained for us on this problem, Simon notes that, "The state of the question has not much improved since the time of Cajetan, except inasmuch as we are no longer tempted to burden intentional forms with subtle duties of a physical character, or to attribute to the sun, or to the heavens, semi-spiritual faculties. The final advice of Averroes remains as timely as ever."[31]

Cajetan's answer maintains Aquinas's distinction between acts proper to the physical being and acts it carries out through participation in the acts proper to separate substances. But this does not seem to get us much further. What kind of participation is involved? Do physical things produce the intentions that are communicated into the medium or not? I think even a cursory summation of Yves Simon's detailed account will reveal that he was able to make a few advances in articulating both the difficulties and,

28. See Decaen, "The Viability of Aristotelian-Thomistic Color Realism."

29. In his "*De Potentia,* 5.8: A Note on the Thomist Theory of Sensation," Klubertanz presents a dissenting position against the interpretations of Aquinas provided by Cajetan, Simon, and Maritain. However, this is not the proper forum for evaluating and dismantling Klubertanz's misdirected criticisms.

30. Simon, *Essay on Sensation,* 79 n. 31.

31. Ibid.

at least, an outline of some answers to the problem of intentions in the medium.[32]

V. Simon on Transitive Intentional Acts

We have already noted Simon's insistence on the confluence of the physical presence of the object's transitive action along with the act of sensation. The *species,* he writes,

> must itself be produced by the physically present object. The "sense impression" cannot be taken for granted. The familiar ways of physical causation account for the alteration of an organ by stimuli, but the thing which acts as stimulus also plays the part of object: the problem is to determine by what ways physical things, in the exercise of their presence and of their transitive action, bring about the means of objective unions which involve the physical presence of the things objectively united with the senses.[33]

Simon brings to our attention that there still must be more involved than the natural transitive act of the physical object and immanent intentional act of sensation. The action of the sensible object must involve a transitive action which is manifested according to the order of nature *and* intention. In other words, in any act of sensation there will be two transitive acts—one natural and one that is intentional—and one immanent intentional act. This additional act—a *transitive intentional act*—might seem superfluous, but Simon's account is particularly instructive as to why it is essential for a realist account of sensation.

> Stating the issue as precisely as possible, let us say that the thing considered to be an object of the external sense can be looked at as the principle of three kinds of actions. First, as a particular thing, the sensible exercises a *transitive material action* on the sense organ, considered as a physical receiver; and the result is a modification of the organ. Second, as an *object* acting intentionally upon the sense faculty, the sensible concurs in the *immanent action* of knowing. But this second kind of action, arising out of the intentionality of the object, is not enough to put the sense faculty in touch with the *physical existence* of the object. For this to happen, a third action is required, which, although it proceeds from the physically existing object, is not a physical but an intentional action, conveying not the object's quality but its existence. Beyond the immanent action of sensing, then, of which

32. Simon, *Metaphysics of Knowledge,* 91–112.
33. Ibid., 79.

it is the co-principle along with the sense faculty (just as the object of thought is, along with the understanding, the co-principle of thought), the sensory object, to make itself present to the sense faculty in its existential reality and to cooperate with it, intentionally, in an act of genuinely experimental knowledge must also exercise on the sense faculty an *intentional transitive action*.[34]

In addition to the sensible object's natural communication of its form it also intentionally communicates its essence-structured activities into the medium through a transitive apsychic intentional act. The sensible object transitively acts on both the psychological sense faculty as well as its physiological substrate. The psychological faculty is activated by this intentional transitive act which communicates the sensible *species* into the sense faculty itself. In other words, the form is not merely present to the sensor in a strictly non-cognoscible natural way, for the transmutation of mechanical to electro-chemical energy of afferent nerves is not sufficient to activate a cognitive act; the initial intentional transitive activation makes the sensible form present *in* the sense faculty in an intentional and potentially cognoscible way.[35] The intentional transitive action, like its natural counterpart, terminates in the other, but whereas the natural immutation results in a subjective union, the intentional transitive action allows for an intentional or objective union through the immanent action of the sense faculty's operation. It is the intentional effect of the *species,* and not the natural effect of the *thing,* that begets the intentional immanent action of the sense faculty.

34. Simon, *Metaphysics of Knowledge,* 93. Emphasis in original. It is this account of sensation that is unfortunately neglected in John Knasas's critique of the epistemological realism of Simon and Maritain. See John F. X. Knasas, "Yves R. Simon and the Neo-Thomist Tradition in Epistemology," in *Acquaintance with the Absolute: The Philosophy of Yves R. Simon,* edited by Anthony Simon (New York: Fordham University Press, 1998), 83–100. Whereas Knasas focuses thematically upon Simon's analogies with memory and sensation, he could have instead found the sort of self-validation of sense realism he was looking for in Simon's account of *intentional transitive action* of the sensible *species.* Further, it also seems that Knasas's "alternative" account of the amplitude of cognitive reception of form over matter finds a complementary account in Simon's treatment of *intentional immanent action* and *autonomic passions,* i.e., the *maintenance* of the form received into a form rather than the *displacement* of a contrary form by the received form. In short, there are more similarities in the doctrine of sense realism found in Maritain, Simon, Gilson, Owens, and Knasas than is commonly found in more recent scholarship. But this contention cannot be justified here.

35. See Sokolowski, *The Phenomenology of the Human Person,* chaps. 12–14; Hacker, *Philosophical Foundations of Neuroscience*; Gibson, *Senses Considered as Perceptual Systems,* chaps. 1–3, 10, 12–13; *Ecological Approach to Visual Perception,* chaps. 3–8.

What we must insist upon at this point is that the intentional transitive action, which is all that goes on in the preparatory phase of sensation, and in which the sense faculty is totally passive, does not cease when the faculty, stirred into initial act, joins with the intentionally present object in the full exercise of the act of cognition.[36]

Without the effect of the intentional transitive action, which makes the sensible form exist *qua species* in the sense faculty, we would be forced to postulate that on the basis of the natural transitive action, the act of sensation generates its own *species*—in some neurophysiological-*cum*-Kantian way—or else take refuge in some variety of occasionalism. The apparent ontological parsimony found in these latter two idealist asylums commits its committed enthusiasts to principles that entail the absurd and fail to provide any explanation of the real. As Simon notes,

> there is absolute irreducibility between intentional transitive action and physical action. Refine the notion of physical action as much as you like, by lightening it, making it invisible, calling it impalpable, and appealing to the unobservable (and often fictitious) entities talked about in modern physics, and you will still have an action that alters the subject that receives it, and that remains therefore, from the ontological point of view, infinitely remote from an action that in communicating an objective quality does not alter its subject. Between becoming *other* and becoming *the other*, the contrast is absolute, exactly as between physical action and intentional action.[37]

The presence of *species* in the sense faculty as the term of the intentional transitive action of the sensible does supply us with an account of *how the sense impression is able to exist in the sense faculty*. But it also explains why Thomist realism can be so insistent that in cognition we are intentionally actualized by the existence of the real.[38] The immanent act of external sen-

36. Simon, *Metaphysics of Knowledge*, 112. "Because this union will ultimately be effected by the soul, this original influence that the object exercises on the knowing faculty cannot be reduced to ordinary causality. And so, even though it is a physical action, it deserves to be called *intentional* action because it is *essentially* designed to give rise to an intentional union. For what the action of the object impresses upon the faculty physically is only the idea [Simon's preferred translation of *species*] in which the object itself is present in a sleep-like state and ready to awake as soon as the soul communicates its own vitality to it. The subjective reception of the idea thus fecundates the faculty and supplies it with everything it needs to move to its terminal act, which will coincide with the awakening of the object present in the idea." Simon, *Metaphysics of Knowledge*, 108–109. Emphasis in original.

37. Ibid., 96.

38. Hence, contrary to some of his critics, Simon quite clearly affirms a thesis that is also cen-

sation terminates in a *species*—an intentional content—which is *other* and whose existence is present in and to sensation, not by any act of sensation itself, but by the transitive intentional act of the existing sensible reality.[39]

And so, we have to conclude that the influence exercised by the physically existing object is necessary not just to produce the union of its idea with the faculty but also to preserve that union. The sensation will persist only as long as this influence

---

tral to the epistemological accounts of Étienne Gilson and Joseph Owens. See Étienne Gilson, *Methodical Realism: A Handbook for Beginning Realists*, translated by Philip Trower (Front Royal, Virginia: Christendom Press, 1990; reprinted by San Francisco: Ignatius Press, 2011); *Thomist Realism and the Critique of Knowledge*, translated by Mark A. Wauck (San Francisco: Ignatius Press, 1986); Joseph Owens, "Aquinas on Cognition as Existence," *Proceedings of the American Catholic Philosophical Association* 48 (1974): 74–85. Let us also note here Gilson's prefatory remarks in his *Methodical Realism* (p. 10): "The essays that follow and most of which have already appeared in various journals are gathered here only to deter a wish conveyed to me by Mr. Yves Simon. May he allow me to express my gratitude and also to share with him in the responsibility, not for the ideas contained in these essays, but for a publication of which, without him, I would not have thought."

39. Maritain's own presentation of this doctrine is too fine to summarize: "[T]he object of external sense, on the contrary, is not grasped in a word or image, but just as it exists outside the mind, in the very extramental action of the thing on the sense: *sensus secundum actum sunt singularium quae sunt extra animam* (St. Thomas, *In de Anima*, lib. II, lect. 12), *sensatio terminatur ad res prout extra sunt* (John of St. Thomas, *Phil. Nat.*, III. P., q. 6, a. 11 and 4). This is to say that, inasmuch as sensation is not a transient action, but an immanent action that is completed in the sense, the term of sensation just like the term of every immanent operation, a term that is contemplated or loved, but not produced, exists in the subject itself, *in ipso operante*. Sensible reality, on the other hand, is in the sense—by its transient action, *actio in passo*—just as it is outside the soul. Sensation, then, while terminating in the sense, terminates in the sensible thing as it exists outside, *prout est extra*, in the thing's very action upon the sense. And the actual existence, outside the knowing subject of the thing present in it through its action, is one of the constitutive conditions of the object of the sense as such. The entirely immanent act of sensation, at the beginning of which there is the *species impressa*, has a term, an object, which implies the actual existence of the thing within its own very objectivity—so much so that in the absence of a thing actually given through its action—(even if a star has ceased to exist at the moment the light reaches us, it is at that moment present by its action)—a sensation properly so called (I do not mean an imaginative perception or a hallucination) is absolutely impossible.... By giving precision to the scholastic theory of sensation in this fashion, i.e., by admitting that the sense's intuition bears upon external reality itself, grasped not from the point of view of nature or essence (for that is the intellect's proper object, but *according as it actually acts* on the sense by its qualities or as it exists outside *in its action* upon the sense (an action that is something real but accomplished in the organ), there is little difficulty in replying to the main objections derived from 'errors of the senses' (the broken stick in water, Doppler's effect, etc.). The sensible quality is perceived, in fact, *as it exists in the action* the body exercises through it and at the instant it reaches the sense after being transmitted through a medium (external or internal). The thoroughly realistic value of sense-perception and, at the same time, the *relativity* it entails—because of the materiality with which it is bound—are thus at one stroke safeguarded." Maritain, *The Degrees of Knowledge*, 125–26 n. 108. Emphasis in original.

is exercised. This is not like the case of the universal, whose form once impressed in the soul stays there and is forever ready for an intentional union with it. The singular sensible exists outside the soul, and the soul can be united to it only under the influence of its external reality.[40]

The medium provides an avenue for the intentional transitive act of the sensible reality. It is through this instrumental role of the physical medium that the sensible object is able to activate the immanent act of sensation by the communication of *species* through the medium. Like the intentional transitive act of the sensible object, the instrumental causality of the medium requires that the *species* in the medium exist intentionally.[41]

Before moving on to the next section, let us take note of a few additional explanatory features that this account of natural and intentional transitive action has with respect to the often-misunderstood distinction between sensation and perception and their physiological processes, that is, the stimulus energy or material causes that undergird these intentional immanent acts. Sensation is the core of perception for human beings.[42] Through a *transitive intentional act* and an *immanent intentional act*, sensation makes consciously present *per se* or *essential sensibles*, whereas perception involves the apprehension and judgment of *per accidens* or *incidental sensibles*. Perception enlists the cogitative power and the intellect which bring

40. Simon, *Metaphysics of Knowledge*, 112 and 89–91 n. 9. N.B. Simon prefers to use "idea" for the Latin term *species* (see Simon, *Metaphysics of Knowledge*, appendix), just as Maritain prefers to use "presentative form" or "objectifying form" (see Maritain, *The Degrees of Knowledge*, 123 n. 102). Maritain also has a very fine treatment of species and signs in "Sign and Symbol" in Jacques Maritain, *Ransoming the Time*, translated by Harry Lorin Binsse, (New York: Charles Scribner's Sons, 1941), chap. 9, 217–54, esp. 218–26.

41. See Simon, *Metaphysics of Knowledge*, 102–103. What Thomists need today is a more perspicuous account of instrumental causality and its various manifestations. A comprehensive treatment of instrumental causality would not only help us understand how intentions present in an apsychic medium can communicate the sensible and quidditative character of things to psychic powers but would also contribute to our appreciation of the secondary causality found in created natures through the divine power and the instrumental role of the phantasms in intellectual abstraction. See Simon, *Metaphysics of Knowledge*, 122–26. Due to considerations of space, I have not taken up Simon's and Cajetan's discussions of instrumental causality in the medium as well as of the progressive immaterialization of the intentions from the sensible form, to the medium, to the act of sensation, to phantasms, and finally, to completely abstract *species intelligibilis*. See Simon, *Metaphysics of Knowledge*, 101ff. For more recent studies on this progressive immaterialization of intentions, see Hoffmann, "St. Thomas Aquinas on the Halfway State of Sensible Being"; Burnyeat, "Aquinas on 'Spiritual Change' in Perception"; and Tellkamp, "Aquinas on Intentions in the Medium and in the Mind."

42. See Simon, *Essay on Sensation*, 56–58; 79–82.

our conscious attention to bear upon the identity (primary substance) and quiddity (essence) underlying the sensible manifold of accidental beings. Through the cogitative power we are able to *perceive* a sensible phenomenon as more than a white shaped magnitude in motion, but as *this man*.[43] Both sensation and perception are conscious acts and both make present what James Gibson would describe as "stimulus information"[44] of an "invariant object" or what Robert Sokolowski would describe as an "identity within the manifold." What is not intentional or conscious are the *natural transitive acts* which involve the neurophysiological substrate of our external sense faculties, the *sensus communis*, and the cogitative power. The interactive stimulation of electrochemical energy through our afferent and efferent nerves is an entirely non-cognitive process. If we were to reduce all sensory or perceptual cognition to the stimulation of nerves we would be left with the puzzle as to how the continuous flux of electrochemical stimulation is able to present a constant invariant intentional content, and *a fortiori* how it can present the non-cognitive as cognitive (i.e., to make *things* into *species*). But on Simon's Thomist account it is the intentional transitive acts of things which make present invariant objects, that is, *species*, amidst the informed flux of varied stimuli, that is, the natural immutations of things. More recently, psychologists like James Gibson have also recognized the significance of this problem.

> The stimulation of receptors ... are variable and changing in the extreme.... The unanswered question of sense perception is how an observer, animal or human, can obtain constant perceptions in every day life on the basis of these continually changing [stimuli].... The active observer gets invariant perceptions despite varying [stimuli]. He perceives a constant object by vision despite changing [stimulations] of light; he perceives a constant object by feel despite changing [stim-

43. See Thomas Aquinas, ST I, q. 17, a. 2; q. 78, a. 4; *In De anima*, 2.13; Cyrille Michon, "Intentionality and Proto-Thoughts," in *Ancient and Medieval Theories of Intentionality*, edited by Dominik Perler (Leiden: Brill, 2001), 325–42; Daniel De Haan, "Linguistic Apprehension as Incidental Sensation in Thomas Aquinas," *Proceedings of the American Catholic Philosophical Association* 84 (2011): 179–96; Cornelio Fabro, "Knowledge and Perception in Aristotelico-Thomistic Psychology," *The New Scholasticism* 12, no. 4 (1938): 337–65; George P. Klubertanz, *The Discursive Power: Sources and Doctrine of the Vis Cogitativa According to St. Thomas Aquinas* (St. Louis, Missouri: Modern Schoolman, 1952).

44. "Different stimulus energies—acoustical, chemical, and radiant—can all carry the same stimulus information. The equivalence of different "stimuli" for perception and behavior has long been a puzzle, but it ceases to be puzzling if we suppose that it results from equivalent stimulus information being carried by different forms of stimulus energy." Gibson, *Senses Considered as Perceptual Systems*, 55.

ulations] of pressure; he perceives the same source of sound despite changing [stimulations] of loudness in his ears. The hypothesis is that constant perceptions depend on the ability of the individual to detect the invariants, and that he ordinarily pays no attention whatever to the flux of changing sensations.[45]

The peculiar character of a thing's intentional transitive acts is not easily eliminated by any principle of parsimony that also respects more fundamental epistemic principles of intelligibility. Theoretical parsimony is worthless without verified intelligibility. To entirely reduce the world to non-cognoscible things, is to eliminate the possibility of explaining why the world is intrinsically intelligible and admits of inquiry, exploration, investigation, speculation, extrapolation, and all other modes of scientific and philosophical questioning, all of which presuppose an initial act of wonder in the presence of the intelligibility of being.

VI. The Vocation of Intentional Beings in Sensible Things and the Medium

In the last section we discussed the natural and intentional transitive acts of physical things. But what is the purpose of this duality found within transitive acts of sensible realities? Why do sensible bodies emanate their form both naturally and intentionally? Intentional acts are proper to higher separated beings, not to physical beings; the existence of intentions in physical things and the medium seems to be superfluous to the nature of corporeal beings. According to Simon,

The [*species*] has physical being, and goodness, not for its own sake but exclusively as an intentional medium whose union with the faculty derives its entire *raison d'être*, with nothing left over, from the intentional union of the faculty and the object. And because of that, transitive action of the object on the faculty and the corresponding passion in the faculty in relation to the object are, by virtue of their essential purpose, something quite different from ordinary action and reception, which always result in the constitution of a composite. The immediate effect of

45. Gibson, *Senses Considered as Perceptual Systems*, 3. Elsewhere, Gibson writes: "Just as the stimulation of the receptors in the retina cannot be seen, so the mechanical stimulation of the receptors in the skin cannot be felt, and the stimulation of the hair cells in the inner ear cannot be heard. So also the chemical stimulation of the receptors in the tongue cannot be tasted, and the stimulation of the receptors in – the nasal membrane cannot be smelled. We do not perceive stimuli." Gibson, *Ecological Approach to Visual Perception*, 55. See Hacker, *Philosophical Foundations of Neuroscience*, 121–47, especially his criticism of David Marr's theory of vision, pp. 143–47.

> the action of the object on the sense is simply to disengage from the potentiality of the sense a form that will determine that potentiality. But this is an intentional form affected to the very depths of its physical reality by what may be called its intentional vocation.[46]

But why do *species* have an intentional vocation at all? Jacques Maritain has provided a cogent answer to this very question. We should not assume that all things in creation act only for their own sake. Once we recognize this, it becomes clear that the intentional vocation of physical *species* is not superfluous with respect to the whole order of being.

> Examine everything entitative about the medium that transmits sensible quality and you will only find the properties and movements—the wave movements and others—that the physicist sees in them. You will no more find quality there than you will find the soul under the scalpel. Yet quality passes through it, *secundum esse intentionale,* since the sense will perceive it when the wave or vibration reaches the organ. It is like a dream of a materialistic imagination to want, with Democritus, to have quality pass through the medium entitatively, or, since it is not there entitatively, to deny, with the votaries of modern "scientism," that it could pass through it at all. Even when *esse intentionale* has nothing to do with the world of knowledge, it is already a way for forms to escape from this entombment in matter.[47]

> The true philosophy of nature honors the mystery of sensorial perception; it knows that such perception takes place only because the immense cosmos is activated by the first Cause whose motion passes through all physical activities so that, at the higher reach where matter awakens to *esse spirituale,* they may produce the effect of knowledge upon an animated organ.[48]

Like Maritain, Simon also recognizes that, "nature anticipates cognition by producing a universe of intentional forms outside the realm of the soul to provide the soul with what the soul needs to 'become all things.'"[49] But what accounts for this generosity of material natures?

These material natures cannot be the ultimate efficient cause of a mode of existence which exceeds their own nature. "[T]he production of intentional forms by the sensible objects ... presupposes a participation on their part of some kind of higher efficient power." God not only gives to material things the causal efficacy to produce effects proper to their nature, "God

46. Simon, *Metaphysics of Knowledge,* 108.

47. Maritain, *The Degrees of Knowledge,* "Critical Realism" § III. 22. [V], 122.

48. Jacques Maritain, *Philosophy of Nature,* translated by Imelda C. Byrne (New York: Philosophical Library, 1951), 84.

49. Simon, *Metaphysics of Knowledge,* 103.

also communicates to them an additional efficacy, designed specifically to make them known to beings who are deprived of innate ideas and who are at once material and cognitive."[50] It is here that we find Simon's benign interpretation of the participation of sensible thing's in separated substances, an interpretation that frees Aquinas's doctrine from any associations it might have had with the older cosmology. Unfortunately for us, Simon does not go into detail on the way in which sensible things participate in divine causality. Nonetheless, Maritain's and Simon's remarks on the vocation of *species* as intentional beings does suggest a possible route for further inquiry. In the next and final section of this study we will attempt to amplify Simon's account of sensible things' participation in divine causality by appealing to Aquinas's doctrine of the transcendentals.

VII. The Transcendentals: Thing and Truth as Sensible Realities and Intentional Beings

Aquinas's appeal to the participation of sensible things in separate substances to account for intentions in the medium should not surprise us, and Simon's interpretation of this account is no doubt accurate. Simon writes, "the endowing of things with the power of intentional as well as physical causality is but the counterpart to or the complement of the creation of animals and of man. It may well be paradoxical, but it is no more so than this participation in the divine infinity granted with the gift of knowledge to angel, man, and the lowest of the beasts."[51] There are many different modes of participation found within the created order that contemporary Thomists, Platonists, and neo-Aristotelians accept with little hesitation. Placing the problem of the intentional transitive act of sensible things within the context of a metaphysics of participation provides a robust ontological foundation for our problem. In what way do the activities of sensible things manifest a kind of participation in separated substances?

Separated substances only interact with one another at the order of intentional immutation; the communication of one form to another by

50. Ibid., 104–105. "What has to be explained here is an effect belonging to an order higher than the whole physical order. As it exists in the inanimate medium, the sensible form, which obviously does not yet possess there an *Erkannt-Sein*, must already be at least an *Erkenntnisbild*, a kind of virtual idea destined to bring about an act of knowledge." Ibid., 103.

51. Ibid., 106.

intentional being is proper to their immaterial mode of being.[52] Sensible bodies only *partake* of this sort of activity; it is not characteristic of material substances as such. But just as all creatures participate in their act of being (*actus essendi*)—since the act of being is not proper to any creature's essence as such—so also do all creatures participate in being as truth. In order to make this kind of participation clear, we will need to present a brief explication of Aquinas's doctrine of the transcendentals.

The doctrine of the transcendentals offers a helpful clarification of Aquinas's introduction of participation into his account of intentions in the medium. Two transcendental aspects of being appear to be especially pertinent to Aquinas's distinction between natural and intentional immutation. First, the transcendental thing (*res*), which highlights that every thing that is, has or is its essence, quiddity, or *ratio*,[53] and second, the transcendental truth (*veritas*) which directs our attention to the conformity of all being to cognition.[54]

The transcendental truth cuts two ways. Human cognition must be conformed to the essence or quiddity of the existent thing in order for truth to be obtained. But the reality that is the measure of our minds also has its own more fundamental measure. The created order of existent essences also conforms to the divine intellect, where all created essences find

52. See Thomas Aquinas, ST I, q. 56, a. 2, ad 3; q. 107, a. 1; Harm Goris, "The Angelic Doctor and Angelic Speech: The Development of Thomas Aquinas's Thought on How Angels Communicate," *Medieval Philosophy and Theology* 11, no. 1 (2003): 87–105.

53. "... non autem invenitur aliquid affirmative dictum absolute quod possit accipi in omni ente nisi essentia eius secundum quam esse dicitur, et sic imponitur hoc nomen res, quod in hoc differt ab ente, secundum Avicennam in principio Metaphysicae, quod ens sumitur ab actu essendi sed nomen rei exprimit quiditatem vel essentiam entis ..." Thomas Aquinas, *Questiones disputatae De veritate* q. 1, a. 1 (Leonine, vol. 22.1:5.131–39). See Thomas Aquinas, *De ente* et *essentia*, chap. 2; *In I. Sent.*, d. 2, 1.5 ad 2; d. 8, 1.3; d. 33, 1.1 ad 1; ST I, q. 39, a. 3, ad 3.

54. "Convenientiam vero entis ad intellectum exprimit hoc nomen verum." Thomas Aquinas, *De veritate*, q. 1, a. 1 (Leonine, vol. 22.1:5.159–61). See Jan Aertsen, *Medieval Philosophy and the Transcendentals: The Case of Thomas Aquinas* (Leiden: Brill, 1998); "'Res' as Transcendental: Its Introduction and Significance'," in *Le problème des transcendantaux du XIVe au XVIIe siècle*, edited by G. Federici Vescovini (Paris: Vrin, 2002), 139–56; "Truth as Transcendental in Thomas Aquinas," *Topoi* 11, no. 2 (1992): 159–71; "Is Truth *Not* a Transcendental for Aquinas?" in *Wisdom's Apprentice: Thomistic Essays in Honor of Lawrence Dewan, O.P.*, edited by Peter Kwasniewski (Washington, D.C.: The Catholic University of America Press, 2007), 3–12; Joseph Owens, "Aquinas on Being and Thing," in *Thomistic Papers*, vol. 3, edited by L. A. Kennedy (Houston, Texas: Center for Thomistic Studies, 1987), 3–24; John F. Wippel, "Truth in Thomas Aquinas," *Review of Metaphysics* 43, nos. 2–3 (1989): 295–326; 543–67; reprinted in John F. Wippel, *Metaphysical Themes in Thomas Aquinas*, vol. 2 (Washington D.C.: The Catholic University of America Press, 2007), 65–112.

an exemplar—i.e., an intelligible pattern for creatable essences—inasmuch as they imitate the perfection of the divine essence.[55] In this respect all creatures participate, not only in *esse,* but also in *essentia*. We all partake in the pattern of being that God has intended for us to be; through each and every act we are becoming what our essence is to be.

> And the very first thing which "to be" does, is to make its own essence to be, that is, "to be a being." This is done at once, completely and definitively for, between to be or not to be, there is no intermediate position. But the next thing which "to be" does, is to begin bringing its own individual essence somewhat nearer its completion. It begins doing it at once, but the work will take time and, in the case of such corporeal beings as men, for instance, it is bound to be a slow process. It takes each of us a lifetime to achieve his own temporal individuality. True enough, essence itself is there from the very beginning, and, in a way, it is whole, but its wholeness is not that of a thing. The essence of the symphony is in the mind of the composer, and, since it is its essence to be a symphony, it will have to be it, but it will not exist until the last bar of its score has been orchestrated, and even that will not be the end of its becoming. So also with natural essences. Each of them is the progressive becoming of its own end. In short the actual perfecting of essences is the final cause of their existences, and it takes many operations to achieve it.[56]

Our essence is what we are striving to become as *things,* yet this same created essence is known by God, and to some degree by ourselves, as the *truth* of what we are, and as the *truth* that measures what we, say, as humans should become, and have often failed to be. With this robust metaphysical context of the transcendentals in mind, it is not unusual for all materially instantiated essences to communicate the quidditative principle of their being according to the order of the transcendentals thing and truth. Just as the formal communication of natural transitive immutation is the face of *thing,* so the intentional transitive immutation of the same form is the face of *truth* insofar as the intentionality of a physical essence is communicated into the medium through the natural existence of the physical essence as truth.

55. "[S]ic ergo intellectus divinus est mensurans non mensuratus, res autem naturalis mensurans et mensurata, sed intellectus noster mensuratus et non mensurans res quidem naturales, sed artificiales tantum. Res ergo naturalis, inter duos intellectus constituta, secundum adaequationem ad utrum que vera dicitur: secundum enim adaequationem ad intellectum divinum dicitur vera in quantum implet hoc ad quod est ordinata per intellectum divinum." Aquinas, *De veritate* q. 1, a. 2 (Leonine, v. 22.1:9.93–102). See Aquinas, *In I Sent.,* d. 2, 1.3; ST I, q. 14, a. 8, ad 3; qq. 15–16; q. 44, a. 3; q. 84, a. 5; Suppl. III, q. 80, a. 4.

56. Étienne Gilson, *Being and Some Philosophers,* 2nd ed. (Toronto: Pontifical Institute of Medieval Studies, 1952), 184.

In short, all physical beings were created by God to be things in relation to themselves and truths for others, for the same material essence acts both naturally and intentionally by participating in the exemplar of that essence as it exists in the ideas of the divine intellect.[57] Accordingly, the doctrine of the transcendentals thing and truth brings into relief the cascading modes of participated being and immutation that essences take on through creation. Beginning with their principal existence as ideas in the divine intellect, such essences are also given natural existence as created physical things; but as truths, the essences of things are communicated through various media and take on a non-cognitive intentional existence as *species*; and finally, these essences take on the cognitional intentional existence of *species* or ideas received into cognitive powers.[58]

There are of course many more details that need to be spelled out to understand the specific modes of participation involved in the ways things and truths in the created order participate in the divine exemplars and how they communicate this to the world around them. This will have to be taken up in a future study. Nonetheless, it should be clear that the integration of the Thomist doctrine of the transcendentals thing and truth, with the doctrines of the intentional transitive acts of sensible things and the communication of the nature of things into the medium, does indeed provide a metaphysical structure for the doctrine of *species* in the medium and also frees it from its unnecessary associations with the older Aristotelian empirical physics and cosmology.

VIII. Concluding Remarks

This paper has only grazed the surface of the philosophical issues that must be clarified with respect to sensation, metaphysics, and the medium, all of which are prerequisites to a proper and more complete treatment of

57. The transcendental truth is the underlying thread that Aquinas has woven throughout the participated perfections, i.e., natural essences, which lead us through the fourth way (ST I, q. 2, a. 3) to their presence as divine perfections (ST I, q. 4, a. 2), as divine ideas (ST I, q. 15), and divine truth (ST I, q. 16), which is causally related to our participated knowledge in the latter, through our knowledge of the material essences of created things (ST I, q. 14, a. 8, ad 3; q. 84, a. 5), which alone gives us the grounds for universal necessary knowledge of dynamic and changing material realities.

58. See Aquinas, *Quodlibet* 8, q. 1, aa. 1–2.

the problem of intentions in the medium. One must also deal with the veridicality of sensation itself, as well as investigate the precise causal relationship that obtains between intentions and the medium, while attending to the relevant discoveries of empirical science. Important questions also need to be addressed concerning privileged states of the medium, as well as what are the proper and optimum dispositions of the medium and the sensory organs that are required for properly functioning veridical acts of sensation.[59] These important problems cannot be addressed here.

In this paper I have attempted to make clear the way in which every sensible *thing* can be said to have an intentional vocation that is fulfilled in its essence-structured activities by which it will naturally and intentionally emanate what sort of thing it is. In other words, corporeal things leave vestiges of truth or *species* in various media in the environment by virtue of their transitive intentional acts. Such *species* are the only scent that is necessary for a rational being filled with a sense of wonder and a natural desire to know to seek out and understand the essence of things through their *species*. Inasmuch as rational beings come to recognize the participated character of such intentional immutations, they also will come to recognize the transcendental character of being, thing, and truth. And every Thomist knows that this road sets out on a direct path of increasing intelligibility towards the Being whose existence is what He is.

This preliminary study was intended to prepare the way for a more extensive future treatment of what Thomists like Simon and Maritain only began. Maritain once wrote that:

> We think it would be of great interest to philosophers to study the role that *esse intentionale* plays in the physical world itself, wherein there undoubtedly arises from such existing, that sort of universal animation whereby motion puts into bodies more than they are, and colors the whole of nature with a semblance of life and feeling undoubtedly derived from it.[60]

I hope that this paper has at least generated some interest in further articulating the ways *esse intentionale* are present in the medium. And if we heed the call of Simon and Maritain, then we should recognize with

59. See Simon, *Essay on Sensation*, 83–91; Decaen, "The Viability of the Aristotelian-Thomistic Account of Color Realism," 214–22.

60. Maritain, *Degrees of Knowledge*, 122.

them that a deeper understanding of the vocation of *species in medio* is of the utmost importance for the doctrine of sensation that is fundamental to Thomist realism.[61]

61. I must acknowledge the helpful corrections and suggestions that I received on earlier versions of this paper from Jörg Alejandro Tellkamp and Steven Jensen. I would also like to thank Anthony and Judy Simon for their kinds words at the 2010 American Maritain Association conference and for supporting the Yves R. Simon Graduate Student Award.

JAMES CAPEHART

Incarnate Spirit

Proper Thomistic Definition of the Human Being or Merely a Description of the Human Soul?

What a creature is man! He is spirit and matter together. He is not an imprisoned angel; he is by nature an incarnate spirit. This is the fact to explain—without changing it and without explaining it away. But the more we are true to the fact of man as an incarnate spirit, to the fact of a subsistent and spiritual soul which is yet by nature a part of man, the more we are driven to ask the why of such a being. And we are equally driven to exclude as impossible all explanations of man which render the facts impossible. What is, is possible; and man is. And because man is an observable reality, he poses the problem of the unity of his being and of his nature.[1]

As the great Thomistic philosopher Anton C. Pegis gives poetic testimony to in the above quotation, the nature of the human being is an awe inspiring mystery. Unlike the brute animals, human beings have a soul which subsists in its own right after death. The soul is indeed a spirit. However, outside of anthropological poetry and hyperbolic rhetoric, is it justifiable to call the *whole human being* a spirit, or even to define it as an Incarnate Spirit? Furthermore, is it justifiable to claim that St. Thomas Aquinas held to the defensibility of such a predication?

In the following account, I hope to show that the answers to both questions are resoundingly in the negative. Nevertheless, there are those philosophers, even Thomists, who maintain, to the contrary, that though St.

1. Anton Pegis, *Introduction to Saint Thomas Aquinas* (New York: The Modern Library, 1948), xxii–xxiii.

Thomas never explicitly used such a definition, his principles make clear that *Incarnate Spirit* is the proper philosophical definition of the human being. Two accounts of such kind which I will address at great length are that of James Lehrberger, in his 1998 article "The Anthropology of Aquinas's *De ente et essentia*,"[2] and that of Pegis, in his 1963 work, *At the Origins of the Thomistic Notion of Man*.[3] In this paper, after examining the arguments from these authors, I hope to show how their predication of *Incarnate Spirit* as the proper definition of *human being* rests squarely upon the consideration of *human being* as convertible with *human soul*, or in other words, upon a consideration of human being as essentially its soul, rather than essentially a composite of both body *and* soul. Once this has been shown through a careful examination of the example arguments of Lehrberger and Pegis, I hope to demonstrate, based upon St. Thomas' own texts, that his thought could not be further from holding such a doctrine—precisely because the doctrine is patently false. Lastly, I will also briefly endeavor to conclude with a consideration of definitions of human being which would, in fact, not fall into the same error as that of Incarnate Spirit, but which also might serve to present the uniqueness and mystery of human nature in a way both true and understandable to the postmodern mind.[4]

I. An Examination of Lehrberger's "The Anthropology of Aquinas's *De ente et essentia*"

Lehrberger begins his treatment of St. Thomas' account of the human being by an explication of the anthropological notions found in *De ente et essentia*, chapters 2 and 3. As he devotes himself primarily in this portion to

2. James Lehrberger, "The Anthropology of Aquinas's *De ente et essentia*," *The Review of Metaphysics* 51, no. 4 (1998): 829–46.

3. Anton Pegis, *At the Origins of the Thomistic Notion of Man* (New York: The Macmillan Company, 1963).

4. The term *postmodern* is indeed a rather loose and subjective one, which is rather fitting for how I am using it here. Broadly speaking, *postmodern* refers to the fact that we are living in an age where the *Cartesian-Modern Project* has thoroughly failed. When I write of the *postmodern mind* here, I am referring to those who see and accept this fact—and those whose thought is deeply influenced by this fact whether they realize it or not—but who still even in going beyond the Moderns have a world view and a vocabulary flowing from the Moderns, both of which are completely at odds with those of the Thomistic-Aristotelian-Scholastic tradition. To have a profitable philosophical conversation about the human being with such thinkers is indeed a difficult task because often we are not speaking the same language.

reiterating Thomas' own words, one finds this section of the article quite helpful for understanding St. Thomas' thoughts on the proper definition for human being. Yet, Lehrberger claims that this earlier treatment in *De ente* is but a stage in the development of St. Thomas' treatment of human nature:

At first, Thomas appears simply to reiterate Aristotle's definition of man as a "rational animal." In doing so Aquinas would seem to restrict himself to a definition worked out in the terms of classical naturalism. Yet in light of the very metaphysical revolution that the *De ente et essentia* itself initiates, it would be surprising if this definition of man is his final word. In fact a careful reading reveals that all the "rational animal" passages cluster in chapters 2 and 3. This definition is nowhere found, explicitly or implicitly, in chapters 4 or 5.[5]

Lehrberger will conclude that this failure to speak of "rational animal" in chapters 4 and 5 is due to a metaphysical turn, of sorts, which will give rise to a metaphysical definition of human being, which for Thomas, he claims, is Incarnate Spirit:

In this paper I hope to show that Aquinas's adoption of Aristotle's "rational animal" understanding of man is partial and limited. Thomas understands that it is not his last word on the subject but his first word. "Rational animal" is the definition proper to physics; Thomas's fuller anthropology is rooted in his metaphysics. I will argue that, in the larger perspective of metaphysics, he understands man to be an "incarnate (difference) spirit (genus)."[6]

Thus, his stated goal is to show that, as St. Thomas proceeds from treating of "Essence as Found in Composite Substances" to a treatment of "Essence as Found in Separate Substances," he will invoke a different treatment of the human being. In the first, "physical" consideration, the human being is properly called "rational animal"; but in the latter, "metaphysical" treatment, the human being is properly called "incarnate spirit." However, Lehrberger has one very important obstacle to overcome: St. Thomas never utters such a phrase as "incarnate spirit," whether in defining the human being or in any other context. How will he be able to overcome such a great obstacle?[7] Let us proceed to follow his argument, step by step.

5. Lehrberger, "Anthropology," 830.

6. Ibid., 831.

7. In and of itself, such an obstacle is not insurmountable. A philosopher who aims to transmit a living Thomism to the contemporary world should not be restricted to repeating only the *conclusions* that St. Thomas explicitly uttered. Yet, if one is to be faithful to Thomas' thought, the

Lehrberger begins the main section of his article with an examination of Thomas' "physical" treatment of human nature, and in doing so summarizes, to our own benefit, several key passages from the *De ente* in which St. Thomas explains the nature of a proper definition. In one such example, Lehrberger explains the very key relationship of whole and part within St. Thomas' treatment of the essence of composite substances:

> *Essentia* signifies the whole composite, neither its matter nor form alone.... The relation of matter and form gives rise to that of genus and difference, though the two relations are by no means identical: they are alike in that both genus and matter are potential respectively to the act of difference and form; they are unlike in that matter and form refer to the parts of the whole, *while genus and difference signify not the parts but the indetermination or determination of the whole.*[8]

Note at this point a very important aspect of definition to which, unfortunately, Lehrberger does not give due consideration as he proceeds to his ultimate conclusions: genus and species alike must refer to the whole *essentia* which is being defined, not just to part. While Lehrberger accepts this in the "physical" treatment of human nature, I believe later on he passes over the fullness of its implications in his so-called "metaphysical" treatment.[9] Commenting upon this relationship of parts to whole and of genus and species in relation to the whole within the "physical" description of human nature, Lehrberger states,

> Man is not defined in the way that he is composed: "Whence [we do not say that man] is a composition of animal and rational as we say that he is a composition

new conclusions reached ought to proceed, either directly or indirectly, from premises which the Angelic Doctor really held. Consequently, the question which is of paramount importance for this treatment is as follows: Are the *premises* which are necessary for arriving at a definition of human being as an Incarnate Spirit truly faithful to the thought of St. Thomas Aquinas? This is what we shall examine in the following pages.

8. Lehrberger, "Anthropology," 832. Emphasis added. Cf. *De ente et essentia* 2, lines 67–84, 195–201, and 211–22. Line numbering in the following *De ente* texts refers to Lehrberger's reference to the Leonine edition. While I have included those line numbers, I have used the Busa edition of the *De ente* for the accompanying Latin texts instead of the Leonine. Also, I have used Lehrberger's own translations of the *De ente* texts found in his article, unless otherwise noted. Cf. *S. Aquinatis Opera Omnia ut sunt in indice thomistico*, edited by Roberto Busa, 7 vols. (Stuttgart-Bad Cannstatt: Frommann-Holzboog, 1980). *De ente et essentia*, in Busa ed., vol. 2, 583–87.

9. I contend that if Lehrberger regards Incarnate Spirit to be a valid definition with regards to the human being, he must hold "spirit" to signify the whole human being even if indeterminately; for were it only a part of the whole, "spirit" could not be the genus. While this is essential for the validity of his argument, he seems to assume its truth without ever addressing the question directly.

of soul and body."[10] Body and soul are the integral parts constitutive of a human being who is neither the one nor the other. "Rational" and "animal," however, signify the whole human *essentia* which at once is both the one and the other. For genus "animal" refers to the entire *essentia* as undetermined in species through the animating form. The difference "rational," on the other hand, precisely signifies the determination of the whole *essentia* through the perfection of its specific form. Accordingly, the species whose *essentia* is expressed in the definition "rational animal" arises from the indetermination of the genus and the determination of the difference.[11]

So, let us make this perfectly clear. Within a proper philosophical definition, genus refers to the whole *essentia* (which for human beings includes *both* matter and form) but *indeterminately*, while the difference refers to the whole *determinately* by means of that key perfection of form, which distinguishes that species from all other species of that genus. While *essentia* can be signified either as a whole or as a part, it is only when signified as a whole that it can be predicated as a definition of singulars. As Lehrberger admits,

When signified as a whole, the human *essentia* stands to each individual like the genus does to the species. Thus the *essentia* is predicable of the individual. In this way, "Socrates is a man." When signified as a part, however, *essentia* stands to individuals as form does to matter. No more than one part is predicable of another is the *essentia* so abstracted predicable of the *ens*—"Socrates is humanity" is false. Socrates is composed of humanity (*forma totius*) and his own flesh, blood, and bones (*materia designata*). Only when *essentia* is taken as a whole can it be signified by definition through genus and species.[12]

Based upon the fact that it does refer to the *essentia* of the whole human being, both indeterminately and determinately, rather than merely referring to its parts, Lehrberger maintains then that "rational animal," from the perspective of natural philosophy, is a perfectly valid definition of human being:

The definition includes all human beings and only human beings while excluding every species of angel and brute. Second, this definition applies to the whole essence as a unity: the parts of the definition are taken from and proportional to, but not identical with, the matter and form of the *definiendum*. "Animal" and "rational"

10. *De ente et essentia* 2, lines 202–204. (Busa edition: Unde dicimus hominem esse animal rationale et non ex animali et rationali, sicut dicimus eum esse ex anima et corpore.)

11. Lehrberger, "Anthropology," 832–33. Cf. *De ente et essentia* 2, lines 159–73.

12. Ibid., 833. Cf. *De ente et essentia* 2, lines 274–90.

are not separate items added to each other, but parts of a definition referring to the whole as indeterminate or determinate.[13]

Seemingly, these are words of high praise for "rational animal" as a proper definition for human being. Yet, Lehrberger is still not satisfied, for such a definition, he says, "is a purely physical definition which takes no account of the riches discovered by the *esse-essentia* analysis of the *human soul*."[14] However, one is abruptly led to ask: How can an analysis of the *human soul*, which is a *part* only, lead to a definition of the *whole human being*? Lehrberger will answer this question through his detailed analysis of chapters 4 and 5 of *De ente.*

For Lehrberger, the key to this "metaphysical" treatment of human nature lies in St. Thomas' inclusion of human soul within his discussion of *Essentia in Separated*[15] *Substances*, "namely, in the (human) soul, the intelligences, and the first cause."[16] In fact, he says that Thomas *must* include the soul in this account because it is a special kind of form:

> The soul must be included among the separated substances because "it is necessary that in every intelligent substance there be complete immunity from matter, so that it neither has matter as part of itself nor is it a form impressed on matter as are material forms."[17] In whatever way the soul is form, it is not form as a material form is. Aquinas is suggesting that the soul may be called 'form' only analogously.[18]

This analogous sense of form is rooted in the fact that the human soul has *esse per se*. Though soul and body form the composite human being, the act of being of the composite is through the soul.[19] Commenting upon this, Lehrberger quite correctly explains that, "In the soul's case the body participates in the soul's *esse*: the soul imparts its own proper *esse* to matter. This does not result in two beings—an intelligence and an animal.... Rath-

13. Ibid., 835.

14. Ibid. Emphasis added.

15. While technically "separated" refers exclusively to human souls and "separate" refers to angelic substances, Lehrberger will translate the Latin *separatis* with the English "separated", applying it to both kinds of beings. Despite the confusion of language, he is trying to prove that separated souls do in fact properly belong within a consideration of *substantiae separatae*.

16. Lehrberger, "Anthropology," 836. Cf. *De ente et essentia* 4, lines 1–3.

17. *De ente et essentia* 4, lines 18–22. (Busa edition: Unde oportet quod in qualibet substantia intelligente sit omnino immunitas a materia, ita quod neque habeat materiam partem sui neque etiam sit sicut forma impressa in materia, ut est de formis materialibus.)

18. Lehrberger, "Anthropology," 838.

19. Cf. *De ente et essentia* 4, lines 185–92.

er there is *unum esse in uno composito*; because there is one act of the soul's existence in which matter partakes, there is one being—man—composed of body through soul."[20] Though having *esse per se*, the soul, as created, is still composed even when considering it apart from matter, as it is in potency to receive that *esse*: "Like all intelligences, however, the rational soul is a receptive potency determining and limiting *esse* as its received act; the human soul, then, receives *esse per se*. Not just Socrates but Socrates' soul subsists; indeed Socrates in his flesh and bones receives existence from his soul, rather than the other way around."[21] As spiritual substances—separated human souls included—are composed of act and potency with regard to *esse* and *essentia*, this composition will be the basis for Lehrberger's method of "metaphysical" definition, as such substances do not have the composition of matter and form (at least when considered in themselves, as in the case of the separated human soul):

> In metaphysical species, there is no matter and form but there is potency and act, *essentia* and *esse*. Genus and difference, accordingly, must be taken from them as referring to the whole in an indeterminate or determinate way: the determinate as potential to many possible determinations, the determinating as specific actualization of the indeterminate. The potential element in spiritual substances, however, is the intellectual *essentia*. The actual element is its finite existence in this or that grade of perfection. Hence the genus of the separated substance must be taken from intellectuality or spirituality. Similarly, the difference must be taken from its finite existence in this or that grade of perfection.[22]

Such a claim as Lehrberger's seems in fact to be quite plausible. As St. Thomas had said earlier in the text, the relation of matter and form gives rise to that of genus and difference. So, in spiritual substances without matter yet still composed of potency and act, the relation of genus and difference could very well be based upon that relation of potency and act within the substance. Quite plausible indeed, but watch what Lehrberger does with it in the following text while attempting to provide a proper definition for the *human soul as a separated, spiritual substance*:

> Hence, in the potency of *essentia* to *esse*, the soul is an intelligence. In the finite *esse* of this or that grade of perfection, the soul is "incarnate," that is, the actuality of the human body. In other words, taking the genus as the whole open to many possible grades of perfection, the soul is intelligence or spirit. Taking the difference as

20. Lehrberger, "Anthropology," 839.
21. Ibid., 840.
22. Ibid., 842–43.

the specific determining grade of perfection, the soul is embodied. Metaphysically, *man* is an "incarnate (difference) spirit (genus)."[23]

Notice the shift in the discussion. He has been commenting upon the characteristics of the separated soul, seemingly preparing to conclude to a definition of *the human soul*, whether separated or not, as an Incarnate Spirit. Considering everything that Lehrberger had said thus far and the principles drawn from St. Thomas, that would have been, I think, a very plausible definition of the human soul with "spirit" referring to the whole *soul* indeterminately and "incarnate" to the whole *soul* determinately, but with the proviso that such a consideration is that of a *privated* being which is only a substance *in a qualified sense* (as I will show later on). However, almost seamlessly, Lehrberger concludes to define "man" as Incarnate Spirit. Though he does not say so explicitly, such a move must, I believe, be based upon a syllogism of this sort: (Major) A human soul is an Incarnate Spirit. (Minor) A human being is essentially its soul. (Conclusion) Therefore, a human being is essentially an Incarnate Spirit. A perfectly valid syllogism, but are the premises true? While the major premise might need further consideration in order to prove or disprove, it at least seems plausible enough to grant for the sake of argument. It is the minor premise for which I am most concerned. Furthermore, if this minor premise is not true, that is, if the spiritual soul is but a part of the whole human being, Lehrberger would be guilty of referring to a part (the soul) indeterminately (as spirit) rather than to the whole human being when predicating its genus, thus invalidating his definition in reference to the whole human being. Thus, to be valid, such a conclusion depends directly upon the convertibility of *human soul* and *human being* in the minor premise. But is that truly the case? Also, does Thomas hold that the human being is essentially its soul, as he must if, as Lehrberger maintains, Thomas subscribes to Incarnate Spirit as the proper metaphysical definition of human being? Before venturing an answer to these questions I would like to examine, though in a briefer fashion, a similar argument to that of Lehrberger's, which likewise defines the human being as an Incarnate Spirit based upon just such a convertibility.

23. Ibid., 843. Emphasis added.

II. An Explication of Anton Pegis' *At the Origins of the Thomistic Notion of Man*

In this short work Anton C. Pegis endeavors to solve the great mystery of the unity of the human being, that is, of how the human being can be composed of both body and spiritual soul and yet, even within that composition, remain truly one. As Pegis explains,

> Not only is [the human being] like other composite substances in nature, one through the unity of his substantial principle, but this principle—the soul—also happens to be a spiritual substance in its own right. The full strangeness of man, therefore, consists in this, that, as a composite reality including an organic body within his being, he exists wholly and radically in and through a spiritual principle.[24]

Thus, that the soul, which is a "spiritual substance in its own right," can also inform a material body, which no other kind of spiritual substance can do, and in so doing impart existence for the composite—this is the core of the great mystery of the human being and of its unity. The soul is both "part" and yet in some sense (and I contend in a very qualified sense) a "whole." And the unity of the human composite is rooted precisely in this mystery of being both "part" and "whole":

> With the aid of Aristotle, but on the premise of transcending his metaphysics, St. Thomas Aquinas decided that man could be one being in nature if soul and body were related to one another as co-parts, that is, as incomplete members of a whole that alone could verify and explain their meaning even as parts. The human soul, therefore, though a spiritual substance in itself, yet had the incomplete nature of a part; it was by nature both a substance and a substantial form, and therefore somehow truly both a whole and a part.[25]

Based upon our considerations of the *De ente* earlier in this paper, Pegis' interpretation to this point seems quite plausible. As neither the body nor the soul is the human being, they must be somehow co-parts if they are not distinct substances in their own right acting upon each other in some kind of contiguous symbiotic relationship with a *per accidens* unity, as Plato contended. As the *esse* of the composite is given through the soul which has

24. Anton Pegis, *At the Origins of the Thomistic Notion of Man* (New York: The Macmillan Company, 1963), 34.

25. Ibid., 38.

that *esse per se*, the soul is somehow a "whole" considered in itself (though again in a very qualified sense, which I will address in a moment). However, similar to Lehrberger's own syllogizing, Pegis will go on, likewise, to call the human being an Incarnate Spirit based upon the same purported convertibility of that quasi-substance, known as soul, with the whole human being. In his own words, Pegis contends:

> *Man* answers to the *soul* as *whole* to *whole* because man is the total reality prefigured in the substance of the soul. And if this means that the soul is by nature destined to be a part of man, it also means that in the unity and concreteness of his being, *man is no more than the soul in the fullness of its nature*—an *incarnated spirit*, whose unity is that *he is wholly spirit* but spirit involved in a discursive intellectual life on the horizon of matter; in rational motion within matter, and in a progressive approach to intellectual formation and spiritual unification.[26]

Thus, it seems as if Lehrberger and Pegis are of one mind on this issue: as the composite human being has *esse* through its soul (which has *esse per se*) informing the body, the human being is essentially its soul (whole answering to whole). As this spiritual soul is a whole that is convertible with the human being, "spirit" is predicable of the whole human being indeterminately, and also "incarnate" as the specific difference of that whole. Also, in both cases, each philosopher claims to have unearthed the true philosophical anthropology of St. Thomas. Returning then to the questions which we posed at the end of our treatment of Fr. Lehrberger's article, we must ask, are the *human soul* and the *human being* truly convertible? In other words, is the soul truly an unqualified whole, such that a term (in this case "spirit") which indeterminately signifies its genus could also indeterminately signify the genus of the whole human being? Does St. Thomas really maintain an affirmative answer to these questions? I contend, and hope to show in the following pages, that the answer to all of the above queries is resoundingly in the negative. In the process of doing so, I hope to show that, in fact, Incarnate Spirit is not in any way a proper definition of the human being, even if a perfectly valid description when considering the soul in itself.

26. Ibid., 45–46. Emphasis added, with the exception of 'man' and the first instance of 'soul' in the first sentence.

III. St. Thomas Aquinas and the Incompleteness of the Human Soul

Against those who attest to the convertibility of *human being* and *human soul,* Jason Eberl counters by emphasizing the importance of considering the human being's sensitive capacities along with its rationality. Quoting St. Thomas in his defense, he says:

> In addition to being rational, a human being is a sensitive, living, and corporeal substance. Human beings have a material nature: "It belongs *per se* to a human being that there be found in him a rational soul and a body composed of the four elements. So without these parts a human being cannot be understood, and they must be placed in the definition of a human being; so they are parts of the species and form."[27]

A consideration of the human being which overemphasizes its rationality without giving due treatment to its materiality would seem then to be bound to run astray, as the human being is not properly understood without considering both its material and its spiritual dimensions. Truly, these two dimensions are not separately existing substances but rather are co-principles of one composite human substance. As Eberl writes, while again also quoting St. Thomas in support:

> A human soul and the material body of which it is the substantial form are not two separately existing substances. A substantial form is the actualization of a material body. Aquinas asserts, "Body and soul are not two actually existing substances, but from these two is made one actually existing substance. For a human being's body is not actually the same in the soul's presence and absence; but the soul makes it exist actually."[28]

A human being's substantiality is *proprie loquendo* as a composite, and cannot be regarded as merely rooted in either the body alone or the soul alone, for neither body nor soul can be regarded properly as an unqualified substance. As Eberl says:

27. Jason Eberl, "Aquinas on the Nature of Human Beings," *The Review of Metaphysics* 58, no. 2 (2004): 334, quoting *Super Boetium de Trinitate* q. 5, a. 3c (Eberl translation). (*Super Boetium de Trinitate,* in Busa ed., vol. 4, 520–39: Similiter etiam per se competit homini quod inveniatur in eo anima rationalis et corpus compositum ex quattuor elementis, unde sine his partibus homo intelligi non potest, sed haec oportet poni in diffinitione eius; unde sunt partes speciei et formae.)

28. Ibid., 335, quoting Summa contra Gentiles (SCG) II, chap. 69, no. 2 (Eberl translation). (*Summa contra gentiles,* in Busa ed., vol. 2, 1–152: Non enim corpus et anima sunt duae substantiae actu existentes, sed ex eis duobus fit una substantia actu existens: corpus enim hominis non est idem actu praesente anima, et absente; sed anima facit ipsum actu esse.)

To summarize, neither a human soul nor the matter it informs alone is a substance. Rather, the two together compose a substance—a human being. A human being is not identical to his soul or his informed material body. Rather, a human being is composed of his informed material body: "A human being is said to be from soul and body just as from two things a third is constituted that is neither of the two, for a human being is neither soul nor body."[29]

But some, agreeing with the positions of Lehrberger and Pegis, might counter that St. Thomas does in fact at times treat the soul as a substance, as we saw with chapters 4 and 5 of *De ente*. How can these two positions be reconciled, namely, the positions that the soul is somehow both a substance and also *not* a substance? It is at this juncture where I think the Lehrberger/Pegis camp makes an especially pronounced disservice to the understanding of St. Thomas' philosophical anthropology, because, despite their selective reading of the texts, St. Thomas is very clear on the fact that the separated soul can only be considered a substance *in a qualified way*, and never *simpliciter*. Eberl comments upon this, focusing upon the key text of the *Summa theologiae* I, q. 75, a. 2, ad 1, where Thomas explicates different ways in which something can be called a substance, or, as he says, a "hoc aliquid":

In his early works, Aquinas took the term "substance" to refer to anything that had *esse*: substance equaled subsistence. In the later works, Aquinas makes a distinction between mere subsistence and subsistence as a substance (*hypostasis* or *suppositum*): "'This something' (*hoc aliquid*) can be taken in two ways: one way, for any subsistent thing; the other way, for what subsists in its complete specific nature. The first way excludes the inherence of an accident or material form. The second way excludes also the imperfection of a part.... Therefore, since a human soul is part of the human species, it can be called 'this something' in the first way, as subsistent, but not in the second—for in this way the composite of soul and body is called 'this something.'"[30]

29. Ibid., 337, quoting *De ente et essentia* 2 (Eberl translation). (Busa edition: Ex anima enim et corpore dicitur esse homo, sicut ex duabus rebus quaedam res tertia constituta, quae neutra illarum est. Homo enim neque est anima neque corpus.)

30. Ibid., 346, quoting ST I, q. 75, a. 2, ad 1 (Eberl translation). (*Summa theologiae*, in Busa ed., vol. 2, 184–926: Ad primum ergo dicendum quod hoc aliquid potest accipi dupliciter, uno modo, pro quocumque subsistente, alio modo, pro subsistente completo in natura alicuius speciei. Primo modo, excludit inhaerentiam accidentis et formae materialis, secundo modo, excludit etiam imperfectionem partis. Unde manus posset dici hoc aliquid primo modo, sed non secundo modo. Sic igitur, cum anima humana sit pars speciei humanae, potest dici hoc aliquid primo modo, quasi subsistens, sed non secundo modo, sic enim compositum ex anima et corpore dicitur hoc aliquid.)

As the separated soul is a substance only in that first *qualified* way as something which merely subsists, it cannot be regarded as a substance *simpliciter*, as it is incomplete in its specific nature apart from the body, having its proper perfection and completeness only within the body that it informs:

> A soul alone is not identical to a human being, nor has it a complete human nature: "No part has its natural perfection separate from the whole. Hence the soul, since it is part of human nature, does not have its natural perfection unless it is in union with the body.... Hence the soul, though it can exist and understand separated from the body, does not have its natural perfection when it is separate from the body."[31]

Due to this incompleteness of nature, the soul can in no way be identical with the human being, and especially not with human person: "Not every particular substance is a *hypostasis* or person, but what has its complete specific nature. Hence a hand or foot cannot be called a *hypostasis* or person; and similarly neither can the soul, since it is part of the human species."[32] This position will lead St. Thomas to conclude, and rightfully so based upon these principles, that "*The soul,* since it is *part* of the human body, *is not the whole human being. My soul is not I.* So even if the soul were to achieve salvation in another life, it would not be I or any human being."[33] Here I shall pause just for a moment to spell out the implications of this for the Lehrberger/Pegis position. Clearly, for St. Thomas, the soul is *not* the whole human being, but is merely a part. Thus, to predicate spirit

31. Ibid., 345, quoting *Quaestio disputata de spiritualibus creaturis* a. 2, ad 5 (Eberl translation). (*Quaestio disputata de spiritualibus creaturis,* in Busa ed. vol. 3, 352–68: Ad quintum dicendum quod nulla pars habet perfectionem naturae separata a toto. Unde anima, cum sit pars humanae naturae, non habet perfectionem suae naturae nisi in unione ad corpus. Quod patet ex hoc quod in virtute ipsius animae est quod fluant ab ea quaedam potentiae quae non sunt actus organorum corporalium, secundum quod excedit corporis proportionem; et iterum quod fluant ab ea potentiae quae sunt actus organorum, in quantum potest contingi a materia corporali. Non est autem aliquid perfectum in sua natura, nisi actu explicari possit quod in eo virtute continetur. Unde anima, licet possit esse et intelligere a corpore separata, tamen non habet perfectionem suae naturae cum est separata a corpore ut Augustinus dicit, XII super Genes. ad litteram.)

32. ST I, q. 75, a. 4, ad 2 (Eberl translation), quoted in Eberl, "Aquinas on the Nature," 346. (Busa edition: Ad secundum dicendum quod non quaelibet substantia particularis est hypostasis vel persona, sed quae habet completam naturam speciei. Unde manus vel pes non potest dici hypostasis vel persona. Et similiter nec anima, cum sit pars speciei humanae.)

33. *Super I ad Corinthios* 15, lect. 2 (Pasnau translation), quoted in Robert Pasnau, *Thomas Aquinas on Human Nature* (Cambridge, Massachusetts: Cambridge University Press, 2002), 386. Emphasis added, except for the first two words. (*Super I ad Corinthios,* in Busa ed., vol. 6, 375–98: Anima autem cum sit pars corporis hominis, non est totus homo, et anima mea non est ego; unde licet anima consequatur salutem in alia vita, non tamen ego vel quilibet homo.)

of human being is not a valid genus for its definition, for it refers not to the whole human being indeterminately but again merely to the part. A human being has a spirit just as it has a body, but it is *proprie loquendo* neither considered separately. Contra Fr. Lehrberger, a "metaphysical" treatment of human nature as a consideration of the human being apart from matter, is not properly a treatment of the human being, for apart from matter there is no human being *proprie loquendo*, even if such a treatment does provide a greater understanding of the human being's spiritual dimension and its place within the whole.

So, I say with confidence that, based upon numerous texts, St. Thomas can be seen to be quite opposed to the position that human being and human soul are convertible. But further textual evidence can be offered to understand his reasoning further still. Yes, he regards the separated soul as incomplete in nature; but the question remains: precisely how can the body it informs help to complete it within the composite? St. Thomas provides a helpful clue in ST I, q. 75, a. 4, where he in fact argues quite explicitly against the claim that the soul itself is the human being. What I would like to make note of is the second half of the *corpus*, where he continues to explain in what ways the soul might be called the human being, and also how, in this as in the other senses mentioned, it is still a false assertion:

> It may also be understood in this sense, that this soul is this man; and this could be held if it were supposed that the operation of the sensitive soul were proper to it, apart from the body; because in that case all the operations which are attributed to man would belong to the soul only; and whatever performs the operations proper to a thing, is that thing; wherefore that which performs the operations of a man is man. But it has been shown above that sensation is not the operation of the soul only. Since, then, sensation is an operation of man, but not proper to him, it is clear that man is not a soul only, but something composed of soul and body. Plato, through supposing that sensation was proper to the soul, could maintain man to be a soul making use of the body.[34]

34. Thomas Aquinas, *The Summa Theologica of St. Thomas Aquinas*, translated by the Fathers of the English Dominican Province, rev. ed., 3 vols. (New York: Benziger Brothers, 1948). (Busa edition: Alio vero modo potest intelligi sic, quod etiam haec anima sit hic homo. Et hoc quidem sustineri posset, si poneretur quod animae sensitivae operatio esset eius propria sine corpore, quia omnes operationes quae attribuuntur homini, convenirent soli animae; illud autem est unaquaeque res, quod operatur operationes illius rei. Unde illud est homo, quod operatur operationes hominis. Ostensum est autem quod sentire non est operatio animae tantum. Cum igitur sentire sit quaedam operatio hominis, licet non propria, manifestum est quod homo non est

Commenting upon and further explicating this very passage, Étienne Gilson maintains:

> But it is quite impossible to hold that the soul alone is the whole man. A general definition of anything is: "that which performs the operation proper to it." In this case man is to be defined as "that which performs the operations proper to man." Man does not perform only intellectual operations. He performs sensitive operations too.... Thus, if sensation is truly an operation of man, even though it is not his proper operation, then it is perfectly obvious that man is not just his soul but some kind of composite of soul and body.[35]

As it is the whole human being which performs the operations proper to human beings, and since the human being has not only intellectual activities which properly pertain to the soul but also sensitive activities which pertain to both the body and the soul, the whole human being, which senses, perceives, and understands in body and soul, must truly be both body and soul. Thus, Thomas' anthropology is rooted not in some a priori, deductive "metaphysical" reasoning, but by means of a posteriori, inductive science which proceeds from the observable animality of human beings, sensing and perceiving through their bodies as all animals do, but with the unique further capability of intellectual knowledge. Any other attempts to define the human being would do well to proceed in like fashion.

IV. Conclusion

In closing, there are numerous points about which I hope to have demonstrated to be not only Thomas' own position, but in fact to be the correct view on the particular matter. First, the soul, as we have seen, is incomplete in nature without the body, and thus when separated is an incomplete substance. Second, even while united to the body, it is not the soul, properly speaking, which performs all the operations proper to the human being, but rather the composite human being which, through its body and soul, senses, perceives, and understands. Furthermore, as soul is truly a *part* of the whole composite human being, no definitions of that part, even if they could very well be properly predicated of the soul, as such, are

---

anima tantum, sed est aliquid compositum ex anima et corpore. Plato vero, ponens sentire esse proprium animae, ponere potuit quod homo esset anima utens corpore.)

35. Étienne Gilson, *The Christian Philosophy of St. Thomas Aquinas* (Notre Dame, Indiana: University of Notre Dame Press, 1994), 191–92.

rightly predicable of the whole composite, because such definitions refer to the part indeterminately and determinately rather than to the whole. Thus, though a human soul may very well be regarded as an Incarnate Spirit, the human being cannot be so defined. For though the human being truly has a spirit, *proprie loquendo*, the human being is not a spirit.

But this gives rise to an aporia: if not Incarnate Spirit, what is the proper philosophical definition of human being? Though "rational animal," as Thomas himself argues in the *De ente* passages we have already seen, fills all the requirements of a proper definition, still this does not mean, as I think Lehrberger correctly pointed out, that this is the only philosophical definition which can ever adequately describe the human being or even that this definition has no limitations to it. Although as a Thomist, I am personally inclined to favor "rational animal," I cannot help thinking that the postmodern mind is bound to be confused by this term. Though such a thinker, when hearing "animal," will, due to the advances of modern biology and biochemistry, have a much better grasp of what an animal is than St. Thomas and his contemporaries, he is unlikely to understand anything like what St. Thomas did by the term "rational," at least not without a great effort at entering into Thomas's premodern mindset.

What term, or terms (for that matter), then, can more adequately express the human being's specific difference, which makes it unique in comparison with all other animals and which can lead the hearer to properly understand what is being defined? Indeed, as the word "rational" attests, it is the human being's *intellectuality*; but in what does that consist which makes the human animal unique in comparison to all other animals? The specific difference of any proper definition of the human being will have to answer this very question both adequately and clearly. To do so, that same specific difference will do well to point toward the human animal's unique ability to consider objects which cannot be sensibly instantiated, an ability which truly distinguishes intellectual knowledge from mere animal perception.[36] Though much more could and should be said on this matter, I will leave that for a later date.

36. I would like to thank Dr. John Deely of the University of St. Thomas (Houston) not only for this insight, but also for his numerous helpful comments on a previous draft of this work. Without his encouragement and guidance, this paper would not have been possible.

MICHAEL NOVAK

Maritain on the Void

I don't remember who first put *True Humanism* into my hands in my senior year at Holy Cross Seminary, across the highway at the University of Notre Dame, but I do recall vividly how it stunned me. That an argument this profound, ranging, and engaged had already been published and had been available for many years—and yet I had not heard of it! Some passages were so beautifully written, and others so down-to-earth and practical, I knew I was in the presence of a master. *True Humanism* offered a new horizon for thought, and a lifetime's agenda for action. My inner motto had already become "To restore all things in Christ." But I had not yet dreamt of a philosophical vision so applicable to this world now, so transformative, so future-oriented, so practical-practical.

One of the things I loved about Maritain from the first was the poetry in his philosophical writing, his sensitivity to nature and the subconscious (and preconscious). Maritain approached his craft as an artist does. In this he was more like Plato than like his beloved Aristotle. (Although doesn't Maritain remark somewhere that Aristotle's dialogues, no longer extant, were esteemed by some contemporaries as highly as Plato's? Tragic, if we have lost the literary works of Aristotle.)

Where other philosophers approach epistemology from sense perception and its deceptions, and in a most pedestrian way, Maritain did not hesitate to approach it from the side of the preconscious and the vivid knowing-in-images connatural to the poet, and also (in a different way) to the athlete, such as Aristotle's archer.

Yet it was not until recently that I was flat-out stopped by Maritain's chapter in *Ransoming the Time* on self-knowledge, natural mysticism, and the void. These are subjects more commonly explored by novelists, poets, and dramatists in our time, than among, say, British logicians and language philosophers of the twentieth century. Maritain's reflections on self-knowledge and the void in this chapter did not wholly surprise me. I had long loved *Existence and the Existent,* and tended to see in Maritain, as in Gabriel Marcel, not a little of the existentialist awareness of the fragility of "becoming." Indeed, Maritain showed more existentialist insight than is usually indulged in by those interested merely in logic, science—in the serene world of essences and concepts.

It is evident that Maritain, as a conscious being in one staccato moment of time, well knew the sharp sense of *existing*. He was painfully aware of how fleeting our consciousness is, a mere flicker against the impassivity of the night. We are, as it were, always "standing out from" nothingness (*ex-sistens*). We know, sharply, what it is suddenly to *be* here and now, and then tomorrow not to be.

Yet Maritain did not approach the void as Albert Camus or Jean-Paul Sartre did. Not for him the haunting, shocking remembrance of murder (as in *The Stranger*) or suicide (as in *The Myth of Sisyphus* and *The Fall*). And yet, we do seem to remember that Jacques and Raïssa had formed a pact to commit suicide together, if a deeper meaning of life did not soon unfold before them. The hundreds of thousands of dead in the trenches during the long years of the First World War cast a pall over their lives. Many of their young friends fell dead on the still smoking fields of that war—Ernest Psichari (with a bullet through his head on his first day of battle) among them. They had experienced the meaningless of the 1920s, and of most of the philosophers, too, except for Bergson.

No, Maritain began not with personal experience, nor with "self-knowledge" in the existentialists' manner, nor even in the Socratic manner. Rather, he began with metaphysical inquiry into the interrelated meanings of intellectual substance, subsistence, contingent existence, and the human subject. This reflection led him to human consciousness, which is such that we see out of the corner of our eye, or with a kind of backward awareness, a glimpse of something unsettling deep within us. Right in the core of our being is the taste of our own nothingness.

Maritain's essay on the void in the last chapter of *Ransoming the Time* is a complex one, and on a then relatively unknown topic. In such cases, it was typical of his method to array on the terrain of argument the pieces he needed to make his point clear. At each stage, he also scouted the terrain, and warned the reader away from traps and swamps in which the advance of his arguments, and their reinforcements, would otherwise be lost.

The reader notices on the first page that Maritain is working in a strange sort of light that comes from outside philosophy itself, namely, his awareness of a theological background that in this essay he cannot pause to explore. What he needs, though, is to hold this light in the background as a measure of the human subject and the void. He needs to show the *difference* between a mysticism that arises out of the nature of the intelligent subject, and a mysticism that arises out of the superabundance of Light and Love that possesses some humans, from beyond nature itself. In order to measure natural mysticism, he needs to keep aware of what is so different from it, the mysticism that springs from God's own freely given, undeserved action.

This supernatural mysticism, which Maritain is aware of in the world around him, he knows, is not *against* human nature but springs from *beyond* it. He knows this from mastering in his youth the reports of his beloved Saint John of the Cross and Saint Teresa of Avila. There is some hint in the chapter (in his clarity about boundaries) that he knows this also from his own experience. But he never goes into that.

As the essay progresses, it becomes clear that Maritain's immediate interest here is not the Western experience of "being and nothingness" that Jean-Paul Sartre writes about. Rather, it is the trustworthy record and fairly detailed reports of the Hindu and Buddhist experience of the *void.*

This experience is what Maritain wishes to explore. Almost right away he notes that the Hindu experience of the void is not the experience of a *superabundance* of Life, Love, and Light. It is, as the word they choose makes vivid, the experience of a void. Nonetheless, can this experience be, in its authentic forms, an analog of the supernatural mysticism? Can it even rank as a valid form of natural mysticism? Rather surprisingly, Maritain's answer to both questions, typically generous but carefully explained, is Yes.

Maritain is not asking these questions in solitude. He is part of a vigorous and very high-level intellectual conversation. He considers two leaders in particular, whose work he has found helpful. The first, Père Maréchal, in answer to a question posed by Maritain at a conference, gives the latter confidence that even his disagreement with that colleague is worth pursuing. The second, Père Gardeil, has a rather more substantial position, about which a longer discussion is necessary. Here, too, Maritain begs to disagree, and advances the discussion quite a lot further with careful argumentation.[1] It is not necessary for us to recapitulate these steps here. But it is important to note that Maritain was working in a powerful collegial enterprise. Not they alone, but also Friedrich Nietzsche, Herman Hesse (*Siddhartha*), and others were writing about the Buddhist and Hindu experience of the void. At least a few in the West were discovering the East.

I. The Preliminary Circling

I have already mentioned that Maritain needed to marshal his troops of argumentation on the table, and to explore the terrain of argument. This latter move required circling back and forth on the climb up the mountain, and it took at least three switch-backs.

The first point Maritain needed to make clear is that human knowing is an act of many kinds and degrees. He needed to remind his readers that knowing is not limited to language and logic, or even to the sense of "empirical" then governing many of the philosophers working in Europe and America. Thus, he made clear that we all have experience of a knowing that comes by "connaturality," that is, a habit shaped to, and shaping, our nature and our actual practices.

For example, take golf and archery. Lying as he is on the short but difficult approach to the fifth hole of a golf course, which club does the veteran and highly skilled golfer choose for his next shot? Which club is best suited to *him*, and to this peculiar terrain (a hill, a clump of trees, the inlet of a small lake) on this particular shot?

Then the experienced and highly skilled archer (a beautiful example from Aristotle). Which arrow from his quiver does the skilled bowman select, and how hard does he strain his bow, and in what manner should he take account of the distance and the wind, in order to "hit the mark"?

Nobody can reasonably deny that there is a certain kind of knowing involved in these actions, in which a neophyte is not likely to share. This knowing is an everyday adaptation of the golfer's and archer's practice of their crafts. The same with the surgeon's craft. The sure knowledge that comes by

1. See Jacques Maritain, *Ransoming the Time*, translated by Harry Lorin Binsse (New York: Charles Scribner's Sons, 1941), 264, 268–69, 272.

experience makes a large difference in outcomes, especially in difficult cases.

Another sort of knowing lies in the art, habit, and practice of the poetic eye and hand. The role of the imagination and the artist's subconscious fund of images and experiences plays here a larger role than in conceptual or logical reasoning. So does a quite different approach to words—in the one case, seeking the univocal and the literal and most economical expression (by the rule of Ockham's razor), suited to impersonal scientific discourse. And, in the other case, seeking the richest possible play of analogy and symbol, in order to awaken the many layers of the subconscious, and to produce an entirely different form of expression. Poetic, not scientific.

Some philosophers, alas, have been known to restrict philosophy, and certainly the empirical sciences, to the barest, cleanest forms available in logic and language. Maritain finds in his own experience that that choice does not do justice to human knowing. When Dante writes: "In His will our peace," and "L'amor' che muov' il sol' ed altre stelle,"[2] he and his readers participate in a knowledge far richer with analogy and implication and networks of human experience and thought than A. J. Ayer's *Language, Truth and Logic.* Maritain discerns a kind of knowing in poetry that is of very high value to the philosopher, and is present in one poet more than in another, and in one poem more deeply and richly than in another.

One of my favorite lessons from my own experience was the distinguished philosopher from Cornell who wrote that it was no form of "knowing" that led him to choose to marry his wife; rather, it was an *emotive* decision. That did not seem to me to be true in fact. The couple seemed to have a steady and well-bonded life together. It seemed to me to tell against his theory of knowing. I for one know quite well how much thought I put into the judgment, and my future wife even more (I came to the conclusion rather more quickly than she did), that Karen and I ought to, indeed must, marry. I know it was not emotive, but reasoned, sometimes painfully reasoned. I even remember making a list of "Why?" and "Why not?" Don't try to tell me I did not know what I was getting into, or that a long self-examination and multifaceted judgment was not involved, more complex than any I had ever put into solving a trigonometry problem, or into discerning the validity of Kant's synthetic and analytic judgments. (I spent a whole semester under Morton V. White on that one.)

2. *Paradiso,* cantos 3 and 33.

So also, Maritain discerns, a kind of knowing of the self occurs in natural mystical knowledge, notably that (less known in the West) of the Hindu sages. By a kind of long and practiced ascesis, not easily learned or mastered, these mystics come at the end of their ascent into highly disciplined intellectual air—to what? What is the fruit of their deepest insight?

Theirs is an extraordinarily disciplined use of senses, imagination, memory, and intelligence itself. Some of the categories of Saint John of the Cross help to elucidate what they are doing—the dark night of the senses, of the imagination, of the memory, and of the searching intelligence.[3] Of course, the dark night of which Saint John of the Cross writes seeks a far different quarry from that sought by these sages.

What they do find, the Hindu sages themselves say, is the void. Not the "nothingness" of which so many in the West write. But something far more emptied out of sense knowledge, images, feeling, memories, or any object of conception. And yet, a certain knowledge worthy of the name "self-knowledge." Maritain analyzes this knowing as a kind of reflexive awareness of, or backward glance at, the self which has been deliberately and with great skill emptied of all knowing.

It is manifest that this sort of natural mysticism, which Maritain is led to judge authentic, is well attested to, and subject to all sorts of, external tests (administered by others, skilled guides themselves) to detect fraud, illusion, and self-deception.

Thus, even while this experience of the void is the direct opposite of the Jewish and Christian experience of the superabundance of the Being, Light, and Love of the divine—and thus is essentially different from it—Maritain still finds it an acceptable analog, here in nature, of the experience of God given to us from beyond our nature. Both involve an obscure knowledge of the self. Both are protected by many tests administered by other skilled guides.

And yet the one comes by way of emptying out the self so as to have as object nothing but the self, emptied of all its perceptions, images, and concepts. The other comes from without, from the in-pouring presence of the Lord of all being, knowing, and loving. But, of course, this Lord is so disproportionate to every form of human knowing—so far beyond our own

3. See Saint John of the Cross, *The Dark Night of the Soul*, translated and edited by E. Allison Peers (New York: Image, 2005).

humble wavelength—that in His possession of us we too are emptied of all other forms of knowing.

As St. John of the Cross puts it in "The Dark Night of the Soul" (I paraphrase):

> I sought Him everywhere,
> Yet as I ascended to the top of the stair
> Where I found Him,
> No one was there.

"No one sees God," Saint John writes in his First Epistle (1 John 4.12). No knowing of ours is on His wavelength. If we did detect Him, our fuses would be blown out, utterly destroyed.

There is a third switch-back necessary to Maritain's advance. He needs to point out the difference between the Idealist and the Realist conception of the subject and the object. In an odd way, modern philosophers after Descartes have separated the two—mind over here, body over there; the subject over here, object over there—and created for themselves the problem of how to re-unite them (the so imagined "mind-body problem"). Despairing of a solution, the strict rationalists go one way, the strict empiricists the other, each choosing its preferred route to "reality." Yet in both, object remains separate from subject. For instance, some speak of "objective" as opposed to "subjective" knowing—and in more than one sense of these, at that.

Aristotle and Aquinas, but not all of the ancients and medievals, have a very different view of knowing. From their own experience, they know knowing as a unity of mind and matter, and also of subject and object. "The mind is in some way all things," Aristotle writes in a breathtaking proposition.[4] And the mind becomes one with all things by knowing them, by letting them come inside ourselves by sense perception and intellection, and then through discernment and judgment casting off what the evidence does not permit. In this way, the knower and the known are one. The subject and the object become one. The mind and the body are one.

For myself, I find Lonergan's experiential description of realism in *Insight* better, more detailed, closer to experience, than Maritain's description (recorded in many places, including *The Degrees of Knowledge*). It is quite clear to me, who loves both writers, that they are playing in the same ball-

4. *De anima* 3.5.

park. Only, in my view, here Lonergan plays with greater precision, with more satisfactory grounding in experiences anyone can replicate, and with a winning crispness. On the other hand, I find Maritain much Lonergan's superior in writing about the archer, the surgeon, the lover, and the poet. And natural mysticism.

Only when all these turns have been made does Maritain's defense of the authenticity of Hindu and Buddhist mysticism ring true. To sum up: Such knowing is a form of natural mysticism, a form of valid and extremely valuable knowing, and it is not the same as the very different supernatural—seized from above—knowing of Saint John of the Cross, Saint Teresa of Avila, and "le altre stelle."

II. The Experience of Nothingness

My account would not be complete if I did not try to place in relation to this chapter my own researches into "nothingness" in a book entitled *The Experience of Nothingness*.[5] There I was not writing about mysticism at all, nor about the void in the Hindu sense, but about a prosaic form of knowing that became utterly common in the twentieth century: the seemingly unshakable sense that even fourteen-year-old girls in Rio Linda have, that our lives are without meaning. "Whaddaya wanna do tonight?" "Dunno. Whaddaya wanna do?"

Some thinkers blame this widespread perception of meaninglessness on atheism and relativism. Some blame it on the technological imprint of our world on human flesh and mind. Some blame it on the tide of gross popularizations of Nietzsche and lesser nihilists. Here is the key text from Nietzsche: "What does nihilism mean? That the highest values devaluate themselves. The aim is lacking; 'why?' finds no answer."[6]

Some philosophers think that ideas govern the world. There is some truth to that. But it is also true that inhibitions and desires, passions and restraints, govern the broad world. Which has more power: ideas, or passions and desires? It is a good question. But Saint Paul is rather convincing when he invites our own self-knowledge onto the field: "The good that I know I

5. Michael Novak, *The Experience of Nothingness* (1970; New Brunswick: Transaction Publishers, 1998).

6. Friedrich Nietzsche, *The Will to Power*, translated by Walter Kaufmann and R. J. Hollingdale, edited by Walter Kaufmann (New York: Random House, 1967), 9.

should do, I do not. Those things that I know I should not do, I do" (Rom 7.15). Knowledge and passions run in different directions.

Even for Aquinas, *caritas* is the form of all the virtues in a way different from the way in which *phronesis* (prudence) is the form of all the natural virtues.[7] For the ultimate seat of *caritas* is the will: to love is to will the good of the other *as other*.[8] (Those last two words are the hard part. No matter how close you are, think how *other* your spouse is from you.)

Thus, in certain recurrent circumstances, the will is a better guide for the intellect than the intellect alone. To love one's best friend well is to hone in on nuances that your intellect alone does not detect. To love the subject one studies is to raise mightily one's probabilities of learning it well. To have a true love, like a North Star, steadies the intellect even when it grows faint, or strays aside. Love very often guides intellect.

Of course, the persuasiveness and decisiveness of intellect are also frequently observed, as we have seen above in the example of judging that this woman, or this man, is the one to commit oneself to for life. Every love, to keep true, very much needs the scrutinizing examination of keen intelligence and sound judgment.

Our present widespread sense of meaninglessness—that invisible, odorless gas seeping everywhere, as Bernanos writes—is implicit in a Godless and reductive materialist worldview. If everything is by chance, down hundreds of millions of years, and there is no purpose, no point but survival, then reason itself is a fraud. It seeks meaning, from a condition of meaninglessness.

And yet Mary Eberstadt has convinced me that we ought to look at this question the other way around. What has led us to imagine that *the world* is meaningless is the lack of reason in *our* desires and *our* passions. Marriage is too difficult, so we too quickly give up its daily grinding of willful subject against willful subject. Raising children eats up far too much time and energy (and money), so we find reasons not to do so.[9]

In this way, marriage declines as an ideal, and an imperative, and a personal asceticism. And so we substitute for it serial monogamy or simply no marriage at all. Or else, we participate in such wholesale male abandon-

7. See Thomas Aquinas, *Summa theologiae* (ST) II-II, q. 23, a. 6.

8. See ST I, q. 20, a. 1, ad 3.

9. See Mary Eberstadt's *Adam and Eve after the Pill* (San Francisco: Ignatius Press, 2013) and *How the West Really Lost God* (West Conshohocken, Pennsylvania: Templeton Press, 2013).

ment of the women whom they have impregnated, that 70 percent of our children in some urban areas (and in large rural areas too) now dwell under the care of a "female householder, no husband present," as the Census Bureau with exquisite sensitivity names them.

Eberstadt argues that it is not the loss of God that causes the breakdown of meaning, and morals, and marriage. Rather, it is the rejection of marriage that has caused the loss of God. When individual lives are disordered by desire and passion, without the simplest and most ordinary forms of asceticism, life does become meaningless. God has no point.

Looked at from another viewpoint, the exceedingly rapid expansion of the realm of personal choices has also, I argue, brought about a kind of vertigo. Saint Augustine wrote that looking up into the multitudes of stars, in the dark nights along the coast of Africa, made him dizzy with glimpses of infinity. He felt much, much too small. Something analogous happens to me when I walk through a university bookstore. There is a dizzying multitude of dazzling books in scores of different areas, subjects, and genres. They stagger me, they make me much too small. I could not possibly read all the books just in one limited corner of my own fields of interest, let alone become well-informed in all these spinning galaxies of subject matters.

It is the same when a young person faces the choice of vocation. She imagines one path, then tosses it aside as not quite right. Then another. Then another. Then another. Finally, it does not seem to matter, really. Life is a dart board, a game of chance, one goes with the flow. All is flux, did not some Greek philosopher write?

The multiplicity of freedoms today causes the dizziness of meaninglessness. By contrast, before they were born, the life courses of my ancestors, and yours, were seemingly laid out for them long in advance, as if by eternal decree or, what comes to the same thing, "just the way things are." Pray, pay, and obey.

Not to put too fine a point on it, democracy and capitalism have blown open a sky-full of choices for our young people. No wonder sophomores feel disoriented, and find it hard just to get out of bed. What does anything matter?

Freedom itself brings a feeling and a fear of meaninglessness. There is so little one *must* do. Life seems to have no direction. Just choices, one damn choice after another. Everyone claims to want liberty, Dostoevsky wrote. Just give it to them. They will start giving it back. Freedom is too much to bear.

That is why nihilism today—relativism if you will—is not just a theory or an idea but a daily experience. I might as well have called my book, *The Experience of Meaninglessness.* But to my ear, "Nothingness" conveyed a much deeper strain in our tradition. In the deepest sense, the sense of nothingness is rooted in our unlimited desire to know. Everything we meet, every answer, we must question. Our minds are made for the infinite. Yet the infinite is so vast, and we are so small. It is not surprising that we all feel moments of weariness, fatigue, dizziness, disorientation. We all feel "the fingers on the windowpane" as the night darkens and the rain falls. We all sense the need for lights, music, action, movement, anything to keep away the insistent silence with its troubling questions. The gnawing of the finitude, the nothingness, within us.

Mostly, in *The Experience of Nothingness,* I argue that this experience is a wonderful experience, a gift to be welcomed. *Creatio ex nihilo.* Nothingness is where creation begins. The fact of relativity does not imply the imperative of moral relativism. It exalts the role of creating our own lives. We begin in nothingness, and of our own choice begin to act in this way, not in that, by the light that is given us. Of course, the choice we make may be wrong; we *could* have chosen a different course. But that is what freedom is, isn't it—risk, fragility, the possibility of learning from experience, corrigibility, and choosing anew?

The fragility of freedom is the road to full womanliness and manliness. That is what humanism is. That is what the free person is, the burden she must bear, the glory of being human in which she basks.

I think that in *The Experience of Nothingness* I also show successfully (although that is for others to judge) that the leading philosophies of nihilism, nothingness, even relativism so far presented, begin in *being.* Nietzsche's first two demands of the brave and the bold who dare to face the meaninglessness at the heart of things is that they be *honest,* and that they then have the *courage* to face what honesty sets before them. Honesty and courage, you can't have the one without the other.

But, then, how do philosophers of nothingness convey this message? *They write books.* But if they really believed that everything is meaningless, why would they undertake such an arduous activity as writing books? What possible meaning is there in telling that to others? What difference does it make?

Furthermore, the writing of books, the presentation of nihilism and relativism in universities, and movies, and songs, could not take place without a commitment to the importance of *community.* Those who have experienced the nothingness (the meaninglessness) in the eyes of others recognize their soul-mates. They live in, form, and try to expand their communities.

Fourth, besides *honesty, courage,* and *community,* those who write about nihilism, the *nada,* the nothingness, assume into their own practice yet another pregnant and important human commitment. They are committed to personal *freedom* "all the way down." Yet in a meaningless world, on what grounds is freedom considered to be superior to subservience? On what grounds do they consider *creativity* to be morally superior to destructiveness? They do call, do they not, for building a new world, a better world, one that flows from their vision.

Did not Hitler with his unflinching nihilism in practice, and with his race of "Super Men," and in his exaltation of "the triumph of the will," call Nietzsche's bluff? What Hitler did, of course, is not what Nietzsche meant. But if everything is meaningless, then what difference does it make *which* meanings Nietzsche chose, or Hitler chose? Where there is no truth, no being, there is only, after all, *The Triumph of the Will.* Intellect has been ruled out of bounds.

In a word, those who claim to be relativists, nihilists, and prophets of the nothingness at the heart of human life are wearing Halloween costumes. They really do have values underneath their discoveries and their expositions and their exhortations. They really do act as if honesty has more being in it than dishonesty, that courage stands out from nothingness more than cowardice does, that community is actually on a superior plane of being than passive, atomic human individuals, blown about like dry leaves (in Dante's image) before the gates of purgatory.

They really do demean other philosophies as anti-human and destructive, rather than (what they honor) creative. They call other philosophies "anti-freedom," as if freedom has more value, more *being* in it than unfreedom.

What do our modern proponents of nihilism lack, then, but self-critical knowledge about their own hidden philosophy, to prevent them from being taken as philosophers of being (though under Venetian disguise). They seem in fact—with their appeals to honesty, courage, community, and freedom—to be heralds of a renaissance of integral humanism, or at least of its beginnings. They preach non-being, but despite themselves and in practice, their arguments will not work without hidden appeals to powerful forms of being and acting: honesty, courage, community, freedom.

Do what they do, not what they preach.

III. Conclusion

The broad popular diffusion of modern nihilism, through the culture of the media, presents us with a marvelous "teaching moment." Buried in the experience of nothingness are important habits of a new humanism—honesty, courage, community, creativity, freedom. On these, a new civilization may be built.

Albert Camus imagines his lifetime task as finding a way out of the ruins of our time, the ruins left behind by the nihilism of Lenin, Hitler, and Mussolini into which he had been thrust. He learned this when a young friend of his in Marseilles was strangled to death with a piano wire by the Gestapo. There are nihilisms, and then there are nihilisms, Camus thought then. And some of them must be opposed till death.[10]

Born into much the same world, Jacques Maritain imagined his lifetime task, and ours, as "Ransoming the Time." No one can say the intellectual opportunity to do so is not in our hands.

10. See, for example, *The Rebel* (1951).

II

THEOLOGICAL TURN

ROGER W. NUTT

Christ's *Esse* and Filiation

Interpreting St. Thomas on the Metaphysical Status of Christ's Human Nature

I. The Filiation of Christ: An Introductory Test Case

As a preface to the body of this essay, which focuses on the debate among Thomists over Christ's *esse,* brief consideration will be given to Aquinas's treatment of Christ's adoption.

In the narrative of the *tertia pars* of the *Summa theologiae,* St. Thomas situates the questions treating Christ's *esse* (17) and adoption (23) within the larger section (questions 16–26) devoted to "those things which follow upon the union."[1] As effects or consequences of the hypostatic union, the topics of Christ's *esse* and adoption shed reciprocal light on each other; indeed, it is difficult to imagine maintaining consistency in Christological doctrine without taking a similar position on both issues. In the four articles of Question 23 on Christ's adoption, Aquinas proceeds in a fashion that is unique in this section of the *Summa.* The first three articles do not, in fact, pertain to Christ directly, but ask whether or not it is fitting for God to adopt sons, whether this adoption is done by the whole Trinity, and whether adoption of the rational creature is especially appropriate.

1. *Summa theologiae* (ST) III, q. 16, *praefacio*: "de his quae consequuntur unionem." All English citations from the *Summa theologiae,* unless otherwise noted, are taken from the translation of the Fathers of the English Dominican Province originally published in 1911 and reprinted in five volumes as *The Summa Theologica of St. Thomas Aquinas* (Allen, Texas: Christian Classics, 1981). All Latin texts, unless otherwise noted, are taken from E. Alarcón's posting of the *corpus thomisticum* at www.corpusthomisticum.org.

After this richly Pauline mini-treatise on adoption by grace, Thomas then asks in the fourth article the specifically Christological question: namely, "Whether Christ, *secundum quod homo,* is an adopted son of God"—the *secundum quod homo* being an important qualifier relative to the question of Christ's *esse.* In light of the fact that Aquinas has already affirmed, earlier in the *tertia pars,*[2] that Christ, as man, enjoyed grace to a superabundant degree, the answer would seem logically to be yes—Christ, as man, having received grace in his human nature, is an adopted son of God. Thomas' answer, however, runs to the contrary: "Sonship," he reasons, "belongs properly to the hypostasis or person, not to the nature.... Now in Christ there is no other than the uncreated person or hypostasis, to Whom it belongs by nature to be the Son."[3] Because adoptive sonship in grace is participatory of natural sonship or likeness, Aquinas concludes that "Christ, Who is the natural Son of God, can in nowise be called an adopted son."[4]

In the fourth book of *Summa contra gentiles,* Aquinas articulates his position against those who deny the eternal and natural sonship of Christ even more sharply and with appeal to the order of being: "It goes without saying," Aquinas declares, "that the son generated by God did not take up a beginning of being from Mary."[5]

The distinction between person or hypostasis and nature thus plays out even in Aquinas's understanding of Christ's singular mode of filiation as the Eternal Son of God. What makes Aquinas's discussion of Christ's adoption a "test case" for the *esse* question is, precisely, that if Christ's human nature did indeed contribute a human *esse* to Christ, the human *esse* of the human nature would, it seems, by virtue of Christ's superabundant grace, be adopted. Aquinas, however, manifestly denies that such an adoption took place. Given Aquinas's position following the Christology of Chalcedon that in Christ there is but a single person and subsistence,[6] the grace

2. See, for example, q. 7, where Aquinas affirms that Christ had habitual grace (a. 1), infused virtue (a. 2), gifts of the Holy Spirit (a. 5), and gratuitous grace (a. 7).

3. ST III, q. 23, a. 4.

4. Ibid.

5. *Summa contra Gentiles* (SCG) IV, chap. 4, no. 11: "Unde relinquitur quod filius a Deo genitus initium essendi a Maria non sumpsit."

6. The discussion of Christ's *esse* by Medieval thinkers is a continuation of the Patristic developments regarding Christ's subsistence. The Councils of Chalcedon (451) and Constantinople II (553), in addition to teaching that Christ's two natures are united in one person also teach that there is a single subsistence. By *esse* Medieval authors wish to consider whether each of Christ's natures contributes existence to the reality of Christ or if the *esse* of the Word pro-

received by Christ's human nature was not adoptive, but merely perfective of that nature. Hence, the adoption question provides a kind of test case for thinking through the *esse* question with consistency.

The remaining sections of this essay examine the acuity of the interpretation of Aquinas on Christ's *esse* by Herman Diepen and Jacques Maritain. Special emphasis will be devoted to the diverse interpretations of the disputed question, *De unione verbi incarnati*, by Maritain and Diepen, on the one hand, and the advocates of the so-called "ecstasy of being theory," on the other.

II. Aquinas's Single-*Esse* Position

St. Thomas consistently articulated a single-*esse*[7] understanding of the reality of the union of the two natures in the one Person of the Word. In the *Compendium of Theology*, St. Thomas offers a concise explanation of his position: "Since there are in Christ one person and two natures we have to examine the relationship between them to determine what is to be spoken of as one, and what is to be spoken of as multiple in Him."[8] Christ is, then,

---

vides and acutates the existence of the human nature. David Tamisiea explains that the sense of *esse* that Aquinas uses in the context of his Christology "means that which causes a thing to exist in reality, and is only attributed to real things contained within the categories of being identified by Aristotle." See David Tamisiea, "St. Thomas on the One *Esse* of Christ," *Angelicum* 88, no. 2 (2011): 383–402, 385.

The decree of the Council of Chalcedon (451) reads as follows: "One and the same Christ, Son, Lord, only-begotten, acknowledged in two natures which undergo no confusion, no change, no division, no separation; at no point was the difference between the natures taken away through the union, *but rather the property of both natures is preserved and comes together into a single person (prosopon/personam) and a single subsistent being (hypostasin/subsistentiam)*; he is not parted or divided into two persons, but is one and the same only-begotten Son, God, Word, Lord Jesus Christ, just as the prophets taught from the beginning about him, and as the Lord Jesus Christ himself instructed us, and as the Creed of the fathers handed it down to us." *Decrees of the Ecumenical Councils*, vol. 1, *Nicaea I–Lateran V*, edited by Norman P. Tanner, S.J. (Washington D.C.: Georgetown University Press, 1990), 86–87. Emphasis added.

7. See *Quodlibet* 9, a. 3; ST III, q. 17, a. 2; *Scriptum in Sententias* III, d. 6, q. 2, a. 2; *Compendium theologiae*, chap. 212. See also Stephen Brown, "Thomas Aquinas and his Contemporaries on the Unique Existence in Christ," in *Christ Among the Medieval Dominicans: Representations of Christ in the Texts and Images of the Order of Preachers*, edited by Kent Emery and Joseph Wawrykow (Notre Dame, Indiana: University of Notre Dame Press, 1998), 220–37.

8. Thomas Aquinas, *Aquinas's Shorter Summa: Saint Thomas's Own Concise Version of His Summa Theologica* (Manchester, Vermont: Sophia Institute Press, 2002), p. 249, n. 212. "Quia igitur in Christo est una persona et duae naturae, ex horum convenientia considerandum est, quid in Christo unum dici debeat, et quid multa."

considered two or multiple "in accord with the diversity" of his natures. While, Thomas continues, "whatever belongs to the *suppositum* or *hypostasis* must be declared to be one in Christ." This unity includes Christ's existence: "if existence is taken in the sense that one *suppositum* has one existence, we are forced, it appears, to assert that there is but one existence in Christ.... [I]f we look upon Christ as an integral *suppositum* having two natures, His existence will be but one, just as the *suppositum*, too, is one."[9]

In ST III, q. 17, a. 2, Aquinas again advocates a single-*esse* understanding of the Incarnate Word. "Since the human nature," Aquinas explains,

> is joined to the Son of God hypostatically or personally, as was said above [in question 2 on the union], and not accidentally, it follows that no new personal being came to the Son of God, but only a new relation of pre-existing personal being to the human nature [came to of the Son of God]: namely, such that the Person of the Son is now said to subsist not only according to the divine nature, but also according to the human [nature].[10]

There is, on this account, one personal being or *esse* in Christ, that of the eternal suppositum of the Word subsisting in two natures.

III. Cajetan, Maritain, and the Ecstasy-of-Being Theory

This articulation of Christ's *esse* is usually associated with the likes of Cardinal Cajetan and, more recently, Reginald Garrigou-Lagrange.[11] It is called the "ecstasy-of-being" theory because (according to Adrian Hasting's summary of Cajetan's position): "[Christ's] human nature possesses

9. Ibid., pp. 249–50, n. 212. "Ea vero quae ad suppositum sive hypostasim pertinent, unum tantum in Christo confiteri oportet: unde si esse accipiatur secundum quod unum esse est unius suppositi, videtur dicendum quod in Christo sit tantum unum esse. Manifestum est enim quod partes divisae singulae proprium esse habent, secundum autem quod in toto considerantur, non habent suum esse, sed omnes sunt per esse totius. Si ergo consideremus ipsum Christum ut quoddam integrum suppositum duarum naturarum, eius erit unum tantum esse, sicut et unum suppositum."

10. ST III, q. 17, a. 2: "Sic igitur, cum humana natura coniungatur filio Dei hypostatice vel personaliter, ut supra dictum est, et non accidentaliter, consequens est quod secundum humanam naturam non adveniat sibi novum esse personale, sed solum nova habitudo esse personalis praeexistentis ad naturam humanam, ut scilicet persona illa iam dicatur subsistere, non solum secundum naturam divinam, sed etiam humanam."

11. For a discussion of Cajetan's reading of *De unione* 4 see Klaus Obenauer's monumental critical edition of the *De unione*, Thomas von Aquin, *Quaestio disputata "De unione Verbi incarnate"* (Stuttgart-Bad Cannstatt: Frommann-holzboog, 2011), 409–412.

no 'esse proprium,' but instead it can be said to have—not only an ecstasy of knowledge and love through the beatific vision—but also a very 'ecstasy of being,' of existence itself; for an ecstasy is literally a being out of oneself."[12]

In his commentary on ST III, q. 17, a. 2, Cajetan defends the superiority of the single-*esse* position by means of the distinction between nature and person or "*quo est*" and "*quod est*." "Nature," Cajetan explains, "is the principle by which"[13] of a thing's *esse* while person is to *esse* "as the subject, or that which has being, or that which is."[14] The distinction between *quo est* and *quod est* leads Cajetan to "two important conclusions" about the *esse* of the Incarnate Word.[15] "First, this lack of personality," in the words of Shawn Colberg, "implies that the human nature can bring no additional *esse* to the person of the Word. Second, the potential humanity of Christ (only in the order of logic) can have no *esse* of its own because it has no person of its own."[16]

Cajetan's position (in his commentary) is developed not only with an eye to Aquinas's text, but also with an awareness of the criticisms against Aquinas's single-*esse* doctrine made by Duns Scotus. A central component of Scotus' critique is that each nature in Christ must have an *esse*. Cajetan explains Scotus' position as follows: "In Christ living was two-fold as is obvious from the fact that he lost one of the living things through death. Therefore, in Christ there was a two-fold *esse*."[17]

Scotus' criticisms of Aquinas and his two-fold *esse* position provide an important context for understanding the impatience that the great com-

12. Adrian Hastings, "Christ's Act of Existence," *The Downside Review*, no. 232 (1955): 153. For a thorough evaluation of the ecstasy of being theory see Helen-Marie Deloffre, *Question disputée L'union du verbe incarné* (Paris: Vrin, 2000), 219–29.

13. Citations from Cajetan are taken from the text of his commentary included in the Leonine Edition of the *tertia pars* of the *Summa theologiae*, vol. 11 (*Comm. on Tertia Pars*) (Rome, 1903). "Natura est principium quo immediatum ipsius esse." (sec. 13, p. 226.). Most of these texts are identified in the helpful study of Shawn Colberg, "Accrued Eyes and Sixth Digits: Thomas Aquinas and Cardinal Cajetan on Christ's Single *Esse* and the Union of Natures," *Nova et Vetera* (English edition) 8, no. 1 (2010): 55–87.

14. Cajetan, *Comm. on Tertia Pars* : "Persona enim est cui primo convenit esse ut subiecto, seu quod habet esse, seu quod est." In *De Christo Salvatore* (Turin: Case Editrice Marietti, 1949), Garrigou-Lagrange explains his view as follows: "Haec thesis sancti Thomae est alta conceptio secundum quam humanitatis Christi habet non solum extasis cognitionis et amoris per visionem beatam, sed *extasis ipsius esse*, prout existit per ipsum esse aeternum Verbi." (314)

15. Shawn Colberg, "Accrued Eyes and Sixth Digits," 76.

16. Ibid.

17. Cajetan, *Comm. on Teria Pars*, sec. 10, p. 225: "In Christo fuit duplex vivere: ut patet ex hoc quod unum per mortem perdidit. Ergo in ipso fuit duplex esse."

mentator has for two-fold *esse* readings of Aquinas's Christology. According to Cajetan, Aquinas's position on Christ's *esse* throughout his *corpus* can be spoken of as two-fold, if by duality one means "according to a duality of natures; in relation to those words a duality of *esse* is indeed less affirmed, though not totally negated."[18]

This Christological point of the Thomist tradition was clearly in the mind of Jacques Maritian, when he penned the fourth appendix of the first edition of *The Degrees of Knowledge*. In this appendix, Maritain explains the "notion of subsistence" in the following way: "We may say that its formal effect is to make the (substantial) nature or essence so possessive of existence that it cannot communicate in the act of existence with anything which is not itself, or which it is not already."[19] This understanding of subsistence, Maritain argues, is superior to the account of subsistence as "that which renders a nature incommunicable to *another suppositum*" because subsistence pertains to "the setting up of the suppositum" and should thus not be used in defining it.[20]

The "*mystery of the Incarnation*" is one case to which Maritain appeals to defend this view of subsistence. "Because the subsistence of the Word is an infinite subsistence," Maritain argues, "It can receive in Itself the human nature of Christ, a created substantial *quo* (without a created personality) which subsists and exists by the Divine Subsistence and the Divine Existence themselves."[21] How is it possible following Maritain's definition of subsistence that the divine and human "communicate" or are united in Christ? The divine subsistence of the Word, Maritain observes, can assume the human nature because "this is a *privilege of the infinite subsistence* of a Person whose nature is identical with His existence and is eminently all things."[22] In short, the Person of the Word, following this account of Maritain, can assume a created nature into his subsistence and be personally united to that nature because of the fullness of existence that He (the Word) enjoys.

18. Ibid., sec. 4, p. 223. J. L. A. West in "Aquinas on the Metaphysics of *Esse* in Christ," *The Thomist* 66, no. 2 (2002): 231–50, rejects this position, arguing that there is no sense in which the *esse secundarium* of the *De unione* can be read without contradicting Aquinas's metaphysics and consistent arguments against the Christological heresies.

19. *The Degrees of Knowledge*, translated by Gerald Phelan (Notre Dame: The University of Notre Press, 2002), 455.

20. Ibid., 455–56.

21. Ibid., 456.

22. Ibid.

The same is not true, however, for created natures. "We must say" of created natures, Maritain explains, "—precisely because subsistence enables them in their very finitude to imitate in some manner the self-sufficiency of divine beings—that none of them, once sealed in its own subsistence, can exist in common with any other nature whatsoever."[23] A finite created nature, contrary to the full perfection of existence enjoyed by the Word, "excludes those others from the existence which actuates it, itself, and which properly belongs to it."[24]

IV. *De unione* article 4

The general position of Aquinas as read by Cajetan and Maritain was normative among Thomists until Aquinas's famous disputed question *De unione verbi incarnati* was read under a new light. In the twentieth century, scholars began viewing the *De unione* as a later work, near to the date of the *tertia pars*.[25] When the *De unione* began to viewed as a mature work, Jean-Pierre Torrell points to the "originality" of Herman-Michel Diepen, who argues that the ecstasy-of-being theory "could no longer claim to follow Thomas directly" because the *De unione* says, in his view, something to the contrary.[26]

The content of the fourth article of the *De unione* is, as a result of these claims, one of the most controversial and commented upon aspects of Aquinas's Christology.[27] In this text Aquinas asks directly: "Whether in Christ there is only one being (*esse*)?" This point logically follows the argument of the previous article (a. 3) on Christ's numeric unity, where Thomas concludes that because of the unity of the suppositum in Christ, Christ is one *simpliciter*, and two only *secundum quid*. Aquinas makes the connection between these two articles in the first line of the body of article four:

23. Ibid.

24. Ibid.

25. For a discussion and defense of the authenticity and date of the *De unione*, see F. Pelster, "La quaestio disputata de Saint Thomas *De unione Verbi incarnati*," *Archives de Philosophie* 3, no. 2 (1925–26): 198–245. Pelster's work is viewed as lying to rest the question of authenticity.

26. See Jean-Pierre Torrell, "Le thomisme dans le débat christologique contemporain," in *Saint Thomas au XXe siècle*, edited by Serge-Thomas Bonino, O.P. Actes du Colloque du Centenaire de la *Revue Thomiste* (Paris: 1994), 379–93, 383–84.

27. The parallel passages, as noted above, in which Aquinas also treats Christ's *esse* are *Quodlibet* q. 9, a. 3; *ST* III, q. 17, a. 2; *Scriptum in Sententias*, III, d. 6, q. 2, a. 2; *Compendium theologiae*, chap. 212.

"It should be said that this question [on Christ's *esse*] is, in a certain sense, the same argument [*ratio*] as the previous because something is said to be [*esse*] one and a being [*ens*] from the same thing."[28]

The heart of Aquinas's argument is as follows: first, "in Christ the subsisting suppositum is the person of the Son of God, who is sustained[29] *simpliciter* by the divine nature." Secondly, "the suppositum of person of the Son of God, however, is not sustained[30] by the human nature." "This is so," Aquinas concludes, "because the person of the Son of God existed before he assumed the humanity, and [his] person was not in any way augmented or perfected by having assumed a human nature." Aquinas points out, however, that "the eternal suppositum is sustained by the human nature in so far as it is 'this man.'"[31]

The central point in this sequence is that the subsisting suppositum "is sustained *simpliciter* by the divine nature." This insight provides the governing principle for the last paragraph of the body of article four—which is at the heart of the interpretive of controversy. First, Aquinas moves from Christ's unity as one established in article 3 to his consequent unity in being: "Just as Christ is one *simpliciter* on account of the unity of the suppositum and two in a certain respect on account of the two natures, likewise he has one being [*esse*] *simpliciter* on account of the one eternal being of the eternal suppositum."[32] This is an important point in the interpretive debate: Aquinas declares there to be one *esse simpliciter* in Christ.

28. *De unione*, a. 4, c. "Dicendum, quod huius quaestionis est quodammodo eadem ratio et praemissae: quia eodem dicitur aliquid esse unum et ens." All citations from the *De unione* are from my own translation, which is forthcoming in a volume on the *De unione* to be published by Peeters Press in the Dallas Medieval Text series. The translation is from the Latin text of Obenauer's volume (see n. 11 above), which is vastly superior to the text of the Marietti edition.

29. The word "sustained" (*sustentificatur*) marks, perhaps, the most significant contribution of the critical Latin text of the Obenauer edition of the *De unione*. The manuscript tradition followed by the Marietti edition has *subsistentificatur*. The difference between the two is subtle but important. *Subsistentificatur* would inaccurately indicate that the Word is made a substance by the divine nature.

30. Ibid.

31. Ibid. "In Christo autem suppositum subsistens est persona Filii Dei, quae simpliciter sustentificatur per naturam divinam, non autem simpliciter sustentificatur per naturam humanam: quia persona Filii Dei fuit ante humanitatem assumptam, nec in aliquo persona est augmentata seu perfectior per naturam humanam assumptam. Sustentificatur autem suppositum aeternum per naturam humanam, inquantum est hic homo."

32. Ibid. "Et ideo, sicut Christus est unum simpliciter propter unitatem suppositi et duo secundum quid propter duas naturas, ita habet unum esse simpliciter propter unum esse aeternum aeterni suppositi."

What, then, is to be made of the existence of Christ's human nature? "There is also another being of this suppositum," Aquinas adds, "not in so far as this other being is eternal, but in so far as the [eternal] suppositum was made man temporally." Aquinas concludes this line of argument with the following hotly-debated formulation: "Although it [the created nature] is not accidental being—because 'man' is not accidentally predicated of the Son of God, as was said above in the first article—it is nevertheless not the principal being [*esse*] of its suppositum, but the subordinated [*secundarium*] being."[33]

V. Does the *De unione* Negate the *Ecstasy-of-Being Theory*?

The controversy sparked by article 4 stems from Aquinas's use of the "*esse … secundarium*" formulation. The introduction of the *esse secundarium* seems to contradict Aquinas's treatment of Christ's *esse* elsewhere in his opera because the *De unione* is the only work in which Aquinas speaks of any other *esse* in Christ than that of the Word.

The interpretive debate over *De unione* article 4 thus stands as a fault-line dividing Thomists, like Cajetan and his followers, including the early-Maritain, from the school of Diepen and the later-Maritain who read the *De unione* as affirming a second *esse* relative to the human nature. Cajetan's reading of the *esse secundarium* in article 4 of the *De unione* in relation to Aquinas's other treatments of Christ's *esse*

> boils down [in the words of Shawn Colberg] to the distinction between *quo est* and *quod est*; specifically, *esse* can be considered in a dual manner *insofar as it relates to the two natures* whereby it exists. This is a necessary flexibility that stems from affirming that a nature gives a thing its quiddity or that it is related to *esse quo est*. As a positive insight, then, Cajetan allows the possibility that *De unione* (and also ST III, q. 17, a. 2, ad 1 and ad 3) can be taken as speaking to the way in which Christ's natures relate to his *esse*, as *quo est*.[34]

Because, however, of his awareness of the Scotist two-fold *esse* position, Colberg notes that "if a reader refuses to interpret Thomas's position in this

33. Ibid. "… est autem et aliud esse huius suppositi, non inquantum est aeternum, sed inquantum est temporaliter homo factum. Quod est, si non sit esse accidentale—quia homo non praedicatur accidentaliter de Filio Dei, ut supra habitum est—, non tamen est esse principale sui suppositi, sed secundarium."

34. Colberg, "Accrued Eyes and Sixth Digits," 81. Emphasis in original.

more supple and generous manner and insists that he posits of Christ's humanity a second *esse quod est*, then the *De unione* should be abandoned as misleading."[35] As a result, Colberg concludes that according to Cajetan, "if one cannot see a way of harmonizing the *De unione* text … then it cannot be regarded as authoritative against the weight of Thomas's other writings on this issue."[36]

The originality of the opposing view, that of Diepen and Maritain, stems from their quest to integrate the consistent *unum esse* doctrine with a reading of the *esse secundarium* of the *De unione* that affirms something unique in Aquinas *corpus*.[37] In the words of Helen-Marie Deloffre, Diepen's position, against that of Cajetan's, works "by the integration and not the elimination of the created existence."[38] Article 4 of the *De unione* is thus central to Diepen's theory, in so far as he holds that this text represents Thomas' most complete formulation of the *esse* question. With traditional Thomists, Diepen maintains Aquinas's real distinction between essence and existence, person and nature, and stands with Cajetan against the *duplex esse* position of Scotus.

However, against Cajetan's rejection of any talk of a human or created *esse*, Diepen maintains (a) that the *esse secundarium* of *De unione* 4 *does indeed* refer to a created *esse* and (b) this created *esse* does not violate the unity of the *esse* of the Word. How so? The two-fold *esse* "is realized by participation and exemplarity, by subordination and integration."[39] The two *esses*, then, do not stand in relation to the person of the Word "*ex aequo*." "There is an essential subordination," Diepen explains, "of the *esse humanum* (which is a non-personalized act of a nature) to the *esse divinum*."[40]

Diepen holds that the affirmation of a two-fold *esse* in Christ along the lines of his reading of Aquinas better renders the revealed mystery of "the

35. Ibid.

36. Ibid., 82.

37. From 1949–1960, Diepen composed a series of influential articles in which he worked out his theory. The fruit of this effort is brought together in his book *La Théologie de l'Emmanuel: Les lignes maîtresses d'une Christologie* (Desclée de Brouwer, 1960); see especially 51–158.

38. Deloffre, *Question disputée L'union du verbe incarné*, 19. For a formidable criticism of Diepen's "integration" theory, see Obenauer, ed., *De unione*, 402–417. Also, ibid., 418ff, has a helpful section on the "conceptual divergences" between *De unione* 4 and ST III, q. 17, a. 2. The use, for example, of *esse personale* in ST III, q. 17, a. 2 is not followed in *De unione* 4. It does not have to be held that such differences result in speculative contradictions between the texts, but they do make the integration thesis difficult to maintain.

39. Diepen, *La Théologie de l'Emmanuel*, 155.

40. Ibid.

natural Son of God in *utraque natura*" than does the "too facile and simplistic" ecstasy-of-being theory.[41]

This examination of Diepen's argument brings this paper back to Jacques Maritain. Maritain famously abandoned the ecstasy-of-being theory which he had supported in the first edition of *The Degrees of Knowledge*. Maritain adopted the position defended by Diepen, as a result of Diepen's criticisms, in a series of "Further Elucidations" appended to the 1954 edition of the same volume. Maritain articulates his position, following the work of Diepen, according to several primary tenets:

1. As the "great Commentators" taught, there is "only one single subsistence" and "*personal existence*" in Christ.
2. Following the *De unione* and Fr. Diepen's argument: "there is ... a created *esse*, by which the human nature is actuated" in Christ.
3. The created *esse* "is only *received* by the human nature, it is not exercised by it."
4. "The created and human *esse* does not at all concur in the constitution of the *esse personale* of Christ."
5. This means that the created *esse* is "integrated ... to the *ens personale*, to the subsistent whole."
6. The created *esse* does not compromise the hypostatic unity of Christ because the eternal person and suppositum subsists "henceforth according to this nature also, and no longer only according to the divine nature."[42]
7. The created "esse" "is received by a human nature without human subsistence, it is exercised by an uncreated supposit which pre-exists it and for whose existing as supposit, or personally (for its existing *simpliciter*), it in no way contributes."[43]

Two immediate observations must be made in light of the position advocated by Diepen and adopted by Maritain. First, more reflection is needed on the meaning of the term *secundarium*. *Secundarium* does not mean "second," as if there were one being of the Word and a second *esse* in Christ of the human nature. Why not? Aquinas is not contrasting that which is numerically first with that which is second, but rather that which is "*prinicpale*"

41. Ibid.

42. Maritain, *The Degrees of Knowledge*, 464–66.

43. Ibid.

with what is "*secundarium*." Aquinas's use of the word *secundarium* elsewhere clearly indicates an order of dependency in which what is *secundarium* depends on what is "*principale*."[44] For these reasons *secundarium* is translated in this essay as "subordinate."[45] "Secondary" can be misleading in English if it is read as indicating a "second" (numeric) *esse* along with that of the Word, while a subordinate *esse* does not posit a second created actuation.[46]

Secondly, Diepen's attempt to integrate and synthesize article 4 of the *De unione* with Aquinas's other works by viewing it as a fuller articulation, which offers a new insight (*esse secundarium*) through which the other texts can be read, fails to discern precisely what Aquinas was seeking to accomplish in the *De unione*. Aquinas's language in the *De unione* more clearly betrays an attempt to modify (and mollify) the position of others, than to introduce something new into his own position.

Sr. Deloffre catalogs the different ways in which the major authors of the thirteenth century, following Lombard's second opinion, the Subsistence Theory, speak of one *esse* in Christ.[47] Reading the *De unione* in light of these attempts is helpful in pinpointing Aquinas's intentions. These formulations include, *inter alia*: *esse simpliciter* and *esse personale* (used by Alexander of Hales, Albert the Great, and Bonaventure) and *esse hypostasis* (Albert and Alexander of Hales).[48] Conversely, many of these same authors, especially the Franciscans, use the phrase *esse humanum* to speak of Christ's human nature.

A problem arose for these authors, however, regarding Christ's unity. How can the unity of Christ be articulated in terms of *esse simpliciter*

44. For example, addressing the order of ends, Aquinas says the following: "just as there is an order in agent causes, so too there is an order in final causes: as, namely, a secondary end [*secundarius finis*] depends on a principal one [*a principali dependeat*], just as a secondary agent depends on a principal one." SCG III, chap. 109, no. 5. The primary and secondary ends are twofold, but the *finis secundarium* does not contribute *finis* to the primary end and the secondary end exists as an end in a relation of dependency on the primary end. The same is true with Christ: there is a genuine *secundarium* of the human nature, but because it depends on the primary *esse* it does not contribute *esse* to the one reality of Christ.

45. Of course, given that the *esse* in question is the created *esse* of Christ's humanity there is no question of Christological subordination.

46. It is also the case, in defense of translating *secundarium* as subordinate, that *A Latin-English Lexicon of Saint Thomas Aquinas*, edited by Roy J. Deferrari (Fitzwilliam: Loreto Publications, 2004), offers the following English choices for *secundarius*, a, um: "coming in second place, subordinate, secondary, the opposite of *prinicipalis*."

47. See Deloffre, *Question disputée L'union du verbe incarné*, 45–50.

48. Ibid., 45.

"without eliminating the reality of the human nature?"[49] To address this problem, Bonaventure spoke of Christ's human nature in relation to the divine *esse* of the Word as "inclining toward an accident" (*vergit in accidens*).[50] Bonaventure offered this position because it has the advantage of safeguarding the substantial and hypostatic unity of Christ, for when a person or suppositum accrues new accidents to itself, the person remains one *simpliciter*.

Albert the Great, on the other hand, rejects the position of those who speak of Christ's human nature as *vergit in accidens*. In so doing, although he speaks clearly of a single *esse simpliciter* in Christ, at times Albert speaks of Christ's human nature in terms of a two-fold *esse* or even hypostasis:

> It should be said that human nature is properly and *per se* assumed, and also united by a certain mode: but it was assumed first and *per se*, and it was united in its hypostasis to the divine hypostasis.[51]

> The *esse* according to this or that nature, however, is the *esse* taken in comparison to the nature making the *esse* in the hypostasis, and from that part the *esse* in Christ is doubled. For, the *esse* of the nature of humanity is in that one, as well as the *esse* of the nature of deity. If we wish to speak properly, then we would say that according to this consideration [the hypostasis] would not have two *esses* but rather one twofold, constitutive *esse* [*unum duplex in constituente esse*].

> The *esse* of the nature is the *esse* that the nature has in itself: for every thing has its own *esse*. The *esse* of the human nature in Christ is not the *esse* of God's nature, but the *esses* are not by that way two as the natures.[52]

Albert is not embracing Nestorianism with this language. He is reacting to the accidental language of Bonaventure and the first and third opinions of Lombard by affirming "the substantial reality of the human nature assumed by noting that the *esse* of Christ's human nature is not the *esse* of the divine nature."[53] Albert does this, as Corey Barnes explains, out of a desire to subordinate

49. Ibid., 46.

50. Ibid., 47. Bonaventure forwards this position in the commentary on Lombard's *Sentences*, III, d. 6, a. 1, q. 3.

51. This text is from Albert's commentary on Lombard's Sentences, *In III Sent.*, d. 5, a. 10. From Corey L. Barnes, "Albert the Great and Thomas Aquinas on Person, Hypostasis, and Hypostatic Union," *The Thomist* 72, no. 1 (2008): 122.

52. The second and third of these passages are from Albert's commentary on Lombard's *Sentences*, *In III Sent.*, d. 6, a. 5. The citation and translation are from Barnes, "Albert the Great and Thomas Aquinas," 131.

53. Barnes, "Albert the Great and Thomas Aquinas,"132.

this duality to the greater unity of Christ in terms of *esse simpliciter,* which is one as the hypostasis in Christ is one. Stressing the unity of *esse simpliciter* in Christ while noting the duality of natural *esse* according as the hypostasis subsists in human nature is an attempt to strike a proper balance between the reality of Christ's singular human nature and the ultimate unity of hypostasis.[54]

In the end, as Barnes points out, "Albert inherited ambiguous terminology with which to address Christological questions along a fluid spectrum of opinions." "His great triumph," Barnes continues, "was to recast pressing questions and concerns in terms of Christ's *esse,* a maneuver that allowed affirmation of Christ's personal unity without undermining the integrity of his two natures."[55]

Aquinas stands in the immediate context of these various attempts to maintain Christ's unity *simpliciter* and the reality of his human nature. As Barnes notes, "Aquinas preserves many of Albert's insights while simultaneously tidying the ambiguous terminology that Albert inherited."[56]

VI. Conclusion

This essay began with a brief consideration of Aquinas's argument against Christ, as man, being an adopted son of God. Maritain, following Diepen, asserts that Christ's human nature possess an *esse* which actuates it. Is it possible to maintain, however, that the created, actuating *esse* of Christ's human nature would not be adopted by the superabundant grace enjoyed by Christ's human nature?

In light of these considerations the following conclusion seems most consistent with both Aquinas's argument and the context in which it was developed: the uniqueness of the *De unione* on the metaphysical status of Christ's human nature is to be explained primarily by Aquinas's attempt to situate his own position on the reality and integrality of Christ's human nature against the *esse accidentale* tendency in Bonaventure and the ambiguities entailed in Albert's position. *Esse secundarium* is therefore not introduced to indicate a second *esse* in Christ according to the human nature, but rather to articulate how Christ's human nature is full, integral, and real without being predicated an accident of the Word or a second hypostasis.

The assessment of Victor Salas on this point seems correct: "Simply

54. Ibid., 132–33.

55. Ibid., 133.

56. Ibid.

put, the human *esse* introduced in *De Unione* seems to be none other than the divine *esse* when considered from the point of view of its subsisting in a human nature."[57] This means that the "*De unione* highlights," Barnes argues, "the *esse* of the Word as determined by the form of human nature. While Thomas's other treatments more narrowly highlight the one *esse* of the Word, this is not to the exclusion of the nature's role in forming that *esse*."[58]

The move by Diepen and, following him, Maritain, to read the *De unione* as affirming a second, received and created *esse* misplaces Aquinas's actual intention. Aquinas was not seeking a new way, nor does he indicate that he ever sensed a need to do so, to affirm the reality of Christ's human nature in the order of *esse*. Rather, by *esse secundarium* Aquinas intends to affirm the real, integral, though subordinate and derivative, existence of the human nature of Christ.

The *esse secundarium* of article 4 must be read in light of the qualification that Thomas makes in the concluding sentence of the previous paragraph, "the eternal suppositum is sustained by the human nature in so far as it is 'this man.'" Had Aquinas wished to say something more, to indicate a second *esse* of the human nature, he could have adopted one of Albert the Great's formulations or selected a word other than *secundarium*, such as *secundum*, to indicate such an intention with much greater clarity.

From the perspective of its relation to the works of his contemporaries, the *De unione* is, in the end, less, not more original, than his treatments of the issue in his other writings.

57. Victor Salas, "Thomas Aquinas on Christ's *esse*: A Metaphysics of the Incarnation," *The Thomist* 70, no. 4 (2006): 592; cited in Barnes, "Albert the Great and Thomas Aquinas," 144.

58. Barnes, "Albert the Great and Thomas Aquinas," 144.

JAMES F. KEATING

The Proper Role of Credibility in the Work of Theology

I. The Current Context

It is commonplace for those who look upon distinctively modern Christian theology as mostly a shabby affair to blame an excessive concern with establishing the credibility of the faith's central claims to self-proclaimed enlightened, secular minds. In Protestant theology, the villains are often John Locke, Friedrich Schleiermacher, and the entire intellectual project known as Liberal Protestantism. In the Catholic world this fault is associated with the Modernists of the early twentieth century condemned by *Pascendi Dominici Gregis,* and, in the minds of some, resurgent in the wake of the Second Vatican Council. The problem with both of these theological approaches, so the argument goes, is that in their quest to present Christian faith as credible within modernity, theologians have allowed systems of thought antithetical to revealed faith to determine and delimit what Christians are entitled to hold about God, Christ, and the nature of human existence. Christian doctrines, therefore, are either translated into a modern idiom denuded of their proper ontological density or eliminated altogether. When this happens, the traditional theological task of "establishing the motives of credibility"[1] for

1. John Lamont offers a nice description: "'Motives of credibility' is the term that theologians have coined to refer to the publicly available evidence accessible to believer and unbeliever alike, that can be used to support the contention that the Christian message is communicated by God. The fact that the motives are accessible to both believers and unbelievers means that they cannot include evidence whose acceptance would presuppose faith." *Divine Faith* (Burlington, Vermont: Ashgate, 2004), 47.

the Church's dogmatic teachings appears to be at odds with the primary vocation of theology as *fides quaerens intellectum*.

One should not be surprised, therefore, that many traditionally minded Catholic intellectuals exhibit less concern than previous generations to attune their presentations of the faith to modern notions and sensibilities. When thought to be faced with a choice between fidelity and convincing non-believers that Church teachings are worthy of their belief, these theologians and philosophers choose fidelity. I would even go further and argue that many traditional Catholic thinkers have developed protective strategies to avoid dealing with the very same issues that motivated modern theologians to devise new, ostensibly more "credible" interpretations to the faith. Foremost among these strategies is the attempted creation of a pre-modern, or perhaps one can say *non-modern*, context for doing theology, a context in which distinctively modern challenges such as the philosophical turn to the subject, the historical-critical approach to the Bible, the ecumenical movement, and religious pluralism play no significant role. The working assumption for such a stratagem is that modern theologians have exaggerated the challenges these developments pose to traditional ways of thinking about God revealed in Christ. Thus one witnesses a resurgence of interest in doing theology as Thomas Aquinas did, sometimes termed "ressourcement Thomism" or as Augustine did, or other premoderns.[2] Another option is to offer as model for new theologians to emulate once almost certainly to be forgotten figures such a Matthais Scheeben and Reginald Garrigou-Lagrange. The attraction seems to be that these men operated before the questions and issues that emerged in the twentieth century, especially during its latter half, had a significant impact on Catholic confidence concerning the adequacy of traditional articulations of Catholic doctrine.[3]

In this vein, two recent converts to Roman Catholicism, R. R. Reno

2. *Ressourcement Thomism: Sacred Doctrine, the Sacraments, and the Moral Life: Essays in Honor of Romanus Cessario, O.P.*, edited by Reinhard Hütter and Matthew Levering (Washington, D.C.: The Catholic University of America Press, 2010).

3. Recent efforts to retrieve Sheeben include: Aiden Nichols, O.P., *Romance and System: The Theological Synthesis of Matthias Joseph Scheeben* (Naples, Florida: Augustine Institute Press, 2010) and Bruce Marshall, "Renewing Dogmatic Theology," *First Things* 23, no. 5 (2012): 39–46. Efforts to retrieve Garrigou-Lagrange include: *Reason with Piety: Garrigou-Lagrange in the Service of Catholic Thought* (Naples, Florida: Sapientia Press, 2008); Richard Peddicord, O.P., *Sacred Monster of Thomism: An Introduction to the Life and Legacy of Reginald Garrigou-Lagrange, O.P.* (South Bend, Indiana: St. Augustine's Press, 2004).

and Reinhard Hütter, have called for a return to Neo-Scholasticism in view of the splintering of Catholic theology following Vatican II. According to Reno, the Neo-Scholastics were convinced "that all modern solutions—from Descartes to Locke, from Kant to Comte, from Rousseau to Mill, from Schleiermacher to Hegel—had failed ... [and that] ... the basic structure of the Thomistic theory of knowledge and the Thomistic account of nature and grace provided a lasting solution."[4] With this confidence of the failure of the modern and the perennial viability of Thomism, Neo-Scholasticism sustained much of Catholic intellectual life from the mid-nineteenth century until the eve of the council. Its collapse was the largely the work of what Reno calls the "heroic" generation, most prominently, Henri De Lubac, S.J., Karl Rahner, S.J., Bernard Lonergan, S.J., and Hans Urs von Balthasar. These figures sought to dethrone Neo-Scholasticism by casting it as a system whose success was premised on a refusal to deal with new trends of thoughts and new cultural development in the world outside the Catholic ghetto. Although their efforts were wildly effective—within a short time the old ways were barely remembered—success came at a high and ironic price. With their Goliath thoroughly defeated, the efforts of these one-time Davids were much less compelling. Moreover, the graduate students of the 1970s, '80s and '90s who were required to study their writings, without any background in the system they opposed, received a truncated version of Catholic theology and not enough to build a fully Catholic theological system. Indeed, with the old enemy nothing more than a dark memory, the following generations found themselves unable to comprehend, much less appreciate, the achievements of these heroes of the conciliar era. Reno's proof of the ultimate failure of the heroic generation is the fact none of them have bequeathed to the Church a unified school of Catholic thought capable of training students in a coherent method. Reinhard Hütter moves in the same direction, but adds that the "discontinuity" with Catholic tradition found in the later work of Rahner has played an especially deleterious role. Rahner's influence helped solidify the notion that Catholic theology could be done apart from a solid grounding in the tradition.[5] For both Reno and Hütter,

4. R. R. Reno, "Theology after the Revolution: A Review of Fergus Kerr's *Twentieth-Century Catholic Theologians*," *First Things* no. 173 (May 2007): 15–21; http://www.firstthings.com/ article /2007/04/100–theology-after-the-revolution-10_(accessed March 31, 2012).

5. "Rahner himself, however, developed in ways that led him to read Vatican II more and more through a hermeneutics of discontinuity and rupture, and this mentality came to define

the solution is a return to the unified system fashioned by Neo-Scholasticism, to a time when Catholic theologians were confident that traditional answers were sufficient to uphold the credibility of the faith.[6]

The allure of returning to a more self-assured, more coherent way of doing theology after the fissiparous creativity that marked much late twentieth-century Catholic theology is plain enough. In the first place, the task of theology is more straightforward when there is no need to worry overly much about, for example, historical challenges to the credibility of biblical accounts of Jesus and the early Church, contemporary philosophical challenges to traditional metaphysics, how certain formulations will sound to non-Catholic Christians, Jews, and so on and on. There are undeniable attractions in the notion that we can go back to a simpler time in which Catholic theology consisted primarily in intramural debates over finely grained theological problems between the different schools of Thomism, with the occasional skirmish with the followers of Soctus. Moreover, there was something undeniably enervating in the anxiety expressed by many theologians after the Council that, apart from serious revision, Catholic belief could no longer be credible to the thoughtful modern.[7] Theology could not long operate on the assumption that the burden fell wholly upon Catholicism to demonstrate that it was not as retrograde as its cultured despisers had so casually concluded. A reaction was inevitable; especially as modernity itself lost its swagger and modernized Christianity its evangelical shine.

Yet, the understandable desire on the part of many theologians to re-

---

the work of most of his American disciples. For them, faithful to the theme of discontinuity, the basic thrust of Transcendental Thomism—to revise and renew a continuous theological tradition—no longer seemed important. As a result, the third generation of American Rahnerians has merged with those who understand systematic theology exclusively as critical reflection on the role of religion in political and cultural contexts, usually in service of a program of liberation, self-realization, and social justice. Today, post-post-Rahnerians treat revision of the Catholic faith and morals—always in pursuit of the paradigmatic modern Protestant goal of relevance—as the main task of Catholic theology." Reinhard Hütter, "The Ruins of Discontinuity: Looking for Answers to the Fragmentation of Catholic Theology in America," *First Things* no. 209 (2011): 37–41; http://www.firstthings.com/article/2010/12/the-ruins-of-discontinuity (accessed, March 31, 2012).

6. Hütter has developed his ideas in "A Forgotten Truth?—Theological Faith, Source and Guarantee of Theology's Inner Unity," in *Dust Bound for Heaven* (Grand Rapids, Michigan: Eerdmans, 2012), 313–46. In this essay, Hütter compares an early work of Walter Kasper on theological method to one by the Neo-Scholastic, Franciso Muñiz, O.P.

7. Examples of such an approach are, of course, legion, but a particularly influential one is Hans Kung's *On Being a Christian*, translated by Edward Quinn (Garden City, New York: Doubleday, 1976).

enact pre- or non-modern Catholic thought and practice in our present context cannot be authentically Catholic if its eschews the responsibility to present the faith as credible to contemporary minds and hearts. The simple fact is that the most influential theologians in the years leading to Vatican II and after were convinced that the credibility of traditional Catholic theology was vulnerable to changes in philosophy, historiography, the appreciation of the Christian and the religious other. They sincerely believed that if Catholicism were not to lose adherents, some revision and adjustment would be required. Whether or not some, many, or most overestimated the power of these challenges and were led to compromise of essentials of the faith, their quest to preserve the credibility of faith in a new context was deeply rooted in Catholic tradition. Accordingly, one must be suspicious when traditional thinkers present themselves as avoiding the mistakes of post-conciliar theology when in reality they are simply avoiding, or excessively downgrading, the questions that motivated revision. The Church needs its intellectuals to face fully and honestly the challenges our modern and postmodern culture presents to the rational credibility of the Catholic faith. To retreat to the comfort of a theological space in which the difficult questions are no longer asked or simply dismissed is to fail the Church, not only in its evangelical mission, but also to neglect the important service theologians can offer believers besieged by a culture hostile to the commitments of faith. In other words, there can be no either/or between fidelity and concern for modern credibility. It will have to be both/and, even if it means running the risk of repeating the mistakes of a repudiated generation.

The modest goal of this essay is to offer a sketch of the history of the question of credibility in Catholic theology as a way to understand the issues involved in any contemporary attempt to uphold a traditional articulation of Catholic faith responsible to reason. Others have presented this history in great detail and sophistication; I am, of course, reliant upon their efforts even as I am not attempting anything like their comprehensiveness.[8] Rather, I am restricting my treatment to two issues. The first is the inherent and perhaps unresolvable tension in claiming that the rational credibility

8. The classic work on the act of faith and its relationship to credibility is Roger Aubert's magisterial survey, *Le Probléme de l'acte de foi: Donées Traditionelles et Résultats des Controverses Récentes*, 2nd ed., revised and corrected (Louvain: E. Warny, 1950). Other important works are: Avery Dulles, SJ, *The Assurance of Things Hoped For: A Theology of Christian Faith* (New York: Oxford University Press, 1994); *A History of Apologetics* (San Francisco: Ignatius Press, 1999); John Lamont, *Divine Faith.*

of the faith is not a proper motivation for accepting it. Although Catholic theologians have been more or less united in asserting that that there are very good reasons, independent of the convictions of faith, to believe that Catholic teaching is vouchsafed by divine authority, they have just as consistently insisted that these reasons are not why a Catholic accepts the faith as true. The salvific assent of faith, what is often termed "divine faith," that God has spoken in Christ and through the Church, is premised upon the authority of the revealing God as first truth and independent of any arguments for the credibility of what has been revealed. The second issue I wish to highlight is the importance of context in determining how theologians over the centuries have gone about establishing the motives of credibility. To argue that a particular belief is "credible" as opposed to "doubtful" or "incredible" is to anticipate an audience with a predictable manner of assessing religious truth claims. In other words, the faith's credibility at any given time or place is determined by particular cultural formations outside the Church. If the Catholic theologian is to retrieve this important aspect of the tradition, he or she will not only need to deal with the tensions between faith and reason but also grapple with determining the characteristics of the contemporary audience with respect to arguments of credibility.

II. Credibility in the History of Theology

Concern that the Christian Gospel be presented and judged as worthy of belief is as old as the faith itself. In the New Testament we find Jesus presented as fulfilling Jewish messianic prophecies and as a miracle-worker.[9] These stories function not merely to witness to what Jesus did and said but also as confirmatory signs to future readers that the Church's claims about Jesus' divinity are to be trusted. The logic is pretty simple and also quite Jewish: if Jesus fulfilled prophecies or performed miracles, it could only be because he was doing God's own work. The supreme instance of this kind of reasoning is the claim that Jesus rose from the dead. Indeed, when St. Paul encounters the risen Jesus, he quickly deduces that since only God has the power over death, the followers of Christ he was sent to persecute were not blasphemers but were proclaiming God's own truth (Acts 9.1; 1

9. "A careful study of the NT throws considerable indirect evidence on the way in which the infant Church carried out its apologetical encounter with Judaism, with paganism, and with deviant tendencies that arose within the Christian community." Dulles, *A History of Apologetics*, 1.

Cor. 15.12–19). Just as the true prophets of Israel had always been revealed as such by God's confirming activity, the resurrection of Jesus was divine validation of the Gospel preached by his followers. Paul's own recounting of the tradition of Jesus' appearance after his death to the apostles and others to the believers at Corinth (1 Cor. 15.1–8) adds an interesting twist. He tells his readers that some of the witnesses to this miraculous event are still alive (1 Cor. 15.6), holding out the possibility that they could check the story for themselves.[10] This apologetical strategy was clearly intended to increase the persuasive power of Paul's witness, to believer and potential believer alike, despite the fact that few or perhaps none of the Corinthians would have been able to take up the challenge. Paul holds out this enticing possibility not because of any incredulity with the miraculous on the part of the letter's audience beyond the normal suspicion against fraud, but because of the importance of the claimed miracle to the faith. Paul's desire is to present a credible argument for the foundational truth of the faith in ways appropriate to the expectations of his audience. This approach finds New Testament sanction with 1 Peter's imperative that followers of Christ "always be ready to give an explanation to anyone who asks you for a reason for your hope" (1Peter 3.15).

Concern to support the credibility of the faith was a significant preoccupation of the Church Fathers, as well.[11] St. Augustine put the necessity for this task in a particularly straightforward manner: "no one ... believes anything unless he has first thought it ought to be believed."[12] Of course, it is a matter of singular importance to discern what informs the "ought." That is, what kinds of evidence render the Gospel more credible and to whom? As Paul makes clear, the audience includes believers as well as unbelievers. Accordingly, the apologetics of the New Testament presume that reports

10. I am following the interpretation of this passage found in Ulrich Wilkens, *Resurrection: What the Early Christians Thought about the Resurrection* (Atlanta, Georgia: John Knox Press, 1978).

11. For Dulles' treatment of the apologetics of "the patristic era" see *A History of Apologetics*, 22–71. Others include: Robert Louis Wilken, *The Christians as the Romans Saw Them*, 2nd ed. (New Haven, Connecticut: Yale University Press, 2003); *The Spirit of Early Christianity: Seeking the Face of God* (New Haven: Yale University Press, 2005). A more technical treatment of Clement of Alexander, Origen, Chrysostom, and Augustine is found in John Lamont, *Divine Faith*, 28–46.

12. Augustine, "On the Predestination of the Saints," in *St. Augustine: Four Anti-Pelagian Writings*, translated by John A. Mourant and William J. Collinge (Washington, D.C.: The Catholic University of America Press, 1992), 221.

of fulfilled prophecies or miracle working will be received as the kinds of things that increase the credibility of the underlying message. Thus, the very act of seeking credibility assumes a culturally particular context in which credibility can be established in certain ways. Part of the wisdom of the Fathers was the recognition that the context had shifted in significant respects from that envisioned by the biblical writers. In addition to miracles and fulfilled prophecies (which still played a significant part of Patristic apologetics), there were also arguments that the new movement deserved tolerance from the Roman authorities, that the refutation of Jewish critics were without merit, and that a deep harmony existed between Christian faith and the best of Greek philosophy. With respect to the last, early Christian intellectuals gave much of their apologetic energy to showing that the God of Israel and Jesus possessed the attributes required of the sole God: immateriality, eternity, impassibility, and so on.[13] While some historians of theology, most notably Adolf Harnack, have argued that this excessive concern for philosophical credibility led to a distorting Hellenization of the God of Bible, others, such as Benedict XVI, have seen a providential encounter between the legitimate insights of Greek thought and the new faith. If the Fathers had rejected the challenges presented by the philosophers, they would have been guilty of failing to see that faith in the Word of God entails commitment to God as "logos."[14] A religion severed from reason is both dangerous and unworthy of adherence. Accordingly, the Fathers had a general sense that Greek philosophy disclosed enough of the truth of things that the faith was well served by presenting itself as credible in light of it.

Yet, while the Fathers confidently asserted the reasonableness of being a Christian, the majority of them was also clear that faith is not a reasoned deduction from the evidence. For example, Clement of Alexandria com-

13. Important studies of this aspect of patristic thought include Wolfhart Pannenberg's "The Appropriation of the Philosophical Concept of God as a Dogmatic Problem of Early Christian Theology," in *Basic Questions in Theology*, vol. 2, translated by George H. Kehm (Philadelphia: The Westminster Press, 1971), 119–83; Jaroslav Pelikan, *Christianity and Classical Culture: The Metamorphosis of Natural Theology in Christian Encounter with Hellenism* (New Haven, Connecticut: Yale University Press, 1993).

14. "John thus spoke the final word on the Biblical concept of God, and in this word all the often toilsome and tortuous threads of Biblical faith find their culmination and synthesis. In the beginning was the *logos*, and the *logos* is God, says the Evangelist." Pope Benedict XVI, "The Regensburg Address," in James V. Schall, *The Regensburg Lecture* (South Bend, Indiana: St. Augustine's Press, 2007), 135.

pared faith in Christ to a student accepting what is taught by a beloved and trusted teacher. Since Christ is the Son of God, the doctrine he teaches can be trusted absolutely. Likewise, Origen, who spent much energy and time refuting the criticisms of the pagan Celsus, denied that a good Christian believer should be unshaken by such criticisms. There was no absolute need to refute Celsus to prove the faith; the spiritual power of the Gospel itself provides sufficient warrant. Chrysostom also rejected any need for evidence for the faith beyond that God has spoken in Christ.[15] John Lamont sums up their common position as follows:

> All of them react to pagan criticism of the irrationality of Christian belief by flatly contradicting it. They claim that it is rational; and the reason they give for its rationality is the fact that it is believing God, who has the highest possible degree of authority. This authority gives faith a certainty that is equal to, or greater than, that of any other kind of knowledge. This certainty is not conferred by the signs or evidence for God's having spoken, although these signs suffice to make the fact of his having spoken beyond reasonable doubt. Faith is not based on these signs, it is based simply on God's spoken word.[16]

This twofold approach of a faith supported by evidence but not accepted for that reason will be followed by the majority Catholic tradition.

During the Middle Ages, working out the rational credibility of faith lay near the heart of Western theology; but, again, one must be careful to note another shift in context. The alien and culturally powerful conceptual framework of polytheism faced by the Church Fathers had disappeared with the creation of Christendom. There was awareness of Islam as a competitor, of course, but it would be a serious mistake to confuse the role arguments for the rational credibility of the faith played in medieval scholasticism with how they functioned in the Patristic period. Yes, the discovery of Aristotle's thought presented a challenge for those convinced by his philosophy to articulate Christian truth, in its terms, whenever beneficial. Nonetheless, even taking into account the Averroists in Paris, the views of Aristotle did not present medieval intellectuals with an opposing thought-world in light of which faith must be established as credible. Aquinas himself alludes to this fact in his *Summa contra gentiles* when he asserts that his job in defending the faith is rendered more difficult than the Fathers because, unlike them, he does not have personal experience of the "sacri-

15. For references, see Lamont, *Divine Faith*, 30–44 and Dulles' *Assurance*, 21–23.
16. Lamont, *Divine Faith*, 46.

legious remarks of individual men," which would tell me which arguments should be used "as the basis of proceeding to a refutation of their errors."[17] Aquinas had to imagine what would count as rationally credible to the intellectual opponents of Christianity.[18]

Such arguments, however imperfect the setting, were seen as necessary, and the master of theology in a medieval university was called upon to engage all possible objections to the truth of the Gospel and provide counter-arguments appropriate to the matter at hand. All are aware of Aquinas's rational arguments for the *preambula fidei*, such as demonstrations that there exists a deity with the proper attributes, the world is a creation, and that the highest form of human happiness is everlasting contemplation of God.[19] When dealing with revealed truths inaccessible to natural reason, however, Aquinas restricts himself to probabilistic arguments for the fittingness of the Incarnation and other revealed mysteries.[20] Reason supports revealed faith by dutifully responding to all objections coming from those who view the faith as irrational or unworthy of God's nature. While such arguments are necessary to demonstrate that the faith is not contrary to reason, Aquinas follows the Fathers in rejecting any notion that the act of faith can be based upon them.

Aquinas's approach to the proper theological placement for rational demonstrations for the credibility of Christianity comes through his analysis of the act of faith and, in particular, his assertion that God's authority as revealer is the formal object of faith (*formalis ratio obiecti*).[21] The formal object of a thing known is the means by which it is known, that is, what motivates the intellect that a judgment is worthily made. Aquinas gives the example of geometry whereby, "the conclusions are the things known

17. SCG I, chap. 2, no. 3.

18. The whole quotation points even more to Aquinas's sensitivity to the contextual character of such argumentation: "To proceed against individual errors, however, is a difficult business.... In the first place it is difficult because of the sacrilegious remarks of individual men who have erred are not so well known to us so that we may use what they say as the basis of proceeding to a refutation of their errors. This is, indeed, the method that the ancient Doctors of the Church used in the refutation of the errors of the Gentiles. For they could know the positions taken by the Gentiles since they themselves had been Gentiles, or at least had lived among the Gentiles and had been instructed in their teaching." SCG I, chap. 2, no. 3.

19. A recent treatment of this aspect of Aquinas's thought is found in Ralph McInerny, *Praeambula Fidei: Thomism and the God of the Philosophers* (Washington, D.C.: The Catholic University of America Press, 2006), esp. 26–32.

20. Aquinas's argument for the fittingness of the Incarnation is in SCG IV, chap. 54.

21. My treatment of Aquinas here follows Aubert, *Le Probléme de l'acte de foi*, 43–71.

materially, while the middle term of demonstration, by which the conclusions are apprehended, are the formal account of the knowing."[22] Things are different, however, when the object of knowing is divinely revealed and therefore beyond the reach of natural reason. Unable to discern the truth of what is revealed by science, believers are motivated to accept the faith as true because it is revealed by God and God is truth itself. As first truth, God is an unimpeachable authority, and in faith the believer accepts what God has revealed for no other reason than because it is revealed by God.[23] Likewise, Catholics believe what the Church professes (the material objects of faith) because they believe that its profession is God's own.[24]

The imperfect character of the act of faith from the perspective of the human knower, that is, that the believer assents to something that she does not see to be true from either first principles or the operations of reason, means that the will must play a role. Accordingly, Aquinas describes faith as "an act of understanding assenting to divine truth by command of the will, moved by God in grace."[25] Yet while this act of volition commands the intellect to assent to what is not certainly known, Aquinas insists the assenting will cannot be without rational motivation, otherwise, its willing would not be a free act. In a move with significant consequences for future theologians, the Dominican master will distinguish between external inducements [*exterius inducens*] and internal causes [*causam interiorem*] leading to faith.[26] "One who believes has a sufficient inducement for believing, for he is led to faith by the authority of God's teaching confirmed by miracles and, still more powerfully, by the interior instinct of God inviting him to believe; thus he does not believe lightly."[27] The internal cause provides a motive for saving faith by leading the will to accept as a desirable good the eternal life that is a reward for belief. This movement of the will is itself the result of an inpouring of God's grace. In addition, God provides external inducements that what is purposed for belief is truly divine, persuasive arguments which give a believer confidence that God stands behind these purported truths and marvels.[28] Among the latter, Aquinas lists the mira-

22. ST II-II, q. 1, a.1. I am using the translation in *On Faith: "Summa Theologiae" 2–2. Qq. 1–16 of St. Thomas Aquinas*, translated by Mark D. Jordan (Notre Dame, Indiana: University of Notre Dame Press, 1990), 33.

23. ST II-II. q. 1, a. 1.

24. ST II-II, q. 5, a. 3.

25. ST II-II, q. 2, a. 9.

26. ST II-II, q. 1, a. 4, ad 3.

27. ST II-II, q. 2, a. 9, ad 3.

28. "In one way, as an outward inducement, such as a miracle seen or a human persuasion

cles of Jesus,[29] as well as the saints.[30] Moreover, in a decision that will have enormous impact on later Catholic apologists, he will point to "the wonderful conversion of the world to the Christian faith" and the consequent effect that even the humble "believe such lofty truths," "accomplish such difficult actions," and "have such high hopes."[31]

Aquinas's approach to argue both for reason's capacity to ensure faith's credibility as revealed truth and that the works of reason belong outside the act of faith was standard among the Scholastics. A number of prominent Franciscans, however, were led to distinguish between acquired and infused faith, the former the product of reason, the latter the product of grace and thereby salvific. Although the category of acquired faith is found in Alexander of Hales, it is given greater prominence by Duns Scotus, who argues that infused faith adds no new evidential content, but merely enables a firmer assent of the will through the power of grace. When addressing the question of why infused faith is salvific but not acquired faith, Scotus offers no reason beyond the testimony of the Bible and the doctors of the Church that this is God's positive decree.[32] Less voluntaristic theologians will seek other reasons, but the effort required to keep acquired and infused faith separate would only increase in the face of the Reformation

inducing one to faith." ST II-II, q. 6, a. 1. Aquinas adds that the insufficiency of the outward inducements requires an "inward cause" [*causam interiorem*], which is the elevating power of grace.

29. "For since those things which are of faith surpass human reason, they cannot be proved by human arguments, but need to be proved by the argument of Divine power: so that when a man does works that God alone can do, we may believe that what he says is from God: just as when a man is the bearer of letters sealed with the king's ring, it is to be believed that what they contain expresses the king's will." ST III, q. 43, a. 1.

30. "But because oral teaching that is offered requires confirmation so that it may be accepted, unless it be evident in itself, and because things that are of faith are not evident to human reason, it was necessary for some means to be provided whereby the words of the preachers of the faith might be confirmed. Now, they could not be confirmed by any rational principles in the way of demonstration, since the objects of faith surpass reason. So, it was necessary for the oral teaching of the preachers to be confirmed by certain signs, whereby it might be plainly shown that this oral teaching came from God; so, the preachers did such things as *healing the sick*, and the *performance of other difficult deeds*, which only God could do." SCG III, chap. 154, no. 8.

31. 'This wonderful conversion of the world to the Christian faith is the clearest witness of the signs given in the past; so that it is not necessary that they should be further repeated, since they appear most clearly in their effect. For it would be truly more wonderful than all signs if the world had been led by simple and humble men to believe such lofty truths, to accomplish such difficult actions, and to have such high hopes. Yet it is also a fact that, even in our own time, God does not cease to work miracles through His saints for the confirmation of the faith." SCG I, chap. 6, no. 4.

32. For discussion of this see Dulles, *Assurance*, 36–37; *Divine Faith*, 83–89.

and the emergence of Enlightenment thinkers certain that reason can be the sole guide in all things, including faith. In other words, the balance begun by the Fathers between motives of credibility and faith as trust in God as revealer was hard to maintain in the ruins of Christendom.

With the onset of the Reformation and the first stirring of Modernity, the context for demonstrating the credibility of Catholic faith became increasingly complex and hostile. To be sure, Catholic apologists of this period no longer had to conjure their opponents out of dusty codices or secondhand accounts of travelers; their opponents stood before them and were armed with clear ideas and relatively predictable standards of assessment. If the opponent was a Protestant, the Catholic could either challenge the rational coherence of *sola scriptura* as a theological principle or defend distinctively Catholic doctrines on biblical grounds. If the opponent was a rationalist, whether attacking revealed religion or religion itself, the terms upon which credibility could be determined were relatively obvious. Not surprisingly, Catholic apologetics thrived in this new environment. Indeed, in the face of these attacks, one can discern an increased confidence that the truth of the Catholic faith could be demonstrated with near certainty. The clearest magisterial expression of this confidence was Vatican I's *Dei Filius*.

Pius IX's council sought to balance faith carefully between the condemned extremes of fideism and rationalism. Accordingly, it described faith, on the one hand, as "a supernatural virtue ... inspired and assisted by the face of God" by which members of the Church "believe that what [God] has revealed is true, not because of the intrinsic truth of things ... recognized by the natural light of reason, but because of the authority of God himself who reveals them."[33] On the other hand, it taught that the supernatural character of faith neither diminishes its "harmony with reason" nor reduces it to a "blind impulse." Rather, a reason open to the truth finds both "exterior helps," such as miracles and prophecies, and the "interior helps of the Holy Spirit." Together, "they are the most certain signs of divine revelation, adapted to the intelligence of all people." The document goes on to add the Catholic Church as itself a sign of the credibility of the message it preserves and proclaims with authority. "The Church by herself, with her marvelous propagation, eminent holiness and inexhaustible fruitfulness in everything that is good, with her Catholic unity and invincible

33. *Enchiridion Symbolorum* (DS), ed. H. Denzinger and P. Hünermann, 43th ed. (San Francisco: Ignatius, 2013), no. 3008.

stability, is a great and perpetual motive of credibility and an irrefutable testimony of her divine mission."[34] Nearly a decade later, the next pope, Leo XIII, will assert along the same lines: "In the same manner, reason declares that the doctrine of the Gospel has even from its very beginning been made manifest by certain wonderful signs, the established proofs, as it were, of unshaken truth; and that all, therefore, who set faith in the Gospel do not believe rashly as though following cunningly devised fables, but, by a most reasonable consent, subject their intelligence and judgment to an authority which is divine."[35]

Although these conciliar and papal statements were clearly intended to set the Church's apologetic strategy in a hostile world on a firm theological footing, it left too many unanswered questions and was too vulnerable to critique to easily serve this function for long. For example, if the credibility of faith was so strong on rational grounds, how could it not play some role in moving the unbeliever to faith? Or, otherwise put, how could an unbeliever presented with this evidence reject the faith and not be guilty of irrationality?[36] On the other side of the ledger, how could the believer's faith not be affected negatively or remain committed to reason when these arguments are cast into doubt? The tensions between the demands of reason and a faith motived by authority had been part and parcel of Catholic theology since the patristic period but they became more acute as the Enlightenment matured and the intellectual challenges to traditional Catholicism gained in strength. Among the many such challenges, we can mention the demonstrable success of empirical rationality and its application to more and more of reality. If this new form of reason had proved so successful in overthrowing traditional thinking concerning nature, why should it not be applied to the claims of religious faith? Of equal importance was the development of a new historiography that eschewed reliance on authoritative witnesses to past events and sought to reconstruct the past in accord with what the new science was revealing about the way the world operated.

34. DS, no. 3013.

35. *Aeterni Patris,* para. 5. http://www.vatican.va/holy_father/leo_xiii/encyclicals/ documents /hf_l-xiii_enc_04081879_aeterni-patris_en.html (accessed April 27, 2012).

36. The danger of one thinking that this is consequence of Catholic teaching explains the following condemnation of Vatican I: "If anyone says that the assent of Christian faith is not free, but that it necessarily follows from the arguments which human reason can furnish in its favour; or if anyone says that God's grace is only necessary for that living faith which worketh through charity, let him be anathema." DS, no. 3035

This not only made any apologetical appeal to miracles problematic, but served to undermine the public's confidence in the historical credibility of the scriptures.

From our contemporary perspective we can discern two basic responses with respect to the credibility of Catholic faith: 1) the assertion of different standards for the educated and the uneducated, and 2) the importation of the motives of credibility into the act of faith itself. The first response is found in the writing and teaching of an influential Jesuit professor at the Gregorian University, Louis Cardinal Billot, S.J. (1846–1931), which reached the public through his popularizer, J. V. Bainvel, S.J..[37] Billot followed the tradition of comparing the assent of faith to the human act of believing something on the basis of another's authority. I believe my doctor when she tells me that my symptoms indicate pneumonia because she is a doctor, and not on account of any personal expertise in such matters. Bainvel termed this kind of faith as one of "simple authority" and offered the exemplar of a child placidly accepting the authority of a loving parent.[38] Yet, given the high claims of rational credibility for faith asserted by Vatican I, Billot is compelled to ask whether this kind of trust in divine authority meets these standards. To answer this question, Billot notes a complexity within the common human experience of trusting the authority of another. That is, the extent to which it is rational to accept the testimony of another without quibble depends on one's access, either through opportunity or education, to potentially supportive or undermining evidence that the one speaking is to be trusted. To return to our example, it is quite rational for me as a patient to accept the diagnosis of the doctor simply because she is a doctor with medical training and not because what she says sounds right to me. Likewise, in faith the believer accepts what God reveals because he is God and to be trusted; the credibility of what has been purportedly revealed plays no role. Yet, while it is true enough that when I am sitting on that examination table covered merely, and inadequately, by a tie-in-the-back smock, I am at the mercy of my doctor's authority and humbly accept it, this acceptance need not be final. I may well have reason to question my

37. Billot's writings were not widely published, but see J. V. Bainvel, SJ, *Faith and the Act of Faith*, 3rd ed., translated by Leo C. Sterck (St. Louis, Missouri: B. Herder, 1926).

38. "To believe is to know and to affirm a truth, not because we see it in itself—that would be *science*;—not because we see the truth of it in the word of God,—that would be *scientific faith*;—but simply and solely *because God has said it*, simply and exclusively, upon the authority of the divine word." Bainvel, *The Act of Faith*, 60.

doctor's prescription later because I have spoken to someone with more medical knowledge than I or because I found a website that explains the issue at hand to me in an understandable and convincing manner. Of course, the credibility I find in the doctor's word shifts as I educate myself further and, consequently, the reasonableness of accepting her authority. In other words, the level of trust I can with reason invest in my doctor's authority changes as I gain expertise. Accordingly, if I have knowledge upon which to assess the competency of my physician it would be contrary to reason not to employ it.

For Billot, if human faith has this dynamic, something akin must pertain to Catholic faith. While true faith is a matter of trusting God's word because he is God, there are also two types of evidence by available to potential or wavering believer capable of providing certitude that whatever God reveals must be true and that God has in fact spoken in Christ and speaks through the Church. With respect to the first kind of evidence, Billot is thinking of metaphysical principles that make the idea of God uttering falsity an impossible. The second kind of evidence concerns the historical credibility of Jesus' miracles, his fulfillment of prophecies, and the resurrection, as well as the moral miracle that the Church has clearly been throughout the ages. These supports do not touch upon the credibility of the content of the purported revelation, but only that the revealer is to be trusted without question. Faith remains a matter of trusting God, therefore, even for the tutored. Yet, what about the person without the capability or the access to the motives of credibility, is her act of faith rational? Yes, because the expectations for aligning one's trust in an authority is relative to one's education. What is not rational for the learned can be rational for the simple.[39]

Although Billot's position, which is more complex than presented here, enjoyed great influence among Catholic theologians during early decades of the 20th century, it left enough ambiguity to allow for a wholly different approach to the matter to arise. In reaction to the problems involved in combining escalated confidence that Catholic faith could be demonstrated

39. Avery Dulles summarizes Billot on this point as follows: Can uneducated persons obtain sufficient rational evidence to exclude the probability of error? Billot and his school reply that such cannot be held to a type of certitude exceeding their capabilities. To accept the fact of revelation on the word of parents and teachers may be prudent for them, although not for more educated Christians. Their rational certitude of the fact of revelation can be 'relative' or 'respective,' in the sense of being adequate for themselves." *Assurance*, 105.

by reason alone with an insistence that such confidence is not the motivation for divine faith, Maurice Blondel and Pierre Rousselot, S.J. shifted the whole question by placing the judgment of credibility within the graced act of faith. In part this involved a reconfiguring of the traditional Thomistic division between nature and grace. The claims made my Billot and others, in an effort to be faithful to Vatican I, for the power of reason to demonstrate the truth of faith seemed to endanger the need for a faith produced by the infusion of grace. Some theologians would even speak of a natural judgment of credentity that expresses a duty to assent to the Catholic faith in light of the evidences of reason.[40] If this is true, what remains for grace to do? To avoid this overlap, Blondel and Rousselot argued that grace is at work in the reasoning about the truth of faith and rejected the idea that someone could come to certainty that Catholicism was the true religion by purely natural means. In his *Letter on Apologetics,* Blondel argues that the effects of grace on the will as well as the intellect is determinative in how any particular person receives the arguments that God has in fact spoken in Christ and through the Church.[41] When presented with the claims of faith, a potential believer must see that what the Church proclaims about God is good for him, meeting his needs as a person. If the judgment leads to assent, it is God's grace at work stimulating and shaping the believer's affections so that the arguments in its favor increase in power. Apart from such divine involvement, the external signs of credibility would not warrant the full surrender that is the nature of authentic faith.[42]

Rousselot's *The Eyes of Faith* makes a similar point.[43] Working off of Thomas' idea that the intellect is drawn toward the true just as the will is drawn to the good, Rousselot postulates that these two faculties work together under the power of grace to arrive at the judgment that the faith is worthy of belief. Whereas traditional defenders of the rationality of faith focus on the evidential force of particular assertions of fact, e.g., miracles accomplished, prophecies fulfilled, and examples of heroic virtues by the

40. Among the theologians who treat of credentity is the Dominican A. Gardeil, *La Crédibilité et L'Apologétique* (Paris: Gabalda, 1908). Aubert treats Gardeil's proposal in *Le Probléme de l'acte de foi*, 393–451.

41. Maurice Blondel, *Letter on Apologetics*, translated by Alexander Dru and Illtyd Trethowan (Grand Rapids, Michigan: Eerdmans, 1995).

42. For treatments of Blondel, see Dulles, *A History of Apologetics*, 271–79, and Aubert, *Le Probléme de l'acte de foi*, 277–94.

43. Pierre Rousselot, SJ, *The Eyes of Faith, Answer to Two Attacks*, translated by Joseph Donceel, S.J. (New York: Fordham University Press, 1990).

saints, they forget that people do not make life decisions in light of a collection of particulars pieces of evidence. Rather, it is the often unarticulated connections among the particulars that together constitute evidence worthy of momentous change of mind.

> The same holds for faith, for the *lumen fidei* ["the light of faith"], when we perceive something as credible. Short of a miracle this light does not provide us with new objects for knowing; *determinatio fidei est ex auditu* ["faith is specified by what we hear"]. But it accounts for our perceiving the connection, making the synthesis, giving the assent. The sufficient reason for these operations, which ... is not located in *representations* entertained.[44]

The intellect, therefore, played a necessary role in gathering the piece of evidence into a convincing whole. This activity for Rousselot is not prior to the act of faith, but rather is within it and under the influence of grace. In other words, "the *reasonableness*" of faith "derives from its very *supernaturality*."[45]

It is difficult to exaggerate the influence Blondel and Rousselot would have on the Catholic approach to the credibility of faith in the twentieth century. Although certain Thomists saw in their approach a collapsing of the natural and the supernatural aspects of the faith and thus, in essence, undermining the rational credibility of the faith, others such as Henri de Lubac and Karl Rahner would follow them in wholly refashioning the traditional distinctions between nature and grace, and faith and reason. To make a very and complex long story very short and simple, these efforts to bring the motives of credibility within the act of faith itself and under the purview of grace appeared in the eyes of many to render the traditional work of establishing the motives of credibility obsolete. It is not too much to say that the standard arguments in support of the Church's claim to be a legate of revealed truths (e.g., miracles, prophecies, the glorious history of the Church) fell almost out of sight and were replaced with anthropological arguments which sought to correlate what had been revealed in Christ with fundamental human desire. The questions over which generations of theologians had energetically debated concerning the proper balance of nature and grace, intellect and will, and faith and reason lost their urgency, and with them a sense of the continued importance of establishing the motives of credibility of faith.

44. *Eyes of Faith*, 28. Emphasis in original.
45. Ibid., 45.

III. Conclusions

What does this history teach the contemporary theologian seeking to maintain fidelity to Catholic tradition in our contemporary context? I find two broad lessons. The first is simply the seriousness with which Catholic theologians have taken to demonstrate the credibility of the faith, i.e., that the option to believe what the Catholic Church teaches is a rational one. Beginning with the New Testament, Christian intellectuals have recognized the importance of showing the reasonableness of the assent of faith, not only in order to counter the attacks of critics but as an aid to the believer. Arguments for credibility serve this purpose even if authentic Catholic faith is not a conclusion from the working of human reason, but a trusting assent to what God has freely revealed of himself and his plan of salvation. As we have seen, maintaining the proper balance between a faith that is well supported by evidence and one that is not accepted for that reason, proved a difficult task, especially as the Church faced the challenges of the collapse of Christendom and the rise of secular reason. Yet, the very fact that theologians exerted so much energy on the problem is testimony to the importance of holding together the supernatural character of faith and its rational credibility. Thus, no theologian hoping to work within the greater tradition can avoid the issues that threaten to undermine the credibility of Catholicism. If the theologians of the conciliar eras all too often exaggerated the revision such challenges required and lost their way, their concern for credibility in the modern age was itself deeply rooted in tradition. Ironic it would be, therefore, if the would-be traditional theologian of today lost touch with this tradition in an effort to avoid the mistakes of their modern predecessors. Yet, any effort to reconnect with the issue of credibility will need to confront the questions raised by Blondel and Rousselot on whether grace and nature should be distinguished to the point of making 'scientific faith' possible. Any return to a time prior to their contributions will require massive efforts to either resurrect the traditional motives or coming up with new ones that neither rely upon a graced intellect or the intrinsic appeal of the content of revelation.

The second lesson is the importance of context for the question of credibility. As we have seen, theologians adjusted their arguments for the faith in light of the anticipated audiences, whether Jewish, pagan, Muslim, Protestant, or secular. Not only did the kinds of argument offered change in light of the chances of a positive reception but also how the arguments were made. For this reason, the contemporary traditional theologian interested in establishing the faith's credibility will first need to determine his or her audience. This will be no easy task. Contemporary societies are marked by what Brad Gregory has described as "a hyperpluralism of religious and secular commitments, not any shared or any convergent view of what 'we' think is true or right or good."[46] While some continue to believe that they have the truth in matters of religion, it is rare that some one believes an objective argument will settle things. Of course, there are still committed atheists roaming the land and the airwaves asserting that no rational person could believe in a supernatural being much less believe that he has spoken a universally significant Word. Yet, such pugnacious secularists are the exception and they appear just as out of step with their age as the most committed believer. Reason, it is thought, simply does not have the power to decide such matters. Ours is time when the surest sign of moral elevation is to allow an easy-going tolerance and let others believe about religious matters what they will unless they directly threaten public life. The would-be apologist seeking an audience for the credibility of the Catholic faith is, therefore, very likely to be disappointed.

Does this mean the end of apologetics? I do not think so, but it does mean that Catholic theologians must develop new and creative strategies. If the theologians of the early modern period had to learn how to operate in the ruins of Christendom, the contemporary Catholic faces the ruins of modernity. The task, however, remains the same: to present the Catholic faith as credible to whomever might encounter its message. This means that the Catholic intellectual must honestly confront every challenge that might obstruct a potential believer's path to faith or threaten the peace of someone already committed to the faith. Any retreat to a more comfortable past is to abandon those who live in the present. Such neglect can find no support from the tradition.

46. Brad S. Gregory, *The Unintended Reformation: How a Religious Revolution Secularized Society* (Boston: Harvard University Press, 2012), 11.

BERNARD DOERING

Jacques Maritain, Charles Journet, and *Humanae Vitae*

When the encyclical *Humanae Vitae* was finally promulgated in 1968, its teachings were widely contested. In preparing for the Second Vatican Council, John XXIII had already appointed the first version of the Birth Control Commission. His successor Paul VI renewed this commission, expanding its mandate and membership, but from the very beginning of his reign, he made it clear that birth control was off the agenda. During the Council under Paul VI, there were some speeches on the floor alluding to birth control, but no substantial discussion of the subject. The differences among the Council Fathers concerning the licitness of certain forms of birth control were so profound and so set that finding an agreement proved impossible, so a commission of lay as well a clerical experts was formed to study the question and help the Holy Father prepare an encyclical after the close of the Council.

In the meantime, by Vatican intervention, the position of *Casti Connubii* was maintained in force. Once this commission was formed, the procedures and discussions were kept under the strictest secrecy. Many prominent Catholic intellectuals, both clerics and laymen, were intensely interested in the workings of the commission. One such layman was Jacques Maritain, who, at the close of Vatican II, had received from the hands of his friend Pope Paul VI the Council's message to the intellectuals of the world; one such cleric was Cardinal Charles Journet, theologian of the papal household and advisor to Paul VI during the Council. These two were intimate friends and from their first meeting in 1920 until Maritain's death in 1973 they exchanged 1,774 letters filling six volumes.[1] Maritain chose this younger Abbé (later Cardinal) as his "confidant-théologien," which he remained during the 51 years of their friendship.

The sixth and final volume of their correspondence appeared in 2008. This completed the enormous collection of letters, some of which reveal their reactions to the Church's position on contraception even before *Humanae Vitae*. A few letters contain their reactions to the teachings of *Casti Connubii* and its interdiction of all forms of birth control except the "natural" Ogino or Rhythm method. Under pressure from Roman authorities and local ecclesiastical superiors, they did not dare to make their reservations public. There was discussion in the Curia of placing some of Maritain's books on the Index, and Journet risked being relieved of his position as professor of theology at the seminary in Fribourg and being returned to parish duties, mainly because of their shared anti-fascist position on the Spanish Civil War. Then there is a long silence on the subject.

During his stay at Princeton in 1958 Maritain once again broached the subject of birth control with Journet. In referring to a recently invented pill that would prevent ovulation, he mentioned a distinction he had made in the past between the *finis operis* (the intrinsic end or purpose of an act) and the *finis operantis* (the end or purpose of the actor). In the former case, he felt it was easy to distinguish between what is natural and what is against nature. In the latter case however, a distinction between the use of the Ogino method and the use of the pill in question seemed to him "vain and futile." At that time he wrote: "I have met young Catholic professors who already have 7 or 8 children and for whom the problem of additional births would be tragic (the Ogino method seems ineffective). It is in thinking of them that I have decided to write to you. Has the Church made a pronouncement on the subject of these pills? Would their use be licit while waiting for the Church to make such a pronouncement?"[2] In reply, Journet sent him a copy of a papal document forbidding the use of the pill for the limitation of births. Maritain found the reasoning "questionable." About the pills, Journet remarked: "I too would hope that their use be permitted: I find your distinction well founded. Alas I see the opinion of the moralists

1. Charles Journet and Jacques Maritain, *Journet/Maritain Correspondance* (J/M Correspondance), vol. 5 (Paris: Editions Saint-Augustin, 2006), and *Journet/Maritain Correspondance*, vol. 6 (Paris: Editions Saint Augustin, 2008). Only volumes 5 and 6 concern *Humanae Vitae*.

2. *J/M Correspondance*, vol. 5, letter 1343 (5:1343).

running in the opposite direction.[3] "With those contraceptive pills, there seems to be an embryo of a solution: if they could be used to regularize the 'periods' one could say that the end is legitimate and in conformity with nature. Then the Ogino method could be used with assurance. But this is still fragile."[4] Maritain's questions showed that he looked forward to a clear pronouncement by the Magisterium.

After the Council, Journet closely followed the proceedings of the Commission, which he found equally conflicted, so he asked for Maritain's help to eliminate the differences. He wrote: "When you have a moment if you could write me a sentence about this nauseous question of the *limitation of births*,[5] I would send it to Carlo Colombo, who will send it on to the Pope, who seems to be waiting for some light in order to escape from this impasse."[6] Maritain expressed sympathy for "*a poor Pope imprisoned* [Maritain's underlining] in the solitude of his sorrows and of his sovereignty, powerless to instill into souls the divine Truth whose cross he is bearing—because, on the one hand, he cannot teach with sovereign authority except in the name of dogma, and on the other, *disciplinary sanctions risk* leading to revolt and insubordination."[7]

There is no further mention of birth control until 1967. Raïssa had died and was buried at Kolbsheim. After a last visit to America in 1966, Maritain joined the Little Brothers of Jesus in Toulouse as a lay philosopher and later took religious vows in that congregation. The proceedings of the Birth Control Commission were kept under sworn secrecy, but naturally there were leaks. Though his last years were plagued by frailty and ill health, Maritain looked for any news he could find. He learned that the committee of theologians during the Council was in a majority for authorization, on the general principle that the intervention of right reason in natural things is evidently legitimate. He wrote to Journet: "It seems to me that the theologians against regulation and those in favor of it, both invoke principles that are *too broad*, and do not take enough account of the means employed. Couldn't they make use here of the classic distinction between *finis operis* and *finis operantis*? There are contraceptive means, which violate

3. Ibid., 5:1344.

4. Ibid., 5:1346.

5. All emphases in the quoted letters are those of the writer of the letters.

6. *J/M Correspondance*, 6:1663.

7. Ibid., 6:1674.

... the very act of the union of the sexes: these are the ones the Church was confronted with when she proclaimed her condemnations. There are others that, without violating the finality of the *opus* itself, are concerned with the *finis operantis*: the Ogino method, the method of temperatures, etc. In my opinion there is no essential difference between the pill and the other methods, between a mental calculation and a medical intervention.... [T]he moral condemnation brought against any means that violate the *opus* should be held as immutable. But the situation has changed with the discovery of *these other means*, and their moral condemnation cannot be justified by reason."[8]

In his reply,[9] Journet suggests that Maritain "may have found a path to the solution of this problem." Then he cites Pius XII's Allocution to Midwives (Oct. 29, 1951), which "condemns any attempt by spouses in the accomplishment of the conjugal act or in the development of its natural consequences, any attempt to deprive this act of the power that is inherent in it and thus prevent the procreation of a new existence." "Can't we get beyond this?" Journet asked. By return mail Maritain wrote: "By means that violate the *opus* itself I understand the means used in the very accomplishment of the act. Aren't these the means that were in use at the time when Pius XII delivered his allocution? And can't his text be understood as having in view *those particular means?*"[10] Two letters later, Journet remarked that, "according to certain moralists, the pill is considered even more pernicious than other contraceptives because it attacks not a transitory act, but a state. The only solution, according to Father Kaelin, is that in which one opts for the lesser evil."[11]

Both Maritain and Journet were very close friends of the Pope: Maritain, as French Ambassador to the Vatican, worked closely with Cardinal Montini, then papal Secretary of State, who later became Paul VI, and Journet as a theologian participating in the Council and advisor to Paul VI. Both were sympathetic to the Pope caught in the impasse of conflicting sides on the question of birth control. Maritain wrote:

> And look at these Cardinals, themselves subject to the censure of the Episcopal Commissions. How frightened these bishops and experts are! How jealous they are of their authority! This is what counts more than anything else (more even

8. Ibid., 6:1727.
9. Ibid., 6:1728.
10. Ibid., 6:1729.
11. Ibid., 6:1732.

than the defense of the faith). But the only thing to do is to speak the truth, and disregard all the rest.... I am thinking of the Pope and the *impossible* situation in which he finds himself.... I imagine that the *opinions* of the theologians who surround him offer scarcely any help. (That of Father Kaelin, about which you spoke to me, is worth nothing. The Church cannot declare as morally permissible by a universal rule something that is morally good in itself, and not a lesser *evil,* which is an affair of prudence in particular circumstances.) ... I believe that the only solution is to say that as long as there is a question of means used in the very accomplishment of the act and at the same time violating the finality of the *opus,* it was necessary then, and will always be necessary, to condemn those means. But how the progress of science has changed things, and—now permitting the use of means which satisfy the *finis operantis* without violating the end of the *opus*—brings it about that the use of these means, if they are used according to right reason, *is not,* in itself, *morally evil,* and could not be condemned as such. So the Church could authorize these means without contradicting itself.

At certain times I say to myself that it is perhaps my duty to compose a note which, if you do not think it ill advised, you could send to the Holy Father on my behalf. But I am horrified at the thought of butting into something that is not my business, and, even more, I do not believe that I could succeed in composing such a note in irreproachable terms. Hence I am rather troubled. Tell me, Charles, if I am right to believe that I *should not involve myself in all this,* and that I should put it all aside in my head, thinking that the Pope has no need of advice from a poor idiot like me.... If this is what you think as well, it would certainly reassure my conscience.[12]

Journet was not as troubled as Maritain about his distinction of ends. "I understand your position," he wrote. "The objection is that the *finis operis,* which you consider only from a physical point of view, is determined by them from a moral point of view, as if it were not able to be deprived artificially of its possible effect." And he advised his friend to "save his strength for what concerns the faith and the truth that is closely connected to it," and "leave all this to the omnipotence of God."[13] Maritain agreed: "Yes, I have to leave all this to the omnipotence of God! The question of birth control is none of my business!"[14]

Yet he seems to have found it impossible to drop the subject, for at the end of this same letter he added a note, a "final word" on the subject, hand-written instead of typed, containing several crossed-out phrases, indicated by parentheses:

12. Ibid., 6:1739.

13. Ibid., 6:1741.

14. Ibid., 6:1745.

Another (final) word (I am stubborn) on birth control. If they consider it morally forbidden to deprive the *opus* of its *possible* effect, then the Ogino method should be interdicted just like the pill. Mental calculation with a view to avoiding that possible effect (by choosing periods of sterility for the *opus*) is something just as 'artificial' with regard to nature as a medication that modifies conditions prior to the *opus* but in no way affects the latter itself. Charles, excuse these deletions. I was trying one last time to defend my idea concerning birth control. But I don't want to talk any more about it.

And he did not, for more than a year. On July 25, 1968, *Humanae Vitae* was promulgated; its teachings were widely contested. On August 16, Maritain wrote in his *Carnet de notes*: "These days I have been reading the encyclical of Paul VI on birth control. A very beautiful document, very noble and very human, but it causes me pain and disappoints me. What a shame that it has come out after the *Credo*."

What *Credo* was Maritain referring to? On June 30, 1968, Paul VI proclaimed the *Credo of the People of God,* a greatly extended text of the existing Creeds, in celebration of the Year of Faith. Paul VI had asked Journet to help him prepare the text. He in turn asked Maritain for help. Maritain, almost within a week, wrote out a text that he sent to Journet, who in turn sent it on to the Pope. Paul VI adopted the text of Maritain almost word for word. The last sentence in Maritain's letter seems to indicate his fear that this new *Credo of the People of God* would receive the same reception as did *Humanae Vitae,* which was promulgated a month later.

On August 24, Maritain received a letter from Journet announcing that Msgr. Paul Phillipe (of the Sacred Congregation of the Faith) had asked him, "*par ordre supérieur*" (from the top down, that is), for an article that would appear in *Osservatore Romano* defending the authority—and hence the competence—of the Holy Father in his encyclical *Humanae Vitae.* He asked for help from his friend: "Jacques, if you see any way to confront this problem or if you have some point to suggest to me I would bless you! I am always afraid of being clumsy in this after-the-Council world!"[15] This request of Msgr. Phillipe came, by way of a Msgr. Benelli, from the Pope himself.[16]

After a few days Maritain, who had claimed he did not want to speak of this subject any more, wrote a long letter to help his friend. Here is that letter[17]:

15. Ibid., 6:1806.

16. Ibid., 6:1806a.

17. Ibid., 6:1807.

It is painful that they asked you for this article. What is more, I myself feel very bothered by the Encyclical: admirable in tone, in elevation, in charity and in courage, I say with all my heart *Roma locuta est.* But if there is question of reasonable arguments, my own reason is not satisfied; they do not hold close enough to what is real and concrete. I am against the pill, but not in the name of too general a metaphysical principle, because in the long run physiologically and psychologically it brings about a kind of disorder in the human being, and puts human genetics in danger....

As to your concerns, may I dare to offer a few suggestions?

1. As much as possible refrain from discussing the basic elements of the question, I mean the subject itself of *Humanae Vitae,*

a. Your competence is elsewhere; in what concerns such a matter, you are like the Pope, in the realm of the abstract, only more so than he; your defense of the encyclical would only redouble the sarcasms it has attracted.

b. No one can say better than the Pope what he had in mind; and if you say something else, or have recourse to other arguments, that would be an offense to him and would only get things all mixed up. So keep yourself in your own particular line, that of a theologian of the Church, and of the general question of the authority of the Pope (on any subject whatsoever).

2. It seems to me that you could take as your point of departure the absurdities spouted off by the priests who are rising up against the encyclical and the aberrations to which they have surrendered.... Behind all this there is a spirit that is *antipapism* and disdain for *obedience* in general and on principle. ([See] Bloy on obedience. There are undoubtedly other texts by Bernanos, by Claudel). React vigorously against all this. Don't go into this fight pulling your punches!

3. Such a polemical introduction would be a natural entry into the *theological exposé* that would make up the heart of your article.

It would be idiotic to demand scientific arguments from the Pope. He knows better than all those puny contestants the dangers for the human species that science and a large number of doctors see in the pill and contraceptive methods. It is out of very pure concern for intellectual vigor that he wanted to stay in his proper domain. The Pope is the successor of Peter and doesn't have to consult anyone. The Council was abused horribly on this matter. Let your article be an implacable defense of the *primacy* of the Pope.

And above all, let him give the explications and the clarifications that are so needed today about the *authority* of the Pope in the sphere of the *Ordinary Magisterium.* The faith does not demand that we adhere only to defined dogmas and to the infallible teachings of the Church. There is also the *spirit of faith* (and faith in the Church itself, and faith in the mission of the Vicar of Christ ...). Personally, I am led to believe that the *conclusions* of the encyclical, condemning the pill, etc., have the value of infallibility and oblige the conscience in the name of theological faith itself.

And even if one contests (and one has the right to do so) this or that consideration or argumentation of an encyclical (which only proves undoubtedly that there are better arguments), or rejects an encyclical because one does not agree about what is based on human reason, it is a stupidity contrary to the spirit of faith. But I am uttering gibberish in speaking of these things. This is your own business, O Theologian. [End of the letter.]

Maritain did not write again to Journet on the subject of birth control; this was the Theologian's business now. However, there are three instances when Maritain communicated, in writing or orally, his reflections on this subject to two individuals and to a small group, communications that were not made public until the 2008 publication of volume six of the *Journet/Maritain Correspondance.* The annexes to volume six of the correspondence contain letters to and from Maritain and Journet to others to whom they wrote or with whom they spoke concerning *Humanae Vitae.* One was Georges Cardinal Cottier, O.P., theologian of the Papal Household, a close friend and disciple of Journet. Another was Msgr. Pasquale Macchi, secretary to Paul VI. The third was a small group of Little Brothers of Jesus, the religious congregation to which Maritain belonged.

As was mentioned above, Journet asked Maritain for help in preparing the defense of *Humanae Vitae* at the request of the Pope. Journet had also asked Cottier for help in composing his defense. Cottier sent a copy of this note to Maritain and discussed it with him before sending the final text of his suggestions to Journet. Cottier's suggestions, shared and discussed with Maritain, are very similar to those of the philosopher, but far more detailed. He began with a consideration of the secondary end of marriage: *conjugal friendship,* in which the refinement of conscience is not identical for both spouses, and he offers some very compassionate advice. He wrote: "It will be a *duty* of [each conscience] to tolerate imperfections, for a time, in this or that particular case, without giving up the struggle for perfection. To me it seems liberating to insist on this, while underlining, in these circumstances, the necessary recourse to the sacraments (whereas so many couples, at the time of such difficulties, withdraw from the sacraments. This would be disastrous)."[18] We all know that the use of any form of birth

18. Ibid., 6:1009.

control except the one nick-named "Vatican roulette" was considered a mortal sin, and most confessors forbade penitents who confessed such a sin to receive communion, unless they renounced the use of any form of birth control except the Ogino method.

Cottier did not send on to Maritain his suggestions for Journet that further develop Maritain's ideas about *finis operis* and *finis operantis,* the legitimacy of a pill that does not harm the health of the woman, a pill for men, the distinction between what is "against nature and what is not." Concerning a pill that would not harm the health of the woman, Maritain had already written in his notes: "as a matter of fact, in the actual state of science, *medical means* involve serious dangers for the woman (a grave carcinogenic risk; and, I believe, a risk of a progressive deterioration of the female organism by what is the equivalent of a continuous series of miscarriages). While becoming permissible once science has triumphed over these risks, they are, in fact, *morally prohibited in the actual state of science.*"[19]

Among Maritain's papers, there is a rough draft of a letter to Msgr. Macchi, Secretary to the Pope, in which he wrote:

> I have heard that the question of birth control is under study in Rome. I would like to take the liberty of submitting to you a few ideas that have come to me on this subject and about which I spoke some time ago to Msgr. Journet who did not seem to disapprove of them.... May I add that each method has its own inconveniences, and that *psychologically* the Ogino method and that of temperatures do not seem to be without notable inconveniences? When two spouses come together in the flesh, the reason is not simply the satisfaction of concupiscence. There are many far more complex psychological and moral factors involved: the desire to seal a reconciliation after a disagreement, the need for a remedy to some kind of anguish [illegible word], or against despair, or the sudden inrush of a wave of tenderness or pity, what do I know? Can it not be asked if the intervention of calculation hindering the satisfaction of such a desire or need at the moment when it rises naturally in the soul, does not risk a psychological or moral imbalance in the life of the spouses?[20]

There are also notes for a conference to some Little Brothers of Jesus after the publication of *Humanae Vitae.* Most of these notes refer to ideas already exchanged with Journet, Cottier, and Macchi, but Maritain did reflect on the specific condemnation of *all acts* that make procreation impossible. He told his audience:

19. Ibid., 6:1004.
20. Ibid., 6:1005–1007.

One sentence in the encyclical seems to me from this point of view contestable:

[That sentence was] "Equally excluded is *every action*, which, whether in anticipation of the conjugal act, or in its enactment, or in the development of its natural consequences, proposes as its end or as its means to make procreation impossible" [No. 14]. If something good—to avoid procreation in a given case—can be done by a mental calculation based on natural processes, why condemn *every action* leading to the same end?

I see only two means of avoiding impregnation that are clearly *good.*

In the first place: a product—yet to be discovered—that would make the feminine cycle absolutely regular.

In the second place: a means to avoid pregnancy that would be used *after* the execution of the sexual act carried out in all its spontaneity and the integral respect for its natural finalities,—I am thinking of a means, which, used rather soon after the accomplishment of the act, would hinder the spermatozoa from joining the ovule (about ten hours are necessary to do this). No one seems to be speaking of this category of means. They ought to exist however, [for example, in the case of] Nuns who have been violated.[21]

In preparing his defense of *Humanae Vitae,* Journet followed Maritain's advice to the letter. He did not discuss the *subject* of the encyclical. He held fast to the *authority* of the Pontiff to make the decision he made. After citing the scriptural foundations for the Pope's supreme authority, he discussed the levels of that authority: *personal* or *collegial, solemn* or *ordinary,* proclaimed by *mediation* through delegated organs or *immediately* through encyclicals. Journet's conclusion was that

one thing is certain: the ordinary magisterium of the sovereign pontiff is in full force here. The theologian who reflects on the gravity of the cause, on the level of light to which it has been lifted to be made clear, on the precision and the certitude with which the response has been given, will be able to think that he finds himself—this is our personal opinion—in the presence of a moral doctrine definable later on and capable of rising one day to the level of an assent of divine faith.[22]

This assent of both Journet and of Maritain was immediate and complete,[23] and this is not surprising. Maritain's conversion to Catholicism was not the result of a rational progression. It was equivalent to being "turned inside out like a glove," as he had written of the conversion of Jean Cocteau.

21. Ibid., 6:1022–25.

22. Charles Journet, "La Lumière de l'Encyclique '*Humanae vitae*,'" *Nova et Vetera* 205, no. 3 (1968): 170–75.

23. *J/M Correspondance,* 6:1000.

He felt the encyclical should not have been promulgated; there were certain points he contested. His "own reason [was] not satisfied." Yet he wrote that his "spirit of faith" obliged him in "conscience," to accept "in the name of theological faith itself," as having "the value of infallibility," what his human reason led him to reject. Journet was a theologian of the Church: its institution, its nature, and above all its authority. He wanted to put an end to the unsettling controversy over the authority of *Humanae Vitae*. In his defense of the encyclical, he wrote: "The preambles and the arguments proposed in the Encyclical can certainly be discussed, weighed, subjected to deliberation. They have no other object than to prepare the conclusion; they are not its basis."[24]

Legitimate discussion, weighing, and deliberation imply the possibility of change, which in turn implies that the conclusions may not be infallible pronouncements, but may be reformable. To stem a controversy that is still unsettling the Church today and leading to numerous defections, Journet seems to have felt that a more authoritative papal proclamation, under the supreme *personal* authority of the sovereign pontiff in a *solemn* declaration, would bring an end to the turmoil. He looked forward to "a point of moral doctrine *ultérieurement définissable*," definable later on, and "requiring" the "assent of divine faith."

That was in 1968. In 1998, Pope John Paul II, in his Apostolic Letter *Ad Tuendam Fidem*, introduced a new category of teaching, called "definitive," and implied that though such a teaching was *not infallible* it was nevertheless *irreformable*. Although the word *irreformable* itself does not actually appear in this Apostolic Letter, the Pope did add a second paragraph to Canon 750 of the 1983 revision of Canon Law concerning the importance of stability. The new paragraph stated:

> Each and every thing which is proposed definitively by the magisterium of the Church concerning the doctrine of faith and morals, that is, each and every point of teaching which is required to safeguard reverently and expound faithfully the same deposit of faith, is also to be firmly embraced and retained; therefore, one who refuses those propositions which are to be held definitively is opposed to the doctrine of the Catholic Church.

Effectively, if not verbally, he transferred some freely debated doctrines from the field of "doubtful things" to the field of "necessary things" where

24. Ibid., 6:1001.

no question must be raised about their unchangeable nature. Journet's expression "*ultérieurement définissable*" shows that the discussion of "definitive teachings" was in the air at the time of *Humanae Vitae* and that he looked forward to its conclusions being declared "*definitive*" to settle the controversy. From Catholics, such a declaration, according to the new paragraph of Canon 750, would require *obsequium* (this word has many meanings: loyalty, respect, submission, obedience) as well as an *assent of faith.*

In 2011, the Jesuit periodical *America* printed an article entitled "Rights of Conscience,"[25] which contains an interesting and important distinction between "noninfallible" teachings and "irreversible" statements. The author Kevin O'Rourke noted that both Thomas O'Meara, O.P., and Nicholas Lash maintain that a doctrinal teaching of the magisterium calling for assent is not the same as a disciplinary statement requiring obedience. Referring to an instruction issued by the Congregation for the Doctrine of the Faith and a commentary on that instruction by Avery Dulles, S.J., the author notes that noninfallible statements are of two sorts: "reformable" or "prudential." "Reformable" does not imply that the statement could be reversed in the future, but that it might be better expressed, the better to be understood and to be more adequate to the truth it conveys. Reformable statements that are formal teaching should be accepted, in the words of the Second Vatican Council, with "religious submission of intellect and will." This form of response is not an act of religious faith in revealed truth; rather it is an internal intellectual assent. The author notes, however, that even prudential teachings have been reversed. In 1990 at a press conference introducing an instruction of the Congregation for the Doctrine of the Faith, then Cardinal Joseph Ratzinger listed several examples of teachings that had been reversed: statements promulgated by the Holy See in regard to ecumenical activities, relations between church and state, personal freedom and the rights of conscience in choosing a religion, and declarations of the Pontifical Bible Commission made at the beginning of the twentieth century. When a person cannot give "intellectual assent," such responses are to be called "personal difficulties." Both Cardinal Dulles and Nicholas Lash indicate that "dissent" is not a fitting term for this type of response. Mr. Lash prefers to label them "disagreements."

In 1970, two years after *Humanae Vitae* and three years before his death,

25. Kevin O'Rourke, "The Rights of Conscience," *America* 205, no. 3 (2011): 13–16.

Maritain published *On the Church of Christ,* in which he distinguished "three manners of adhering to an encyclical.

> The first is to make a bow full of reverence, while inveighing against it and judging it inopportune and badly founded. I prefer, in order not to give offense, to abstain from qualifying this first manner.
>
> The second manner is to adhere to it *as if* from one end to the other it was an infallible document. He who reads an encyclical in this way gives more than is asked of him. But since he does so in a spirit of faith, it can be for him an occasion of great graces.
>
> The third manner is the one ... which I believe normal. It asks that one make an effort of the intelligence (is it possible to live by faith, even if one were a village illiterate, without having to exercise one's intelligence?) But this third manner does not make the adherence given to the pontifical document a condition for the success of the effort in question.[26]

Maritain died in 1973 and Journet two years later. With *loyalty* and *respect,* both gave their *assent of divine faith* to the teachings of the encyclical. Whether or not they accepted them as irreformable or *irrevocable* we will never know. The status of "definitive teaching" was not then and is still not settled. Much ink will flow and words be spoken over the question of how a proposition that is not infallible can at the same time be irreformable, such as the conclusions of *Humanae Vitae.*

"In necessary things unity, in doubtful things liberty,
in all things charity."

26. Jacques Maritain, *De L'Eglise du Christ, La Personne de l'Eglise et son Personnel,* (Paris: Desclée de Brouwer, 1970), 249.

JOHN J. CONLEY, S.J.

Sign, Symbol, Initiatory Sacrament

In his essay "Sign and Symbol" in *Ransoming the Time*, Jacques Maritain devotes a scant five paragraphs to the special problem of the sacraments in a semiotic context. In this paper, I would like to take Maritain's sketch of sacramental sign and apply it to a semiotic account of the three sacraments of initiation: baptism, confirmation, and the Eucharist. To perform this application, I will refer to the standard ecclesiastical presentation of the three sacraments found in *The Catechism of the Catholic Church.*

I. Semiotic Theory

Maritain situates his theory of the sacraments within his broader consideration of the practical sign. In developing his theory of the practical sign, Maritain follows the Aristotelian-Thomistic distinction between the speculative and the practical intellect. "The good proper to the speculative intellect is purely and simply the true; the good proper to the practical intellect is the true as leading to right action. In one way or another—that is to say, for reasons and to degrees which differ greatly with cases—the practical intellect presupposes the will; its object, in so far as it is known as object, is something to be put into existence, something to be made concrete in action."[1] The emphasis of this definition of the practical sign on will and action recurs in Maritain's treatment of the particular problems associated with the status of the sacrament.

In his consideration of the sacrament, Maritain treats it as the preem-

1. Jacques Maritain, *Ransoming the Time,* translated by Harry Lorin Binsse (New York: Charles Scribner's Sons, 1941), 222.

inent and exceptional example of the practical sign. "[The sacrament] is a practical sign ordered to interior sanctification.... Being something external and sensory which signifies an effect of interior sanctification to be produced, it is a conventional sign founded in fact on a certain analogy (a practical symbol.)"[2] In this definition, the sacrament is more than a practical sign; it is a practical symbol, inasmuch as there is an analogical resemblance between the external sensate face of the sacrament and the transformation it is designed to effect. The water of baptism is thus a symbol of the purification from sin, not simply the sign of such a spiritual liberation. The sacrament is distinguished from most other practical signs by its unique focus on an internal transformation, even if this transformation has clear consequences in social action.

The sacrament also raises unique problems of authorship and authority. Maritain insists on the broad spectrum of sacramental instances. In this conception, there are "natural" sacraments, the sacraments of the Old Law (Judaism), and the sacraments of the New Law (Christianity). All enjoy divine authority but in different modes. In the natural sacraments, present in societies outside the reach of the divine law, the civil authorities often establish rites of a religious nature to encourage growth in natural virtues by its members. Maritain insists that such natural sacraments reflect a real but indirect and easily distorted divine inspiration.

The sacraments of the Old Law are instituted by the direct and pure inspiration of God. Such Jewish rites as circumcision, the sacerdotal anointing of the Aaronic priest, and the celebration of the Passover meal are authentic sacraments, instituted by God to bring about internal sanctification of those who participate in them. Nonetheless, the efficacy of the sacraments of the Old Law is limited. Of themselves, these sacraments do not confer the spiritual transformation they signify; rather, by offering persuasive external signs, they encourage the devout participant to pursue the moral and spiritual goods they represent. (In passing, it should be noted that Maritain's sympathetic and detailed defense of the properly sacramental nature and supernatural source of the rites of the Mosaic law is very much of a piece with his combat against anti-Semitism, prominent in other essays in *Ransoming the Time*, notably "The Mystery of Israel."[3])

The sacraments of the New Law distinguish themselves by their unique

2. Ibid., 225.
3. See ibid., 141–79.

efficaciousness. They represent such an unusual type of practical sign that they break apart the category of sign itself. "Not only are "the sacraments [of the New Law] sacraments; they are sacraments in a super-eminent manner; they effect that which they signify. . . . This comes to be by virtue of the superabundance coming forth from Christ's passion, and because the major element in the new Law is the grace of the Spirit operating from within. The sacramental sign is no longer merely a *practical* sign; it becomes an *instrumental cause* of which the very Cause of being makes use to produce grace in the soul, just as an artist makes use of the violin or flute to produce beauty. And to be thus a cause (instrumental) is extrinsic to the idea of the sign, even of the practical sign."[4] Through its divinely authored capacity to cause what it signifies, the New-Law sacrament breaks the limits of moral invitation which hedge about other practical signs, even those of a natural or Old-Law sacramentality. Given his longstanding aesthetic concerns, Maritain interprets the sacrament's efficaciousness through an artistic, specifically a musical, analogy.

The Eucharist represents the summit of this sign-breaking efficaciousness of the sacrament to effect what is signifies. The Eucharist does not operate on the basis of a physical resemblance between its external signifiers (bread and wine) and its internal significance (the Body and Blood of Christ). Rather, it effects an ontological change (through transubstantiation) which has no parallels in nature or even in the other sacraments. "Far from resting upon an identity between the sign and the signified, the sacrament of the Eucharist adds to the relationship of sign to signified that of cause to effect and implies the intervention of the first Cause producing the most radical change we can conceive, a change which affects being in so far as it is being."[5]

Despite its supernatural realism and account of divine efficaciousness, Maritain's account of the sacrament does not ignore the question of human will, which he posits as central to the exercise of all practical signs. Although, when properly celebrated, the sacraments effect what they signify, their proper grace can only be received "if the subject does not put obstacles in their way by his contrary disposition."[6] Sacramental efficaciousness is thus in no way comparable to magic, a predominantly imaginary form of spiritual instrumentality severed from questions of moral disposition and

4. Ibid., 226.

5. Ibid.

6. Ibid.

one which Maritain treats at length in the closing section of his meditation on sign and symbol.

II. Sacrament and Initiation

Maritain's theory of the sacraments can provide a useful grid for understanding the semiotic and symbolic dimension of the sacraments of initiation. Conversely, the *Catechism*'s treatment of the initiatory trinity of baptism, confirmation, and Eucharist can complement and expand the sacramental theory outlined by Maritain in *Ransoming the Time.*

The *Catechism's* opening treatment of the sacraments in general stresses their symbolic nature. Like Maritain, the text emphasizes the analogy between the natural world and the supernatural world represented by the sacraments. "The seven sacraments touch all the stages and all the important moments of Christian life: they give birth and increase, healing and mission to the Christian's life of faith. There is thus a certain resemblance between the stages of natural life and the stages of the spiritual life."[7]

In its treatment of baptism, the *Catechism* stresses how the external sign of water used in the sacrament is rooted in a faith-inspired view of water in the divine economy of salvation; the link to nature as such is minimal. The water of baptism is tied to the waters of creation in Genesis, of the great flood, of the exodus of Israel from Egypt, of the baptism preached by John the Baptist, and of the baptism of Christ in the Jordan. Baptism thus appears as more of a conventional (specifically ecclesial) than a natural sign of purification. Grasping the nature of baptism's use of water to signify purification from sin requires an understanding of how God has used water in analogous episodes of creation, redemption, purification, and mission in the history of salvation. Outside this faith-based framework of reference, the external rite of baptism easily becomes a simple enigma to the onlooker. It is in this context that one can grasp how the plunging into the waters of baptism represents a spiritual immersion into the death and resurrection of Christ and how baptism "signifies and realizes the death to sin and the entry into the life of the Most Holy Trinity through configuration to the paschal mystery of Christ."[8]

Like Maritain, the *Catechism* stresses the internal purification effected

7. *Catechism of the Catholic Church* (CCC) (New York: Doubleday, 1995), no. 1210.
8. CCC, no. 1239.

by the celebration of baptism. In particular, it emphasizes how baptism infuses the theological virtues, empowers the new Christian through the gifts of the Holy Spirit, and strengthens the pursuit of the moral virtues by the baptized. But it also describes the external, social dimension of the effects of baptism. Through baptism, the Christian enters upon the mission proper to the common priesthood of all believers. Baptism must be expressed by participation in the various external apostolates proper to the Church. This stress on the external mission conferred by baptism on the Christian carries the echoes of Maritain's emphasis on the will and action as central to the operation of all practical signs, even if Maritain's presentation of the finality of the sacrament remains confined to a narrower category of internal sanctification.

In its treatment of confirmation, the *Catechism* treats the external sign of the sacrament in a more naturalistic account of symbol. The action of anointing with oil is interpreted in the light of both ancient and biblical history. It emerges as a natural symbol of a substance and action which cleanses, limbers, heals, and polishes. The external sign appropriately points to the spiritual cleansing, healing, consecration, and burnishing which the sacrament effects in the soul. The external sealing with oil points to the internal sealing in the Holy Spirit which confirmation operates.

As in its treatment of baptism, the *Catechism*'s account of confirmation delineates the external as well as internal effects of the sacrament. Internally, the sacrament unites the believer more firmly to Christ and increases the gifts of the Holy Spirit within the soul. Externally, it propels the believer to "spread and defend the faith by word and action as true witnesses of Christ, to confess the name of Christ boldly, and never to be ashamed of the Cross."[9] One might well regret the post-conciliar abandonment of the old complementary gesture of the episcopal slap on the cheek, which underscored the price of this militant witness to the faith before the contempt of the world.

In its presentation of the Eucharist, the *Catechism* reverts to a more biblical interpretation of the external signs used in the sacrament. While the text briefly cites the generic status of bread and wine as "fruit of the earth and of the vine,"[10] echoing the prayers of the Offertory, it devotes far greater attention to the roots of this bread and wine in the history of

9. *CCC*, no. 1303.
10. *CCC*, no. 1333.

salvation. In particular, it evokes the centrality of bread and wine in the redemptive history of Israel: the bread of the Passover meal, the manna in the desert, the cup of blessing in Jewish feasts. Like Maritain's insistence on the authenticity of the sacraments of the Old Law, the *Catechism*'s catalogue of the Eucharist's precedents in Judaism emphasizes the deep and precise roots of even the external signs of the Eucharist in the economy of Israel, especially in its experience of the Exodus. It also stresses the link to the miracles of Christ. The Eucharistic bread echoes the multiplication of the loaves while the wine echoes the transformation of the water into wine at Cana.

Despite the rich biblical echoes of its external signs, the Eucharist effects a reality which transcends the feeble external signs. Through the epiclesis and words of institution, the priest transforms the bread and wine into the substance of the Body and Blood of Christ. The unique sacrifice of Christ on the cross becomes present in the church's sacrifice of thanksgiving and praise. In its supernatural transformation of the external signs it employs, the Eucharist operates its effect in a manner markedly different from the other sacraments. It is this preeminence in divine authorship and efficaciousness that constitutes the Eucharist as the source and goal of the other sacraments.

The *Catechism*'s account of the fruits of proper reception of the Eucharist emphasizes how the internal transformation wrought by the sacrament alters the communicant's relationship to society and to the future. Internally, the Eucharist augments union with Christ, charity, opposition to sin, and union with the Church. Externally, it frees the communicant to embrace the neighbor in several specific ways. The Eucharist strengthens commitment to the poor. "To receive in truth the Body and Blood given up for us, we must recognize Christ in the poorest, his brethren."[11] It also commits the communicant to work for the unity of Christians. "The more painful the experience of the divisions in the Church which break the common participation in the table of the Lord, the more urgent are our prayers to the Lord that the time of unity among all who believe in Him may return."[12]

The Eucharist also reorients the believer's relationship to the future. In the celebration of the Eucharist, the believer looks forward to the comple-

11. CCC, no. 1397.
12. CCC, no. 1398.

tion of the Eucharistic sacrifice in the heavenly kingdom of God. "If the Eucharist is the memorial of the Passover of the Lord Jesus, if by our communion at the altar we are filled 'with every heavenly blessing and grace,' then the Eucharist is also an anticipation of the heavenly glory."[13] The internal sanctification wrought by the sacrament thus alters the communicant's relationship to time as well as to space. A greater love of the neighbor and a greater hope in the final triumph of God's kingdom emerge as the fruits of worthy reception.

III. Conclusion

To conclude, Maritain's semiotic treatment of the sacraments in *Ransoming the Time* permits us to grasp something of the signification and symbolism inherent in the sacramental acts of the church. Ratifying certain of Maritain's insights, the *Catechism* permits us to recognize a broader social finality to the sacraments' grace and to grasp how deeply even the external signs of the sacrament are rooted in an ecclesial memory of the economy of salvation. Perhaps Maritain's most significant contribution to semiotic discussions of the sacraments is to remind us how the sacraments, especially the Eucharist, ultimately defy the limits of even the most robust religious signs and symbols. At a certain moment, semiotic analysis must yield to adoration.

13. *CCC*, no. 1402.

III

HISTORICAL TURN

RANDALL B. SMITH

Hope and History

I. False Hope and Man's Search for Meaning: On Faith as the Basis for Hope

1. *The Problem of False Hope*

Hope is a funny thing. And it is odd the different things people use to give themselves hope. So, for example, not everything that we think will give us hope actually does. There is such a thing as *false* hope. That is because hope, as I will argue in what follows, needs to be tied to *truth*—the truth about the world and the truth about the human person.

When it comes to hope, there are, of course, the simple, everyday human hopes, such as: "I hope I get a raise at my job," or "I hope I won't have any unexpected medical expenses this year." These often enough turn out to be "false hopes." And then there is what is sometimes called the "theological virtue" of hope by which we are directed to union with God in heaven as our last end. One question we might ask is whether the hope which directs us to this supernatural end provides any help *in this life*? Does our hope for eternity help us when it comes to our hopes in time and in history? Or is our hope for eternity merely (as Feuerbach and Marx, among others, have argued) merely a *distraction* from human history—an "opiate of the masses."[1]

1. The famous phrase "opium of the masses" (*das Opium des Volkes*) is Marx's and originates from the introduction of his proposed work, *A Contribution to the Critique of Hegel's Philosophy of Right.* Although this work was never completed, the introduction (written in 1843) was published in 1844 in *Deutsch-Französische Jahrbücher.* Cf. also Ludwig Feuerbach, *Das Wesen des Christentums* (The Essence of Christianity), translated into English by the famous novelist Marian Evans (who wrote under the more recognizable pen name "George Eliot").

In what follows, I wish to argue that all human hopes must find their ultimate foundation in the theological virtues of hope and faith; otherwise, these hopes will remain false and empty—"distractions" (*divertissements*) as Pascal would call them[2]—not sure guides to the future or the present. Indeed, as we will see, false hopes can even, at times, do great damage.

So, for example, in his now-classic book *Man's Search for Meaning*, author Viktor Frankl tells how his senior block warden at Auschwitz, "a fairly well-known composer and librettist," confided to him one day that he had had a dream that the camp would be liberated on March thirtieth of that year, 1945. Sadly, says Frankl: "When F— told me about his dream, he was still full of hope and convinced that the voice of his dream would be right. But as the promised day drew nearer, the war news which reached our camp made it appear very unlikely that we would be free on the promised date. On March twenty-ninth, F— suddenly became ill and ran a high temperature. On March thirtieth, the day his prophecy had told him that the war and suffering would be over for him, he became delirious and lost consciousness. On March thirty-first, he was dead." "To all outward appearances," says Frankl, "he had died of typhus." And yet, "Those who know how close the connection is between the state of mind of a man—his courage and hope, or lack of them—and the state of immunity of his body will understand that the sudden loss of hope and courage can have a deadly effect."[3]

Frankl confirmed his thesis with the chief doctor of the concentration camp who reported that "the death rate in the week between Christmas, 1944, and New Year's, 1945, increased in camp beyond all previous experience." The explanation for this increase "did not lie in the harder working conditions or the deterioration of our food supplies or a change of weather or new epidemics. It was simply that the majority of the prisoners had lived in the naive hope that they would be home again by Christmas."[4] When it became clear to them that they would not, they lost all hope and, with it, the will to live.

Recognizing the dangers presented by the loss of hope, the senior block warden asked Frankl to say some words to his fellow prisoners to restore their hope when the mood had become especially low. Not an enviable task. How does one speak about hope to men facing prolonged daily suf-

2. Cf. Pascal, *Pensées*, 139.
3. See Viktor Frankl, *Man's Search for Meaning* (New York: Beacon Press, 1959), 96–97.

fering, sitting in the dark at Auschwitz with the white ashes of their dead comrades spread all about them on the ground like snow? While hope was necessary to the prisoners' survival, *false* hope could be fatal.

Perhaps T. S. Eliot had it right, then, in "East Coker," the second of the *Four Quartets*, when he wrote:

> I said to my soul, be still, and wait without hope
> For hope would be hope for the wrong thing; wait without love,
> For love would be love of the wrong thing; there is yet faith
> But the faith and the love and the hope are all in the waiting.[5]

Frankl, however, I am glad to report, did *not* read them Eliot.

2. *Hope and Meaning*

What Frankl actually said to his fellow prisoners was this: namely, that "human life, under any circumstances, never ceases to have a meaning, and that this infinite meaning of life includes suffering and dying, privation and death." He implored them not to lose hope, but rather to "keep their courage in the certainty that the hopelessness of our struggle did not detract from its dignity and meaning."[6]

Frankl is of course known and revered—rightly, to my mind—for the many inspiring passages in *Man's Search for Meaning* such as this one:

> Any attempt to restore a man's inner strength in the camp had first to succeed in showing him some future goal. Nietzsche's words, "He who has a *why* to live for can bear with almost any *how*," could be the guiding motto for all psychotherapeutic and psychohygienic efforts regarding prisoners. Whenever there was an opportunity for it, one had to give them a *why*—an aim—for their lives, in order to strengthen them to bear the terrible *how* of their existence. Woe to him who saw no more sense in his life, no aim, no purpose, and therefore no point in carrying on. He was soon lost.[7]

Much of Frankl's post-war psychological practice of logotherapy was based on this insight.

And yet, with all due respect to Frankl's real achievements, is there not a danger lurking here as well—something Frankl conveniently skirts over in his otherwise excellent book? Namely, that the goal or purpose one adopts in life is not unimportant. After all, one can live for revenge as well as for

4. Ibid., 97.
5. T. S. Eliot, "East Coker," III, 23–26.
6. Frankl, *Man's Search for Meaning*, 104.
7. Ibid.

love. And in getting the prisoners to focus on a future goal to which they could look forward, was Frankl not risking encouraging in them precisely the sort of false hope that might in the long run be deadly?

So, for example, Frankl suggests (rightly in my view) that, "A man who becomes conscious of the responsibility he bears toward a human being who affectionately waits for him, or to an unfinished work, will never be able to throw away his life. He knows the '*why*' for his existence, and will be able to bear almost any '*how*.'"[8] That's true, I have no doubt, as long as the man remains convinced the person affectionately waiting for him is still alive. And yet, so many of the relatives of those in the camps were already dead, and the men in the camps either knew it or at least suspected it. And as for "unfinished work," imagine a young medical intern such as Viktor Frankl in Auschwitz in 1945: What chance was there of finishing that medical degree now? Of entering into an honored profession with esteemed colleagues beside one's beloved spouse? If those were the sort of things that had been giving a man the "why" for his existence, the decreasing likelihood of ever realizing these hopes could certainly have given him cause to doubt whether he should continue bearing with the terrible "how."

Frankl is on firmer footing, or so it seems to me, when he makes clear later on in his book that "there could be no earthly happiness which could compensate for all we had suffered." Indeed, "We were not hoping for happiness," he tells us; "it was not that which gave us courage and gave meaning to our suffering, our sacrifices, and our dying."[9] This is not an unimportant point, I think, for those of us who imagine ourselves proponents of what is sometimes called a eudaimonistic (or "happiness"-based) ethics. For there is reason to suspect that what Aristotle and St. Thomas meant by *eudaimonia* and *beatitudo* is so far from what we currently mean when we use the word "happiness," that perhaps we should cease using it. But if not happiness, then what?

Frankl's answer is intriguing. The typical reply with which a man lost in despair would respond to all encouraging arguments, says Frankl, went something like this: "I have nothing to expect from life any more." "What sort of answer can one give to that?" asks Frankl. None, in fact. Because "what was really needed," he says, "was a fundamental change in our attitude toward life.

8. Ibid., 101.
9. Ibid., 114.

We had to learn ourselves and, furthermore, we had to teach the despairing men, that it did not really matter what we expected from life, but rather what life expected from us. We needed to stop asking about the meaning of life, and instead to think of ourselves as those who were being questioned by life—daily and hourly. Our answer must consist, not in talk and meditation, but in right action and in right conduct.[10]

Right action and right conduct: here is the first pillar. One key element of *eudaimonia* leading to man's ultimate human flourishing is right action and right conduct. As the philosopher Aristotle put it: "happiness is a certain activity of soul in conformity with perfect virtue."[11] So, too, in the Christian tradition, this insight is not negated, but deepened. Pope John Paul II, for example, in his encyclical *Veritatis splendor*, commenting on the passage in the Gospel of Matthew in which a rich young comes to Jesus to ask the question, "What good must I do to have eternal life," says this:

The question which the rich young man puts to Jesus of Nazareth is one which rises from the depths of his heart. It is *an essential and unavoidable question for the life of every man*, for it is about the moral good which must be done, and about eternal life. The young man senses that there is a connection between moral good and the fulfilment of his own destiny.[12]

And yet this insight, that the moral life, the life of "right action and right conduct," is a *sine qua non* for human happiness and human flourishing, is merely a first step. Christianity shares this insight with pagan philosophy. Does Christian faith offer anything more? Can it deepen this insight in fundamental ways?

I suggest it can, especially with regard to one of the great challenges to pagan morality: What to do when bad things happen to good people? What do we say about the virtuous man who suffers as though he were evil? And about the evil man who enjoys benefits as though he were virtuous? This is the question Glaucon poses to Socrates in book 1 of *The Republic* which generates the rest of the discussion in the book.[13] And it is a question Aristotle too poses in book 1 of the *Nicomachean Ethics* when he grants that one needs not only complete virtue, but also a complete life from which grave external misfortunes are absent.

10. Ibid., 98.

11. Aristotle, *Nicomachean Ethics*, translated by H. Rackham (London: W. Heinemann, Putnam's, 1934), 1.13, 1102a1. All quotations from the *Nicomachean Ethics* are from this translation.

12. John Paul II, *Veritatis Splendor* (1993): no. 7.

13. Plato, *The Republic* 2, 359d-361d.

For many reverses and vicissitudes of all sorts occur in the course of life, and it is possible that the most prosperous man may encounter great disasters in his declining years, as the story is told of Priam in the epics; but no one calls a man happy who meets with misfortunes like Priam's, and comes to a miserable end.[14]

Now admittedly the question of whether Aristotle believed that external misfortunes can destroy human happiness—or to put this another way, whether human happiness is at least to some extent dependent upon external conditions and chance—is one scholars continue to debate. The particulars of that debate need not detain us here. It is enough for our purposes simply to note that Aristotle's comments open up the question of the problem of suffering, and it is a question that, rather famously, remains unresolved. It is precisely here, I would suggest, with regard to the question of external misfortune and undeserved human suffering, where the perspective of Christian faith can offer a new perspective from which one can speak meaningfully of authentic "hope."

Consider Viktor Frankl's situation in Auschwitz from a solely Aristotelian perspective. He had set out years earlier to be a psychologist and physician, a good husband and father, and a respected citizen serving his community. As he walked among the grey blockhouse buildings of Auschwitz with the burnt ashes of his dead comrades covering everything, what was he to think? That right action and right conduct lead to human happiness and human flourishing? Although Frankl affirms this, it hardly seems adequate to the tragic irony of the camps. Good, virtuous men were dying left and right all around him, and some of the most vicious men history has ever known were being lauded as the heroic saviors of Europe. If nowhere else, certainly at the gates of Auschwitz, the vision that informs Aristotle's *Ethics* has reached its natural limits, and we must turn to another way of seeing the world. Christian faith, far from being a flight *from* the world, as Marx and Feuerbach and so many others have insisted, is, I would suggest, humanity's proper embrace *of* the world—in hope and love.

3. *Faith: Seeing the World Anew, "From the Perspective of Eternity"*

Later in his book, Frankl speaks of "sacrifice" and its meaningfulness. "It was in the nature of this sacrifice," he admits, "that it should appear to

14. Aristotle, *Nichomachean Ethics* 1.9, 1100a5–9.

be pointless in the normal world, the world of material success. But in reality our sacrifice did have a meaning. Those of us who had any religious faith ... could understand [this] without difficulty."[15]

It would be interesting to propose this question as a test of religious faith: Do you believe that a sacrifice appearing pointless in the normal world, the world of success, can in reality be meaningful and significant? And are you willing to bet your life on the truth of that claim? If not, what does this fact say about your faith—not to mention the hope founded on it?

"It is a peculiarity of man," says Frankl, "that he can only live by looking to the future—*sub specie aeternitatis*."[16] This last little "tag"—*sub specie aeternitatis*, "under the aspect of eternity" or "from the perspective of the eternal"—is noteworthy, and much depends upon how the whole sentence is construed. "Looking to the future," as Frankl has made clear, is *not* necessarily the same as looking at events *sub specie aeternitatis*. One can "look to the future" with an eye to getting out of prison by Christmas, and when that date passes, one's sense of purpose is lost. It is quite different, however, I would suggest, to look at the future, as well as the present, and indeed perhaps even the past, as Frankl suggests, *sub specie aeternitatis*.

What does this looking at history from the perspective of the eternal entail? This is a difficult question, as the reader can imagine, and not one to which we can give a sufficient answer in a brief space such as we have here. But in order to make a first stab at an answer, I propose we shift our focus a bit and come at it from a slightly different angle. The fundamental question, to my mind, is how we can view the world of time and change and suffering in which we live and move and have our being *now* from the perspective of *the eternal*, which is a perspective we will not truly share until we are fully united with God at the end of time? Is this even possible? It is, I would suggest, but it is a divine perspective only made possible by *faith*.

Josef Pieper poses a similar problem in his book *In Tune with the World: A Theory of Festivity*. How it is possible to be festive and joyful, he asks, in the face of the world's sufferings and given the reality of death? "Consolation exists," according to Pieper, "only on the premise that grief, sorrow, death, are accepted, and therefore affirmed, as *meaningful* in spite of everything."[17] So,

15. Frankl, *Man's Search for Meaning*, 105.

16. Ibid., 94.

17. Josef Pieper, *In Tune with the World: A Theory of Festivity*, translated by Richard and Clara Winston (South Bend, Indiana: St. Augustine's Press, 1999), 28.

for example, says Pieper: "We can't festively celebrate [even] the birth of a child, if we hold with Sartre's dictum that 'It is absurd that we are born.'"[18] If the world is meaningless, if life is meaningless, if existence itself is meaningless, then on what basis would we festively celebrate anything—birth, marriage, college graduation, job promotions, *anything*? You go to a wedding; the bride and groom look happy; everything *seems* joyful; and then you say to yourself: "They'll probably just get divorced. He'll cheat on her, or she'll cheat on him. Their children will hate them. One of them will get Alzheimer's, and in the end, they'll both be dead, anyway."

Now, one obvious response to this sort of thing might be simply to reply: "Oh, grow up!" That might be fine, as far as it goes, but it will need to be fleshed out a little bit. Plenty of grown-ups have such thoughts at weddings—don't tell me no because I've heard them—so we will have to think more seriously about what real "grown-ups" understand that the people who make such comments do not.

So, for example, another sort of response might go like this: "Look, why *not* celebrate? Sure, you're going to die; sure, you're going to suffer; sure, there are going to be bitterness, pain, and sorrow, but that's no reason not to celebrate *now*?" Yes, but that's precisely Pieper's point: we do festively celebrate major events in life in spite of suffering, pain, and death. The question is not, "Are those things sufficient to make us *not* celebrate?" The question is: "Is there any reason *to* celebrate?"

Note that I did not ask whether there might be good reasons to drink heavily or, as Walker Percy suggests in a famous essay on bourbon, whether it might be advisable to employ sufficient quantities of bourbon to relieve the malaise.[19] That is not the question. Rather, the question is whether there is any reason to celebrate. And since we generally do not take the certainty of sorrow, suffering, and death to be especially good reasons to celebrate, the problem we have posed recurs: If the world is meaningless, if life is meaningless, if existence itself is meaningless, then on what basis would we festively celebrate anything—birth, marriage, college graduation, job promotions, *anything*?

18. Ibid., 25.

19. See Walker Percy, "Bourbon," in *Signposts in a Strange Land* (New York: Picador, 1991), 102–107.

4. *"Dover Beach": Love in an Age without Faith*

Perhaps a literary example of the problem is in order. One of the purest expressions of the modern sense of the pointlessness of celebration can be found in Matthew Arnold's 1851 poem "Dover Beach," written on the occasion of his marriage to Frances Lucy, a woman for whom he, wishing to marry but unable to support her on the wages of a private secretary, sought and obtained a position as one of Her Majesty's Inspectors of Schools, a job that required him to spend long hours in dreary railway stations and small-town hotels, and even longer hours listening to children recite their lessons and parents their grievances. Arnold often described the duties connected with his job as pure "drudgery," and given the job description, it strikes me that one need not care for Arnold's prose or literary criticism in the slightest to sympathize with his plight. I mention these details about his marriage simply to make clear in advance that Arnold was, in his own way, neither unromantic nor undevoted to the woman he had just taken as his wife when he wrote this poem. Indeed, he would go on to father half-a-dozen children with the woman to whom he composed the following lines. As a love poem, it begins promisingly enough:

> The sea is calm to-night.
> The tide is full, the moon lies fair
> Upon the straits; on the French coast the light
> Gleams and is gone; the cliffs of England stand;
> Glimmering and vast, out in the tranquil bay.
> Come to the window, sweet is the night-air!
> Only, from the long line of spray
> Where the sea meets the moon-blanched land,
> Listen! you hear the grating roar
> Of pebbles which the waves draw back, and fling,
> At their return, up the high strand,
> Begin, and cease, and then again begin,
> With tremulous cadence slow[20]

Good so far. With the sea waves coming in and going out and coming in again, Arnold almost manages to strike an erotic note—or about as erotic

20. Here and below, I am quoting from the version at *The Poetry Foundation* website: http://www.poetryfoundation.org/poem/172844.

as this buttoned-down Victorian Englishman of the academic establishment is capable of getting. But at this point, the poem takes a more sinister turn:

> Listen! [he tells his wife] you hear the grating roar
> Of pebbles which the waves draw back, and fling,
> At their return, up the high strand,
> Begin, and cease, and then again begin,
> With tremulous cadence slow and bring
> The eternal note of sadness in.

This man is on his honeymoon; whence comes that "eternal note of sadness"? Indeed, in the next stanza, things go quickly from bad to worse, from "sadness" to "human misery."

> Sophocles long ago
> Heard it on the Agaean, and it brought
> Into his mind the turbid ebb and flow
> Of human misery [this is going downhill fast]; we
> Find also in the sound a thought,
> Hearing it by this distant northern sea.

Poor Arnold. He is married to the woman he loves; he is on his honeymoon; they are looking out at a beautiful ocean vista; and all he can think about is Greek tragedy and "the turbid ebb and flow of human misery." Not exactly the sort of cheery fellow one generally looks for in a husband.

But give the man credit for this: He understands that something is not right, that something has been lost, and that this loss has serious consequences for the possibilities of human joy and fulfillment. What is equally interesting is that he even recognizes what it is that has been lost.

> The Sea of Faith [he says]
> Was once, too, at the full,—and round earth's shore
> Lay like the folds of a bright girdle furled.
> But now I only hear
> Its melancholy, long, withdrawing roar,
> Retreating, to the breath
> Of the night-wind, down the vast edges drear
> And naked shingles of the world.

On Arnold's view, it appears that when the "Sea of Faith" enveloped the earth, then one might have looked upon this physical sea with joy. But as that Sea of Faith has withdrawn, it has left a world disenchanted and dreary, merely bits and pieces of "stuff" here and there, no longer enfolding the world, but merely "naked shingles of the world."

> Ah, love, let us be true
> To one another! [says Arnold finally] for the world,
> which seems
> To lie before us like a land of dreams,
> So various, so beautiful, so new,
> Hath really neither joy, nor love, nor light,
> Nor certitude, nor peace, nor help for pain;
> And we are here as on a darkling plain
> Swept with confused alarms of struggle and flight,
> Where ignorant armies clash by night.

So Arnold *was* an incurable romantic, as it turns out. It is simply that his romantic appeal to his new wife was rather grim: "Ah, love, let us be true to one another"—not because the world is sweet and you are sweeter, yet; nor because love is the world's rhythm, and to its tune I must dance; no, but because so much of the world is so thoroughly and completely terrible, we must hold on to one another for dear life. What does a newlywed wife say to a husband who tells her that the world only *seems* "so various, so beautiful, so new," but has in reality, "neither joy, nor love, nor light, nor certitude, nor peace, nor help for pain." It is likely he may have heard what many husbands hear on their wedding night: "It's time to stop talking now, dear."

And yet, to be fair to poor Matthew Arnold, is "Dover Beach" not precisely the proper sort of poetic embodiment of the view of the universe expressed by contemporary philosopher Quentin Smith who insists that, in light of contemporary scientific theories about the origins of the universe, "the fact of the matter is that the most reasonable belief is that we came from nothing, by nothing and for nothing.... Our universe exists without cause or without explanation.... [It] exists non-necessarily, improbably, and causelessly. It exists for absolutely no reason at all."[21] If existence itself is meaningless, then certainly festivity, joy, and hope are empty and ultimately illusory.

21. Quentin Smith, *The Felt Meanings of the World: A Metaphysics of Feeling* (West Lafayette, Indiana: Purdue Research Foundation, 1986), 300. To be fair to Smith, although he denies that the universe can have any *rational* meaning, he does grant that it can have "felt" meanings.

5. *The Perspective of Faith: The Necessary Foundation of Authentic Hope*

"To have joy in anything," says Josef Pieper, "one must approve everything. Underlying all festive joy kindled by a specific circumstance there has to be an absolutely universal affirmation extending to the world as a whole, to the reality of things and the existence of man himself."[22] What, then, is this act of will born of love by which we can affirm the world as a whole and the ultimate meaningfulness of human life and human history? For Christians, they call this affirmation of the world and its ultimate meaningfulness *faith*. And being able to make this sort of loving affirmation of human existence is, I would argue, a necessary foundation for authentic *hope*.

In his book *Introduction to Christianity*, the then-Cardinal Joseph Ratzinger asked "What is belief really?" His reply was that

> it is a way of taking up a stand in the totality of reality, a way that cannot be reduced to knowledge and is incommensurable by knowledge; it is the bestowal of meaning without which the totality of man would remain homeless, on which man's calculations and actions are based, and without which in the last resort he could not calculate and act, because he can only do this in the context of a meaning that bears him up. For in fact man does not live on the bread of practicability alone; he lives as *man* and, precisely in the intrinsically human part of his being, on the word, on love, on meaning. Meaning is the bread on which man, in the intrinsically human part of his being, subsists. Without the word, without meaning, without love, he falls into the situation of no-longer-being-able-to-live, even when earthly comfort is present in abundance.[23]

"[M]eaning is not derived from knowledge," Ratzinger continues elsewhere.

> To try to manufacture it in this way, that is, out of provable knowledge of what can be made would resemble Baron Münchhausen's absurd attempt to pull himself up out of the bog by his own hair. I believe that the absurdity of this story mirrors very accurately the basic situation of man. No one can pull himself up out of the bog of uncertainty, of not-being-able-to-live, by his own exertions, nor can we pull ourselves up, as Descartes still thought we could … by a series of intellectual deductions. Meaning that is self-made is in the last analysis no meaning. Meaning,

22. Pieper, *In Tune with the World*, 26.

23. Joseph Ratzinger, *Introduction to Christianity*, translated by J. R. Foster (San Francisco: Ignatius Press, 2004), 72.

that is, the ground on which our existence as a totality can stand and live, cannot be made but only received.[24]

It was just such an act of affirmation of the ultimate meaningfulness of things, I would suggest, that Viktor Frankl made in the camp when he consciously chose to help and support his fellow prisoners, not out of a calculation for survival or personal benefit, but simply out of the un-stated conviction that "Doing this is what life is *for*." Each such act of self-less courage and love reveals—and *a fortiori* in conditions where they stand forth as "signs of contradiction" to everything around them—that the actor has taken a stand on the notion that, in the end, love and self-sacrifice matter; that within the whole vast scope of the universe, this small, seemingly insignificant, act of love and sacrifice is and will remain, in spite of everything, meaningful. And if within the whole vast scope of the universe, this act of love and self-sacrifice matters, then there is at least this one thing in the universe that actually does matter, and it will no longer remain "the most reasonable belief" to say anymore that "we came from nothing, by nothing, and for nothing," and that the universe "exists for absolutely no reason at all." This one eternally significant act, along with all the others like it wherever and whenever they occur, proclaims a decisive "no" to certainty about the meaninglessness of the universe. Like a candle flame in the night, it reveals that not all is darkness.

And yet, the darkness remains. It has not gone away. There are still a whole lot of "in-spite-ofs" remaining here: there is meaning, we say, *in spite of* pain, sorrow, suffering, death, disease, evil, Nazi concentration camps, and all the rest. When one says with one's life and one's actions, "This I know; this I am willing to take a stand on: that things like courage and love and self-sacrifice are meaningful—indeed perhaps the only meaningful things in this world—not in some other, imaginary, ideal world, but *this* world," then such a person will also be forced to admit that this act of affirmation (what Christians call "faith") is not something that could have been deduced or inferred from any set of experiences of the world, especially a world that contains a place like Auschwitz.

And yet, *somehow*, when I extend my sight beyond the here-and-now so as to be able to see the here-and-now *sub specie aeternitate*, it allows me to see the here-and-now in a new way and to live in the here-and-now in

24. Ibid., 73.

a new way: a way that involves care and love and self-sacrifice. Why and how the human spirit reaches beyond the visible in this way to the ultimate source of meaning is hard to say. But the witness of individual acts of courage, self-sacrifice, mercy, and love proves it does. The love and care and self-sacrifice are not made necessary by the world, just as they are not logically deducible from it. Rather one discovers the love and care and self-sacrifice superabundantly breaking in upon the world, enveloping it with a logic beyond the logic of the world of war and survival and power and prestige and "who's up and who's not." Existence, though still ultimately a mystery, the way love always remains a mystery, is no longer merely a puzzle to be solved or a mathematical equation to be completed. It is a gift to be celebrated and enjoyed. But also a gift to be loved and cared for. To the untrained eye, this faith in the meaningfulness of the world and the hope and love it makes possible will seem absurd precisely because it cannot be deduced from the world. And it is precisely the degree to which this act of love is not made possible by the world and not reducible logically to any string of data or inferences from the world, that we call this act of faith, hope, and love "supernatural."

Hope—if it is to be real, authentic hope of the sort that can be the foundation for human flourishing and not the sort of "false hope" that will damage us in the end—needs to be tied to truth: the truth about the world, the truth about the nature and dignity of the human person, and ultimately, to the truth about history.

6. Faith, Hope, and the "Good News" of Jesus Christ

But who tells us the truth about the world and the human person? Where do we find the truth about history, the real "story-behind-the-story" of history, the context within which history makes sense and can thus teach us truthfully and not merely fill us with false hopes?

1 Peter 3.15 instructs Christians that they should be ready to "give a reason for the hope" that is in them.[25] For Christians, the reason for their hope is found in God's revelation of Himself as the Creator who has created the world out of His infinite goodness and love, and as the Redeemer who rescues His People from slavery and makes a covenant with them, a covenant ratified ultimately by the blood of His Son sacrificed on the cross at Calvary.

25. Quoted from the King James Version.

This message, the "Good News" of Christ crucified and risen, is meant to provide a reason for the hope that is in those who have chosen to affirm the meaningfulness of acts of self-less love and courage in an otherwise empty and seemingly meaningless universe. Like Paul coming to the Areopagus to give a name to the god who has heretofore been left unnamed, the Christian story says: We can give substance to your hope; we can give evidence of that unseen thing beyond and behind history, that only "the backward look behind the assurance / of recorded history / the backward half-look / over the shoulder / towards the primitive terror" can reveal.[26]

What Christianity has to offer a man like Viktor Frankl, and the rest of mankind caught in our contemporary cosmic concentration camp, is this: The reassurance that the story handed over to us, and that we are commissioned to hand over to others, helps to make sense of the sort of life that in their best moments they know they want to lead—the sort of life that makes sense of the world and makes it something other than a miserable chaos. When human beings act in such a way as to affirm the meaningfulness of self-less courage and love, they testify to a certain truth about the world. The Christian *logos* gives reason for that hope and provides the undergirding substance for the truth that they affirm by their actions and embody in their lives.

Commenting in the Spanish newspaper *El País* on what he took to be the significance of World Youth Day, Peruvian Nobel Prize winner for literature and self-described "agnostic" Mario Vargas Llosa wrote recently that:

> For a long time it was believed that religion, this elevated form of superstition, would disappear with progress in knowledge and democratic culture, and that science and culture would amply substitute it. This, we now know, was another superstition which reality has gradually demolished. Moreover we also know that culture, especially today, is incapable of carrying out this function which the free thinkers of the 19th century attributed to it with such great generosity and an equal amount of ingenuity. This is because in our day culture has ceased to be a serious and deep response to the great human questions about life, death, destiny and history as it sought to be in the past. On the one hand it has become an inconsequential light entertainment and on the other, a cabal of incomprehensible and arrogant experts, who have taken refuge in unintelligible jargon, light years from common mortals.[27]

26. T. S. Eliot, "The Dry Salvages," ll. 53–55.

27. Quoted from "God in Madrid," an English translation of the address re-printed in *L'Osservatore Romano*, April 9, 2012.

"Culture has not been able to replace religion and will not be able to do so," claims Vargas Llosa, because "the majority of human beings finds answers—or at least the feeling that a higher order exists, of which they are a part and which gives meaning and tranquility to their existence—solely through a transcendence that neither philosophy, nor literature nor science have managed to justify rationally."[28]

What is important to note for our purposes, as well, is the way in which the Christian revelation has opened up a new, authentically *historical* horizon for human aspirations, often misunderstood or otherwise missing. The late Fr. Richard John Neuhaus used to say that the world had forgotten its story and that Christianity's duty was to remind the world of its story.[29] By this I take it he meant that by telling the world the Christian story of salvation history, Christians might help restore that sense of meaning and purpose for which so many in our post-modern world yearn, who, having succumbed to the allure of so many of modernity's empty hopes and promises, both ideological and technological, have been left ever more subject to the dual temptations to meaninglessness and despair. As I've suggested several times above, the life of faith on this view is not a flight *from* the world, but an embrace *of* it, with all its sufferings and misfortunes. It involves viewing the world of time and change from a new perspective and with a new basis for hope and care.

In this regard, it will be instructive to compare the basis of hope we've sketched out above with what I suggest are the two most common ways that we human beings customarily try to give ourselves hope: the first is by attempting to predict and control history, and the second is by attempting to escape from it.

II. The False Hope that Comes From Attempting to Predict and Control History

Let us begin with the first of these: namely, prediction and control. Many people throughout history have been convinced that if they could see the future—if they could predict what was coming—then perhaps they could control events for their own benefit. That, at least, was the hope. This

28. Ibid.

29. See, for example, Richard John Neuhaus, "Telling the World Its Own Story," reprinted at: http://catholiceducation.org/articles/apologetics/ap0081.html.

sort of faith and hope explains the perennial appetite for consulting predictive instruments such as horoscopes, tarot cards, and oracles.

Unfortunately, some people suffer from the misconception that the Old Testament prophets were in the business of predicting the future. An earnest study of the Old Testament would reveal that this was not the case. The Old Testament prophets almost always speak about the meaning of present events and where they are leading. The Old Testament prophets sometimes speak about what God will do, but they never do so in anything but the most general terms. Thus, as John Haught suggests in *Mystery and Promise: A Theology of Revelation*, the prophets "speak to us of the meaning of history, not in the mode of prediction, but in that of promise."[30] More on this point shortly.

In the meantime, it is important to note that there is an odd irony involved in wanting to know the future, as the wiser Greeks in the ancient world understood. If the predictions you are given are true, then they cannot be changed. If it truly is your fate, then it cannot be avoided. The presumption that it can be avoided is based on the hubris that assumes I and I alone can escape the causal nexus of history that will envelope everyone else. The false hope is that no one else will use his or her knowledge and free will to change the future, only me. The hope is that I will become, in effect, for a time at least, the lord of history. And that is something, I am afraid, the real Lord of History simply will not allow.

Consider, in this regard, the example of Oedipus who, having learned that he was fated to kill his father and marry his mother, and having left his home in a vain bid to escape his fate, set in motion a tragic chain of events that led him to do unwittingly all that had been foretold. Attempting to avoid his fate, he rushed headlong into it.

Foolish men like Oedipus imagine that wisdom comes from those like the oracle at Delphi or the blind seer Tiresias who can see the future. If one can see the future, they imagine, then one can control history—or so it would seem. True wisdom, however, means understanding that history cannot be controlled and that seeing the future can be a curse and not at all the blessing many people suppose it to be. So it is that when Tiresias is led into Oedipus's presence, the seer cries out:

30. This is a wonderful little book, but is nearly impossible to obtain in print. Fortunately, it is easily accessible online. For this quotation, see chapter 9, paragraph 3, at: http://www.religion-online.org/showchapter.asp?title=1947&C=1802.

> Alas, alas! How dreadful it can be
> to have wisdom when it brings no benefit
> to the man possessing it.[31]

Seen or unseen, fate will have its way in the end.

In this regard, it is important to note that we are not so distant from our ancient forebears as we might like to imagine. Do we not often play very similar cat-and-mouse games with history and destiny, justice and virtue be damned? History, we are told, has been the story of continual progress ever since the advent of modern science. We evolve. The universe evolves. Technology evolves—in fact, at ever faster rates. Greater understanding of nature brings with it greater ability to predict and control it by means of technological progress. And such developments give rise to the hope that, increasingly, we will be able to escape suffering and, eventually, perhaps even death, either by genetic manipulation or some other technological invention.

That certainly sounds hopeful. But not, of course, if you are one of the prisoners in Auschwitz on whom scientific experiments are being done. And not, one might imagine, if you are dying of cancer *now*. What a cruel fate: to die just before that last great scientific discovery makes death obsolete. If only science had been a little faster, if only there had been more money for research, if only there had been fewer restrictions, you too might have avoided death. Damn those religious fanatics with their irrational objections to scientific research! They cheated me—history cheated me—of the immortality I might have enjoyed. If it ever comes, that is. Modern science often holds out this promissory note of unlimited progress in some mythic future. The question is whether that promissory note is a source of authentic hope or a distraction from the realities of the here-and-now.

And what about the life that we live now? Well, it is a paradox, is it not? While, on the one hand, modern science seems to hold out the promise of unlimited freedom and control, by the same token, it often enough tells a story of "fate" and "determinism" as unavoidable as any ancient Greek tragedy. We are not fated by the gods, of course, but by our genes or by a combination of genes and society. But if we are "fated" by any of these—let us say, our genes—then will we not face the same quandary the ancient

31. Sophocles, *Oedipus the King*, translated by Ian Johnston (Arlington, Virginia: Richer Resources Publications, 2007), ll. 374–76. See also the same online at: https://records.viu.ca/~-johnstoi/sophocles/oedipustheking.htm.

Greeks faced about knowing their fate, wondering whether we should count ourselves blessed for having such knowledge or cursed?

Take for example Harvard professor Steven Pinker who wrote recently in *The New York Times Magazine* that, "One of the perks of being a psychologist is access to tools that allow you to carry out the injunction to know thyself."[32] And how does Pinker propose to "know himself?" Well, says the *Times*, he has had himself tested for things like "vocational interest (closest match: psychologist), intelligence (above average), personality (open, conscientious, not too neurotic) and political orientation (more libertarian than authoritarian)." He has had M.R.I. pictures done of his brain—"no obvious holes or bulges" (nice to know, I suppose)—and will soon undergo what the *Times* describes as "the ultimate test of marital love." "Children?" you ask. "Twenty years of waiting for a husband who is away at the Trojan War while suitors eagerly court you?" No. "The ultimate test of marital love," according to the *Times*, is to have your brain scanned while your spouse's name is subliminally flashed before your eyes. Well, that does test *something*, I suppose. But personally, before I would put too much stock in the results, I would want to correlate the brain scan data with the husbands who remain faithful and wives who actually wait patiently for their absent husbands while they were away at war. Only an intellectual could believe that a brain scan would be a better test of love.

But whatever the pros and cons of these various tests, the *Times* articles goes on to say that Professor Pinker has also taken advantage of what they describe as "the ultimate opportunity for self-knowledge." And what *is* the "ultimate opportunity for self-knowledge?" "Raising children?" you ask. "Fighting a hopeless battle against tyranny?" No again. Pinker, as it turns out, has had his genome sequenced and allowed it to be posted on the Internet, along with his medical history. "Affordable genotyping," reports Pinker enthusiastically, "may offer new kinds of answers to the question 'Who am I?'—to ruminations about our ancestry, our vulnerabilities, our character and our choices in life."

And yet, it is interesting that, even with all this information available to him, Pinker faced his own tough choice, one that his test results could not help him with: namely, whether to learn what, if any, genetic markers for

32. See Steven Pinker, "My Genome, My Self," *The New York Times Magazine*, January 7, 2009.

"horrible conditions that you can do nothing about," such as Huntington's Disease or Alzheimer's, the genetic sequencing had turned up? Pinker's reply was this: "I figured that my current burden of existential dread is just about right," so he chose to have this information withheld from him. Well, "know thyself," I guess.

But is selective ignorance the same as the Stoic acceptance of one's fate? Or is remaining ignorant in this way merely a form of denial—a way of prolonging the illusion of control, a way of avoiding the truth that life includes suffering and dying, privation and death?

Indeed, given the modern myth of scientific control, a "heroic" life tends to be seen, not as one where, like Epictetus or Aeneas, I accept my fate, but rather as one where I do battle with nature and fate to the last moment. My colleague Christopher Martin at the University of St. Thomas did some research in newspaper obituaries and found that phrases that involve "battling" death, such as "died after a long struggle," have largely replaced older formulations such as "rest in peace" or "died peacefully at home."

The ancient Greeks had their heroes, and we have ours: theirs learned to accept their fate with courage and still persevere in virtue, ours "struggle against death" to the last moment. They do not "give up" or "give in." They "rage, rage against the dying of the light," and "go not gentle into that dark night."[33]

And yet, when such people "lose hope"—that is, when they realize that technology will not restore an adequate quality of life that has come to characterize the young and upwardly mobile American upper-middle class—then they seek to have death administered to them. Suicide then becomes the last "heroic" act: the last act of "control" over nature and fate. But is this freedom? When many people—especially those who are young—increasingly understand suicide to be the ultimate act of self-affirmation, we know we have a culture that has lost much, if not all, of its hope in history.

III. False Hope in an Escape From History

Pain and suffering were supposed to be things of the past, as soon as we had ridden ourselves of the superstitions of Christianity and gave ourselves over fully to the sure guidance of science. And yet, the continued pain and suffering that characterizes the modern world has caused many of our con-

33. Dylan Thomas, "Do Not Go Gentle Into That Good Night."

temporaries to give way to new forms of gnosticism—so-called "New Age" *spiritualities*—which offer an escape from the busy-ness, and messiness, of our historical existence.

I will not say much here about the "new gnosticism" of these New Age spiritualities other than to observe that, ever since the days when men and women were encouraged to "leave it all behind" and go "find themselves" on a mountaintop in Tibet, or as was more likely, an ashram in Nevada, such spiritualties all too often seemed to involve forsaking all one's obligations and responsibilities to family, friends, and society. In this way, they seemed to me then, as they do now, well-attuned to the individualistic, ego-centric culture of the American bourgeois-bohemian classes, and not so much to the blue collar steelworkers and construction guys I grew up with near Pittsburgh.

Be that as it may, another way to "escape from history," Haught suggests in *Mystery and Promise*, is "the gnostic path of dreaming up some radically other world, to which we 'essentially' belong by virtue of an esoteric knowledge or 'gnosis,' membership in which therefore keeps us from having to dwell fully within the messiness of historical existence."[34] If history is essentially suffering, if time and change are the sources of disruption, perhaps wisdom, then, involves recognizing that the changing world of history is illusory, and beatitude is to be found in an escape from history—into an eternal or timeless or mythic realm.

Unfortunately, some people mistake this view with the Christian view of history. Life is but a "valley of tears," it is said. Our hope lies in an escape from history into the beatitude of heaven. Indeed, when I was a college student, contemplating my entry into the Catholic Church, my cradle-Catholic friend Dan Brennan said to me: "Smith, you've got a great opportunity now. After you're baptized, you'll be entirely free from sin. So if at the moment you leave the church, you get hit by a bus and killed, *bang*!—you'll go right to heaven."

"That's good to know, Dan," I told him. "But I think I'll try to stick around for a while, just in case there's something useful I can do on this end."

"Well, okay," he told me. "But it would be a shame to miss out on the chance. You never know whether you might end up falling into mortal sin and losing it all."

34. Haught, *Mystery and Promise*, chap. 9, para. 9.

"It's a risk," I admitted.

But he had a point. If heaven is so good, and this life is nothing but a "valley of tears," why not just get there? In fact, why has God put us here in this world at all? Just to torment us? Just to give us more chances to fall into mortal sin and make ourselves even more unworthy of heaven?

The existential challenges presented by views of the afterlife are twofold. On the one hand, if death is oblivion, it seems we need a notion of life after death in order to make this life meaning-*ful*. All this life, all this love, all these experiences, and then ... *nothing*? On the other hand, we cannot then rely upon a notion of life after death that in its own right makes this life meaning-*less*. My friend's get-out-while-the-gettin's-good view of the afterlife would, I suggest, *make* life meaningless. Authentic Christian faith does not.

IV. Faith, Hope, and History: Salvation History as the Basis for Human Meaning and thus for Human History Properly Speaking

Unlike some religions, Christianity does not describe events as occurring in some "mythical" time. Nor does it follow "the gnostic path of dreaming up some radically other world, to which we "essentially" belong, membership in which therefore keeps us from having to dwell fully within the messiness of historical existence. As T. S. Eliot insists:

> A people without history
> Is not redeemed from time.
>
> If all time is eternally present
> All time is unredeemable.
>
> Only through time time is conquered.[35]

Christian faith is not an escape from history and time; it is, rather, that "absolutely universal affirmation extending to the world as a whole, to the reality of things and the existence of man himself" described by Josef Pieper. "The Bible," writes Haught, "forbids our searching for meaning, salvation, or fulfillment completely apart from historical existence."[36] That is precisely the importance of speaking about salvation history. God's revelation of

35. See "Little Gidding," 233–34; "Burnt Norton," 4–5; "Burnt Norton," 90.
36. Haught, *Mystery and Promise*, chap. 9, para. 18.

Himself as the Creator who creates out of His infinite goodness and love, and as the Redeemer who rescues His People from slavery and makes a covenant with them, a covenant ratified ultimately by the blood of His Son, sacrificed on the cross at Calvary, opens up a new historical horizon for human aspiration.

> "Earth's the right place for love," wrote the poet
> Robert Frost,
> "I don't know where it's likely to go better."[37]

We must learn to live, therefore, says Haught, "by promise rather than prediction or tragic resignation."[38] That is to say, we must resist the two great human temptations to escape the mystery of history. The first is the temptation to attempt to control history for our own purposes by refining our skills at *prediction*. The second is the temptation to give way to *tragic resignation*, wash my hands of all responsibility for history and take refuge somewhere beyond it. We must learn to live, rather, by faith and hope in God's *promise* of His continuing providential care. To live in faith and hope means neither seeking to control history and subject it to our will nor simply escaping from it. It consists, rather, in seeing within history—even in its sufferings—a meaningful sacramental foretaste of a beatitude that is yet to be fully realized. Our task as humans is to live in the tension between being fully present to reality *now* while living forward toward that which is *not yet*. Hope is what allows us to live faithfully and authentically in that tension.

The reason Christians give for this hope lies neither in their greater predictive powers about the future, nor in a superior spiritual ability to quiet the self in the midst of turmoil. It lies, rather, in receptive hearts open to the love of the Lord of History, whose love was so great, we believe, that He entered into history to redeem history (and us) from its slavery to sin and its subjection to futility. And so, too, must we enter into history, neither seeking to escape from it, nor simply accepting its faults. Our faith in the ultimate meaningfulness of what will seem to most people to be "absurd," "utterly foolish" acts of self-sacrifice makes possible a hope that can give rise to a love that is neither passive, nor entirely needy, but which can instead be *transformative*.

37. Robert Frost, *Birches*, ll. 52–53.
38. Haught, *Mystery and Promise*, chap. 9, para. 10.

Allow me, if I may, to quote in this regard from one of my heroes: G. K. Chesterton. "Let us suppose," writes Chesterton, that "we are confronted with a desperate thing—say Pimlico," a once-fashionable London suburb that by Chesterton's time was considered part of the west-London slums.

> If we think what is really best for Pimlico we shall find the thread of thought leads to the throne or the mystic and the arbitrary. It is not enough for a man to disapprove of Pimlico: in that case he will merely cut his throat or move to Chelsea. Nor, certainly, is it enough for a man to approve of Pimlico: for then it will remain Pimlico, which would be awful. The only way out of it seems to be for somebody to love Pimlico: to love it with a transcendental tie and without any earthly reason. If there arose a man who loved Pimlico, then Pimlico would rise into ivory towers and golden pinnacles; Pimlico would attire herself as a woman does when she is loved.... If men loved Pimlico as mothers love children, arbitrarily, ... Pimlico in a year or two might be fairer than Florence. Some readers will say that this is a mere fantasy. I answer that this is the actual history of mankind. This, as a fact, is how cities did grow great. Go back to the darkest roots of civilization and you will find them knotted round some sacred stone or encircling some sacred well. People first paid honour to a spot and afterwards gained glory for it. Men did not love Rome because she was great. She was great because they had loved her.[39]

Consider the perspective that would make this transformation of Pimlico possible. It would not be a vision of Pimlico that avoids the reality of Pimlico's problems, its sufferings and shortcomings. That would be a flight from reality to un-reality, and whatever hope we might have for Pimlico's future would likely be illusory and empty—as empty as the slogans one often hears from politicians and public relations officials about "better times ahead" and "the best is yet to come."

Neither is the needed perspective one that would view Pimlico purely as *material* to be molded into the "ideal" town by those with superior technical skills. That would be to attempt to cut-and-form Pimlico to one's own image, not to love it for what *it is*. This would be a mere *conditional* sort of love, one that says: "I will love you Pimlico if you become the sort of thing I want you to be"—in other words, if and to the extent that I see you becoming *worthy* of my efforts on your behalf by allowing yourself to be molded by me. This is the short-road to the well-intentioned tyranny of the rational planner.

It hardly needs saying that these hopes are also likely to reveal themselves as ultimately empty and illusory in the long run, given the undeni-

39. G. K. Chesterton, *Orthodoxy* (New York: John Lane Company, 1909), 122–23.

ably "messy" character of particular, instantiated historical realities and their resistance to being forced into all pre-conceived, idealized mental schemes. So, for example, often when the past character of the place or the people begins to impinge on the purity of "the plan," planners often lose hope, as will many of those who put their faith in them and their plans. For in such cases, who could blame the plan, given its rational perfection and the purity of the motivations that created it? But this, too, is in its own way a flight from reality to unreality—the abstract unreality of "the plan." For even if Pimlico could be made to fit "the plan"—even if it could be shaped to fit my mental mold—what then? "The plan" is static; it exists outside of time. It is an end, not a beginning, as it must be, opening up to the (often uncertain) future.

In a similar way, all "happy endings" are the same; the time-line of the story must end there. If the story points to an uncertain future, then the ending is, to that extent at least, not "happy." But as all mature adults know, all such happy endings are based on false hopes. They are based on the illusion that the newly-married couple will never have problems; the newly-reconciled lovers will never argue again; or that the villagers brought together by struggle will not fall out with each other over the next petty difference. If the ending is to be "happy," it cannot be an end. It must be a beginning of something more, something new. "Happy endings" are thus profoundly anti-historical. They force an unnatural flight from the changeableness of history into an idealized state that can never in reality be maintained. The love people have for a place or a person will have to be fully *now* and *not yet*. One cannot love truly only for what someone or someplace might be *in the future*. And yet one's love is always "forward-looking" toward a more profound union and a deeper communion, one that present sins and infidelities can often stifle and obscure.

Thus what if instead of the various ways of fleeing from the reality of Pimlico, we could see Pimlico clearly and truly say of it: It is good that it exists. Even with all its problems and difficulties, it is *good*. And because it *is* good, we can love it, warts and all. I can see Pimlico now, not outside of or beyond time or reality, but precisely as something *real* and *in time*; and because *in time*, thus also *on the way* toward an end not yet in sight. The love that affirms that Pimlico is good, and that it is good that it exists, can see Pimlico's own inherent potential in ways that I, who wish only to shape Pimlico according to my own limited vision and plans, often cannot.

Instead of seeing Pimlico as the perfect matter to be molded by my genius, let us say that I begin to see it rather as something *beloved,* and so something to be treasured and cared for. Then it no longer serves *me* and *my* plans; rather I see myself in service *to it.* Now I no longer avoid its imperfections or see them as potential obstacles to "the plan," threats to my ever-expanding will-to-power, but as *particularities* that give the place its own special character and beauty. Before seeking to *change* it, I must first seek to *understand* and *appreciate it.* Then the transformation I wish for it will be in accord with its own proper nature and character—one that proceeds from within the special "genius of the place" (*genius loci*), not one that is merely "imposed" from without, even if imposed with the best of intentions. Instead of desiring that Pimlico become something *other than it is*—something more like Oxford or Cambridge or the Harvard Yard—now I wish for Pimlico *to be Pimlico,* but the Pimlico the one who truly loves it would want it to be: its inherent beauties unveiled, its inherent goodness demonstrated, the best elements of its character realized.

And yet it is precisely this sort of *faith* in its ultimate goodness—the goodness grounded in its very *being*—that would allow me to believe in its future without denying the difficulties and problems of its present. When it fails to live up to my expectations, I would not lose hope for it any more than I could lose my love of it. When I see clearly what it is, I see more clearly what it can be when it can finally express what is best in it, not merely what I can make of it. When I love Pimlico in this way, I do not attempt to control it, nor do I flee it for some idealized reality outside of or beyond time: the "spiritual" Pimlico apart from its embodied existence, or the "ideal" Pimlico of my dreams. Rather I begin to see Pimlico, as I should see the rest of the world, *with love,* as something *on the way* within time and history to an ultimate, unseen end, one that I believe in but cannot fully envision, faith being "the substance of things hoped for, the evidence of things unseen."[40]

Thus when I struggle to help Pimlico transform itself, I struggle in the knowledge that my job is not to see to it that all of Pimlico's shortcomings are destroyed or that they are rationalized into some overarching idealized plan. Rather, my job is simply to struggle, in the faith and with the hope that its shortcomings and sufferings, as well as mine, are all meaningful

40. Hebrews 11.1, KJV.

when viewed *sub specie aeternitatis*. The world is God's, and He alone is the Lord of History. My task is more limited, but not therefore unimportant nor unmeaningful. Perhaps, then, it is true, as T. E. Eliot suggests, that "the faith and the love and the hope are all in the waiting."[41]

Hope is what bridges the divide between the limited realities of the "here-and-now" and the infinite promise of the "not-yet." Hope is what enables us to connect the past stories of our lives with an uncertain future. For Christians, the reason for this hope is to be found in their faith in the Creator Who made this world at its origins and proclaimed it "good, very good," and who has redeemed that same fallen world with the blood of His Son and who sanctifies us with the gift of His Spirit. The one who died on the cross and rose from the dead holds out the promise of hope that life is meaningful even in the midst of sin, suffering, and the dark reality of death.

41. T. S. Eliot, "East Coker," III, 26; cf. n. 5 above.

≈IV≈

AESTHETIC TURN

C. A. TSAKIRIDOU

Spiritual Expressionism

Léon Bloy, the Maritains, and the Mystery of Israel[1]

"The Mystery of Israel" is included in *Redeeming the Time,* a collection of essays first published in 1943. Maritain's view of Israel in this period should be seen through the prism of his and Raïssa's encounter with the idiosyncratic spirituality of Léon Bloy (1846–1917), the French author and self-professed mystic, who became their godfather when they converted to Catholicism in 1906. Bloy's apocalyptic, anti-modern, and anti-bourgeois ideas, his conflicted personality, and claims of divine election and extreme suffering, gave him unprecedented psychological authority over the young couple and captured their imaginations for years to come. In reading what Jacques and Raïssa wrote about Israel and the Jewish people, we encounter elements of a spiritual expressionism that emphasizes intense psychological and emotional states and intimates a Manichean world: dark, pathetic and overwhelmed by sin, where holy souls do battle with evil. Bloy's identification of sainthood with artistic genius and his view of Israel as the protagonist of a great redemptive drama centered on the Passion of Christ, helped define the Maritains' vision of a vital, creative, and revolutionary Christianity.[2]

1. For Paul and Margot Soven.

2. John Howard Griffin and Yves R. Simon, *Jacques Maritain: Homage in Words and Pictures* (New York: Magi Books, 1974), 4–5.

I. The Jewish Passion

Maritain had discussed the persecution of European Jews a few years earlier in a lecture titled "A Christian Looks at the Jewish Question," given in Paris in 1938 and later that year in New York. In a 1921 essay, "On the Jewish Question," he presented Jews as being alien and adverse to a Christian civilization and as aligned with international finance and Masonic intrigues.[3] In his study of the development of Maritain's thought on this subject, Richard Crane has put these views in their proper historical and social context, pointing out, among other things, that Maritain's friend and mentor, Charles Péguy, an adamant defender of Captain Alfred Dreyfus, easily divided Jews between those governed by a spirit of avarice and those who embraced a spirit of poverty.[4] These divisions and the ambiguities they imply remained with Maritain in the pre-World War II period and are very much present in "The Mystery of Israel." The essay examines the spiritual and philosophical aspects of the problem, specifically the notion that Israel has a divine vocation and that anti-Semitism is a spiritual phenomenon. Maritain's approach is "metaphysical and religious" and is concerned with the "hidden and sacred meaning" of events affecting Jews living in Europe and elsewhere in the world.[5]

There are two obvious difficulties with what Maritain is trying to do in this essay. The first is that, as Zygmunt Bauman has shown in his book *Modernity and the Holocaust*, anti-Semitism in itself, as a ubiquitous phenomenon in many societies and especially dominant in late nineteenth-century France, is not sufficient to explain the systematic extermination of Jews under the Nazi regime.[6] What is needed, according to Bauman, is an understanding of the political and social mechanisms by means of which anti-Jewish violence was organized and dispensed on this catastrophic scale.[7] Even though Bauman's argument targets the Holocaust, it can be extended to other acts of violence aimed at Jews and their institutional and ideo-

3. Richard Francis Crane, *Passion of Israel: Jacques Maritain, Catholic Conscience and the Holocaust* (Scranton, Pennsylvania: University of Scranton Press, 2010), 10.

4. Ibid., 13–14.

5. Jacques Maritain, *Redeeming the Time*, translated by Harry Lorin Binsse (London: Geoffrey Bless, 1946), 124.

6. See Zygmunt Bauman, *Modernity and the Holocaust* (Ithaca, New York: Cornell University Press, 1989), 31–32.

7. See ibid., 33.

logical contexts. By approaching anti-Semitism as a "spiritual disease" and largely ignoring these factors, Maritain was depriving his analysis of the critical perspective that, according to his friend and student, the philosopher Yves Simon, was essential to understanding the scope and range of French Catholic anti-Semitism.[8]

Secondly, Maritain assigns to Jews a collective destiny because of who they are or what they have done, and explains, on that basis, acts of violence and oppression committed against them. By stating, for example, that "the mystical body of Israel is a Church fallen from a high place," he is in effect saying that all Jews, wherever they are, are subject to this collective failure or error.[9] The fact that by "Israel" here is meant a spiritual state and not a race or people as such, does not alter the concrete historical and political consequences which necessarily follow from this condition. Thus analogies between the Diaspora and the Body of Christ in Communion—where Israel, like the Host, must be broken and shared by humanity ("the earthly leavening of the world")—point at the necessity of Jewish dispersion, fragmentation, and suffering.[10] Furthermore, when Maritain writes in 1938 that Israel's persecution will end "only with the reconciliation of the Synagogue and the Church," what he means by reconciliation is not co-existence but conversion.[11] From an eschatological standpoint, Jewish suffering is therefore justified and inevitable: justified because of the rejection of Christ, and inevitable because of a divinely ordained imperative of conversion through suffering which, set in motion like a Hegelian dialectic, gradually clears the "obscuring mist" of Jewish piety and brings it to Christ.[12]

In an essay published in Robert Royal's *Jacques Maritain and the Jews* (1994), John Hellman has argued that at least prior to World War II, Maritain believed that Jews could only find spiritual fulfillment in Christianity and that their inadequate spiritual state was the cause of the subversive role that they played in society. He also showed how indebted this view was to the writings of Bloy and specifically his book, not translated in English, *Le*

8. See Maritain, *Redeeming the Time*, 126; John Hellman, "The Jews in the 'New Middle Ages': Jacques Maritain's Anti-Semitism in Its Times," in *Jacques Maritain and the Jews*, edited by Robert Royal (Notre Dame, Indiana: American Maritain Association, 1994), 89–103.

9. Maritain, *Redeeming the Time*, 134.

10. Ibid., 134, 136.

11. Jacques Maritain, *A Christian Looks at the Jewish Question* (New York: Longmans, Green, and Company, 1939), 33.

12. Maritain, *Redeeming the Time*, 135.

Salut par les Juifs (1892). Hellman's characterization of this work as Bloy's "most vitriolic and anti-Semitic diatribe," is accurate and hard to challenge, particularly when considering his description of Jews as "venomous parasites," or of Jewish merchants that he encountered in Hamburg as "impure profiteers whose obsequious howling clings to me."[13] Bloy's revulsion for Jewish physical existence is supposedly mitigated by his recognition of Israel's spiritual majesty, a majesty, however, that is possible only when Israel and the Jewish people are seen as progenitors of Christ and their religion is assimilated into the life and destiny of the Church.

It is true that the Jewish critic and journalist Bernard Lazare, a friend of Péguy, considered Bloy a "philosemite" who at least allowed Jews to survive as unwilling witnesses to the divine Passion and catalysts to salvation.[14] Lazare's view is an important reminder of the need to appreciate the cultural and ideological environment in which Bloy's and Maritain's ideas were developed and thus to avoid an anachronistic assessment of their thought. Indeed, when compared to other Christian writers of the time, especially the anti-Semite Edouard Drumont (1844–1917), Bloy clearly embraced the co-existence of Jews and Christians and idealized the religious Jew. Still, the fact that Lazare's surprising endorsement of *Le Salut* in 1892 did not stop Bloy from reasserting his view of Jews as justly oppressed for being the most "despicable" oppressors of the poor, points at the conflicted nature of Bloy's attitudes.[15] The same applies to Maritain. His claim in the essay that "Israel has quit reality for an illusory image, money," an idea that he assigns to Bloy as one of his "most profound themes," shows clearly that he had not at the time abandoned dangerous stereotypes.[16]

Like Bloy, who saw in the religious Jew a reflection of the genealogy of Christ and his Mother, and thus as a type of holy image that Christians should reverence, Maritain condemns anti-Semitism because it is essentially an affront to Christ. It is Christ that sanctifies the Jewish race "despite itself."[17] Judaism is thus deprived of its distinct theological and spiritual voice and the Jews of the right to a Jewish salvation, while in their social existence Jews are viewed as compulsive capitalists, whose inordinate pas-

13. Hellman, "The Jews in the Middle Ages," 90.

14. Nelly Wilson, *Bernard-Lazare: Antisemitism and the Problem of Jewish Identity in Late Nineteenth-Century France* (Cambridge: Cambridge University Press, 1978), 87–88.

15. Ibid., 237 n. 37.

16. Maritain, *Redeeming the Time*, 153.

17. Ibid., 155

sion for the world ("materialized Messianism") leads to the exploitation of the poor.[18] Israel is "mystically" drawn to money, "the poor man's blood," a Bloy expression that Maritain adopts.[19] But Israel is also drawn to the service of God's justice on earth ("Israel's other center of attraction").[20] Jews, in other words, have replaced their passion for God either with a passion for wealth or with a passion for worldly justice. Unwilling members of a divine drama, they exist in a state of alienation from God.

For Maritain, the conversion of Jews to Christianity is preordained, as is the suffering that their rejection of Christ brings upon them, such as the Diaspora, persecutions in the hands of gentile nations, and enslavement to materialism. In the Royal volume, Rabbi Leon Klenicki uses Martin Buber's expression to describe Maritain as a "metaphysical anti-Semite."[21] On the other hand, Crane describes Maritain's attitude to Jews as "ambiguous philosemitism." After taking a thorough look at the intellectual, religious, and social context that informed Maritain's views, Crane concludes that he "wrestled with a theological mystery that cannot be avoided when examining the long story of Jewish-Christian relations."[22]

Crane actually quotes a passage which, far from settling the matter, as he thinks, shows exactly where the problem lies. Writing in 1944 to his friend and future Cardinal, Charles Journet, Maritain confesses that he finds the suffering of the Jews unbearable and expresses his frustration with how Christians "have not comprehended the divine tragedy, the sacred horror of this Golgotha of a people."[23] The extermination of Jews is here a Christian rather than a Jewish tragedy. It is seen through "Golgotha" rather than "Egypt" or "Babylon." Jewish suffering is sanctified and we are presented with the spectacle of a "sacred horror," an unfolding sacred drama. Why didn't a Catholic intellectual, an advocate of Thomistic catholicity, see in Jewish suffering a simply human suffering, the direct result of human prejudice and malice? Why was he drawn, instead, to the image of Jews grafted onto the Passion of Christ, a perpetual reminder of their role in deicide? Didn't the bestowed honor affirm the offense and even exaggerate it?

18. Ibid., 147.

19. Ibid., 140.

20. Ibid., 140–141.

21. Leon Klenicki, "Jacques Maritain's Vision of Judaism and Anti-Semitism," in *Jacques Maritain and the Jews*, 72–88.

22. Richard Francis Crane, "Jacques Maritain, the Mystery of Israel and the Holocaust," *The Catholic Historical Review* 95, no. 1 (2009): 25–56.

23. Ibid., 56.

The notion that the state of Israel is an exception to the "law" that drives the majority of the Jews to live in the Diaspora, outside "temporal society," and that neither nationhood nor statehood is appropriate to a people charged with a "mysterious historic mission," seems to condemn Jews to perpetual exile while depriving them of a homeland and the right to self-determination.[24] Certainly Maritain did not oppose the existence of a Jewish state and certainly the idea that only God can establish a state for Israel in his own good time has been entertained by Jewish sages and rabbis. The idea itself is not problematic. What is problematic is the fact that consideration of the dangers affecting stateless peoples and especially those persecuted for their otherness is entirely absent from Maritain's vision of Israel, a vision which the "consecrated tribe," bound, as he puts it, to "the law of the desert," wanders in the wilderness until, like a decimated prodigal son, it returns home to the God of Christianity.[25]

We cannot help but wonder why the Maritains did not approach Israel from the standpoint of Maritain's 1927 essay "Primacy of the Spiritual." In this essay, in what was to become one of the dominant themes of Vatican II (1962–65), Maritain embraces a universal rationalism mediated by Christ and promulgated by the Church, in which all nations, even those that are not Christian, can participate by virtue of the "hidden stepping stones" that God has placed in every corner of the world.[26] "Man and reason," he writes in that spirit, "are everywhere the same."[27] Anticipating Benedict XVI in Regensburg, Maritain warns that the evils of history are the result of human error; of the abandonment of "the absolutism of truth and charity," rather than the unfolding of a divine drama.[28] There is, to be sure, a sense of apocalyptic urgency in what Maritain writes in this work that recalls Bloy, but the overall approach is optimistic and centers on the illuminating and salvific work of Christian reason and of a Christian humanism that in the end will prevail.

Instead of integrating Israel in this humanistic and lucid vision, Jacques and Raïssa chose a far more obscure alternative, a vision in which unconverted Jews are subject to dramatic, if not catastrophic, spiritual and mate-

24. Maritain, *Redeeming the Time*, 129.

25. Ibid., 130, 151.

26. *The Social and Political Philosophy of Jacques Maritain*, edited by Joseph W. Evans and Leo R. Ward (New York: Image Books, 1965), 150.

27. Ibid.

28. Ibid., 151.

rial consequences, and the excruciating suffering caused by their rejection of Christ is in reality the expression of divine mercy. True, the notion of divine punishment for disobedience is found in the prophetic tradition and in the Old Testament, as is God's mercy for the punished. But why, given the virulent anti-Semitism of French society at the time, rely on such politically and viscerally charged notions of Jewish separation, opposition, and punishment? This lack of discernment is puzzling. And so are the ideas that history at once punishes and redeems Jews by assimilating them to Christianity through centuries of suffering—every suffering Jew being an *alter Christus*—and that Nazi anti-Semitism is actually an opposition to Christ. The Jews are hated and killed, Maritain argues, because they gave Christ, a Jew, to the world. This makes Nazis Christophobes and murdered Jews de facto Christians: a conversion by death in which they have no say. Why would Jacques and Raïssa think this way?

II. A Soul Oppressed by Genius

Bloy's view of Israel shaped the Maritains' first encounter with Christian spirituality and their subsequent conversion. The young couple's friendship with Bloy was sealed by *Le Salut par les Juifs*. The book's subject was of more direct relevance to Raïssa (née Oumancoff), a Jewish émigré, than to Jacques, but the two had been impressed earlier by Bloy's novel *The Woman who was Poor* (1897), in which abject poverty became a supernatural virtue and the antidote to bourgeois charity.[29] Like the novel's wretched heroine, an equally destitute Israel was to find redemption in unmitigated suffering and rejection.[30] There were, of course, other factors involved, such as Maritain's attraction, during that period, to the reactionary politics of *L'Action Francaise*, the association of neo-Thomist thought with that movement (e.g., in Father Humbert Clerrisac, whom the Maritains admired, or Father Reginald Garrigou-Lagrange, in the case of the Pétain regime), and the popularity of anti-Semitic ideas and stereotypes in late nineteenth-century and pre-World II France. But the psycho-spiritual and aesthetic elements are essential for understanding the persistence of

29. See Julie Kernan, *Our Friend Jacques Maritain: A Personal Memoir* (New York: Doubleday, 1973), 29.

30. See Stephen Schloesser, *Jazz Age Catholicism: Mystic Modernism in Postwar Paris 1919–1933* (Toronto: University of Toronto Press, 2005), 66–67.

these themes in their thought and their inability to see Bloy's spirituality for what it really was.

The Maritains' emotional and intellectual vulnerability to this self-professed prophet and mystic is undoubtedly related to the tragic circumstances of their conversion to Catholicism: the suicide of Maritain's father in February of 1904, and Raïssa's life-threatening illnesses in the winter of 1906 and again in 1907—a pattern that would continue throughout her life. These events exacerbated the sense of displacement and disorientation that the two were experiencing at the time, especially in the case of Raïssa, the daughter of Jewish immigrants from Russia who arrived in Paris in 1893, one year before the eruption of the Dreyfus affair (1894). Coupled with their little knowledge of Catholicism and Judaism, they created a psychological and spiritual vacuum in which the exaggerated religiosity of Bloy, expressed in an imagery of prophetic rage and self-immolation, would find little resistance let alone critical judgment.[31] When Raïssa's life was placed in the hands of Our Lady of La Salette, whose personal emissary Bloy claimed to be, the newly converted Maritains found in her recovery and Bloy's explosive piety the certainty that had eluded them in their university years. They also found themselves immersed in a cosmic drama, in which their personal lives could be totally absorbed and transfigured.

The influence of Bloy on Raïssa and Jacques has been discussed extensively in this connection, but the aestheticism involved in their fascination with Bloy has not. Bloy's morbid and Manichean view of Christ's Passion, coupled with his manipulative narcissism and decadent piety, had a lasting impact on the Maritains, who became his awe-struck audience and eager patrons. This entry in Bloy's diary on June 20, 1921, on the day that he received their letter of interest, is quite revealing: "a young man and his wife suddenly offer themselves to become our friends, at the same time expressing their ambition to *make themselves useful* (emphasis added)."[32] In his response the next day, in a letter that Raïssa included in her anthology of his works, he mentions his dire financial situation three times and thanks them for the money they already sent him.[33] In 1906, days before Raïssa's illness and a few months before their conversion in June of the same year,

31. See ibid., 71.

32. Raïssa Maritain, *We Have Been Friends Together: Memoirs*, translated by Julie Kernan (New York: Longmans, Green and Company, 1942), 117.

33. See ibid., 116.

she and Jacques paid for the re-publication of *Le Salut par les Juifs*, which the grateful Bloy dedicated to Raïssa. Later the Maritains also financed the publication of *Celle Qui Pleure*, Bloy's book on the La Salette apparitions.[34]

"The Mystery of Israel" is heavily indebted to *Le Salut*. Even though, as expected, its arguments are more sophisticated and sober, the iconography of Israel remains the same. Thus, on the one hand we have the universality and transcendent unity of the Church, and on other the "mystical body" of Israel which has been condemned to be "disjointed from itself, broken and dispersed" because of its unfaithfulness.[35] This brokenness also takes a spiritual form since Jewish piety, according to Maritain, is in reality nothing more than the exiled Jew's unconscious embracing of Christ's passion, "without realizing what he does."[36] The Jew, then, is not really a Jew. Maritain takes a dialectical perspective when he writes that the Jews are the spiritual cause of the "misfortunes" that "activate history" and thus its natural "scapegoats."[37] Even the most lenient reader must try hard to justify these ideas and the image of Israel as a people that is both opposed to and grafted into Christ, and tries hopelessly—since nothing can stop this divinely ordained progression—to bring salvation to an unwilling and hateful world: "Israel thus suffers the repercussion of the activation it produces, or which the world feels it is destined to produce."[38] The most generous thing that we could say about this statement is that it paints Jews as the mystically sanctified victims of the enemies of Christ.

The idea of extreme suffering and degradation for the sake of God was one of Bloy's signature themes (or obsessions). From a fierce and fearless prophet ("I obey a command from on high"), to a destitute and tormented mystic ("buffeted, spit upon, scourged, crucified"), Bloy was convinced of his divinely ordained mission and supernatural gifts, and his "mysterious affinity" with the saints.[39] It was a strange mixture of self-pity and arrogance, megalomania and humility, an image that Bloy carefully cultivated throughout his life and one that had a powerful attraction for Jacques and Raïssa, as can be easily seen in Raïssa's recollections of that time. In her memoir, *We Have Been Friends Together* (1942), she explains statements like

34. See Emmanuela Polimeni, *Leon Bloy: The Pauper Prophet* (New York: Philosophical Library, 1951), 53.

35. Maritain, *Redeeming the Time*, 134.

36. Ibid., 135.

37. Ibid., 136.

38. Ibid., 137, 130.

39. Raïssa Maritain, *We Have Been Friends Together*, 106, 117, 114.

"anyone who is not instinctively disgusted by the Synagogue is unworthy of a dog's respect" as flamboyant rhetoric and hyperbole, and marvels at Bloy's "adamantine impartiality" because he heaps similar insults on Christians, describing them as "swine" who like the "pigs of the Synagogue" are being fed by Christ's blood.[40]

Her admiration for Bloy has a devotional quality that is hard to miss: "Grandeur, simplicity, unshakable conviction, disdain for contingencies, singleness of purpose likened him in our eyes to one of those sturdy and magnificent messengers of God."[41] She compares him to "a torrent which drags the rocks and trees from its banks and carries them headlong with the mud and the pebbles from its bed."[42] "Life," she writes of their first encounter, "cast him upon our shores like a legendary treasure—immense and mysterious."[43] His medieval vision of Jews in *Le Salut* may have expressed "inadmissible" detestation but it was to be excused because of its mystical artistry.[44] Bloy, Raïssa explained, "painted a picture of the Jewish people which was a contrast in light and shadow. The picture he purposely blackened at times, so that its light might shine forth all the more brightly."[45] Bloy was sublime, immense, a force to be reckoned with, a modern day Jonah, a man of genius who "suffered the captivity of misery, the anguish of solitude, the harsh contact with mediocrity," in short an avant-garde genius who painted what God revealed to him in dramatic and violent tones, who delighted in extremes and loved to shock his readers with a morbid and vulgar imagery.[46]

He was not the last narcissist to have seduced the Maritains. Jean Cocteau, as I have shown elsewhere, appealed to them for a very similar combination of qualities: Christ-like suffering stemming from a life-long opium addiction and a misunderstood and vilified genius (much like Bloy).[47] The Maritains were introduced to the work of Cocteau through Georges Auric, who was also a frequent guest in the Bloy household. Like Bloy, Cocteau was a master of self-promotion and particularly adept at performing the role of the immolated soul to an eager audience. The title of his 1930 film, *Blood of a Poet* echoes, as was Cocteau's habit, Bloy's *Le Sang du Pauvre* (1909), and so do other Bloy expressions that he and Maritain used in

40. Ibid., 125.
41. Ibid., 106.
42. Ibid., 109.
43. Ibid., 120.
44. Ibid., 124.
45. Ibid.
46. Ibid., 111–112.

their correspondence, like that of a glove turned inside out, an image that in Bloy describes the conversion of Israel and that Cocteau later adapted to his own homoerotic fantasies and verse.[48]

As Schloesser has shown, Cocteau succeeded in enchanting Maritain and convincing him that his was the genuine avant-garde aesthetic, one that centered on the notion of the artist as a sacramental being that penetrated through unconscious processes, deeper realities, and profound truths.[49] Maritain's praise of Cocteau in a 1923 letter as "a soul sought out by the angels," is typical of the kind of exchange between the two that culminated in their published correspondence, *Art and Faith: Letters between Jacques Maritain and Jean Cocteau* (1948).[50] Only later would Maritain realize the frivolous nature of Cocteau's anti-modernism and Catholic fervor.

Maritain's introduction to the 1947 English edition of *Pilgrim of the Absolute*, a collection of Bloy's writings edited by Raïssa, presents his godfather's manic personality and penchant for vitriol as evidence of mystical and artistic gifts granted to him by divine grace: "In this violence one must see, first of all, the effect of a very special kind of abstraction, certainly not philosophical but *artistic*, or, if one prefers a very special kind of typification; every event, every gesture, every person, here and now, was instantaneously transposed . . . and transformed, in the eyes of this fearful visionary, into the pure symbol of some devouring spiritual reality."[51] Bloy is portrayed as a man possessed by God who sees people and the world around him as divine signs, a mixture of prophet and artist, whose incinerating visions create a supreme spiritual art. In the same essay, Maritain describes his godfather as "a soul whom genius oppressed."[52]

Here, spirituality becomes an aesthetic condition, and one can almost

47. See Cornelia Tsakiridou, "'Redeeming Modernism': Jacques Maritain and the Catholic Vocation," in *The Vocation of the Catholic Philosopher*, edited by John P. Hittinger (Washington, D.C.: American Maritain Association, 2010), 94–109.

48. See Hellman, "The Jews in the Middle Ages," 93; Jacques Maritain, *Art and Faith: Letters Between Jacques Maritain and Jean Cocteau*, translated by John Coleman (New York: Philosophical Library, 1948), 21.

49. See Schloesser, *Jazz Age Catholicism*, 148.

50. Ibid., 177.

51. Bloy supporter, Emile LaDouceur, writes: "It is difficult indeed to condone or to justify his unwise polemics and his intemperate outbursts of temper." Bloy was incapable of holding a job, which explains his poverty. Léon Bloy, *She Who Weeps, Our Lady of La Salette*, translated and edited by Emile LaDouceur (Fresno: Academy Library Guild, 1956), 12–13. Also see Raïssa Maritain, *Léon Bloy: Pilgrim of the Absolute* (New York: Pantheon Books, 1947), 11.

52. Raïssa Maritain, *Léon Bloy: Pilgrim of the Absolute*, 9.

see Bloy as a grand master of visions and visitations, or perhaps more accurately, a spiritual conjurer and master of "mystical keys" that tries to make the tangible sing for God.[53] Another expressionist icon follows: "the feeling of mystery, so pure in itself, so lofty in Bloy, sometimes translates itself by means of lighting flashes and a darkness which is too material."[54] Bloy, Maritain writes, lived in a "spiritual universe," immersed in a sorrow that followed him from his early childhood, and suffered visions that made him impatient with the world's "perishable forms," which he did not hesitate to angrily deplore.[55] Bloy's Pythic explanation, "my anger is the effervescence of my pity," recalls the self-ennobling aphorisms used by Cocteau, and resonates with Maritain who comments: "he felt he could treat men like signs or counters with which his art spelled out the mercy or the indignation of God."[56]

In his remarks, Maritain urges the reader who wishes to understand Bloy's struggle for sanctity to read a letter he wrote to Jean de la Laurencie. In it, Bloy professes humility but with a clear conviction of his supernatural gifts, "the feeling, the need, the instinct ... of the Absolute, ... an extremely rare gift," which he confesses to have wasted.[57] Suffering in his vocation as a writer, failing in his call to be a saint, ever in tears, but never in doubt of his prophetic and literary genius, Bloy delights in seeing Christian life as a perpetual course of misery, pain, and darkness, and elevates his suffering to a mystery worthy of contemplation. As observed Sister Mary Rosalie Brady in her incisive 1945 study of Bloy's thought, his was a Tertullian vision that degraded the body and saw no merit in improving the condition of the poor through social and economic means—contrary to Church teaching (Leo XIII's *Rerum Novarum*).[58] Rather than celebrate the joyful mysteries of the Church, Bloy saw them as occasions for even more intense suffering. "In all these reflections," Brady writes, "he puts a natural pathology on a supernatural level."[59] Bloy's claim that he was the recipient of a supernatural secret (for which, apparently, a confessor's approval was never sought or given), as well as his bragging (apropos of the baptism of

53. Ibid.

54. Ibid.

55. Ibid., 12.

56. Ibid., 13.

57. Ibid., 293.

58. See Sr. Mary Rosalie Brady, *Thought and Style in the Works of Léon Bloy* (Washington D.C.: The Catholic University of America Press, 1945), 29.

59. Ibid., 32.

Jacques and Raïssa) that his books "were approved not by a Bishop or a Doctor but by the Holy Spirit," raise serious questions about the integrity of his Catholicism.[60]

One of the most revealing examples that Brady cites is Bloy's identification of genius with the Holy Spirit: "Talent, which everybody in the world loves, belongs to the Father and the Son. Genius, which everybody in the world hates, belongs exclusively to the Holy Spirit."[61] The self-referential nature of this statement is hard to miss since it was Bloy himself who, like the Holy Ghost, was a genius hated and misunderstood by the world. Here, the tormented and vilified artist or mystic (the two are actually interchangeable) participates in the life of the Holy Spirit. When he suffers, so does the Holy Spirit. In this passage from *Pilgrim of the Absolute*, Bloy claims extraordinary insights into the mystery of the Trinity: "Remember also this thing which long ago was revealed to me, and which I *alone* in the world have been able to say, namely, that this Sign of suffering and ignominy is the most expressive figure of the Holy Ghost."[62] Read together, the two statements paint a picture of spiritual and artistic election that is inundated with theological error and grandiosity.[63]

Like a somnambulist and a clairvoyant, Bloy, as he writes to Jacques, discovers truths that elude philosophy, "tripping blindly over a threshold and being thrown flat on one's stomach into the House of Light."[64] Sanctified by the "Absolute," the direct sight of which makes him godlike and allows him to see in the souls of others, he travels back to the time of the Jewish patriarchs and recognizes Raïssa's Christian soul.[65] Or, he turns to Israel and sees the "constant lingering" of the Holy Spirit Who manifests Himself in the wretched of the world. Thus "the very abjectness of that Race is a divine sign," Bloy writes, reminding us of Maritain's attempt to explain his penchant for vulgarisms and the grotesque as a mystical code or a spiritual symbolism of a literary genius.[66]

It is clear that Bloy felt at liberty to create his own theological imagery.

60. Ibid., 27, 52, 64–65.

61. Ibid., 53 (my translation).

62. Raïssa Maritain, *Léon Bloy: Pilgrim of the Absolute*, 338.

63. See Rayner Heppenstall, *Léon Bloy* (New Haven, Connecticut: Yale University Press, 1954), 47–48, 54.

64. Raïssa Maritain, *Léon Bloy: Pilgrim of the Absolute*, 278.

65. See ibid., 277.

66. Ibid., 269.

Apocalyptic visions of the Cross as the Holy Spirit revealed only to him, and given in flashes of revelation ("the very tip of the arms of lightning") that illuminate a dark and condemned world accompany the familiar theme of deicide where Jews nail the Word of God on the Cross as a sign of "crushing Love."[67] Part Symbolist, in its effort to interiorize and reconfigure reality, part Expressionist, in its fascination with distortion and emotional intensities, it is an imagery that draws its energy from an undisputed center: the ineffable and inexplicable subject immersed in its own sublimity (Bloy himself). Maritain's attempt to explain Bloy's genius shows how little he understood the play of these elements in Bloy's work and perhaps more significantly how indebted his own views of the spiritual life and art remained to Bloy's ideas.

Bloy's style, Maritain writes, uses words "to procure, as he used to say, the feeling of mystery and of its actual presence."[68] Everything is intended to "express reality in the very darkness that joins it to this feeling," and the language therefore, as St. Thomas would concur, "endeavors primarily to make you divine reality, to make you touch it without saying it."[69] Compare Heppenstall's view of Bloy's work: "In modern times no Frenchman has written prose so riotously excessive."[70] Maritain describes Bloy as a mystical illustrator who strives to make the divine realities that are revealed to him visible to others. Language in his hands becomes an instrument for creating similes and figures which are meant to awaken the mind to this hidden world. And he concludes with a poetic remark of the type that often appears in his writings about art: "All his literary efforts," he says of Bloy, "consisted in projecting in the mirror of enigmas and similitudes the rays of this substantially luminous night."[71] It is hard to tell what Maritain is describing here.

The image of Bloy as the archetypal Christian artist-mystic is easily identified in *Art and Scholasticism* but is less pronounced in *Creative Intuition in Art and Poetry* (1953). The former's third and final revision in 1935 pairs Bloy with Rembrandt as examples of great artists who have the license not to work for a living and support their families.[72] Statements like

67. Ibid., 253.

68. Ibid., 19.

69. Ibid., 19–20.

70. Heppenstall, *Léon Bloy*, 45.

71. Raïssa Maritain, *Léon Bloy: Pilgrim of the Absolute*, 20.

72. Jacques Maritain, *Art and Scholasticism and the Frontiers of Poetry*, translated by Joseph W. Evans (New York: Charles Scribner's Sons, 1962), 15–16.

the following fit Bloy perfectly: "The Artist is subject, in the sphere of his art, to a kind of asceticism, which may require heroic sacrifices.... He must pass through spiritual nights, purify himself without ceasing, voluntarily abandon fertile regions for regions that are barren and full of insecurity."[73] Cocteau is recalled in this context for yet another of his pan-artistic aphorisms that apparently impressed Maritain (it was repeated in *Creative Intuition*), who seems to overlook the significance the term "angel" had in Cocteau's poetry (e.g., his 1925 *L'ange Heurtebise*): "We shelter in ourselves an Angel whom we constantly shock. We must be the guardians of this angel. Shelter your virtue."[74]

Aesthetic virtue, comparable to that of the ascetic, is justified by art's intrinsic prudence. The artist's sanctity is art's work. But some artists, Maritain observes, still "opt for the devil," something that apparently art's prudence cannot prevent.[75] Among the few who choose Christ, "Léon Bloy and Paul Claudel have particular historical significance. Through them the absolute of the Gospel has entered into the sap of contemporary art."[76] The influence of both men and of Bloy, in particular, on modern art is here overestimated. Maritain's enthusiasm and spiritual aspirations influence his judgment.

III. A Darker Picture

In his 1953 study Rayner Heppenstall, the British novelist and critic (himself a Catholic convert and once fascinated by Bloy's poverty mysticism), gives one of the most negative portraits of Bloy as a man troubled by "symptoms of persecution mania and other recognized forms of psychosis," including "coprophilia, sado-masochism and narcissism."[77] Heppenstall's analysis systematically uncovers the inconsistencies and contradictions in Bloy's statements and actions, from the more benign tendency to exaggerate his self-importance and literary legacy, to his belief that his mistress Anne-Marie Roulet had apocalyptic visions about the Day of Judgment in which he was destined to play the role of St. John the Baptist.[78] Roulet be-

73. Ibid., 78.

74. Ibid. Also see Jacques Maritain, *Creative Intuition in Art and Poetry*, Bollingen Series, vol. 35.1 (Princeton: Princeton University Press, 1953), 392.

75. Maritain, *Art and Scholasticism and the Frontiers of Poetry*, 138.

76. Ibid.

77. Heppenstall, *Léon Bloy*, 37.

78. See ibid., 12, 40.

came the character Véronique in Bloy's 1887 novel *Despairing,* who in an ultimate act of chastity tries to nullify her lover's passion by parting with her hair and teeth.[79] In real life, Roulet (who was a prostitute when they met) and Bloy ended their relationship and lived as spiritual partners before she was overcome by madness and committed to the Bon-Saveur asylum outside Paris, where she died in 1907. According to Heppenstall, Bloy may have sent money to the asylum but never visited her in the 25 years that she spent there.[80]

His habit of soliciting money from friends and first acquaintances is well-documented, as we saw in the case of the Maritains. Bloy could actually be quite pressing, as happened in the case of a wealthy donor, a woman who gave him 200 francs, and was reproached for not offering a higher amount to support the publication of one of his books.[81] He apparently lied about payments that he received from his publisher and his own contribution to his poverty, whether due to incapacity or choice or both.[82] This self-imposed poverty becomes an aesthetic element in his novels, which like the early paintings of his friend Georges Rouault, are obsessed with unmitigated depravity, darkness, and sin.

The last chapter of *The Woman who was Poor* (included in Raïssa's anthology), paints a gothic portrait of the heroine Clotilde as she "walks from cemetery to cemetery," her head "covered only with the hood of a large black cape," moving around on her knees, "her eyes burned out with the tears that have furrowed ravines in her face."[83] Bloy's equation of poverty with utter destitution leads him to absurd conclusions like this: "woman only *exists,* in the truest sense, if she is without food, without shelter, without friends, without husband, without children.... [O]nly thus can she compel her Saviour to come down."[84]

The novel concludes with Clotilde's occasional visits to Lazare Druide, a painter of grotesque and morbid paintings of passion, who was "like Delacroix, reproached for the poverty of his drawing, the frenzy of his colouring."[85] Druide painted a picture titled *Andronicus Delivered to the Populace of Byzantium,* a picture of torment, blood, and death in which Andronicus

79. See ibid., 11.

80. See ibid., 11–12.

81. See ibid., 37–38; Brady, *Thought and Style in the Works of Léon Bloy,* 36.

82. See ibid., 39.

83. Léon Bloy, *The Woman Who Was Poor,* translated by I. J. Collins (Lanham, Maryland: Sheed and Ward, 1947), 353.

84. Ibid., 353, 355.

85. Ibid., 169.

appears like a "Redeemer" figure as the hateful crowds, "their eyes dazzled with the sun of torture," delight in his demise.[86] The narrator marvels that the "composition, vast as its scale is, bursts with its content, and the breathless drama overflows it, and surges out, like a dragon, into the midst of the terrified spectators themselves."[87] In what seems like a self-portrait, Bloy describes Druide in these terms: "swift as a volcano, and no less sonorous, when some boor was disrespectful, his fury, instantly pathetic, would burst forth, to the confusion of the Philistine, from the heart of a politeness so exquisite."[88]

It was this kind of bipolar sensibility that the Maritains encountered in 1905. Raïssa quotes Jacques' description of their first encounter with Bloy from his Preface to the *Letters of Léon Bloy to his Godchildren* (reprinted in the 1947 edition of *Pilgrim of the Absolute*). It reads like a fairy tale: "June 25, 1905, two children of twenty mounted the sempiternal stairway."[89] They were destined to meet the "strange beggar who, distrusting philosophy, cried divine truth from the rooftops," and whose "unsheltered greatness" would fill them with compassion. Bloy, Maritain recalls, "seemed almost timid, he spoke but very little and very low." Writing in 1942, Raïssa remembers that they felt "enriched by a unique friendship, *so gentle on the part of this violent man*, that all *fear* had left us from the day of our first meeting, and our respect became daring and familiar, like that of children who feel that they are loved (emphasis added)."[90]

It is interesting that she describes an equally intimidated Rouault reacting to Bloy's denigration of his work: "How many times in the following years did not we see Rouault at Bloy's house, standing and leaning against the wall, with a slight smile on his closed lips, his gaze far off, his face apparently impassive but with a pallor that increased when the question of modern painting was broached."[91] Her attempt to portray Bloy's abusive behavior as an expression of his spiritual and aesthetic authority and the painter's need for correction is far from convincing but represents accurately how she and Jacques chose to rationalize the man's darker side and idiosyncratic spirituality: "It seemed as if he [Rouault] sought from Bloy

86. Ibid., 171.
87. Ibid.
88. Ibid., 171–72.
89. Raïssa Maritain, *We Have Been Friends Together*, 118.
90. Ibid., 120.
91. Ibid., 158. Pierre Courthion, *Georges Rouault* (London: Thames and Hudson), 104.

the very indictments that tormented within him that which he held most dear ... to test against them the strength of that instinct that impelled him toward the unknown."[92]

But what troubles Heppenstall the most is the misanthropic and misogynist satisfaction Bloy seems to draw from the deaths of prominent Parisian women in the 1897 Charity Bazaar fire that killed 121 people. As Bloy describes it, "A large number of handsome ladies were reduced to ashes, last evening, within less than half an hour. *Non pro mundo rogo,* saith the Lord."[93] In a letter to Andre Rouveyre that Raïssa reproduces in *Pilgrim of the Absolute,* he finds imagining the stampede of these "chaste lilies" and "tender roses" as they struggled in vain to escape the incinerating furnace, delightful.[94] Not even the blessing of the papal nuncio, minutes before the inferno, could save "the dainty and voluptuous carcasses which those full dress clothes covered" from the "black and terrible aspects of their souls."[95] In Bloy's esoteric pneumatology, the nuncio's blessing is "sacrilegious" and the fire to which it is condemned is nothing else than "the roaring and wandering abode of the Holy Spirit."[96]

And his recollection of that day becomes even more bizarre: "On reading the first news of this fearsome event I had the clear and delicious feeling of an immense weight lifted from my heart. The small number of victims, it is true, set limits to my joy. At last, I said to myself, all the same, at last! AT LAST! Here then is a beginning of justice."[97] The fire's "unbelievable *swiftness*" and the gruesome images that followed were God's infernal punishment of the rich: "The uniform appearance of the bodies on which the Symbol of Charity hurled itself with a kind of divine rage ... was obvious enough."[98] Bloy was to express similar views about the sinking of the Titanic and the fire at the Iroquois Theatre in Chicago in December of 1903.[99] Ignoring the hundreds of children that were among the fire's 605 casualties, he praised the demise of the Theatre's proprietors.

Mystical literature has the license to paint its subjects in vivid colors and graphic forms, for such is often the nature of the ecstasies, stigmatizations, and sweeping visions that it describes. Bloy had the Maritains read

92. Raïssa Maritain, *We Have Been Friends Together*, 158.
93. Raïssa Maritain, *Léon Bloy: Pilgrim of the Absolute*, 196.
94. Ibid. Heppenstall, *Léon Bloy*, 38–39.
95. Raïssa Maritain, *Léon Bloy: Pilgrim of the Absolute*, 198.
96. Ibid.
97. Ibid., 197.
98. Ibid., 199–200.

Anne Catherine Emmerich's mystical writings and there is little doubt that he saw himself as a mystic of the same order, whose mission was to exaggerate the depravity and excruciating suffering of human life and the ugliness and demonic darkness of sin.[100] The prevalent racial stereotypes of Jews provided him with a framework for translating this vision into prophetic terms, painting images of appalling depravity (as he did of the Hamburg market), and excruciating expiation (the crucified Jew that Maritain adopted and saw in Marc Chagall's paintings).[101]

But as Brady wisely pointed out, the line between the pathological and the spiritual can be very fine. A morbid, and obsessively dolorist spirituality, arbitrarily exercised and dispensed, and prone to the exaggerations and extremes that we find in Bloy, lacks the moderation, humility, and joy that permeate the great Mysteries of the Trinity, the Incarnation, and the Person of Christ himself, and seems oblivious to the healing power of love with which Christ transfigures all beings. It is not an accident that the Druide character—who fits Rouault perfectly—paints terror and death rather than joy and life. There is in Bloy an oppressive monotony, something that we also see in the work of Rouault. Rouault, termed a Fauve and an expressionist (by Maritain), was criticized in the 1904 *Salon d'Automne*, for eliminating light from his "black pictures" (*tableaux noirs*) in contrast to the Impressionists, "for whom light was everything."[102]

The Bloy-Rouault relationship is important because it serves as a key link to Maritain's aesthetics and his idea of the artist as a saint and mystic. Having read Bloy's the *Woman Who Was Poor* in 1904, Rouault was enthusiastic about meeting him. A very impressed Rouault met Bloy in April of 1904 and as Pierre Courthion writes in his magisterial volume on the painter, the two soon discovered that they "shared the same vision of reality, apparently terrible and relentlessly sordid."[103] Courthion in fact notes: "Bloy's style was loaded with the same explosive expressiveness that marked Rouault's new manner of painting." And he considers the prostitutes that populate his canvasses in that period (and roughly until 1908), "to a certain extent, sisters and daughters to Bloy."[104]

Contrary to what any rational person would expect, Bloy's response to

99. See Brady, *Thought and Style in the Works of Léon Bloy*, 47.
100. See Raïssa Maritain, *We Have Been Friends Together*, 151.
101. See Maritain, *Redeeming the Time*, 156.
102. Courthion, *Georges Rouault*, 102.
103. Ibid., 98.
104. Ibid.

these paintings that so resembled the world he created in his novels, was not one of approval. In November of 1904 he accused the artist of suffering from "some unbelievable mental aberration."[105] Then in 1905, after seeing a triptych of prostitutes in which one panel depicted a grotesque couple inspired by characters in the *Woman Who Was Poor,* he lashed out at Rouault for painting "atrocious, vengeful caricatures."[106] And in 1907, in a letter to Rouault, he was even more vehement and abusive: "I have two things to say to you ... the last I shall ever say, after which, for me, you'll be merely a chunk of likable meat.... [Y]ou are attracted solely by the ugly.... [Y]ou have a vertigo of hideousness.... [I]t is time for you to stop."[107] But Bloy, who in his younger days had entertained the thought of becoming an artist, could easily swing to the other side. When in 1904, *Le Figaro* published a review that criticized Rouault's work for its "unmitigated blackness," Bloy advised the artist that he was God's chosen victim. "You will not be more flagellated than I," he wrote, shifting the subject to himself.[108]

Maritain admired Rouault and wrote about his work as early as 1910, at a time when his knowledge of art was very limited. Having met Rouault through Bloy, the Maritains became even closer to him and his wife, when they moved into the same neighborhood (Versailles) in 1909. In his preface to the exhibition catalogue, Maritain, struggling with the grotesque character of the artist's work but ever generous, praises the "exaggeration of his forms" for their ability to penetrate the reality of things while giving them the dramatic forms this reality assumed in the artist's inner world.[109] According to Schlosser, he "portrayed Rouault as being simultaneously medieval and contemporaneously expressionist."[110] In a 1924 review, and in subsequent editions, Maritain described Rouault's prostitutes and clowns rather opaquely with a visual poetry of his own, as "precious transparencies ... the wound of Sin ... the misery of fallen nature" and the painter as imbued with a mystical spirit, "passing through the world of human abysses," filled with "creative emotion" and a "genius" by virtue of "his poetic force."[111] This shift to the creative subject and its spiritual energies was to remain at the core of his aesthetics. But Rouault, like Bloy, according to

105. Ibid., 103.

106. Ibid.

107. Ibid., 104.

108. Schloesser, *Jazz Age Catholicism,* 218.

109. Ibid., 221–22.

110. Ibid., 221.

111. Jacques Maritain, *Art and Poetry,* translated by R. de P. Matthews (New York: Philosophical Library, 1943), 28–29.

Maritain, was also "a stubborn hermit," whose "gift of pitiless observation" explains the "true meaning of his vehemences."[112]

Here Bloy and Rouault fuse into one persona. In a later essay, Maritain describes the Rouault that he met in 1905 in terms that would apply equally well to Bloy. He is tormented by "ferocious images through which he discharged his anger; he depicted heartless and ugly judges, pitiable clowns, prostitutes, shrews, smug and arrogant upper-class ladies."[113] Rouault is "the painter of original sin and of the misery of wounded humanity."[114] For Maritain, creative emotion is the mark of the great artist but it must be mediated by suffering. Great art is impossible without the "steady struggle inside the artist's soul, which has to pass through trials and 'dark nights,' comparable, in the line of the creativity of the spirit, to those suffered by the mystics in their striving union toward God. Such was the case with Rouault."[115]

Maritain's characterization of Rouault as "the greatest religious painter of our time," is questionable largely because his evaluation of the painter's work lacks a credible aesthetic basis and instead relies on the spiritual states that he associates with the creative process.[116] There are tangential references to features of Rouault's paintings but they are overwhelmed by spiritual considerations which lead Maritain to assign to them a grandeur and expressive intensity that they clearly do not have: "In his scenes of the Passion, paroxysmic deformation has been superseded by the majesty of a suffering which, before coming from the wickedness of tormentors, comes from the very will of the Lamb of God offering Himself by love."[117] Rouault's 1918 painting of the *Crucifixion* and his 1932 *Christ Mocked by Soldiers* are grotesque, somber and solemn—the latter is chromatically more expressive and dynamic—but nothing like what Maritain describes.

IV. Conclusion

In writing about Maritain's affiliation with *Action Française,* Ralph McInerny draws our attention to his philosophical passion for "atemporal things," in which is implied an innocence or naivety when it comes to

112. Ibid., 25.
113. Ibid., 26.
114. Ibid.
115. Jacques Maritain, *Georges Rouault* (New York: Harry N. Abrams Publishers, 1969), 16.
116. Ibid., 32.
117. Ibid.

the practical realities of politics.[118] A contrast may be drawn here between Maritain's poetic vagueness in these matters and Simon's notion that philosophy errs when it "uses a term whose meaning cannot be reduced to being."[119] But Simon's assessment of his friend's contemplative and artistic nature and "gifts of intuitive familiarity," should put what may appear as a weakness in a different light.[120] In what was to be his last public lecture, Simon said this: "He [Maritain] has always been in warm contact with the existential man, and his excellence in the rational analysis of the soul has never interfered with his *intuitive relation to men such as they are here and now, such as they have been shaped by history, by grace and by suffering, and such as they behave with regard to their eternal destiny.*"[121] We may infer from this statement and from the text of Simon's homage to Maritain, that his philosophical examination of spirituality and art was rooted in the existential conditions of the time, and that he saw in these conditions, and in the grave moral and spiritual challenges they posed, the ground where a vital Thomism would take root. This means that whatever obscurities one might encounter in that path would eventually give way to the lucidity and charity of reason.

In the case of Israel, Bloy, and avant-garde art, Maritain's "practical opacity," as McInerny so aptly called it, was informed by the spiritual world that he and Raïssa encountered in the early years of their conversion to Catholicism.[122] The figure of Léon Bloy, painted in the extreme and explosive colors of mystic, genius, martyr, and prophet, stands at the center of this encounter. Destitution and majesty, sacrifice and glorification, rage and meekness were polarities that informed his spiritual and literary persona, creating an amalgam of radical faith and art that the young Maritains found irresistible. Projecting into that experience not only their Bergsonian intuitionism but also their sympathy for the anti-establishment art of the avant-gardes, they naturally saw in Bloy a rebellious spirit who could perceive reality in its purest and most sacred forms and embody these forms in a language that only few could decipher. This was also the dream and

118. Ralph McInerny, *The Very Rich Hours of Jacques Maritain* (Notre Dame, Indiana: University of Notre Dame Press, 2003), 64.

119. Walter Nicgorski, "Yves R. Simon: A Philosopher's Quest for Science and Prudence," *The Review of Politics* 71, no. 1 (2009): 68–84.

120. Griffin and Simon, *Jacques Maritain: Homage in Words and Pictures*, 7.

121. Ibid., 4. Emphasis added.

122. McInerny, *The Very Rich Hours of Jacques Maritain*, 64.

claim of many avant-gardes. It was thus easy for Jacques and Raïssa to see in painters like Rouault, whose work shocked bourgeois and academic art sensibilities, the toils of holy souls seeking redemption in the name of a transcendent purity.

Far away from her native Russia and having abandoned the religion of her ancestors, Raïssa was especially vulnerable to the aestheticism of this vision in which Israel too becomes a mystery to be deciphered and the great masterpiece of divine providence. In her memoirs, she draws attention to the last chapter of *Le Salut,* where Bloy improvises on the La Salette prophecies. She calls the text "magnificent and obscure" and blames hers and Jacques' youthful ignorance for failing to understand "Bloy's complex symbolism" when they first read it. Still, "its beauty," she recalls, "was obvious."[123] She remains confident that, just as Bloy had predicted, the "Passion of Israel will be the reflected image of this agony of Love. And in this unspeakable community of suffering, Israel will recognize Him of Whom it is the symbol."[124]

Having noted the problematic aspects of Maritain's essay, it is important to keep in mind the nature and scope of the spirituality that informs it. This is not to deny the presence of anti-Semitic elements in its imagery and vision, especially when considering both from the sophisticated understanding of anti-Semitism that we have today. It is, rather, to place them in their proper context. From this perspective, it is fair, I think, to conclude that the Maritains' fascination with the world of Bloy and his views of the Jewish people, was part of a long journey to clarity and an attempt to reconcile the radical hope and charity of Christianity with a broken world.

123. Raïssa Maritain, *We Have Been Friends Together,* 135.
124. Ibid., 136.

JOHN MARSON DUNAWAY

Maritain's Influence on American Literature

While I was in graduate school, I enrolled in an extraordinarily stimulating class on French literary criticism. The professor, Wallace Fowlie—who happened to be one of Maritain's innumerable godchildren—assigned to each of us an oral book report. For some reason, as I looked over the list of standard books in the field—Bachelard, Barthes, Poulet, Thibaudet—I was intrigued by a dusty old tome by a philosopher who called himself an anti-modern, and whose aesthetics was based, of all things, on the quaint old notions of the medieval Schoolmen.

Ever since that first reading of *Art et scolastique*,[1] I have tended to see modern literature in the light of Aristotle, Aquinas, and Jacques Maritain. At that time in my life, I thought I was only interested in modern literature. Anything that came before 1900 had to be thoroughly outdated and puerile. But eventually I discovered that the twentieth-century writers who interest me the most are almost exclusively the most anti-modern.

When I wrote my book on Maritain in the mid-seventies,[2] I devoted a chapter to his influence on writers and artists. I began to compile a list of those who found his aesthetics important enough to mention the debt. I sent letters to writers in England, Canada, and the United States, asking to what degree and how they were influenced by Maritain. As a matter of fact this particular part of the project turned out to be one of the most rewarding. I received some fascinating responses, some of which included

1. Jacques Maritain, *Art et scolastique* (Paris: Librairie de l'Art catholique, 1920).
2. John M. Dunaway, *Jacques Maritain* (Boston: Twayne, 1978).

further leads that I was able to pursue on the topic. Since that time I have continued to run into examples of Maritain's profound impact on modern literature.

Later I wrote letters to several more American writers and critics inquiring about the Maritain connection. What I propose to do in the next few pages is first to review briefly the most pertinent findings I published in my Twayne book on Maritain, then to suggest several possible areas for further exploration, and finally to concentrate on two examples of a truly profound Maritain influence: Caroline Gordon and Flannery O'Connor.

The United States had a special place in Maritain's heart. He was persuaded that the hand of God was what led him to this country and that his vocation as Christian philosopher gave him a message that should be heard among American Catholics. In articulating his Christian humanism, he expressed great faith in the potential of American democracy as an example of sociopolitical justice for the whole modern world. He devoted an entire book to this country.[3] In the realm of aesthetics, *Art and Scholasticism* had been available in translation as early as 1947;[4] *Art and Faith*[5] and *The Situation of Poetry*[6] by 1948 and 1955, respectively. And, interestingly enough, his masterwork of aesthetics, *Creative Intuition in Art and Poetry*,[7] as well as *The Responsibility of the Artist*[8] were among the few books he actually composed directly in English. They were, thus, written primarily with the American public in mind.

Clearly, Maritain was aware of his role as philosophical conscience to a whole generation of American Catholics, and it is probably a fair supposition that few Catholic writers active in this country during the 1940s, 50s, and 60s went untouched by his ideas on art.

Princeton University was the site of Maritain's most lengthy residence

3. Jacques Maritain, *Reflections on America* (New York: Charles Scribner's Sons, 1958).

4. First published in English by Sheed and Ward. An improved translation by Joseph W. Evans (and requested by Maritain) was published as *Art and Scholasticism and the Frontiers of Poetry* (New York: Charles Scribner's Sons, 1962). The original translation in English was made by J. F. Scanlan (New York: Sheed and Ward, 1947).

5. Jacques Maritain, *Art and Faith: Letters Between Jacques Maritain and Jean Cocteau*, translated by John Coleman (New York: Philosophical Library, 1948).

6. Jacques and Raïssa Maritain, *The Situation of Poetry*, translated by Marshall Suther (New York: Philosophical Library, 1955).

7. Jacques Maritain, *Creative Intuition in Art and Poetry* (New York: Pantheon, 1953).

8. Jacques Maritain, *The Responsibility of the Artist* (New York: Charles Scribner's Sons, 1960).

in America (1948–1961), and it was there that he gathered around himself perhaps his most enduring and personally significant American literary acquaintances. The most prominent members of this Princeton group were Francis Fergusson, Allen Tate, Caroline Gordon, and the Maritains. All traditionalists by temperament, they found in Saint Thomas Aquinas a well-articulated philosophy to serve as a foundation for their diverse fields: Fergusson the critic, Tate and Raïssa the poets, Gordon the novelist, and Jacques the philosopher of art. Tate has said: "Jacques Maritain's influence on me was pervasive from the time I first knew him in 1940 until his death.... Jacques was a very great man. Not only a great intellect, but a warm and friendly human being who had he been a clergyman would no doubt be canonized."[9] Fergusson, who knew Tate and Maritain quite well at Princeton, told me that the influence was not only personal and spiritual in nature but also directly literary. In a personal interview in the seventies, Fergusson told me it was through Maritain that Tate read Aquinas. He added that "The Seasons of the Soul" was perhaps the clearest example of a direct literary influence. And Tate himself, in "The Symbolic Imagination" and "The Angelic Imagination," acknowledges a great debt to Jacques and Raïssa in his thinking on the angelism of such poets as Edgar Allan Poe.

Fergusson's own writings did not escape Maritain's influence. The major thrust of his criticism and art theory was a basic revitalization of the modern perspective on art through the use of Aristotle, Aquinas, Plato, and other ancients who seemed to have been too often neglected. The other writer in this group at Princeton was Tate's first wife, Caroline Gordon, whom I shall discuss in a moment.

T. S. Eliot had considerable contact with Maritain at Princeton, but although he called Maritain "probably the greatest force in contemporary French philosophy," Maritain's Aristotelianism and Thomism were too rigidly systematic for Eliot's taste. John Howard Griffin's *Black Like Me*[10] was what he called a living out of Maritain's ideas on racism, and his friend Thomas Merton attributed his conversion to Gilson and Maritain. *The Seven Storey Mountain* gives an idea of the immense importance of Maritain's aesthetics and his thinking on the relationship between art and morality for the late Trappist poet.

9. Letter to the author, dated 4 May 1976.
10. John Howard Griffin, *Black Like Me* (New York: Houghton Mifflin, 1961).

When Sally Fitzgerald came out with *The Habit of Being*,[11] I learned of Flannery O'Connor's great debt to Maritain. And I had attended the 1980 American Maritain Association conference in Louisville, where Father Daniel Berrigan, as one of the principal speakers, mentioned how much he too owed to Maritain. I proceeded to add the following names to my list: Robert Penn Warren, William Styron, Reynolds Price, Peter Taylor, James Dickey, Randall Jarrell, Robert Lowell, and Walker Percy.

In the case of those who were still living, I simply wrote directly to them. For Jarrell and Lowell, I wrote to their biographers and critics. The results were as follows: Styron replied that Maritain is "terra incognita to me, despite my fairly good acquaintance with modern French literature."[12] I quote Percy's note in its entirety, since it was short:

> Art and Scholasticism: Valuable to me in setting forth art as a Cognitive enterprise, e. g.—"art as a virtue of the practical intellect." J. M.'s writings on Descartes: Valuable in clarifying for me, both as a novelist and an amateur philosopher, the radical and enduring effect of Cartesian philosophy on Western thought (e.g., my novel *Love in the Ruins*).[13]

Lowell and Jarrell, too, appear to be dead ends. I did not get responses from Berrigan, Warren, Price, Taylor, or Dickey, but I believe the most likely directions for further study most probably would be Berrigan and Warren.

Caroline Gordon felt greatly indebted to Maritain as both a personal and a literary influence. Her novel *The Malefactors*[14] is dedicated to him, and *The Glory of Hera*[15] was based largely on *Art and Scholasticism*, in which she found "the most profound and complete aesthetic of the novel."[16] In a letter to me, she said she was persuaded that many of Maritain's ideas were in circulation without being credited to him. "One of the things," she wrote, "that most impressed me about Jacques was that he read novels as if he were a novelist, read poetry as if he were a poet and looked at pictures as if he were a painter.... Maritain knew more about the novel, I think, than anybody I have ever known."[17] The letter I'm quoting here was four pag-

11. Flannery O'Connor, *The Letters of Flannery O'Connor: The Habit of Being*, edited by Sally Fitzgerald (New York: Farrar, Straus and Giroux, 1979).
12. Postcard to the author, dated 3 July 1984.
13. Note to the author, undated.
14. Caroline Gordon, *The Malefactors* (New York: Harcourt, Brace and Company, 1956).
15. Caroline Gordon, *The Glory of Hera* (New York: Doubleday, 1972).
16. Letter to the author, dated 25 July 1976.
17. Ibid.

es long. Miss Gordon [this is how she told me to address her] wrote with boundless enthusiasm about her respect for Maritain and the impact his ideas had on her life, declaring herself one of his most dedicated disciples. She enclosed a copy of the letter that Maritain had written to her in 1955 after having read *The Malefactors*. Interestingly enough, Flannery O'Connor, who corresponded with Gordon and admired her work, was also aware of this letter from Maritain. In *The Habit of Being* she not only mentions it but discusses the strengths of *The Malefactors* in practically the same terms Maritain used.[18]

Caroline Gordon's *How to Read a Novel*[19] contains several references to Maritain's special conception of the novel as having to do with the conduct of life, a point we shall discuss below in relation to Flannery O'Connor. And I believe Maritain's idea of the *roman à clé* must have been a favorite of hers. It was not her own image, but I think Miss Gordon might have agreed that a good *roman à clé* is a little like a chef's casserole, whose ingredients are a carefully guarded secret. In her letter to me she wrote of Henry James's understanding of the matter: "Henry James has treated the subject more explicitly than any other author when he refused to again receive a young novelist, Vernon Lee, who had satirized him in a novel. 'I do not care to care,' he wrote his fuss budget of a brother, William, who was all for 'taking steps.' 'But I will not see her again. She has committed two crimes. She has invaded my privacy and she has put a human being into a novel without re-imagining him.'"[20]

Gordon's *The Malefactors* is replete with Christian imagery; the story is even haunted, I would say, by the aspiration to sainthood. The canonized historical figures that appear in it include Saint Eustace, Saint Ciannic, and Saint Catherine of Siena. And their contemporary counterpart is Catherine Pollard, who is patterned after Dorothy Day. The principal action of the novel is the slow and mysterious movement of the main character, Tom Claiborne, from a detached skepticism to the all-transforming light of grace. One of the most intriguing interpretive questions concerning Maritain's influence on *The Malefactors* is the rather mystifying epigraph chosen by Miss Gordon. It is a quotation from Maritain: "It is for Adam to interpret the voices that Eve hears."[21] Frederick McDowell suggests that these words refer to "Claiborne's

18. O'Connor, *The Habit of Being*, 157–160, 166.
19. Caroline Gordon, *How to Read a Novel* (New York: Viking, 1957).
20. Letter to the author, dated 25 July 1976.
21. Maritain, *The Frontiers of Poetry*, 141.

failure until the end to bring his mind into a fruitful relationship with intuition."[22] Another possibility is that they have to do with a traditionalist understanding of the spiritual authority vested in the husband and his responsibility to judge the prophetic visions that come through his spouse.

It is always difficult to write a novel about a religious conversion without allowing it to stray off into hagiography or sentimentality. Maritain, however, declared in *Art and Scholasticism* that only a Christian, indeed a mystic, could become a complete novelist, "un romancier complet," because one would need to know first-hand all that is within the human heart.[23]

Other than Gordon and Flannery O'Connor, one might think of Julien Green, François Mauriac, Georges Bernanos, and Vladimir Volkoff as examples of this kind of novelist. Maritain himself believed that Green was the best exemplar of that model in France. O'Connor, in a letter in *The Habit of Being,* comments rather strongly on a novel she especially disliked, specifically because it appeared to her to be "just propaganda and its being propaganda for the side of the angels only makes it worse. The novel," she goes on, "is an art form and when you use it for anything other than art, you pervert it. I didn't make this up. I got it from St. Thomas (via Maritain) who allows that art is wholly concerned with the good of that which is made; it has no utilitarian end. If you do manage to use it successfully for social, religious, or other purposes, it is because you make it art first."[24]

Here is the reason, I believe, that both Caroline Gordon and Flannery O'Connor found such enlightenment in Maritain. First, he saw that the novel has to do with the very conduct of life, and that in this respect the novelist is different from all other artists. For the end that is served by all the means at the disposal of the artist is the work to be created, but with the novelist, the work to be created is a world in itself, and her relationship to this fictional world is analogous to God's relationship to his creation. The multifaceted interrelations among the characters are to be handled with utmost care, one should even say with compassion.

This is why Maritain admired Bernanos, who was said to have identified so deeply with his characters that he prayed for them. A second of Maritain's insights on the novel that seems to have especially impressed Gordon and O'Connor grows directly out of the first. Since the novel has to do with

22. Frederick P. McDowell, *Caroline Gordon* (Minneapolis, University of Minnesota Press, 1966), 41.

23. Maritain, *Art and Scholasticism*, 266.

24. O'Connor, *The Habit of Being*, 157.

the very conduct of life, and since the characters are autonomous, the novelist must never consider them as puppets to be manipulated. Julien Green said that for this reason he never made a preliminary outline of the action and never put words in his characters' mouths. He preferred to write down what he witnessed them doing and saying of their own volition.

To quote again from *The Habit of Being*:

> Maritain says that to produce a work of art requires the "constant attention of the purified mind;" and the business of the purified mind in this case is to see that those elements of the personality that don't bear on the subject at hand are excluded. Stories don't lie when left to themselves. Everything has to be subordinated to a whole which is not you. Any story I reveal myself completely in will be a bad story.[25]

The third major idea of Maritain that especially influenced novelists is a bedrock-fundamental principle of art that he got from Saint Thomas, one that underlies the other two notions discussed above. Art is a virtue of the practical intellect, says Maritain, first in *Art and Scholasticism,* and then throughout his aesthetic writings. As such it must always be distinguished from prudence, another virtue of the practical intellect. "Prudence works for the good of the one acting.... Art works for the good of the work made."[26] Prudence belongs to the sphere of doing (*agibile*), that is, the pure exercise of our free will. Art, on the other hand, operates in the domain of making (*factibile*), where an action is good only insofar as it conforms to the work to be made. Hence the absolute purity and independence of art in relation to morality. Brenna Moore has recently suggested that this strong refusal to allow art to serve morality not only made the Maritains particularly appealing to avant-garde artists in interwar Paris; it also was the occasion of some concern and even disfavor from ecclesiastical authorities.

Yet Flannery O'Connor agreed with Maritain that, in the Thomistic conception of art, there is an intimate analogy between the vocations of artist and saint. "Art is a virtue of the practical intellect," she says in *Mystery and Manners,* "and the practice of any virtue demands a certain asceticism and a very definite leaving-behind of the niggardly part of the ego."[27]

Clearly, Maritain's philosophy of art was formative to Flannery O'Connor and to her view of the fiction writer's special role. I have quoted from *The Habit of Being* and also from *Mystery and Manners*. This latter book is

25. Ibid., 15.

26. Maritain, *Art and Scholasticism,* 15.

27. Flanner O'Connor, *Mystery and Manners: Occasional Prose,* edited by Sally and Robert Fitzgerald (New York: Farrar, Straus and Giroux, 1970), 81.

composed of talks and essays on writing that O'Connor composed for various occasions during her brief career. In a 1957 letter, O'Connor wrote that *Art and Scholasticism* was "the book I cut my aesthetic teeth on."[28] And of course, the very title of Fitzgerald's collection of letters is explicitly derived from Maritain. The *habitus* of art, as Maritain termed it in *Art and Scholasticism,* was a notion that was rich in meaning for O'Connor. She used it several times in the essays of *Mystery and Manners.* It refers not to mindless routine practices we call habit, but rather to a mental or spiritual attitude that must be trained and cultivated through rigorous discipline. According to Ms. Fitzgerald, we may not only find a luminous example of the habit of art in Flannery's fiction; her letters amount to a striking example of the equally rare habit of being.

In a favorable review of Maritain's *The Range of Reason,* O'Connor called him "one of the major voices in modern philosophy to reassert the primacy of reason."[29] And one O'Connor scholar notes that Maritain was one of the seven religious writers whose works appear most prominently in her personal library. In a 1960 letter to Robert Giroux, she requested that he send a copy of *The Violent Bear It Away* to Maritain because she had heard that he had been quite taken with *Wise Blood.*[30]

Frederick Asals's interpretation of *Wise Blood* is an excellent example of the intimate link between O'Connor's fiction and Maritain's philosophy. In *Flannery O'Connor: The Imagination of Extremity,* he claims that Hazel Motes "compellingly illustrates Maritain's notion of post-Cartesian man as 'an angel inhabiting a machine.'"[31] His analysis of the dualisms in *Wise Blood,* especially in the movement toward pure body in Enoch Emery and pure spirit in Hazel, makes extensive use of Maritain's *Existence and the Existent* as a gloss.[32] He also points out that two chapters of Maritain's latter book were earlier published in the *Sewanee Review* in the same issue in which O'Connor's story "The Train" appeared.[33]

28. O'Connor, *The Habit of Being,* 216.

29. Lorine M. Getz, *Flannery O'Connor: Her Life, Library and Book Reviews* (New York: The Edwin Miller Press, 1980), 72.

30. See O'Connor, *The Habit of Being,* 417.

31. Frederick Asals, *Flannery O'Connor: The Imagination of Extremity* (Athens, Georgia: University of Georgia Press, 1982; reprinted in 2007), 4.

32. Jacques Maritain, *Existence and the Existent,* translated by Lewis Galantière and Gerald B. Phelan (New York: Pantheon, 1948).

33. See Jacques Maritain, "From Existentialist Existentialism to Academic Existentialism," *The Sewanee Review* 41 (1948): 210–29, and Flannery O'Connor, "The Train," 261–71.

Maritain students will find a wealth of material in the issue of *Renascence* which was devoted entirely to the topic of Maritain's aesthetics. Published in commemoration of his centenary in 1982, this volume features an excellent article by Neal Oxenhandler. Oxenhandler believes that Maritain's most significant contribution to literary theory was in this country rather than France. His case study is the New Criticism of Ransom, Brooks, Warren, and Tate. He suggests that it was Maritain who provided the philosophical framework for their movement, specifically in their emphasis on the autonomy of the text. This central tenet of the New Criticism may indeed be perceived as arising out of Maritain's emphasis on the sovereignty of the work to be produced by the artist, since art for Maritain is a virtue of the practical intellect to be distinguished from prudence. "There can be little doubt," concludes Oxenhandler, "that Maritain's presence in this country and his writings on literature and art had a powerful influence on the members of the New Criticism."[34]

This essay would not be adequate without mention of Dana Gioia. Author of the seminal *Can Poetry Matter?*[35] and of course a growing corpus of brilliant poetry, as well as President George W. Bush's hand-picked Chair of the National Endowment for the Arts, Gioia gave an extended eloquent testimony of his debt to Maritain at the American Maritain Association's 2001 conference in Boca Raton, Florida.

To assess the influence of one writer on another is, of necessity, rather speculative. Often it is more a case of a meeting of like minds. Yet in Jacques Maritain we find a man with a mission, a man whose calling was characterized by an effort to reinterpret modern problems—whether political, theological, or literary—in the light of half-forgotten truths. His return to the wisdom of the ancients was a philosophical program that he consciously sought to disseminate, a revival for which he deliberately sought adherents from the days of the literary gatherings at Meudon right down to his last years of solitude along the banks of the Garonne. And it is in American writers like Gordon, O'Connor, and Gioia that we see perhaps the most far-reaching effects of a truly profound literary influence.

34. Neal Oxenhandler, "Maritain and Recent Critical Thought," *Renascence* 34, no. 4 (1982): 263.

35. Dana Gioia, *Can Poetry Matter? Essays on Poetry and American Culture* (St. Paul, Minnesota: Graywolf Press, 1992).

JOSHUA HREN

The Sound and the Fury, Symbolizing Something

Maritain and Percy on the Paradoxical Miracle at the Limits of Language

For my son, Søren

In *Ransoming the Time,* Jacques Maritain suggests that, "a treatise on the sign and on the symbol, such as I hope someday may be written, would on the one hand endeavor to winnow out what is essential in the extensive intellectual elaboration to which medieval thinkers subjected this matter," and on the other hand would link the conceptual procedure thereby established with, "the scientific investigations of our own time."[1] We who live under an extremely perspectivist sky, where the pantheon of academic gods giddily or cynically proclaim a total fissure between sign and signifier, recognize the scholastics' now subversive understanding of a "really intrinsic proportion between signs and that which they signify."[2] As Stanley Rosen relates, those who are obsessed with language in our time tend to come to the conviction that there is, finally, nothing but interpretation, that "there is nothing 'out there' but ghosts of uninteresting truths; truth is superstition."[3] Against this Maritain insists not that there is a literal link

1. Jacques Maritain, "Sign and Symbol," in *Ransoming the Time,* translated by Lorin Binsse (New York: Charles Scribner's Sons, 1941), 217.

2. Ibid., 219.

3. Stanley Rosen, *Hermeneutics as Politics* (New York: Oxford University Press, 1987), 192.

between sign and signifier, but that there is a, "certain presence—presence of knowability—of the signified in the sign; the former is there *in alio esse,* in another mode of existence."[4]

Signs, while used by humans, play a great part in the psychic life of animals. For animals, as for humans, signs *do something,* and yet the sign is also, "the keystone of intellectual life."[5] In order to trace how this key to the intellect is turned, one must sort out the distinct meaning of a sign. "An animal employs signs without perceiving the relationship of meaning. To perceive the relationship of meaning is to have an *idea*—a spiritual sign."[6] Maritain contends that the miraculous quality of the perception of meaning is most remarkably evident in the awakening intelligence of blind deaf-mutes, "imprisoned souls."[7] The philosopher-novelist Walker Percy, who in many ways worked out Maritain's requested "treatise on the sign and the symbol" also pauses before the blind deaf-mute's consciousness of *meaning,* considers it singularly important in the study of signs and symbols. Helen Keller's teacher could help her to interpret the word as a *signal* that "*did* something," but what she "could not make [Helen] understand was that the word *water* was not a command to *do* something with water, but *meant,* denoted water."[8] Once, by a mysterious flash of insight, Keller understood that this "is" water, "what she had to know immediately was *what everything else was!*"[9] Consciousness, moving from sign to symbolized meaning, requires that everything *be* something, but finds paradoxically that the "one thing in the world which by its very nature is not susceptible of a stable symbolic transformation is *myself.*"[10]

A hermeneutic informed by both Maritain and Percy's philosophies of language, sign, and symbol, will guide us as we engage with Percy's novel *The Moviegoer,* in which the protagonist Binx Bolling articulates creative intuitions regarding the "miserable, anxious awareness" paid for the gift of language, and comes to find in his mentally disabled but linguistically luminous brother Lonnie an almost holy truth about our use of symbols. Percy and Maritain find in those who suffer from limits in language a revelation of the miracle of symbols that *mean* something.[11] By bringing the semiotic

4. Maritain, "Sign and Symbol," 220.

5. Ibid., 221.

6. Ibid., 220.

7. Ibid., 220–221.

8. Walker Percy, "Symbol as Hermeneutic in Existentialism," *Philosophy and Phenomenological Research* 16, no. 4 (1956): 525. Emphasis in original.

9. Ibid; emphasis in original.

10. Ibid., 527; emphasis in original.

11. See Peter Augustine Lawler, *Postmodernism Rightly Understood: The Return to Realism in American Thought* (New York: Rowman and Littlefield, 1999), 192.

treatise Maritain calls for and the creative intuition in Percy's poetry into dialectical relationship, we will perhaps fall in love with language, perhaps come to see that love is impossible outside of human symbolization, outside of *homo symbolificus*—man the symbol-monger.

Peter Augustine Lawler notes that Percy, "agrees with Aristotle and Saint Thomas that discovering the truth and communicating it to others may be the greatest of the human pleasures," even as, "man experiences himself as an alien because he cannot, through language or thought, formulate or locate his own place in a cosmos that is otherwise dyadic."[12] *Dyadic* is a word used by Percy's semiotic mentor Charles S. Pierce to mean composed of "stimulus-response sequences."[13] Percy, with Pierce, distinguishes *dyadic* (response-stimulus) from *triadic* behavior in order to differentiate human use of language. In *triadic* behavior the self stands *apart* from stimulus-response sequences and uses symbols to navigate through them.[14]

In order to distinguish between dyadic sign use and triadic symbol use, Percy establishes the two categorizations of *environment* and *world*. He first sets before us the organism as an open system that maintains homeostasis in spite of all changes in an environment. The organism responds to those segments of its environment to which its genetic code has been predisposed to through evolution.[15] In such a case, segments of the environment without biological significance are ignored. Learning, in an environment, consists of modifying certain neurons in the organism's central nervous system in such a way that it will "respond to certain signals in an environment by a behavior oriented toward other segments of the environment."[16] An environment allows for only dyadic relations.

The triadic moment occurs when organism B understands sign A as "meaning" something, as more than a signal to flee or approach.[17] While a signal is *received* like any other stimuli in an environment, a symbol or a "sign requires a sign-giver."[18] When the sign and symbol user crosses the triadic threshold, she has, in addition to her environment, a *world*.[19] Important for Percy is the crossing as it happens in blind-deaf-mutes, a crossing that contains great meaning and mystery. In *The Message in the Bottle*

12. Ibid., 81.
13. Walker Percy, *Lost in The Cosmos* (New York: Washington Square Press, 1984), 86.
14. See ibid.
15. See ibid., 91.
16. Ibid., 91.
17. Ibid., 96.
18. Ibid., 97
19. See ibid.

he muses that, "three short paragraphs in Helen Keller's *The Story of My Life* veiled a mystery, a profound secret, and ... if one could fathom it, one could also understand a great deal of what it meant to be *Homo loquens, Homo symbolificus,* man the speaking animal, man the symbol-monger."[20] Helen had always responded to stimuli like any good animal. If she wanted cake, she spelled it in the hands of her teacher Miss Sullivan. But one day on a walk a threshold was crossed:

> We walked down the path to the well-house, attracted by the fragrance of the honeysuckle with which it was covered. Someone was drawing water and my teacher placed my hand under the spout. As the cool stream gushed over one hand, she spelled into the other the word *water,* first slowly then rapidly. I stood still, my whole attention fixed upon the motion of her fingers. Suddenly I felt a misty consciousness as of something forgotten—a thrill of returning thought; and somehow the mystery of language was revealed to me. I knew then that "w-a-t-e-r" meant the wonderful cool something that was flowing over my hand. The living word awakened my soul, gave it light, hope, joy, set it free! There were barriers still, it is true, but barriers that could in time be swept away.
>
> I left the well-house eager to learn. Everything had a name, and each name gave birth to a new thought. As we returned to the house every object which I touched seemed to quiver with life. That was because I saw everything with the strange, new sight that had come to me. On entering the door I remembered the doll I had broken.... I felt my way to the hearth and picked up the pieces. I tried vainly to put them together. Then my eyes filled with tears; for I realized what I had done, and for the first time I felt repentance and sorrow. I learned a great many new words that day.[21]

Maritain, considering the blind-deaf-mute experience, maintains that in order for one to *know* the relationship of signification of which they are to make use,

> some external help is indispensible.... The miracle of awakening to the life of thought will come to pass precisely when—thanks to the patiently repeated attempts of the teacher who refuses a desire and suggests a sign, an *artificial, conventional* sign, intended to obtain the satisfaction of the refused desire—the child suddenly will *discover* by some sort of sudden eruption of the idea, the signification of this conventional sign ... and from that moment on progress proceeds with astonishing rapidity.[22]

20. Walker Percy, *The Message in the Bottle* (New York: The Noonday Press, 1993), 30.
21. Ibid., 35.
22. Maritain, "Sign and Symbol," 221; emphasis in original.

Keller's experience intersects with the scholastic insistence (which in a sense is both pre- and post-modern) that there is a, "certain presence—presence of knowability—of the signified in the sign; the former is there *in alio esse*, in another mode of existence."[23] For Ferdinand de Saussure, the sign is "a union of signifier (the sound-image of a word) and signified (the concept of an object, action, quality)."[24] Percy calls the relation between the sign (signifier) and referent (signified) "a particularly mysterious property."[25] This mystery is located in the "troublesome copula 'is,' when Helen said that the perceived liquid 'is' water (the word). According to Jacques Derrida's deconstructionist linguistics, "the referent of a signifier is merely another signifier."[26] Derrida is in this way an echo of the ancient rhetorician Gorgias, who argued that "that by which we reveal is logos [words], but logos is not substances and existing things. Therefore, we do not reveal existing things to our neighbors, but logos, which is something other than substances."[27] Michel Foucault, laboring in this non-vineyard of deconstruction, argues that what is needed is to think *difference*, discontinuity, "to dissociate the reassuring form of the identical" because, "we are difference."[28] But, cautions Rosen, this rejection of the metaphysics of presence, of, we can add, the medieval theory of *in alio esse*, places us as players in a nihilistic world of absence. "If the world is a text written by *difference*," he writes, "it is a tale told by an idiot, a nonsubjective subjectivity or idiot savant, hence a tale full of sound and fury, signifying nothing."[29] Percy grants deconstructionist postmoderns of Derrida's ilk a nod, and then he shakes his head, no: The word "water" *is water*, but then again it is not.

Percy dramatizes the problem of organisms in environments responsive to signals versus humans in worlds using signs and symbols in his novel *The Moviegoer*. One Sunday when the narrator Binx, a film-ingesting stock market agent, is home visiting his mother and family, he attends Mass with them. Although the family falls into a great commotion over getting to Mass, the moment it begins they become, in a sense, the pre-symbolizing "imprisoned souls" described by Maritain, deaf and mute to the meaning around them: "it is as if it [Mass] were over before it began—each has

23. Ibid., 220.

24. Percy, *Lost in the Cosmos*, 103.

25. Ibid., 97.

26. Stanley Rosen, *Hermeneutics as Politics* (New York: Oxford University Press, 1987), 47.

27. Quoted in Alice Gillam, "Classical Rhetoric," in *Theorizing Composition*, edited by Mary Lynch Kennedy (London: Greenwood, 1998), 16–26.

28. Rosen, *Hermeneutics as Politics*, 47.

29. Ibid., 66; emphasis in original.

lapsed into his own blank-eyed vacancy."[30] In this context we witness a purely dyadic response when, "the bell rings for communion," that is, when the bell signifies that the bread and wine are now body and blood.[31] Roy, Binx's stepfather, responds to the bell as though it is what Percy comes to call a "signal."[32] For a dog, the word "ball" is merely a "signal" to which the dog responds like many other stimuli from his environment. When you say "ball" the dog goes to look for it. Roy behaves a bit like a Pavlovian dog. The bell rings, signifying that the Eucharist, source and summit of grace, *is*. And yet when the bell rings, "Roy gets heavily to his feet and pilots Lonnie [Binx's handicapped half-brother] to the end of the rail," where he is to receive the sacramental host.[33] All Binx sees of Lonnie is "a weaving tuft of red hair." We know that Lonnie, in the presence of the Eucharist, begins to tremble, because "when the priest comes to him, Roy holds a hand against Lonnie's face to steady him. He does this in a frowning perfunctory way, eyes light as an eagle's."[34] We, with Binx, are in a sense spectators seeing only a shade of what is happening at the communion rail. Is Roy dutiful but disengaged while Lonnie, shaking, experiences something mystical connected to the Eucharist? Does Roy move from a moment of stimulus-response to a moment in which he understands that Lonnie, or communion, simply *is*? The metaphor "eyes light as an eagle's" offers both clarification and confusion. Are Roy's eyes glazed-over-light or sharpened-light, like an eagle's? Either way, Percy estranges the experience of Eucharist by juxtaposing the signal-response to the bell with the real presence of the Eucharist, which, more than a signal or symbol, is a sacrament.

In "Sign and Symbol," Maritain describes a sacrament as "something external and sensory which signifies an effect of interior sanctification to be produced."[35] In the Catholic tradition, sacraments are signs "in a supereminent manner: they effect that which they signify (if the subject does not put obstacles in their way by his contrary disposition)."[36] Friedrich Theodor Vischer, seeking proof for his hypothesis, read in the sacrament of the Eucharist a central instance of the identity between the sign and the signified. Against this imposition of theory, Maritain insists that:

30. Walker Percy, *The Moviegoer* (New York: Avon Books, 1961), 129.
31. See ibid.
32. See Percy, *Lost in the Cosmos*, 88.
33. Percy, *The Moviegoer*, 129.
34. Ibid.
35. Maritain, "Sign and Symbol," 225.
36. Ibid., 226.

The sacred words, "This is my body" in no way assert an identity; they operate (as an instrumental cause) a change (transubstantiation). Far from resting upon an identity between the sign and the signified, the sacrament of the Eucharist adds to the relationship of sign to signified that of cause to effect and implies the intervention of the First Cause producing the most radical change of which we can conceive, a change which affects being in so far as it is being.[37]

We will soon see that this change *in being* of which Lonnie partakes is paralleled, *in alio esse*, in his language. "Lonnie's monotonous speech gives him an advantage," Binx says, "the same advantage foreigners have: his words are not worn out. It is like a code tapped through a wall. Sometimes he asks me straight out: do you love me? And it is possible to tap back: yes, I love you."[38] "Language is the house of Being," as Heidegger famously and succinctly phrases his philosophy of the word as it relates to human being-in-the world.[39] Lonnie's language, more than most of our language, seems to authentically house being.

After Mass, Lonnie finds Binx, who tells him "I don't think you should fast.... You've had pneumonia twice in the past year. It would not be good for you."[40] Lonnie says he is fasting "to conquer a habitual disposition." He uses the peculiar idiom of the catechism in ordinary speech. Once [Binx relates], "he told me I needn't worry about some piece of foolishness he heard me tell Linda, since it was not a malicious lie but rather a 'jocose lie.'"[41] With his particular language, Lonnie can, like a poet, recover mystery, can, in a sense, "wrench signifier out of context and exhibit it in all its queerness and splendor."[42]

Before we can speak of this recovery of signifier and signified, we must trace the devolution signs undergo. Percy argues that at first the "signifier serves as the discovery vehicle through which the signified is known," as in the case of Helen Keller, "discovering water through *water*."[43] Afterward, the signifier is transformed by the signified. The signifier *water* becomes informed by the utterly loose-substance-spray of chill when a shower is first

37. Ibid.

38. Percy, *The Moviegoer*, 131.

39. Martin Heidegger, *On the Way to Language*, translated by Peter Hertz (San Francisco: Harper, 1982), 63.

40. Percy, *The Moviegoer*, 131.

41. Ibid.

42. Percy, *Lost in the Cosmos*, 106; emphasis in original.

43. Ibid., 105.

turned on, by the heavy, down-ward tending rush of water going down the throat. Finally there is, "a hardening and closure of the signifier, so that in the end the signified becomes encased in a simulacrum like a mummy in a mummy case."[44] For instance: FIRST TOURIST: What is that? SECOND TOURIST: Oh that, that's only Niagara Falls. In such an instance, Percy observes, "a devaluation has occurred," as the thing itself—in this case water—has, "disappeared into the sarcophagus of its sign."[45] The unique looseness and soft-hardness flow or spray of water is, "assigned to its class of signs, a second-class mummy in the basement collection of mummy cases."[46]

Nietzsche posits roughly the same semiotic process in "On Truth and Lying in a Non-Moral Sense," although his primary aim is to critique scientific abstraction. Humans first generalize sensuous perceptions, transforming these sensations into concepts, cool concepts that convince them they can master the world. "Something becomes possible" he writes, "in the realm of these schemata which could never be achieved in the realm of those sensuous first impressions, namely the construction of a pyramidal order based on castes and degrees, the creation of a new world of laws, privileges, subordinations . . . something regulatory and imperative."[47] Nietzsche cherishes the transformation of sense-perceptions into metaphor, because, he contends, every metaphor is individual and unique and therefore beyond classification, beyond scientific good and evil. Scientists construct a great edifice of concepts, an edifice that resembles in its rigid regularity the "Roman *columbarium*."[48] Percy seems to see Nietzsche's devolution via science as something performed more popularly—by all humans. Still, Nietzsche in prescription and Percy more in practice posit poetry as the source by which the world undergoes a rebirth that ransoms it from its tragic, conceptual coma. Whereas for Nietzsche concept-making is part-in parcel with the human will to truth, driven by a will to use words to make man more powerful than he actually is, for Percy man, who has devalued language through symbolization now dead, is more reminiscent of the "Last Man" we meet in *Thus Spoke Zarathustra*. For we can wonder if it is in part at least because the symbols "love," "creation," "star," and "hap-

44. Ibid.

45. Ibid.

46. Ibid.

47. Friedrich Nietzsche, "On Truth and Lying in a Non-Moral Sense," in *The Birth of Tragedy and Other Writings*, translated by Ronald Speirs (New York: Cambridge University Press, 2000), 146.

48. Ibid., 147.

piness" have been devalued through deadening use that the Last Man asks, "What is love? What is creation? What is longing/What is a star," blinking as he asks, blinking still as he says, "We have invented happiness," a happiness called so with words but hollow.[49]

Percy contends that the "semioticist most acutely aware of this devolution of the sign and its renewal through the defamiliarization of art is the Russian formalist Victor Schklovsky."[50] For Schklovsky, as perception becomes habitual it also becomes automatic, unconscious. Were someone to compare the sensation of speaking in a foreign tongue, for instance, for the very first time, "with the sensation of performing this same operation for the ten thousandth time, then he would no doubt agree with us. It is this process of automatization that explains the laws of our prose speech with its fragmentary phrases and half-articulated words."[51] Through this "algebraic" method of thinking, "objects are grasped spatially, in the blink of an eye. We do not see them, we merely recognize them by their primary characteristics. The object passes before us, as if it were prepackaged."[52]

We are given a glimpse of this mode of language and its accompanying thinking in *The Moviegoer*, in Binx's mother. Binx tries to "shake her loose from her elected career of the commonplace" by asking her whether his deceased father was a good husband. "Was he!" she says. "And what hands! If anyone ever had the hands of a surgeon, he did."[53] Binx takes this in: "My mother's recollection of my father is storied and of a piece. It is not him she remembers but an old emblem of him."[54] For a moment, because of Binx's prodding, she is shaken from her commonplace, and she recalls a time when her husband would not eat: "It was like he thought eating was not—*important* enough. You see, with your father, everything, every second had to be—."[55] She breaks off, and upon prompting responds, "I don't know. Something." Binx again asks what was wrong with him, but she only replies, "He was overwrought" in "her regular mama-bee drone and again my father disappears into the old emblem."[56] Most of the time, his mother knows not her husband but sarcophagusic signifiers pointing not to him but to, in Binx's

49. Friedrich Nietzsche, *Thus Spoke Zarathustra*, translated by Adrian Del Caro (New York: Cambridge University Press, 2006), 9–10.

50. Viktor Shklovsky, "Art as Device," in *Theory of Prose*, translated by Benjamin Sher (Elmwood Park, Illinois: Dalkey Archive Press, 1990), 106.

51. Ibid., 5.

52. Ibid.

53. Percy, *The Moviegoer*, 123.

54. Ibid.

55. Ibid., 124.

56. Ibid.

words, "an old emblem." Again: for Percy and Shklovsky, art is a prime device through which the object, hidden behind the emblem, disappeared into its sarcophagus, can be recovered. In Shklovsky's infamous rendering:

> And so, in order to return sensation to our limbs, in order to make us feel objects, to make a stone feel stony, man has been given the tool of art. The purpose of art, then, is to lead us to a knowledge of a thing through the organ of sight instead of recognition. By "enstranging" objects and complicating form, the device of art makes perception long and "laborious." The perceptual process in art has a purpose all its own and ought to be extended to the fullest.[57]

Derrida ends with the devolution of the signifier that can do nothing but point us to another signifier. Shklovsky and Percy grant this devolution but the virtue of hope obtains in their souls: they believe in the resurrection of signification, that what the sarcophagus once contained *in alio esse* will be raised from its deadness. In *The Moviegoer*, Percy leads us to knowledge of the Eucharist through the organ of sight instead of recognition. He estranges the Eucharist through art in the scene of Lonnie's shaking tuft of red hair and Roy's accompanying eagle eyes. Literally in *The Moviegoer*, Lonnie leads us to knowledge of a thing, but not quite through the organ of sight as opposed to recognition. He *estranges* objects by using the "peculiar idiom of the catechism in ordinary speech."[58] Shklovsky writes of the artist who, rather than *naming* things, describes them as if seeing them for the first time. Lonnie, like Hellen Keller, *names* things in such a way that they are seen as if for the first time, and it is in this Edenic moment that we stand in a sense as if beside Adam as he named animals for the first time. Lonnie, like Adam, names things in order to master them. Of course Lonnie is speaking of quite the animal—sin, and (again) he does not get at it by means of a metaphorical snake. Listen as he further interacts with Binx over the question of conquering a "habitual disposition":

> "What disposition is that?" [Binx]
> "A disposition to envy."
> "Envy who?"
> "Duval."
> "Duval is dead."
> "Yes. But envy is not merely sorrow at another's good fortune: it is also joy at another's misfortune."[59]

57. Shklovsky, "Art as Device," 6.
58. Ibid., 131.
59. Ibid., 131–32.

Binx suggests that Lonnie is not hurting the dead man Duval with his envy, but Lonnie says: "It is hurting me. You know what capital sin does to the life of the soul."

"Yes. Still and all I would not fast. Instead I would concentrate on the Eucharist. It seems a more positive thing to do."

"This is true … but Eucharist is a sacrament of the living," Lonnie says somewhat mysteriously, implying that, *symbolically*, he is dead due to envy.[60]

Humans and animals both exist in environments, both use and respond to signs. Humans and animals die. But, just as only humans know the *meaning* of signs, only humans know the natural fact that death is certain. For Percy, Lawler gleans, "That miserable, anxious awareness is the price to be paid for the gift of language, for thinking about the mystery of human existence."[61] Through his singular relationship to language, to the symbol, to the possibility therefore of symbolic death, of death *in alio esse*, Lonnie reveals an awareness that is anxious and a lexicon with which he can ransom that mystery, and can therefore find redemption of everyday sins from the environment they have been held captive in as simple stimulus-response actions beyond human symbolization and therefore beyond human freedom. In Keller's account, immediately after she experienced language as a symbol, she experienced sorrow over shattering the doll: "my eyes filled with tears; for I realized what I had done, and for the first time I felt repentance and sorrow."[62] Lonnie's relationship to the language of the catechism remains *living*, and therefore he is able to "discover" sin, to *name* sin in even subtle situations.

"When I name an unknown thing or hear the name from you, a remarkable thing happens," Percy notes. "In some sense or other, the thing is said to 'be' its symbol. The semanticists are right: this round thing is certainly not the word *ball*."[63] But until it becomes at least in some sense the word *ball* in our consciousness, the ball will remain unknown to us. Percy, like Maritain, points to the Scholastics, whose theory of symbolic meaning he sees as far more adequate. He too touches John of St. Thomas' observation, what is fast becoming a sort of chant for us: "symbols come to contain

60. Ibid.
61. Lawler, *Postmodernism Rightly Understood*, 82.
62. Quoted in Percy, *The Message in the Bottle*, 35.
63. Ibid., 155–56.

within themselves the thing symbolized *in alio esse*, in another mode of existence."[64]

When a man names a thing, says "this is water and is cool," an unprecedented thing happens. Here man goes beyond merely interacting with things: "He stands apart from two things and says that one 'is' the other. The two things which he pairs or identifies are the *word* he speaks or hears and the *thing* he sees before him."[65] Until this point, until man utters *A is B*, "he will never know A or B; he will only respond to them."[66] In a Percyan key: man is more foolish than a bee, but the bee cannot tell the truth; it can merely respond, react, to its environment. Unless Lonnie articulates his "habitual disposition to envy," until he articulates envy as, "not merely sorrow at another's good fortune" but also "joy at another's misfortune" he would not *know* envy, and would only respond (with joy) at the stimuli (another's misfortune) of his environment.

Soon the conversation breaks off, and the two part. After Binx kisses his half-brother goodbye, however, the latter calls him back. But, Binx narrates, "he doesn't really have anything to say," at least, he does not have anything to signal.

> "Wait." [Lonnie]
> "What?"
> He searches the swamp, smiling.
> "Do you think that Eucharist—"
> "Yes?"
> He forgets and is obliged to say straight out: "I am still offering my communion for you."
> "I know you are."
> "Wait."
> "What?"
> "Do you love me?"
> "Yes."
> "How much?"
> "Quite a bit."
> "I love you too."[67]

Here we witness a parallel to a scene in John's gospel. Just as Binx and Lonnie have just finished communion, Jesus and his disciples have just eaten breakfast:

64. Ibid.
65. Ibid., 157.
66. Ibid.
67. Percy, *The Moviegoer*, 133.

> When they had finished breakfast, Jesus said to Simon Peter, "Simon, son of John, do you love me more than these?" He said to him, "Yes, Lord, you know that I love you." He said to him, "Feed my lambs."
>
> He then said to him a second time, "Simon, son of John, do you love me?" He said to him, "Yes, Lord, you know that I love you." He said to him, "Tend my sheep."
>
> He said to him the third time, "Simon, son of John, do you love me?" Peter was distressed that he had said to him a third time, "Do you love me?" and he said to him, "Lord, you know everything; you know that I love you." (Jesus) said to him, "Feed my sheep." (John 21.15–17).

Again there is something singular about Lonnie. As Binx notes earlier, Lonnie's words are, "not worn out. It is like a code tapped through a wall. Sometimes he asks me straight out: do you love me? and it is possible to tap back: yes, I love you."[68] In a sense, Lonnie is a sign pointing us to Jesus. Percy posits a sign as "something that directs our attention to something else," and this directing of our attention is, "brought about by past association."[69] In another sense, Lonnie is a symbol, a symbol that "does not direct our attention to something else, as a sign does. It does not direct at all. It 'means' something else. It somehow comes to contain within itself the thing it means."[70] Having just received Eucharist, Lonnie could be read as a symbol, containing in himself the thing he means—Christ. Maritain reminds us that "the sacramental sign is no longer merely a *practical sign*, it then becomes an *instrumental cause* of which the very Cause of being makes use to produce grace in the soul."[71] Having received the sacrament, Lonnie becomes a symbol.

At the end of his essay, "Sign and Symbol," Maritain argues that, "Nothing is clearer than the importance of the sign in social life," because the sign, "invests human affairs with *meaning* (signification) and fills them with something more than they physically are, makes out of men and their gestures a mirror, a sign, a symbol through which passes *another thing*, and to this extent gives social life an intellectual and indeed a poetical *quality*."[72] In *The Moviegoer*, Lonnie may be a "Helen Keller" helping us to discover signification and therefore sin. He may be a sign mirroring Christ for Binx. Dwelling on the wonder of signification, Maritain argues that it is in

68. Ibid., 131.
69. Percy, *The Message in the Bottle*, 153.
70. Ibid.
71. Maritain, "Sign and Symbol," 226; emphasis in original.
72. Ibid., 250–51.

a sense of little importance that a sign's significance be forgotten over time, or is morphed, or is indistinct. What is essential is that there be sign and signification: "Not knowing precisely what a given sign signifies, I am free to have it signify *everything* for me. In a sense, poetical joy and affective exaltation will then only be more vast and more indeterminate."[73] And yet, on the other edge of this *everything* hangs the great *nothing* spoken of by Shakespeare's Macbeth, for whom all of life, *everything,* is "a tale/Told by an idiot, full of sound and fury,/Signifying nothing." Amidst the sound and fury of *The Moviegoer,* Lonnie may signify many things, but there is one thing he symbolizes more than any other.

Wrestling with three incarnations of the literary term "Christ-figure," Robert Detweiler "speaks of the *sign,* where the character is but Christ in disguise, of the *mythological archetype,* where the character and Christ are seen as representing the same recurring life-pattern, of the *symbol* in which a character's redemptive role in a story is indicated through some overt parallels to the Biblical Christ."[74] Lonnie is a symbolic sign. At the novel's end, Lonnie dies of hepatitis. The day before he is gone, Binx visits him to find that "he had conquered a habitual disposition"—his envy.[75] He became a living man before he died. The day his breath finally expires, Lonnie's half brothers and sisters are left outside in the car all morning, while his mother stays at her dying son's bedside. Binx, until this point an observer and interpreter, comes urgently out of the hospital room: "I have to find the children," he says hastily.[76] Binx comforts the children with kisses and, becoming Lonnie in another mode of existence, becomes thereby a catechetical hope:

"Binx," one of Lonnie's brothers asks, "When our Lord raises him up on the last day, will Lonnie still be in a wheelchair or will he be like us?" Binx says, "He'll be like you," to which young Donice replies, "'You mean he'll be able to ski?' The children cock their heads and listen like old men./'Yes.'/'Hurray' cry the twins."[77] Binx offers to take the children to the Audubon park. The children scream *Yes!* and say, "Binx, we love you too!"[78] Piecing together the work of Percy and Maritain, I propose Lonnie is a sign

73. Ibid.

74. Christine Dowling, "Typology and the Literary Christ-Figure: A Critique," *Journal of the American Academy of Religion* 36, no. 1 (1968): 25; emphasis in original.

75. Percy, *The Moviegoer,* 189.

76. Ibid.

77. Ibid., 190.

78. Ibid.

symbolizing Christ and maintain that in him we find a, "certain presence—presence of knowability—" of what we find in the unbloody sacrifice of the Eucharist and in the bodily sacrifice of his life.[79] Christ is in Lonnie *in alio esse.*

Lonnie is both sign and symbol in the story, but his meaning bleeds beyond both in that he receives the Eucharist. Lonnie offers up the sacrament, which effects a *change in being* in him, for Binx. In the final scene, where Binx interacts with the children, we see, more than a mere change in behavior, a change in being. We see him respond to Christ's direct (and Lonnie's implied) command to "feed my lambs," and "tend my sheep." Of course the shift is not and should not be *storied.* We see him, even after his contact with what Lonnie and what the children signify, even after the remarkably childlike interaction with the children, move into a movie-like image of his beloved Kate in his mind "until my brothers and sisters call out behind me."[80]

Percy begins *The Moviegoer* with a quote from Kierkegaard's *The Sickness Unto Death*: "[T]he specific character of despair is precisely this: it is unaware of being despair."[81] Percy also contends that consciousness, from *con-scio,* "I know with," comes about through language. For he calls consciousness an "act of attention to something under the auspices of its sign ... an act which is social in origin."[82] One who lives in despair without knowing he is in despair is like the deaf mute who only lives through signals. They live, to use Kierkegaard's metaphor of the self, *only in the basement* for their entire lives. The basement is the *aesthetic* way of life in which one is in despair so as not to be conscious of having a self. He who lives in the basement lives in obedience only to desires, and never reaches the ethical first floor, a life lived in obedience to the required, or the religious, second floor, what he calls the ideality of actuality, where all things are made new. Binx lives in the basement, is a practitioner of the aesthetical way. He lives for the fiction of the movies, but *The Moviegoer* reveals that the harmful fictions which distract us are not limited to the second rate blockbusters we live our lives by.

Rather, as Simone Weil shows us in her essay "Morality and Literature," "the substance of our life is almost exclusively composed of fiction.

79. Maritain, "Sign and Symbol," 220.

80. Percy, *The Moviegoer,* 191.

81. Ibid., 7.

82. Percy, *Lost in the Cosmos,* 106.

We fictionalize our future, and, unless we are heroically devoted to truth, we fictionalize our past, refashioning it to our taste. We do not study other people; we invent what they are thinking, saying, and doing."[83] Reality may provide us with raw material, but we tend to refashion it until all values are reversed. Explicating Weil's essay, John M. Dunaway notes that "a law of human psychology perpetuates this tendency until we are confronted with a violent shock of reality—such as contact with a saint or with affliction or crime. The only other thing that can overcome the force of fiction in our lives is the work of great literary genius" which, though fiction, is filled with the density of the real, in part because it ransoms the significance of symbols that give to us *worlds* that, existing within good and evil, grant to us the possibility of *conversion*—conversion at the level of language and conversion at the level of the soul.[84] Remember Maritain's insistence that in order for one to *know* the relationship of signification of which they are to make use, "some external help is indispensible."[85] For Weil, this external help can come from contact with saints, criminals, and great literary works. In *The Moviegoer*, Binx's aesthetical, basement existence is interrupted by contact with the saintly Lonnie, and, in an entirely connected sense, with his contact with children.

While we await those encounters with affliction, criminals, and saints that can administer to us the shocking significance of the real, we are left with great poetry, poetry like Percy's which serves pedagogically as the "external help" that makes the stones feel stony, that helps us perceive the "architecture of the abyss" behind our banally evil fictions, that shows us the Good *in alio esse.* When we are lost in our Pharisaical fictions, those "unseen graves over which people unknowingly walk" that Christ speaks of, when we succumb to sin—signs that signify nothing but other signs—great poems can serve as natural sacraments, can prepare spaces in our language which do not yet exist, opening our very being to the gravity-suspending, despair-defying, language-illumining action of grace.

83. Ibid.

84. John M. Dunaway, "Simone Weil on Morality and Literature," in *The Beauty That Saves: Essays on Aesthetics and Language in Simone Weil*, edited by John M. Dunaway and Eric O. Springstead (Macon, Georgia: Mercer University Press, 1996), 100–101.

85. Maritain, "Sign and Symbol," 221.

V

SOCIAL TURN

ANNE M. WILES

Maritain on Education

In this relativistic and (paradoxically) scientific age, a prominent trend in education is to offer a smorgasbord of courses instead of a well-designed and sustaining menu. Emphasis is placed on standards of learning, psychological tests, and measurements and standardized assessments while classical languages, music, and art are abolished from the curriculum. Higher education is often valued merely as a means to earning a living. In such an environment, the question, "What is a human being?" seems strangely out of place, not a question that has anything to do with education.

Yet, Maritain, in the series of lectures titled *Education at the Crossroads*, given at Yale in 1943 and later issued as a book,[1] urges that this is a foundational question, a question that must be asked and answered correctly, if education is to fulfill its fundamental task of guiding the individual to a fully human life.

The title of the book, as well as the title of the last essay, "The Trials of Present Day Education,"[2] might lead one to suspect that the purpose of the four essays is merely to offer a critique of educational practices and to suggest ways in which education in the United States should move forward from the "crossroads" at the end of the second world war. However, as Maritain mentions at the beginning of the first chapter, he had thought of titling the lectures, *The Education of Man*—not primitive man, or Western man, or the man of the Renaissance, but simply man.[3] Clearly, he is inter-

1. Jacques Maritain, *Education at the Crossroads* (New Haven, Connecticut: Yale University Press, 1943). This work was re-issued as a Yale Paperbound in 1960. All references in this paper are to the paperbound edition, fourth printing, 1961.

2. Ibid., 88–118.

3. Ibid., 1.

ested in more than specific educational practices. The two central lectures also show that Maritain's focus is on matters more fundamental and universal. He is, in fact, offering a philosophy of education founded on Greek, Judaic, and Christian sources, and especially on the writings of Aquinas. Beginning with the fundamental question, "What is a human being?" these lectures on education contain time-transcending truths about the nature and value of education.

The purpose of my essay is to reflect on the principles Maritain invokes, and also on the rich experience and insight he brings to the art of teaching. Following Maritain, this essay considers the nature of the human person, the role of tradition in education, the importance of personal freedom and its relation to external freedom, what self-perfection is and how it is to be sought, the importance of the humanities and liberal education, and concludes with some observations on the personal aspects of teaching.

While the term "education" has connotations ranging from pre-school play through university studies, and from informal interactions within a family or a group of friends or colleagues, to highly specialized technical or professional training, underlying all these is the question, "What is a human being?" If we lose sight of, or fail to answer, this question correctly, we endanger ourselves and others, as well as the educational and social structures of which we are a part.

Humans are not merely animals of nature like a skylark or bear, but animals of culture. Pindar says the task of education is to "become who we are."[4] Maritain says this is possible only in a society, within a civilization, within a tradition. A human being is a political animal, but also an historical animal. Humans by nature desire to know, and while the power of knowing is unlimited, or as Aristotle says, "capable of becoming all that is," nonetheless, the power advances only step by step so that one can progress neither morally nor intellectually unless aided by tradition, understood as "collective experience previously accumulated and preserved, and regularly transmitted."[5] Maritain holds that tradition is necessary for self-determination, not passively accepted tradition, but tradition that weighs heavily upon one and strengthens one to struggle against it. The struggle to understand and appropriate the tradition strengthens the person and enriches the tradition

4. Pindar, *Pythian* 2, line 72.
5. Maritain, *Education at the Crossroads*, 2.

itself; it leads to a continual, and ever-increasing spiritual enrichment of both the individual and the tradition.[6]

Starting from the truth that education is an art, Maritain draws attention to the nature of art in general, and then specifically to the art of education. Every art is "a dynamic trend toward an object to be achieved, which is the aim of this art,"[7] and if the end of education is disregarded, or not clearly conceived, education will not achieve its end. If underlying each specific educational task is the aim of helping and guiding each individual to his own distinct human achievement, the question "What is the nature of a human being?" must be addressed.

Is a human merely an intricate machine whose behavior can be exhaustively measured by empirical methods, totally explained by causal accounts, and consequently completely predictable? If this materialistic (sometimes *erroneously* called "scientific") view of the nature of a human being is accepted, questions about the human spirit, or freedom, or, even acting for reasons—as contrasted with causal explanations of behavior—are ruled out. Maritain points out that trying to build education on such a "scientific" idea of man, having at our disposal only what emerges from sense observation and measurement, would be trying to draw a metaphysics from science,[8] but science is not metaphysics, and however valuable the results of science for human life, the nature of a human being can no more be encapsulated in a merely scientific account than can the nature of love or a work of art. Moreover, from the practical point of view, this spurious metaphysics, "disguised as science," denies or misconceives realities "without which education loses all human sense, or becomes the training of an animal for the utility of the state."[9] Both science and politics have a role to play in human life and education, but it is not the proper role of either to give an ontological account of the nature of the human being.

The only adequate account is the philosophical-religious account. Although Maritain endorses, and unabashedly writes from, the Catholic point of view, he recognizes that there are many different philosophical and religious conceptions of man. However, Maritain's own view is that in order to be completely well grounded, education must be based on the Christian idea of man. The essential features of this account are that a hu-

6. See ibid.

7. Ibid., 3.

8. See ibid., 6.

9. Ibid.

man being is an animal endowed with reason, a free individual in personal relation to God, and an imperfect being who can become more perfect through knowledge, love and grace.[10]

At the center of Maritain's philosophy of education is the concept of human "personality," a concept to be distinguished from "individuality." Each human is a part of the physical universe, an instance of the species, and is inescapably subject to cosmic, ethnic, and historic laws. This set of characteristics belongs to what Maritain identifies as "individuality," an undeniable aspect of a human being.[11] Certain practices in education such as developing "psychophysical habits, conditioned reflexes, and sense memorizations" are related to this "material individuality," and play a part in education.[12] However, a human being—shall we say, "person"—does not exist merely as a physical being. Education is not animal training; rather, it is "a human awakening."[13]

A person has a spiritual aspect that enables a more rich and noble existence through knowledge and love. Aristotle held that the psyche was the first principle of life in any organism, and specifically differentiated the human psyche by its capacity for reasoning. Christianity appropriated this Greek tradition and came to understand the human psyche as "the dwelling place of God and as made for eternal life."[14]

While a person is subject to the slightest accidents of matter, it is the existence of the psyche (soul, intellect, spirit) that is the root of personality. To say that one is a person implies a certain wholeness and independence not captured by the concept of "material individuality." Maritain writes, "It is this mystery of our nature which religious thought designates when it says that the person is the image of God. A person possesses absolute dignity because he is in direct relationship with the realm of being, truth, goodness and beauty, and with God, and it is only with these that he can arrive at his complete fulfillment."[15]

The concept of personality has wide and resounding implications for education. One of the most important is that the educator must have a respect for the person, as well as the body, a sort of "sacred and loving attention" to the mysterious identity of the other, an identity not reachable by mere techniques. This approach is not limited to the liberal arts, but can be

10. See ibid., 7.
11. Ibid., 9.
12. Ibid.
13. Ibid.
14. Ibid., 8.
15. Ibid.

used at every age, and in every type of education, including physical training; it is, in fact, a way of humanizing education.[16]

According to Maritain, the central aspiration of a person is freedom understood as spontaneity, expansion, or autonomy. To the independence one gains by means of intellect and wisdom, he adds the possibility of perfection by love, articulated by St. Paul as, "the freedom of those moved by divine love."[17] Thus, the principal goal of education is for the person to become who he is, "through knowledge and wisdom, good will and love."[18] This is an internal and spiritual perfection, not totally reachable, but to be continually sought. The love of wisdom is not itself wisdom, but, as Plato noted in the *Symposium*,[19] it is an indispensable condition for becoming as wise as is humanly possible.

Education is a spiritual activity and therefore is intentional. The intellect seeks truth, which Maritain refers to as "the conquest of being." In a passage that perfectly captures this sense of freedom, and speaks to the value of liberal education, Maritain writes, "This conquest of being, this progressive attainment of new truths, or the progressive realization of the ever-growing and ever-renewed significance of truths already attained, opens and enlarges our mind and life, and really situates them in freedom and autonomy."[20]

Human thinking begins with difficulties, but also with insights; it ends in insights that then require support by argument and/or experience. Without trust in the intellect's capacity to attain truth about what and how things are, there is no effective human action. It is by having knowledge *into*, not merely *about*, the nature of things that makes possible both speculative and practical wisdom and action that strives, in however limited a way, towards unlimited good.[21]

Certain basic dispositions of human nature that aid one to achieve personal freedom need to be cultivated as early as possible in childhood. The first, which Maritain characterizes as the primary tendency of any intellectual nature, is the love of knowing the truth.[22] Also important is the love of good and justice and "even the love of heroic feats."[23] A third disposition is simplicity and openness with regard to existence, which Maritain describes as the attitude of existing gladly and accepting the natural limitations of

16. Ibid., 10.
17. Ibid., 11.
18. Ibid.
19. Plato, *Symposium* 204b1–7.
20. Maritain, *Education at the Crossroads*, 12.
21. See ibid., 13.
22. See ibid., 36.
23. Ibid., 37.

existence.[24] The fourth disposition is a deep respect for the job to be done and faithfulness and responsibility in doing it.[25] Finally, a disposition closely related to external freedom and political obligation is the disposition of co-operation with others.[26] Here, we must keep in mind that Maritain is not giving a description of the dispositions that most people actually *have*; in fact one might suspect that few adults have cultivated these dispositions. Rather, as is appropriate for a philosophy of education, he is identifying the dispositions that *ought* to be cultivated.

A person naturally desires not only personal freedom, that is, intellectual and spiritual freedom, but also what may be called "external" freedom, a freedom that is linked to social life. Given that a person is a "political" animal by nature, how is personal freedom to be understood in relation to the demands that living in a society places on one? Is there a conflict between personal freedom and political obligation? Maritain answers that in fact there is not, or should not be, a conflict between these two freedoms. Social life, correctly understood, he says, subordinates the person to the common good, not in a tyrannical fashion, but in order that the common good flow back so that each person can enjoy the freedom of expansion and independence made possible by "economic guaranties of labor and ownership, political rights, civic virtues, and the cultivation of the mind."[27]

Development of the skills and civic virtues that enable a person to perform normal, useful, and co-operative roles in the social sphere is an *essential* goal of education, but it is not the *ultimate* goal. Far from being in conflict, the development of personal freedom is actually the foundation for social life. Human society, Maritain says, is most appropriately viewed as a group of human freedoms, accepting obedience and self-sacrifice and a common law for the general welfare. The purpose of the social group is to make it possible for each of these freedoms (persons) to reach a truly human fulfillment. The person and the social group are interrelated and surpass each other in different respects. The person serves the social group; tyranny can be avoided only if it is recognized that the person, "has secrets which escape the group and a vocation which is not included in the group."[28] It is in this inner core, the freedom of the person, that idealism, generosity, and respect for others are developed as well as a deep-rooted

24. See ibid.

25. See ibid., 38.

26. See ibid.

27. Ibid., 14.

28. Ibid., 15.

independence from the opinion of others. One of the ways Maritain recommends to develop this independence is the reading of books, not textbooks, but books that will increase the pleasure of the spirit, the joy of knowing, and the joy of beauty.[29]

Concerning the utilitarian aspect of education in the practical aim of gainful employment, Maritain admits such practical education is necessary because "the children of man are not made for aristocratic leisure."[30] The caution here is that specialized training must never endanger the ultimate goal of internal and spiritual freedom and that the practical aim of education is best provided by the development of the general human capacities. That many large conglomerates do not accept this view is easily born out by a close look at the inner workings of the U.S. Postal Service or the TSA, to mention but two agencies. Even in colleges and universities where one might expect to find liberal education valued along the lines suggested by Maritain, overspecialization and narrowness of outlook often prevail. However, that such conditions exist does not vitiate Maritain's view; rather, these very conditions make it more imperative that his view, and the tradition within which he writes, be better understood and more widely promulgated.

Maritain observes that specialization is increasingly needed by the technical organization of modern life, but warns that education which takes as its only, or highest, aim the formation of specialists who know only their own field and are unable to pass judgment on any matter beyond their specialized competence, would endanger the very existence of "government of the people, by the people, and for the people," the assumption being that a truly well-functioning republic requires that its citizens be generally educated. He asks, "How could the common man be capable of judging about the good of the people if he felt able to pass judgment only in the field of his own specialized vocational competence?"[31] He projects what he thinks would be the consequences of such specialization: "the real life of man would consist of producing in a perfectly pigeonholed manner economic values and scientific discoveries, while some cheap pleasure or social entertainment would occupy leisure time, and a vague religious feeling, without any content of thought and reality, would make existence a little less flat, perhaps a little more dramatic and stimulating, like a happy dream."[32] The

29. See ibid., 16.

30. Ibid., 10.

31. Ibid., 19.

32. Ibid.

only remedy, if there is one, he concludes, is an early and more vigorous education in the liberal arts. The democratic way of life "demands primarily liberal education for all and a general humanistic development throughout society."[33] The consequences Maritain merely projected are now evident on every hand. Is this a failure of the education system? Or caused by the materialistic bent of our times? Or, a natural result of the normal curve of human intelligence? Or of all of these? The causes are complex and the implementation of the cure does not look promising. However, philosophy is not practice, and, as Plato learned from his attempts in Syracuse,[34] putting true insights into practice is not a task that philosophy by itself can achieve.

Maritain's philosophy of education is not an elitist view that values only liberal education. The ideal of *homo sapiens* and the ideal of *homo faber* are integrally related. The intelligence of man is not only in his head, but in his fingers, too. Sense perception is not the end of understanding; it is, however, the beginning. In a homey metaphor, Maritain suggests, "there is no place closer to man than a workshop."[35] Manual work provides psychological equilibrium; it also furthers ingenuity and accuracy of the mind and is the "prime basis" of artistic activity. The Socratic question, *Tis estin*? ("What is it?") that asks for an account of the nature of something is an old question; the companion question, "How does this work?" may be even older. The point, Maritain says, "is to disengage from experience the rational and necessary connections with which that experience is pregnant, and which become visible only by means of abstraction and universal concepts, and in the light of intuitive first principles of reason."[36]

Maritain is writing from within a rich tradition and from his unique appropriation of that tradition. He is, as he himself claims, a Thomist, but he is also a Platonist, an Aristotelian, a French intellectual, and a philosopher, who, by the time he wrote the Yale lectures on education, had already been a professor of philosophy (of the contemplative sort who reflects on the art he practices) for some 30 years. He had thought about and written extensively on the principles that inform his reflections on education.

Drawing on this tradition, Maritain understands that education is an art, an especially difficult art that naturally falls within the sphere of ethics and practical wisdom. As an art, it is a dynamic process towards an end or

33. Ibid., 20.

34. See Plato, *Seventh Letter* 339a-352a

35. Maritain, *Education at the Crossroads*, 30.

36. Ibid., 46.

ends to be achieved.[37] From the foregoing account, it is evident that Maritain has a clear conception of the ends, taken generally, that ought to be sought by the person and by the educational structures in which the person participates. He is also aware of the attendant dangers.

In the early twentieth century, when Maritain was writing *Education at the Crossroads*, there was, especially in the public schools, a tendency to emphasize the methods of education, sometimes to the detriment of the student and the subjects to be studied. Maritain writes, "the child is so well tested and observed, his needs so well detailed, his psychology so clearly cut out, the methods for making it easy for him everywhere so perfected, that the end of all these commendable improvements runs the risk of being forgotten or disregarded."[38] The educational landscape has changed. Since the 1980s, the emphasis has moved from detailed testing of the student to an emphasis on the teacher. How to prepare the teacher? How to test the effectiveness of the teaching? Colleges and universities now have established centers to help teachers learn how to teach. Although the focus is altered, the emphasis is still on the method, on the *means* rather than on the *end*, or purpose, of education. It is not that the methods are bad; they may, in fact, be quite good. And herein precisely lies the danger, both in Maritain's time and in our own; the means may be so good and so interesting to pursue that one loses sight of the end. If the means are pursued and cultivated for the sake of their own perfection, and not as means to achieve the aims of education, they cease to perform their own appropriate function. The supremacy of means over ends leads to the collapse of any clear purpose in education and the loss of real efficiency.[39]

In closing, I quote two passages from Maritain's Yale lectures that show the aspects of teaching Maritain takes to be central to the education of the person, aspects that by all accounts were evident in Maritain's own teaching.

The first occurs early in the lectures where he is speaking of the education of the young. He writes that one of the greatest helps towards self-perfection is to have "the comforting assurance of being in some way recognized by a human personal gaze, inexpressible either in concepts or words."[40]

The second is a passage in which Maritain speaks of the role of intuition in teaching: "If a teacher himself is concerned with discerning and

37. Ibid., 2–3.

38. Ibid., 3.

39. See ibid.

40. Ibid., 41.

seeing, with getting vision, rather than with collecting facts and opinions, and if he handles his burden of knowledge so as to see through it into the reality of things, then in the mind of the student the power of intuition will be awakened and strengthened unawares."[41]

Both these passages are concerned with the education of youth, yet education can go on until death, and these observations are no less true of any interaction that is educative in the ultimate sense that Maritain mentions.

It is impossible in a brief essay to capture the richness and complexity of Maritain's views on education. For that, one must go to Maritain and to the tradition he appropriates, yet the principles identified in this paper, in virtue of their truth and universality, do constitute a philosophy of education worth thoughtful consideration.

41. Ibid., 45.

SAMANTHA BERTRAND

Aristotle's Gentleman

A Good and Noble Philosophy of Education

I. Introduction

"You *can't* legislate morality!"—cries the average, educated modern as she defends private lives and bedrooms from the prying eyes of lawmakers, judges, and the obnoxiously religious; for everyone knows that such tyranny over private conscience, such callous disregard for diversity of values, would be *immoral.*

For Aristotle, this attempt to claim individual moral authority over some areas of human activity is arbitrary and nonsensical. To legislate "morality"—that is, to enact laws that encourage just and prohibit unjust behavior wherever such behavior may occur—is for Aristotle precisely what it means to legislate, period. As he says early in the *Nicomachean Ethics,* "legislators make the citizens good by forming good habits in them, and this is the wish of every legislator, and those who do not effect it miss their mark, and it is in this that a good constitution differs from a bad one."[1] One cannot succeed in creating and maintaining a good constitution if the "good" is left to individual preference. This is not to the detriment of the individual; in fact, it is precisely the central importance of the individual in the polis that demands an objective standard of the good, for it is only

1. Aristotle, *Nicomachean Ethics* (NE), translated by William David Ross, in *The Basic Works of Aristotle,* edited by Richard McKeon (New York: Random House, 1941), 2.1, 1179b25. Throughout the *Politics,* Aristotle especially criticizes the Spartans for missing the mark in this regard.

through the cultivation of good and noble *individual* citizens according to such a standard that a good polis can possibly exist.

In this paper, I will interpret and defend Aristotelian political, ethical, and educational ideals and illustrate what the Aristotelian gentleman,[2] as the product of these ideals, looks like in order to counter misperceptions characteristic of our modern viewpoint. Specifically, I hope to demonstrate the necessity of good liberal education both in the lives of free men and in the life of a free polis.[3] Through the educated, good, and noble man—the gentleman—the relation between citizen and city will be illuminated. After analyzing this noble embodiment of Aristotle's political philosophy, I will compare him to the modern "men without chests"[4] and show thereby the strengths of what is at first glance crippling in Aristotle—such as the apparent sacrifice of individual good for that of the state and the insistence on an absolute moral standard, neither of which is considered acceptable to modern thought—as well as the weaknesses of what is assumed empowering in the modern approach to education, politics, and law.

II. The Inseparability of Law, Ethics, and Education

In his frequent emphasis of the good life and good citizens in the healthy functioning of the polis, it is clear that Aristotle's political thought is continuous with and inseparable from his ethical thought.[5] An appreci-

2. On the use of the word "gentleman": "[O]ne of Aristotle's theses, as fundamental to the *Ethics* as to the *Politics*, is that only the noble is ultimately well and correct and good and that anything that is not noble is not really well or correct or good. The *kaloikagathoi*, however, or those who are literally "noble and good" I refer to as gentlemen, since that is what true gentlemen are." Peter Simpson, *A Philosophical Commentary on the "Politics" of Aristotle* (Chapel Hill, North Carolina: The University of North Carolina Press, 1998), xxvii. Following Aristotle in his frequent use of analogy, I understand "gentleman" to refer to: the morally perfect; those on their way to moral perfection; those who have perfected the degree of virtue possible for them in their particular circumstances.

3. As Leo Strauss explains: "The chief purpose of the city is the noble life and therefore the chief concern of the city must be the virtue of the members and hence liberal education." Leo Strauss, *The City and Man* (Charlottesville, Virginia: The University Press of Virginia, 1964), 31.

4. Following C. S. Lewis' brilliant *The Abolition of Man* (New York: Harper Collins Publishers, 1944).

5. Stanford Cashdollar points out that "there is far more continuity between *EN* X and *Politics* I or II than between almost any two consecutive books of the *Politics*." He continues, "*EN* and *Politics*, or more accurately, the political inquiry is viewed as having as its goal the attainment of the most choosable or desirable life for man (*EN* I. 7, X. 6.; *Pol.* 1323a16, 1325a16–bl). It is not

ation of the continuity of these two works is absolutely necessary in understanding Aristotle's political philosophy; the *Ethics* is "the immediate and particular context of the *Politics*,"[6] apart from which context misunderstanding is inevitable. It is imperative to remember that Aristotle considers his ethical inquiry to be a political one.

One area in which the developments of the *Ethics* are especially key is in Aristotle's recommendations regarding law and education. It is clear from his discussions in book III of the *Ethics* that moral agents must be free in order to be virtuous or vicious, for it is "by choosing [voluntarily] what is good or bad" that "we are men of certain character."[7] At the same time, "it does not follow that if [the unjust man] wishes he will cease to be unjust and will be just." The conviction that goodness and wickedness are ultimately matters of personal, *individual* responsibility is never forgotten throughout Aristotle's political inquiry; it remains a grounding principle even when he advocates ultimate supremacy of the law[8] and the jealous maintaining of "the spirit of obedience to law."[9] Rather than limiting the freedom of the citizen, as seems to be the case at first glance, good laws provide guidance for truly free actions: "in its ordaining of what is good [the law] is not burdensome"[10]—"men should not think it slavery" to live by the constitution, for it is their "salvation."[11] We moderns may cringe as visions of Big Brother loom in our heads when we hear Aristotle say:

> No one will doubt that the legislator should direct his attention above all to the education of youth; for the neglect of education does harm to the constitution. The citizen should be moulded to suit the form of government under which he lives.... Neither must we suppose that any one of the citizens belongs to himself, for they all belong to the state, and are each of them a part of the state, and the care of each part is inseparable from the care of the whole.[12]

However, keeping in mind—as we always should—the investigations of virtue in the *Nicomachean Ethics*, and the vital importance Aristotle places

---

a distortion to say that the ten books attempt to define that life and what is required for its attainment while the subsequent eight books attempt to describe the processes by which these desirable or choosable goals are insured through the actions of the political practitioner." Stanford Cashdollar, "Aristotle's Politics of Morals," *Journal of the History of Philosophy* 11, no. 2 (1973):158.

6. Peter L. Phillips Simpson, *A Philosophical Commentary on the Politics of Aristotle* (Chapel Hill, North Carolina: The University of North Carolina Press, 1998), xxii.

7. NE 3.2, 1112a2.

8. See NE 3.5, 1282b3.

9. NE 5.8, 1307b31.

10. NE 10.9, 1180a24.

11. *Politics* 5.9, 1310a35.

12. *Politics* 8.1, 1337a7–28.

on the freedom of the individual to voluntarily act in the development of virtue therein, it is clear that the men being "moulded" in the ideal city—that is, the men being trained in, by, and for the noble and the good—look nothing like those raised on a Huxleyian assembly line. They are free, noble, virtuous moral agents. Still, it is hard for us to part with the extreme democratic sentiment fuelling a negative reaction to such a view of education and the state; the "false idea" that "freedom means the doing what a man likes" and "every one lives … 'according to his fancy'"[13] is exactly the kind of illusion proper education allows a man to overcome. As the Catholic tradition puts it, "freedom consists not in doing what we like, but in having the right to do what we ought."[14] Acting on the ability to indulge whatever passions may move one is not freedom at all, Aristotle makes clear, and it is in fact enslavement worse than physical chains. Thus, the modern, in pursuing a shallow and false concept of freedom, renders himself unable to enjoy actual liberty and condemns himself to slavery and mediocrity. This is especially problematic in a society built upon a foundation of true autonomy and excellence. As will be discussed in greater detail below, a primary difficulty in the predominant modern political views is that citizens trained according to a doctrine of false freedom cannot maintain a good polis—a free society without truly free citizens will necessarily self-destruct. Hence the need for an education rooted in noble pursuit of the good—anything less will fail to support the continuation of democracy.

Again, the city exists for the sake of the *good* life, not life simply—otherwise "brute animals might form a state."[15] For the citizens to be more than content animals, to be truly happy men (which is what the good life of a city consists in), there need to be good laws, keeping in mind that "the best laws, though sanctioned by every citizen of the state, will be of no avail unless the young are trained by habit and education in the spirit of the constitution."[16]

II. Aristotle's Gentleman

In this section I seek to illustrate the full-fledged good and noble man, who is the guiding ideal the legislator (who in the ideal city is such a man

13. *Politics* 5.9, 1310a25–36.

14. John Paul II, "Homily in Orioles Park at Camden Yards," October 8, 1995. http://www.catholic-forum.com/saints/pope0264is.htm (accessed by author July 4, 2011).

15. *Politics* 3.9, 1280a32.

16. *Politics* 5.9, 1310a14.

himself) has in mind when he makes laws concerning his primary priority: education. In human affairs the ideal is rarely realized, but if it is not at least aimed at, not even a limited approximation will be possible. In educating all freemen as if they could be ideal statesmen—though nature does not seem to provide for such equality—each is at least prepared to maximize the excellence in his power, that is, attain that "state of character which makes a man good and which makes him do his own work well."[17]

1. The Gentleman is Free

Aristotle firmly holds that a city is only as good as its citizens—what else could motivate writing the *Ethics* as the first half of his political inquiry?—saying at the outset of book VIII of the *Politics*, "and always the better the character [of citizens], the better the government."[18] Shortly thereafter he also says, "Neither must we suppose that any one of the citizens belongs to himself, for they all belong to the state."[19] This sounds quite harsh to our individualist ears. However, in the next chapter, Aristotle is quite clear that the state's molding of citizens is producing free men who learn for their own sake (or the sake of friends or excellence) and who avoid the menial and the vulgar.[20] This highlights what is perhaps the first quality of the gentleman that stands out—he is *free.*

The gentleman is truly free; he is not a slave to the false freedom mentioned above; rather, his parents and city having nurtured "the development of reason and autonomous virtue ... guided by reason, 'fostering their best part with their own'"[21] since his earliest youth; he is capable of freely desiring the good and noble. As Burnyeat argues, such habituation—which is central to the early stages of education and key for all future learning—is "actually a way of grasping [the noble and just] on a par with, though different from, induction, perception, and other modes of acquisition."[22] The virtuous being so pleasant to him as a result of this habituation, the law which exists for the sake of encouraging virtue is no burden to him. His upbringing, education, and law are all united in the common political

17. NE 2.6, 1106a22–23.

18. *Politics* 8.1, 1337a7–13.

19. *Politics* 8.1, 1337a28.

20. *Politics* 8.2, 1337b11–24.

21. Randall Curren, *Aristotle and the Necessity of Public Education* (Lanham, Maryland: Rowman and Littlefield, 2000), 49. Curren highlights Aristotle's close following of Plato regarding the Socratic "principle of fidelity to reason."

22. M. F. Burnyeat, "Aristotle on Learning to be Good," in *Essays on Aristotle's "Ethics,"* edited by Amélie Oksenberg Rorty (Berkeley: University of California Press, 1980), 73.

mission to put into practice the understanding of the good discovered in the *Ethics*.[23]

Return now to Aristotle's unsettling claim that "no citizen belongs to himself"—not only does the gentleman belong to the state in such a way as to not contradict his freedom, but it is in fact in and through "belonging" to the state that he attains and maintains that freedom; again, "men should not think it slavery to live according to the rule of the constitution; for it is their salvation."[24] It is the state and its laws that educate the gentleman, that nurture in him "a capacity going beyond the application of general rules, to tell what is required for the practice of virtues in specific circumstances," so that he may in turn legislate and provide for citizens when he participates in ruling. While Aristotle himself only offers a rough sketch of things in these political works, in his outline of the dynamics of constitutional rule, wherein free men alternate between ruled and ruler, we see the beginnings of what his philosophical descendant Maritain develops as a "relation between two wholes":

> For justice and law, by ruling man as a moral agent, and appealing to reason and free will, concern personality as such, and transform into a relation between two wholes—the individual and the social—what must otherwise be a mere subordination of the part to the whole.[25]

Again, while Aristotle would not have formulated it in personalist terms, he did see that the state to which citizens belong is primarily concerned with making them good and obedient to laws. The latter part is not to be interpreted as any kind of legalism—for Aristotle, the law is authoritative insofar as it is in accord with virtue. The ultimate goal of political inquiry is human happiness (action in accordance with virtue), so law must facilitate the achievement of this end; otherwise, it is not (ideally speaking) law.

Thus, when Aristotle says that the state is prior to the individual,[26] or that it is "finer and more godlike"[27] to attain or preserve the end of a state than that same end (happiness) of a single man, it is with the understanding that the relation between city and citizen is *not* one of subordination; a

23. Randall Curren, "Afterword for Aristotle," in *Philosophy of Education: The Essential Texts*, edited by Steven M. Cahn (New York: Routledge, 2009), 148.

24. *Politics* 5.9, 1310a35.

25. Jacques Maritain, *Scholasticism and Politics*, edited by Mortimer J. Adler (New York: Macmillan Company, 1940), 77.

26. See *Politics* 1.1, 1253a19–27.

27. NE 1.2, 1094b7.

city is only good insofar as its citizens are noble and good, and citizens are noble and good insofar as the city enables virtue (i.e., insofar as *it* is good), which is determined in large part through its laws written and unwritten.

2. *Good Man, Good Citizen: The Ideal in a Non-Ideal World*

A problem arises when a gentleman finds himself in a less than ideal city, as the virtue of the citizen in such a city is different from that of the gentleman—while the latter lives in accord with true justice, the former is guided by a constitution and animated by a people deficient in justice. Some conclude from this difficulty that there cannot be gentlemen in a non-ideal city,[28] for it is through his political activity that he is virtuous and, again, the politics of a less-than-ideal city is necessarily deficient.[29] It seems the modern focus on this problem, which Aristotle largely neglects (discussed in further detail below), misses the ultimate guiding end of the legislator: to make men good. If the mediocre legislator is making mediocre laws, the good and noble gentleman will "play the part of a good citizen as best he can, given that his allegiance to the laws and the constitution of his city is not unconditional,"[30] for his ultimate allegiance is to virtue; the city has claim to his cooperation only as far as it "tend[s] to produce and preserve happiness and its components for the political society,"[31] without, of course, inhibiting or contradicting his noble and good character.

Collins argues that the problem for Aristotle is not so much a tension between city and citizen, but a tension "within moral virtue itself between its orientation toward the common good [in justice] and activity as an independent end."[32] With this distinction, we can understand that, again, the interesting problem is not what the gentleman does in the less than ideal city—for he of course will do whatever justice and virtue demands, whether that is in accord or contrary to what the city demands—but what the

28. "[W]ithout the ideal city there will be no good men," Terence Irwin as quoted in David Keyt, "The Good Man in Aristotle's Ethics and Politics," *Social Philosophy and Policy* 24, no. 2 (2007): 221. Also, Eugene Garver argues that Aristotle's understanding of the activity of virtue as *political* yields the "radical and unlikely thesis: *All and only those activities are part of the human good which are activities of good citizens in the good polis.*" Garver, *Confronting Aristotle's Ethics* (Chicago: University of Chicago Press, 2006), 128. Emphasis in the original.

29. *Politics* 3.5, 1278a40–b5.

30. Keyt, "The Good Man in Aristotle's *Ethics* and *Politics*," 240.

31. NE 5.1, 1129b19–20.

32. Collins, "Moral Virtue and the Limits of the Political Community," 57.

city does when it accomplishes its goal of leading a citizen to the truly good life. That is to say, what does the city do when its citizen succeeds not in the secondary good of political activity, but primary human fulfillment in self-sufficient wisdom? We will come back to this later.

3. *All-Around Awesome: The Gentleman is Magnanimous*

Magnanimity, (μεγαλοψύχια) says Aristotle, "seems to be a sort of crown (κοσμός) of the virtues; for it makes them greater, and it is not found without them."[33] Thus only a good man can be truly great-souled—magnanimity is not what it may look like, arrogance or disgust for lower people, but the extra greatness that comes to the honorable, noble, just, liberal, courageous, and completely virtuous man. It is, in Hoffmann's words, "appropriate self-esteem," which is in no way the kindergarten self-esteem that is preached in contemporary culture—that irreproachable regard for oneself regardless of actual virtue or merit, but the appropriate awareness of the capacity for greatness, as well as the desire to achieve and maintain not honors, but honorability itself.[34] This requires real goodness and virtue—no arrogant jerk is a true exemplar of magnanimity, only the exceedingly good and noble gentleman. This necessity of great virtue explains why magnanimity or "true pride" (as opposed to vanity [χουνοτής] or, more appropriately, undue humbleness [μικροψύχια]) is so rare, and why in contemporary culture—in which virtue is all but completely forgotten—it is practically unheard of. The kindergarten variety is much easier.

As magnanimous, the gentleman is the "highest *nonphilosophic* human type,"[35] he is "virtue's exemplar and champion."[36] He is self-sufficient in this insofar as his magnanimity pushes him to continue to be virtuous, while the "humble" "actually seem to make themselves worse,"[37] since they

33. NE 4.3, 1124a1.

34. "[T]he magnanimous person considers himself worthy of honor, but what he desires is honorability, i.e. virtue as the basis of rightly deserved honors. Cf. Ernst Schmidt, 'Ehre und Tugend: Zur Megalopsychia der aristotelischen Ethik', *Archic für Geschicte der Philosophie* 49 (1967), 149–168." Tobias Hoffmann, "Albert the Great and Thomas Aquinas on Magnanimity," in *Virtue Ethics in the Middle Ages: Commentaries on Aristotle's Nicomachean Ethics, 1200–1500*, edited by István P. Bejczy (Boston: Brill, 2008), 103 n. 4.

35. Harry V. Jaffa, *Thomism and Aristotelianism* (Chicago: University of Chicago Press, 1952), 116.

36. Susan D. Collins, "Moral Virtue and the Limits of the Political Community in Aristotle's *Nicomachean Ethics*," *American Journal of Political Science* 48, no. 1 (2004): 57.

37. NE 4.3, 1125a25.

refrain from doing the great things they think themselves unworthy of and thus have a limited opportunity to grow in virtue. This highlights the difference between modesty and improper deficiency in pride—the deficient do not want to appear vain and thus err on the side of lacking pride, which turns out to be in fact a false humility and a manifestation of pride in the pejorative sense.

Aristotle's analysis of the "great-souled" or "proud" gentleman, it is important to remember, is a *pre*-Christian analysis, and thus is not to be understood as necessarily anti-Christian despite the translation of μεγαλοψύχια as "pride." In fact, one could argue that Christian humility has a lot in common with Aristotle's greatness of soul,[38] for the Christian, like the proud pagan, knows himself and knows his due; he despises those honors that are inappropriate to him, namely, "honour from casual people on trifling grounds" or, for the Christian, the honors of the world. Further, the unduly humble or small-souled is understood as more opposed to pride than is vanity. Aristotle says that these pusillanimous ones are "unduly retiring," οκνήροι—they shrink, hesitate, hold back, etc., which is just as much a defect in the pursuit of Christian sanctity as in the pursuit of Aristotelian virtue.[39]

As the exemplar of virtue, the magnanimous gentleman possesses all the virtues in a unified way that distinguishes him from the simply courageous man, as Collins highlights. He is courageous, just as he is liberal, magnificent, temperate, just, etc. but in such a way that he does not separate his own good ends from the noble; rather, they are identical.[40] From this, the "crown" of his virtue is not so much the self-appreciation he can enjoy in the recognition of his own goodness, but rather the extra something that arises out of the harmony of mind, body, and soul that fully perfected virtue entails.[41] Much like the pleasure that completes an activity, which Aristotle

38. As Hoffmann highlights, Aquinas saw magnanimity and humility as partners in tempering and perfecting the passion of hope: "magnanimity orders the passions of hope *and* despair with a view to the attainment of one's own good, whereas humility orders them out of submission to God." Hoffmann, "Albert the Great and Thomas Aquinas on Magnanimity," 127.

39. Of course that is *not* to say that the gentleman is a saint—far from it. But much like the concept of 'moral' does not make sense apart from a divine lawgiver, saintliness and true humility and charity do not make sense apart from an understanding of God as love. Apart from that grounding, without the divine stronghold that is source and anchor, as Kierkegaard explains in *Works of Love*, man's love would not exist. Thus, Aristotle's proud pagan is much more consistent than the atheistic moralist; consequently, the latter has little justification for his objection to the lack of charity of the former.

40. Collins, "Moral Virtue," 48.

41. "[T]he virtuous person's conception of what is truly pleasant is now shaped by his inde-

tries to articulate in the *Nicomachean Ethics,* the gentleman in his magnanimity has crossed a threshold into a new level of virtue which approaches the supernatural. Similar is the case of the problematic philosopher who comes close to divinity in his contemplation of God, mentioned in the previous section.

4. *Gentleman Philosopher?*

> Moral virtue shows that the city points beyond itself but it does not reveal clearly that toward which it points, namely, the life devoted to philosophy. The man of moral virtue, the gentleman, may very well know that his political activity is at the service of noble leisure but his leisurable activity hardly goes beyond the enjoyment of poetry and the other imitative arts.[42]

The gentleman is not the philosopher. Or at least, he is not a philosopher qua gentleman. The gentleman is the perfection of moral virtue and, in the fullest exercise of that virtue, a statesman. However, throughout his education he would have been exposed to a great deal of philosophy and would understand to some extent its primary importance as the primary end of man. This exposure is integral to the well-being of the city, though it may not seem to be. For, if the highest fulfillment of man lies in philosophical activity, and the city is for the ultimate happiness of citizens, the legislator must provide for philosophy, though he himself may never enjoy or fully understand its importance. Further, only philosophy can properly convey knowledge of the virtues, which Aristotle emphasizes ought to be an integral part of the legislator's education, as they make laws in accord with what makes their citizens virtuous. But if the gentleman is the active statesman and not the philosopher, then what *is* the philosopher, and where does he and his near-complete self-sufficiency fit into the city?

Here it is important to understand the role of development, the role of process in stages of the gentleman in Aristotle's view. A gentleman is not born, he is formed. With an appreciation of this, one could further alleviate the tension of theoretical versus moral virtue. Strauss mentions the

pendent, reasoned conception of what is good, just as it was earlier shaped by his father's or his teacher's advice about what is noble. . . . the noble is that which, being good, is pleasant because it is good (cf. *EE* 1249a18–19) And with all three categories in harmony, then, and then only, nothing will tempt or lure him so much as the temperate or brave action itself." Burnyeat, "Learning to be Good," 88.

42. Strauss, *The City and Man,* 27.

"enlightened statesman," the gentleman who has been affected by his philosophical training and takes that with him into his rule[43]; from here one can go a step further and see that problematic loner philosopher as a kind of *ascended* statesman. He could not have made it to that level without the previous virtue, and his leaving it behind does not negate its value—there is no contradiction to resolve; the city is not gravely harmed by this passing of a citizen from the political to the fully contemplative life, for it could only come after decades of very human wisdom-seeking, during which time the city was benefited by those years of virtuous political action, teaching, etc. To adjust the city so that no man could ascend beyond it would destroy its orientation toward the good and, thus, its very reason for existence.

III. Modernity's Men without Chests

While the gentleman's life is marked by a harmony of soul which frees and energizes him in the pursuit of the good, the modern man's life is one of dissonance and crippling insecurity. This is directly related to the modern insistence highlighted in the introduction above on the separation between law and ethics. The primary result of such a bifurcation is the loss of that grounding that Aristotle assumes throughout his reflections, namely, the good and noble, which renders law essentially and fundamentally non-ethical, that is, neutral with regard to ethical concerns. This neutrality in effect neutralizes law itself. For if, as Aristotle holds, law derives its authority from the good it defends and promotes, and if the good is no longer accepted as objective, what does law have left to stand on? What is law for if not the safeguarding of, and guidance in light of, ethical standards? And by what is one to judge which laws are "rightly framed," that is, "commanding some acts and forbidding others … rightly"?[44] The problems that Anscombe saw with modern moral philosophy are (necessarily) the same problems with modern political philosophy—integral concepts like human rights, equality, universal suffrage and education are grounded in assumptions that have been rejected by relativist and materialistic thought. It is only a matter of time before practice catches up with theory and law's relation to ethics is either recovered or eradicated. "If we shatter this basic order [of real justice] which links things human to the divine stabilities of

43. Ibid.

44. NE 5.1, 1129b24.

the universe," says Maritain "even the strongest empirical defenses of the social order will remain vain."[45]

Since law in the Aristotelian understanding is also educative, there result two additional crimes against the legislative art (and consequently, against man and the good); the first is nothing new to Aristotle: non-ethical education. This is the source of the good citizen versus good man dilemma, for in educating a "good" citizen in accordance with the unjust laws of the non-ideal city, one does not educate an unqualifiedly good man.[46] This would seem to contradict the essential purpose of education and learning. The second offence is more complicated and uniquely modern: in the *deliberate* splitting of ethics and law, executed in such a manner as to result in separate public and private spheres of morality, the city goes beyond having a defective justice typical of the non-ideal state; rather, the imperfect justice of the city is acknowledged and even accepted *as* injustice. The pursuit of a just and good city is given up in cynical despair and a corrupt one is instead tolerated in exchange for comfort and security. This is a deviant move Aristotle seems not to have foreseen—which is perhaps why he does not pursue the problem of how a good man in a non-ideal city is supposed to act, which is, to the modern reader, of utmost interest[47]—for he says, "all men cling to justice of some kind, but conceptions are imperfect."[48] But with the Machiavellian turn of modernity being highlighted, this no longer seems to be the case. There is no clinging to justice, but resigning oneself to inevitable injustice.[49]

With the acceptance of injustice as the rule of the city, the man in public service is now held to a standard different from individual's private conceptions of justice.[50] In other words, the city is accepted as inevitably and perhaps inherently unjust—politicians are assumed corrupt and often are proven to be with few consequences affecting their political career. While Aristotle claims that "the state exists for the good life" and "those who care

45. Jacques Maritain, *Ransoming the Time*, translated by Harry Lorin Binsse (New York: Charles Scribner's Sons, 1941), 37.

46. Keyt, "The Good Man," 238.

47. Keyt, "The Good Man", 221.

48. *Politics* 3.9, 1280a10.

49. Which resignation is done for the sake of security, and "To prefer injustice to disorder, as Goethe put it, is to prefer disorder to disorder, disorder in the root to disorder in the flower." Maritain, *Ransoming the Time*, 37.

50. See *Public and Private Morality* for a discussion of Machiavellian politics and its impact on the relation between public and private spheres. Edited by Stuart Hampshire (Cambridge: Cambridge University Press, 1978).

for good government take into consideration virtue and vice in the states,"[51] the modern sees the state and government as inevitably corrupt, and thus is forced to look elsewhere for the good life. With this, the citizen and city are cut off from one another, severely disabling the natural and proper function of both. This is the problem facing the modern: if the legislator, whose first priority is supposed to be the good of the city and thus the virtuous education of individuals, is himself a villain, how can he be trusted to educate? And if the city and city leaders cannot be trusted to educate or make good laws, but are left in charge of lesser, material concerns, what is there to unify the citizen and the city? Only the material. Only security and economics. Again, imperfect justice—which is open to gradual improvement—is thus replaced with sheer injustice as the guiding rule, leaving citizens to find their own versions of good, if they choose to bother. This differs in a small but tremendously important way from Aristotle's gentleman who finds himself under an unjust regime; while both the gentleman and the cynical modern may have to find their own way to the good, largely without city and legal guidance, the gentleman: i. recognizes this as a perversion of the city, while the modern accepts it as the natural and inevitable way of power; and ii. seeks to heal the city through getting involved in legislation himself, while the modern resigns himself to the fact that the state will always be unjust.

1. θυμός and the Modern

Given Aristotle's account of the natural generation of the city and thus its natural orientation to the good life, the normalization of Machiavellian outlook has serious ramifications on the inner life of man. As observed above, Aristotle understands the state to exist for the good life of its citizens, that is, it exists for their exercise of virtue in political life. The splitting of the good life between the necessities for survival provided by society and moral perfection pursued individualistically results in a split within the very soul of man, out of which his spirited element, his θυμός, escapes him.

As Fukuyama explains, θυμός in the form of *megalothymia* (drive for superiority) has been replaced in modernity with the economization of life to fulfill ever increasing material desires, as well as *isothymia,* the desire for acknowledged equality.[52] However, man is not satisfied with these substitu-

51. *Politics* 3.9, 1280a31b5.

52. Francis Fukuyama, *The End of History and the Last Man* (New York: The Free Press, 1992), 190.

tions, and still yearns for a struggle for superiority; so he finds this struggle in business, sports, politics, and art.[53] It seems that these largely "contentless" endeavors only delay or distract from what really satisfies man—the struggle for virtue, which, end of history or not, always remains essential to the good life.

2. *Men without Chests: the New Ideal*

In contemporary society, the gentleman has been jettisoned and replaced with a less offensive model, the "Intellectual." C. S. Lewis says of modern "Intellectuals"—who have replaced the gentleman as the ideal: "It is not excess of thought but defect of fertile and generous emotion that marks them." These are the Men Without Chests, whose heads appear so large and smart only in reference to their stunted chests, their withered spirit. They are the heroes of the Enlightenment who, with Dostoevsky's villain, gleefully sneer at tradition saying: "Science now tells us, love yourself before all men, for everything in the world rests on self-interest."[54] Courage, liberality, even true friendship are rendered incomprehensible by these new gentlemen-models of modern education, who are "content to sit at home and congratulate themselves on their broadmindedness and lack of fanaticism."[55]

Unfortunately for modern man, the spiritedness these Men Without Chests lack is that very thing which drives men to virtue and happiness. Aristotle says, "passion is the quality of soul which begets friendship and enables us to love."[56] Thus, when Lewis' "Conditioners" work to squash spirit for the sake of control, or the democrat does so for the sake of feel-good mediocrity, they squash what makes man *man*, and what makes life worth living. Of course, as Garver explains, without the guidance of Aristotle's polis, "the emotions rooted in thumos, assertiveness and competition, are destructive and bellicose."[57] This is why θυμός must be cultivated and tamed if liberal democracy is to survive.[58] Otherwise, the result is, as has been the case, what Aristotle would call living "Cyclops fashion": each as he pleases. When this is the accepted end of the city—to live like Cy-

53. Ibid., 320.

54. Fyodor Dostoevsky, *Crime and Punishment*, translated by Constance Garnett (New York: Bantam Books, 1981), 140.

55. Fukuyama, *The End of History*, 307.

56. *Politics* 7.7, 1328a1.

57. Eugene Garver, *Confronting Aristotle's Ethics* (Chicago: University of Chicago Press, 2006), 121.

58. See Fukuyama, *The End of History*, 183.

clops—the pluralistic legislator of this amoral polis, having no right to legislate a good and noble education, is faced with either allowing the degeneration of the city into rebellion by neglecting education entirely, or setting up an education that drains θυμός and demands mediocrity of citizens. This cuts to the heart of the difference between modern education and Aristotle's model of guidance: where modern education seeks to fill the head with culturally acceptable and safe facts, the Aristotelian approach, following Plato, seeks to direct their attention and energy toward truth; where modern education instills a consequentialist attitude toward the world in preparing youth for work, the Aristotelian develops "an educated perception, a capacity going beyond the application of general rules, to tell what is required for the practice of virtues in specific circumstances."[59]

IV. What is Needed: A Gentlemen's Education

At the heart of Aristotle's political inquiry is the reality that "argument and teaching ... are not powerful with all men, but the soul of the student must first have been cultivated by means of habits for noble joy and noble hatred, like earth which is to nourish the seed."[60] This image of nourishment or cultivation is an important one; in the ideal city's education of gentlemen—from gymnastics and music in early childhood onward through political and philosophical studies in adulthood—is the realization of *individual* flourishing of *political (social)* animals. That is to say, Aristotle's education is meant to prepare and enable the moral virtue that is the natural end of man. The result is not a slave of the state but a free, just, magnanimous friend that, in a free society, *is*, in a way, the state.[61]

Aristotle makes very clear that education is necessary to the survival and well-being of the polis,[62] which again exists for the good life of its citizens. As Tessitore explains, "the failure to develop one's capacities for both reason and excellence precludes the possibility of lasting happiness despite

59. Burnyeat, "Learning to be Good," 72. 60. NE 10.9, 1179b25.

61. In contrast, the isolation of Rousseau's Emile renders him unable to attain *eudaimonia* in the activity of virtue because he does not receive the guidance necessary to habituate him to anything outside his own passions and material environment. However, the idea is somewhat understandable, for the limited education he would have received in the city, which filled the mind but neglected the soul and body, would not have left him any closer to happiness. Cultural insensitivity aside, the point that Aristotle makes when he applauds the Greeks as having the right amount of spirit and reason is a good one—human perfection lies in balancing spirit and rationality.

62. *Politics* 5.9, 1310a13–36.

whatever advantages of wealth, birth, or position an individual might enjoy."[63] Virtue does not arise by nature nor contrary to nature[64]; rather, it requires cultivation from youth. The modern system, with its neglect of moral virtue that a free society necessarily requires in order to survive, is no better off than the Spartan, which found itself dependent on a virtue their education did not foster."[65] As Fukuyama observes:

> The doctrine that says that there is no privileged perspective dovetails nicely with democratic man's desire to believe that his way of life is just as good as any other. Relativism in this context does not lead to the liberation of the great or strong, but of the mediocre, who were now told they have nothing of which to be ashamed.[66]

In such a society—where everyone has their own personal "bag of virtues"[67] and the purpose of the city is not to promote what it finds to be virtue but rather to facilitate the smooth coexistence of multiple moralities[68]—the proposition that a high standard of moral virtue be incorporated into public education is a hard sell. Additionally, there is a somewhat legitimate fear that "those in charge of [civic education] may wish to indoctrinate students rather than educate them."[69] However, given the previous elucidation of the kind of men a democracy *needs* to survive, (as opposed to the mediocre *wants* of democracies) namely, magnanimous, virtuous, wise gentlemen, it is hard to see how such men can be the products of indoctrination.

V. Conclusion

Given the stark contrast between the modern men without chests and the gentleman of Aristotle's philosophy, it is understandable that the "sensible man" of today would respond to the gentleman's excellence with "an

63. Tessitore, "Aristotle's Ambiguous Account of the Best Life," 211.

64. NE 2.1, 1103a23.

65. As Richard Bodéüs highlights in "Law and the Regime in Aristotle," in *Essays on the Foundation of Aristotelian Political Science*, edited by Carnes Lord and David K. O'Connor (Los Angeles: University of California Press, 1991), 234–48.

66. Fukuyama, *End of History*, 307.

67. Lawrence Kohlberg, *The Philosophy of Moral Development*, vol. 1 in *Essays on Moral Development* (San Francisco: Harper and Row, 1981), 184. The enlightened psychologist, of course, knows better—"virtues and vices are labels by which people award praise or blame to others, but … are not the ways in which they think when making moral decisions themselves." Ibid., 226.

68. See Garver, *Confronting Aristotle's Ethics*, 127.

69. Jack Crittendon, "Civic Education," in *Stanford Encyclopedia of Philosophy*, edited by Edward N. Zalta, http://plato.stanford.edu/archives/fall2010/entries/civic-education/.

urge to kick Aristotle's *ho megalopsuchos*."[70] The promotion of this "bag of virtues" sensibility is *the* goal of modern education. Greatness is offensive. Rather than the gentleman of leisure, we want worms that will kick that sort of arrogance. But we do not want them to actually act on the spiritual deficiency, oh no—

> In a sort of ghastly simplicity we remove the organ and demand the function. We make men without chests and expect of them virtue and enterprise. We laugh at honor and are shocked to find traitors in our midst. We castrate and bid the geldings be fruitful.[71]

70. A "Scotch commentator" quoted by Robert S. Brumbaugh and Nathaniel M. Lawrence, "Education as Self-Realization," in *Philosophers on Education: Six Essays on the Foundations of Western Thought* (Boston: Houghton Mifflin, 1963), 64 n. 2.

71. Lewis, *The Abolition of Man*, 26.

BERNADETTE E. O'CONNOR

Two False Theories of Human Equality Identified by Jacques Maritain

Applied to Feminist Issues

In the essay "Human Equality," which first appeared in French in 1939[1] and is the first chapter of *Ransoming the Time,* Maritain considers two false theories of human equality and opposes to them what he calls the "realist"[2] and "Christian"[3] view of human equality. Maritain treats both false theories as "practical attitudes rather than philosophic schools," attitudes deriving "from concrete attitudes of the intelligence that are of basic practical importance."[4] At the roots of the false theories are sometimes unconscious or only obscurely conscious "instinct and passion"[5] and "restless emotionalism."[6]

I will describe the two false theories of equality and then show where something like the errors of the two false theories enter into feminist concerns. As I address the second set of feminist concerns, I will touch on what Maritain says concerning the relationship between the sexes in "Let Us Make for Him a Helpmate Like to Himself," published in English in *Untrammeled Approaches.*[7] And I will raise some possible difficulties, both

1. See Donald and Idella Gallagher, *The Achievement of Jacques and Raïssa Maritain: A Bibliography, 1906–1961* (Garden City, New York: Doubleday, 1962), 65, 90, and 128. The essay appeared under the title "L'Égalité Chrétienne" in *Études Carmélitaines* 24, no. 2 (1939): 172–94 and in *Les Hommes sont-ils Êgaux?* (Paris: Desclée de Brouwer, 1939), 172–94. The identical pagination for these two publications shown here is as it appears in the Gallaghers' work.

2. Jacques Maritain, *Ransoming the Time,* translated by Harry Lorin Binsse (New York: Charles Scribner's Sons, 1941), 2.

3. Ibid., 17.

4. Ibid., 2.

5. Ibid., 5.

6. Ibid., 16.

7. Jacques Maritain, *Untrammeled Approaches,* translated by Bernard Doering (Notre Dame,

speculative and practical, with his theory of subspecific masculine and feminine types of a modal-essential order and the complementarity of men and women he bases on them.

The first false theory of human equality Maritain calls an "anti-Christian philosophy of enslavement."[8] In this false theory of human equality, a radical empiricism leads to a nominalist concept of humanity in which the real "identity" or "equality" of human beings in sharing one species is reduced to "only a word,"[9] to a mere name. The true equality of human beings—Maritian prefers to speak of the "unity" of human beings—is grounded in their sharing in a real human "*nature* or essence."[10] But the empiricist, limited in knowledge as he or she is to the data of sense experience, cannot conceive this human unity or equality in essence because that essence "is not visibly perceived"[11] but "is perceived by the intellect with the help of the senses, and by transcending the senses."[12]

What is readily apprehended by the empiricist, Maritain posits, are the human "inequalities, which are themselves manifest and tangible, often in a very painful fashion."[13] And, inasmuch as these inequalities, be they natural or social, are real—they "do exist; they cry out; they cover the whole expanse of human reality"[14]—the empiricist makes no mistake in remarking them. The error of empiricist nominalism is not that it sees real differences among human beings but that it sees only them and not the real unity or equality in human nature.[15] The error of empiricist nominalism is to see and to state *only* these differences "and in practice deeming as nothing the reality and ontological dignity of that *nature* or essence which all ... [humans] have in common."[16]

The empiricist blindness to humans' sharing in a real essence or nature, which sharing is the ontological foundation for human unity or equality, manifests its pernicious effects first in the practical realm. By an ironic "sort of recurrence of the instincts and needs of the intelligence," "on a level lower than that of fully-formed intelligibility and of essences properly so-called,"[17] the empiricist raises up pseudo-essences or pseudo-species

Indiana: University of Notre Dame Press, 1977). According to the Editor's notes (151 n. 1, and 163 n. 8) this essay was originally "an informal talk given at Kolbsheim. Cf. published in *Nova et Vetera*, 1967, no. 4: 241–254," the postscript being added in 1972.

8. Maritain, *Ransoming the Time*, 3.
9. Ibid.
10. Ibid., 4.
11. Ibid., 3.
12. Ibid., 4.
13. Ibid., 3.
14. Ibid.
15. Ibid., 4.
16. Ibid.
17. Ibid.

among human beings on the bases of differences or inequalities among humans. Then the empiricist treats these pseudo-essences as if the differences between or among them were of the same value as the differences between two species, such as loins and asses or ants and eagles.[18] The practical mind of the empiricist bent thus "sets up arbitrary groups" "in the fluid mass of individual peculiarities" and attributes to them "the character of specific categories"[19] or of species in their own right.

Maritian mentions both biological and social inequalities or differences among human beings as the bases on which empiricist nominalism raises pseudo-essences, hardening "the natural or social inequalities to which ... [humans] are heir into the differences of species between those groups, existing in fact or arbitrarily imagined, into which they sort ... [humankind]."[20] The false hierarchies and cleavages among the pseudo-essences thus created lead to unjust discrimination among human beings in which accidental differences among human beings replace the "unity or equality"[21] of sharing in a real human "*nature* or essence."[22]

As an example of natural or biological differences on the bases of which essences can be created, Maritain refers to racism and explicitly cites "the racist theses proclaimed at Nuremberg."[23] One of these racist theses claims: "'there is a greater difference between the lowest forms still called human and our superior races than between the lowest man and monkeys of the highest orders.'"[24] Maritain explains that "the biological pseudo-essences may arise in ... [humans'] imaginations by virtue of an unconscious process, the origin of which lies in the obscure workings of the will to power."[25]

And Maritain offers four examples of social differences on the bases of which pseudo-essences can be created: i. layers within a society brought about by "successive conquests"[26]; ii. "privileges of birth normal in a society of the aristocratic or feudal type"[27]; iii. "privileges of wealth in normal society of the mercantile or bourgeois type,"[28] and; iv. "privileges of a purely cynical 'elite' normal in a society of the totalitarian type."[29]

Thus, by "a process, pleasing to instinct and passion,"[30] the empiricist

18. Ibid., 4–5.
19. Ibid., 4.
20. Ibid., 7.
21. Ibid., 3.
22. Ibid., 4.
23. Ibid., 8.
24. Ibid.
25. Ibid.
26. Ibid., 7.
27. Ibid., 8.
28. Ibid.
29. Ibid.
30. Ibid., 5.

creates among human beings "pseudo-scientific cleavages," or "false hierarchies of pseudo-specific gradations."[31] Whether the pseudo-essences are based on differences of the biological or social type, the hierarchies constituted among persons sharing in these false species have certain characteristics in common. First, Maritain mentions, as we have seen, the workings of a covert will to power and insists that the "pseudo-logic" that leads to these false hierarchies "is not at all disinterested."[32] For "just as the life of our instincts constantly underlies and affects that of our intelligence, so the burning inclination toward great sins constantly excites within us the inclination to great errors."[33] Maritain asserts that "the royal race," on top in the hierarchy it creates by a false logic, "in effect concentrates in itself... all the privileges and dignity of human nature."[34] And "the lower categories ... are only partially or inchoately human. They are midway between beast and ... [human]."[35] The fulfillment and happiness of those on the lower rungs of the hierarchy depend upon making their superiors fulfilled and happy:

If they obey their masters, if they work for them, if, through the toil and trial of the lowest categories, their masters succeed in gathering the fruits and joys of supreme human knowledge or supreme human power, and in conquering the life of the free and the strong, their masters will make them happy.[36]

Maritain's outraged sense of justice is almost palpable when he writes that these masters punish their underlings "for their own good"; maintain "them for their own good in a state of slavery"; refuse "them for their own good the rights and liberty of which they are not worthy"; make "available to them the necessities of life and the half-animal, half-human joys which alone they are capable of appreciating."[37] And, finally, Maritain asserts, the "masters can bestow no higher benefit upon ... [the inchoate humans in the lowest categories] than to teach them to find their pleasure and the best reward for their faithfulness in the happiness of those they serve."[38] Maritain asserts that "this philosophy of enslavement is the pure form toward which tends every kind of moral or social empiricism which disregards ... [humans'] equality as a species in nature and sees in it only a word."[39]

The creation of false cleavages and hierarchies appears first as a func-

31. Ibid., 4.
32. Ibid., 7.
33. Ibid.
34. Ibid., 8.
35. Ibid.
36. Ibid., 9.
37. Ibid.
38. Ibid.
39. Ibid.

tion of practical intellect and of the perhaps unconscious instincts and passions that can distort it. But the creation and justification of false cleavages and hierarchies then extends to the speculative sphere, where driven by the same perhaps unconscious forces, is born "a pseudo-science, taking for its object of study the pseudo-essences in question,"[40] and seeking "to justify the privileges or domineering ambitions of those categories judged to be superior."[41] Social Darwinism and Nazi race theory would be examples of pseudo-sciences.

The second false theory Maritain calls "the pure idealist notion of human equality ... the philosophy of egalitarianism."[42] Maritain characterizes this theory, too, as a "concrete" attitude of intelligence that "is of basic practical importance."[43] "The egalitarian error is at once less hateful and more treacherous than the error of the philosophy of enslavement; less hateful, because it preserves an element of that which is naturally Christian in the human soul; more treacherous, because it corrupts that very element."[44]

The idealist egalitarian error is enamored of something like the Platonic Form Humanity Itself. This practical idealism sets up against real "natural inequalities a speculative denial."[45] Practically speaking, the idealist denies these natural inequalities: Humanity Itself must be equal to itself; "the equality in species among ... [human beings] alone becomes the reality, alone has the right to exist, alone is recognized by the mind."[46] Idealist anthropology would transport humans "into the heaven of separated essences ... [which concentrate] in the unity of the hypostasized Species [Humanity Itself] all the qualitative perfection and all the nobility of human nature."[47] Thus the idealist egalitarianism entertains only a "purely logical and not ontological conception of the community-in-essence between reasoning creatures."[48]

For this idealistic and false egalitarianism, natural inequities among humans are "a pure accident ... without value for the mind and from which the mind can learn nothing."[49] The essential dignity of Humanity Itself "is outraged each time one individual is unequal to another and, in short, each time one individual differs from another."[50] For this pseudo-Christian egal-

40. Ibid., 5.
41. Ibid.
42. Ibid., 2.
43. Ibid.
44. Ibid., 16.
45. Ibid., 11.
46. Ibid., 10.
47. Ibid., 13.
48. Ibid., 10.
49. Ibid., 11.
50. Ibid.

itarianism "all natural privileges and the privileges of the mind, natural gifts or acquired virtues, must be rigourously leveled."[51] The poetic, the artistic, and the contemplative gifts "are not exactly denied"[52] but "are refused consideration, pushed aside by the mind beyond any sphere of existence worthy of the name,"[53] and "culture as such must be flattened out."[54] Thus Maritain observes among egalitarian devotees of the Platonic Form Humanity Itself "an uneasy touchiness regarding any possibility of a hierarchy of value among . . . [human beings], whatever it may be."[55]

The error of idealist egalitarianism is thus the mirror opposite of the error of positivist nominalism. Nominalism errs, not in remarking the differences among human beings but in regarding only them and not also the essential unity and equality of human beings. Egalitarianism errs, not in remarking the unity and equality of human beings in sharing one nature but in regarding only this unity and equality and not also the real natural and social differences and inequalities that obtain among them.

Maritain locates the origins of the practical attitude of idealist egalitarianism in both base and noble motives. The attitude can arise from the instinctual tendencies of "hatred of all superiority, collective envy and resentment, a thirst to impose a punishment on others for the setback and humiliations one has suffered."[56] But a leveling egalitarianism can arise also from "generous instincts and truly human aspirations which, although in the end inefficacious, are none the less the attempts at or vestiges of a Christian disposition."[57]

And Maritain observes that a tendency toward leveling egalitarianism arises not only among the "'popular masses,'"[58] where one might expect it to arise. A tendency toward leveling egalitarianism is "rampant all the more among individuals in a given social group as that group is more differentiated and advanced."[59] Maritain identifies the error of idealist egalitarianism with the Communist state.[60] "The cult of . . . [Humanity Itself] demands an absolute egalitarianism"[61] and "ends, in the empirical world, by bringing about an utter uniformity of . . . [human beings] under the law of Number and Quantity, and by transferring to the masses the dignity of the human

51. Ibid. 13.
52. Ibid., 10.
53. Ibid.
54. Ibid., 14.
55. Ibid.
56. Ibid., 13.
57. Ibid., 15.
58. Ibid., 13.
59. Ibid.
60. Ibid., 14–15.
61. Ibid., 12.

person."[62] Thus, in the real world, the two false theories, empiricist nominalism and idealist egalitarianism, these "opposing divagations,"[63] "give rise to each other"[64] and issue in the same bitter fruit: "for, by an effect of the very dialectic of error, that very totalitarianism which belongs in itself to the philosophy of enslavement, is also the last achievement as well as the destruction of egalitarianism."[65]

I turn now to a consideration of how these practical attitudes might be related to feminist concerns. And I begin with what I perceive to be the error of idealist egalitarianism as it afflicts the practice—first, I believe—and then the theory of certain feminists. When the practical consciousness of women and of minorities is raised regarding their unjust oppression under patriarchy and other systems of irrational domination, a possible response is to decry the hierarchy that has unjustly put them in subordinate positions. While victims of unjust hierarchies correctly object to the failure of those at the top of these hierarchies to recognize their co-participation in real, ontological human nature, some victims go further and reject, in practice and subsequently in theory, all forms of hierarchy, even those founded on real differences and inequalities, and thus fall into the mentality of leveling egalitarianism.[66] As Maritain states, however, the false theories of

62. Ibid., 13.

63. Ibid., 10.

64. Ibid.

65. Ibid., 14.

66. Here are five quotes from feminist theorists that illustrate the speculative rejection of hierarchies:

> "The reinterpretation of women's experience in terms of their own imagery of relationships thus clarifies that experience and also provides a nonhierarchical vision of human connection. Since relationships, when cast in the image of hierarchy, appear inherently unstable and morally problematic, their transposition into the image of web changes an order of inequality into a structure of interconnection." Carol Gilligan, *In a Different Voice: Psychological Theory and Women's Development* (Cambridge, Massachusetts: Harvard University Press, 1982), 62.
>
> "The proclivity of women to reconstruct hypothetical dilemmas in terms of the real, to request or to supply missing information about the nature of the people and the places where they live, shifts their judgment away from the hierarchical ordering of principles and the formal procedures of decision making." Ibid., 100–101.
>
> "Our culture is set up according to this basic hierarchical structure [what this author calls "the White Male System"]:
>
> God
> Men
> Women
> Children
> Animals
> Earth
>
> God is dominant over men, women, children, animals, and the earth. Men are dominant over

equality manifest themselves first and more basically as practical attitudes. So consider this example of the leveling attitude, drawn from the practical life we share in a social "group that is more differentiated and advanced"[67] than the common masses: university professors. Sometimes we hear at faculty meetings, by way of a negative evaluation of some proposal for governance, a statement like this: "But this proposal is hierarchical." The explicit statement serves as the minor premise of a syllogism, the major premise and conclusion of which we all infer:

All hierarchies are evil.
But this proposal is hierarchical.
Therefore, this proposal is evil.

And, concerning another issue, some of our colleagues may object to honors programs because they discriminate, in the commitment of university resources, against students who cannot meet the criteria for admission to them.

---

women, children, animals, and the earth. Women are dominant over children, animals, and the earth. The earth is at the bottom of the hierarchy; it is seen as powerless and submissive.

"Along with this dominance goes a tendency to rape and control those who are below one in the hierarchy. There is also a feeling that one should constantly strive to move upward to the next rank; that one's present position is never good enough. Men try to be like God; women try to be like men; children try to be like adults. We also force those below us in the hierarchy to be more like us." Anne Wilson Schaef, *Women's Reality: An Emerging Female System in a White Male Society* (San Francisco: Harper and Row, 1981), 164–65.

"Somehow, we must begin to realize that the theology of our culture—White Male System theology—forces us into a static system of hierarchy and exploitation. We must begin to see how current theological assumptions serve to perpetuate the White Male System and limit human freedom and growth." Ibid., 169.

"'Patriarchy,' 'the family,' 'bureaucracy,' 'management' name hierarchical ways of organizing what people do. They name the way groups are supposed to be organized in going about their activities, not the way they actually do, for they describe groups in terms of roles and role relations. Those words describe hierarchical structures, not the real human activities going on under their supposed control. For example, an organizational chart of a corporation shows lines of authority and responsibility. Does the chart serve as a true description of reality? Does it show what part many secretaries really play in the work of the corporation? Does it show who really has influence and how the work really gets done and how plans really get made? Or does it, rather, picture lines of an ideal coercion: What those at the top like to think is the reality—or perhaps, what they want those at the bottom to think is the reality? Isn't it a sketch of the way things 'ought to be,' the way some people would like them to be, not the way they are?" Kathryn Pyne Addleson, "Words and Lives" in Ann Ferguson, Jacquelyn N. Zita, and Kathryn Pyne Addelson, "On 'Compulsory Heterosexuality and Lesbian Existence': Defining the Issues," in *Feminist Theory: A Critique of Ideology*, edited by Nannerl O. Keohane, Michelle Z. Rosaldo, and Barbara C. Gelpi (Chicago: The University of Chicago Press, 1982), 182–83.

67. Maritain, *Ransoming the Time*, 13.

Remember that Maritain acknowledges that the error of leveling egalitarianism can arise from noble motives: some colleagues grade "encouragingly" for fear of what acknowledging real differences in students' achievements might do to the self-concepts of students at the lower end of that hierarchy. Some universities have a department, staffed with feminist theorists, that manifests "an uneasy touchiness regarding any possibility of a hierarchy of values among ... [human beings], whatever it may be."[68] This uneasiness with a hierarchy of values manifests itself on awards day with prizes for all or, if necessary not to leave anyone out, with "ties" for prizes.

Thus the leveling egalitarian error appears among some feminists and others who have found themselves at the bottom of hierarchies created among pseudo-essences that fail to take into account all human beings' sharing in the unity, equality, and dignity of human nature. But this error refuses to accept the reality of all differences and inequalities, natural or social, differences which, Maritain asserts, "are in themselves as necessary for the development and flowering of human life as [are] the diversity of the parts for the perfection of a flower or a poem."[69] And, while the results of the egalitarian error in academia may not be of the world-historical significance that the sway of Communism was, they can, nevertheless, create what Maritain called the "uniformity of emptiness,"[70] and they fill our halls, if not the world, with what he called "unhealthy fermentations."[71]

Next I want to consider feminism's critique of one false and unjust hierarchy constructed, à la empiricist nominalism, on the pseudo-essences of man and woman. This is the hierarchy that subordinates woman *qua* woman to man *qua* man. Maritain appears to side with the feminist critique in rejecting this error in the essay "Let Us Make for Him a Helpmate Like to Himself." There he writes of "the unity of human nature and equality in nature and dignity of man and of woman."[72] Maritain even characterizes Aristotle's[73] and St. Thomas Aquinas's[74] subordination of women to men as "contrary to philosophical reason which, by the fact that it proclaims the

68. Ibid., 14.

69. Ibid., 12.

70. Ibid., 30.

71. Ibid.

72. Maritain, *Untrammeled Approaches*, 153.

73. See ibid., 154. The parenthetical reference in Maritain's text is to "*De generatione animalium*, chap. 3" without a book or Bekker number. At *De generatione animalium* 4.6, 775a16, the Stagirite writes: "the perfecting of female embryos is inferior to that of male ones." Aristotle, *Generation of Animals*, translated by A. L. Peck (London: William Heinemann, 1943), 459.

74. See ST I, q. 92, a. 1, c., and ad 1 and ad 2.

unity of human nature, proclaims at the same time the equality of value in the very things which constitute the specific human difference."[75] And Maritain acknowledges that the "like to himself" of the second chapter of Genesis, the essential likeness of the two sexes, was "so vexing ... for a long tradition of commentators that held masculinity ... [in] such profound veneration,"[76] attributing to men a superiority of nature over women, "an error that has for such a long time been committed in favor of man."[77] Mary Daly could not have said this better.[78]

Let us consider some examples from our tradition of this kind of unjust subordination based on the pseudo-essences of man and woman that Maritain joins with feminists in condemning. There is an implication of what Aristotle had to say that I want to consider. Aristotle set up a "fearful symmetry" between the body-soul or matter-form relationship and the female-male relationship. Just as the body is inferior by nature to the soul, so too is the female inferior by nature to the male. Just as it is natural and proper for the soul to rule the body, so too is it natural and proper for the male to rule the female.[79] But if for Aristotle the human is distinguished from the other animals by the capacity for deliberation, and if deliberation has as its principle the rational soul,[80] then the male, who is identified with the form or the soul, is fully or properly human and the female, who is identified with matter or the body, is not fully or properly human. Another implication of the proportion matter:form::body:soul::female:male is that just as the soul is the final cause or goal of the body,[81] so too is the male the final cause or goal of the female. The proportion would seem to rob the woman of the personal dignity of being an end in herself.

The scripture scholar Roland de Vaux remarks that among the Jews of old a man could repudiate his wife but a woman could not divorce her husband and that, in effect, a woman remained a minor all her life.[82] And thus her full sharing in rational and self-determining human nature was not

75. Maritain, *Untrammeled Approaches*, 154. 76. Ibid., 156.

77. Ibid., 155.

78. She treats the misogyny in Old and New Testaments and in the ecclesiastical fathers and doctors up through Pope Pius XI in *The Church and the Second Sex* (Boston: Beacon Press, 1985), upon which I depend for the examples below.

79. See Aristotle, *Politics* 1.5, 1254a33–1254b15.

80. See ibid., 7.13, 1332b4–5, and Aristotle, *Nicomachean Ethics* 6.1, 1138b35–1139a15.

81. See Aristotle, *On the Parts of Animals* 1.5, 645b14–19.

82. See Roland de Vaux, *Ancient Israel, Its Life and Institutions*, translated by John McHugh (New York: McGraw Hill, 1961), 39.

acknowledged. And Clement of Alexandria must have had some pseudo-essence in mind when he wrote to the effect that it should be shameful for a woman to reflect on her nature.[83]

St. Thomas Aquinas seems to discount the woman's full sharing in humanity's specific difference of reason when he asserts: "It was necessary for woman to be made, as the Scripture says, a helper to man; not, indeed, as helpmate in other works, as some say, since man can be more efficiently helped by another man in other works; but as a helper in the work of generation."[84]

I am going to make a gigantic leap here, in this flying survey of our tradition, from the thirteenth century to the twentieth. Those of us who were educated in Catholic schools in the 1940s and 1950s know that such a leap is not all that improbable. In his 1929 Encyclical Letter on *The Christian Education of Youth,* Pius XI wrote: "there is not in nature itself, which fashions the two [sexes] quite different in organism, in temperament, in abilities, anything to suggest that there can or ought to be promiscuity, and much less equality, in the training of the two sexes."[85] Again there does not seem to be any real appreciation of the fact that women share fully in rational human nature.

Many of us are familiar with the work of Louis Bouyer, a French priest who has written beautifully on liturgy and the history of spirituality. In an article published originally in France in 1976, Bouyer writes: "let us say bluntly that it would have been monstrous if the Son of God had become a woman."[86] For one who has mediated often on the mystery of the Incarnation, this assertion is simply outrageous. It implies that there is a greater gap between maleness and femaleness than there is between the divine and human natures. We are reminded here, of course, of the Nazi proposition, which Maritain cites, that annunciates a greater difference between the lowest humans and the master race than between a monkey of a higher order and the lowest human. Bouyer appears to insinuate a greater dif-

83. See Clement of Alexandria, *Paedogogi,* in vol. 8 of *Patrologiae Graeca,* edited by Jacques-Paul Migne (Paris, 1857), II, 2, 430 at C.

84. St. Thomas Aquinas, *Summa Theologica,* translated by the Fathers of the English Dominican Province (New York: Benzinger Brothers, 1947), I, q. 92, a. 1.

85. Pius XI, *Divini Illius Magistri* ["Christian Education of Youth"] (31 December, 1929), in *The Encyclicals of a Century* (Derby, New York: Daughters of St. Paul Press), 95.

86. Louis Bouyer, *Woman in the Church,* epilogue by Hans Urs von Balthasar and essay by C. S. Lewis, translated by Marilyn Teichert (San Francisco: Ignatius Press, 1979), 72.

ference between men and women than between God and human beings. He accepts the divine wisdom that made the eternal Word incarnate in a male but would find it a "monstrous" humiliation of the divine to incarnate in a female. Let this suffice for some examples of unjust subordination of women as a pseudo-species to men as a pseudo-species. It is rampant in our tradition and as Maritain remarks, it "does not cease to exert its power in our subconscious,"[87] where it gains power over actions and their rationalizations precisely because it is unconscious.

I now want to consider Maritain's theory of "two *subspecific* types, masculine and feminine, which share the same human nature."[88] At first Maritain characterizes this typology as a "subspecific typicity of an essential order."[89] Then in a footnote, perhaps recalling the error of creating pseudo-essences he had denounced earlier, he indicates that a better expression for this typology would be "subspecific type of a modal-essential order."[90] I want to consider the advantages and possible disadvantages of understanding men and women as subspecific types of a modal-essential order.

Clearly these subspecific types are created on the basis of real differences between women and men, differences Maritain understands as much more profound than merely biological differences.[91] Men and women, "the members of the human species,"[92] are "persons who at the same time are constituted by their soul and its particular qualities in their masculinity or femininity."[93] Maritain identifies these differences in the following way: women have as their "share the most delicate qualities, those of the highest value for the human race,"[94] while men have qualities that are "at the same time more powerful and more directed toward action leading to a good end in the realm of the world as in the realm of thought."[95] Men, by "right of nature," have authority but not domination over women.[96] Notice how the language of nature or essence has a way of insinuating itself even

87. Maritain, *Untrammeled Approaches*, 154–55.

88. Ibid., 158.

89. Ibid.

90. Ibid., 158 n. 5.

91. See ibid., 158–160.

92. Ibid., 161.

93. Ibid.

94. Ibid, 153. We must note, however, that some women would consider this elevation of women to the possession of the most delicate qualities of highest value to humanity as a form of pedestalization. Pedestalization occurs when, on the one hand, a woman or woman in the abstract is elevated and romanticized for some special trait while, on the other hand, her concrete reality and needs are ignored. Statues of the Blessed Virgin Mary on campuses that make no provision for maternity leave or childcare would be examples of pedestalization.

95. Ibid.

96. Ibid.

into Maritain's discussion of differences between men and women. But inasmuch as men and women share the same human nature, these different natures could not be on the level of species.

Maritain argues for the complementarity of men and women on the spiritual level as well as on the physical and sexual levels.[97] He asserts "the evident complementarity of the feminine and masculine types, as well as the fact that their differential qualities are those of the spiritual soul itself which informs the body according as it is individualized in one direction or another."[98] And, to his credit, Maritain asserts that the complementarity of men and women works in two directions: being-woman complements being-man, and being-man complements being-woman.[99]

Given that Maritain has insisted so strongly on the unity in human nature of men and women and therefore on their equality in that nature, his theory of the complementarity of men and women is the kind of complementarity that Prudence Allen, R.S.M., characterizes as "integral gender complementarity" or a complementarity in which each is wholly a person.[100] This is the complementarity of men and women that recent popes have written about, celebrating the evident differences between men and women while insisting on their unity in human nature. In this last section of my paper I want to suggest some possible difficulties, both theoretical and practical, with the concept of integral complementarity or the complementarity of wholes.

The first difficulty is verbal, but words are expressive of ideas and ideas are our grasp of realities. Is there not, at least literally, that is, etymologically, something oxymoronic about the complementarity of wholes? The Latin verb *complēre* means to fill up, to complete, or to make perfect. If a man or a woman shares fully in human nature, in what precise sense does his or her soul need to be completed? And can the specifically spiritual complement one person needs be supplied only by a person of the opposite sex?

And I must ask: is there an ambiguity in the expression "subspecific types of a modal-essential order"? On the one hand, a sub*species* would still have to be a universal that grasps a whatness, and an essential order certainly suggests an essence or nature. But, on the other hand, *modal* qualifies

97. See ibid., 156, 159–60, 162–63.

98. Ibid., 162.

99. See ibid., 160.

100. Prudence Allen, R.S.M., "Man-Woman Complementarity: The Catholic Inspiration," *Logos* 9, no. 3 (2006): 95.

the essential order. I think Maritain means that the masculine and the feminine are ways of being human. But Mary F. Rousseau, in her presidential address at the 1992 American Catholic Philosophical Association meeting, struggled with the nature of "the differentiation of the sexes"; it has, she asserted, "an odd logical, predicable status."[101] To say someone is a woman and another is a man is to assign predicates to them that are neither accidents nor specific differences or properties.

I ask: in this matter of creating masculine and feminine types, could something like what Gilson described in the last chapter of *The Christian Philosophy of St. Thomas Aquinas* as the professorial "tendency to abstract and to confine ourselves to the abstract concept,"[102] to dwell in the realm of pure, stable and unchanging essences, be ironically operative in Maritain's "struggling with words to designate this mutual complementarity"?[103] I say "ironically" because Maritain himself was, of course, a great proponent of the concretely existential character of Thomistic thought. But Gilson reminds us that, while philosophy must transcend concrete, sensible realities in the direction of essences or quiddities, to be fruitful it must return to concrete existing realities.[104] Gilson quotes St. Thomas to the effect that "the properties of the essence are not the same when it is taken abstractly in itself as when taken in state of concrete actualization in a really existing being."[105] And how many real, concretely existing men and women fulfill their human nature and achieve happiness without instantiating the particular qualities that Maritain assigns to their subspecific types of a modal-essential order?

This question brings to mind the obvious, empirically verifiable differences that exist both among women and among men. There are continua of strengths and weaknesses and of gifts and afflictions, continua existing both among women and among men. Because of these real differences among individual men and individual women, some men, in some ways, are more like typic woman than like other men, and some women, in some ways, are more like typic man than like other women. Given this, could isolating male

101. Mary F. Rousseau, "The Primacy of Gender," *Proceedings of the American Catholic Philosophical Association* 66 (1992): 1.

102. Étienne Gilson, *The Christian Philosophy of St. Thomas Aquinas*, translated by Laurence K. Shook (New York: Random House, 1956), 364.

103. Maritain, *Untrammeled Approaches*, 159.

104. See Gilson, *The Christian Philosophy of St. Thomas Aquinas*, 365.

105. Ibid. The source in St. Thomas is *In II Boethii De hebdomibus*.

and female types with set spiritual characteristics require something like what Maritain characterized as the logical error of "attributing, without realizing it, the character and value of specific categories to arbitrary groups set up in the fluid mass of individual peculiarities"?[106]

Maritain softens his critique of St. Thomas's having made woman the helpmates of man in procreation *only* by stating that, in writing about the relations between men and women, "the pressure of the cultural milieu exerts such force on the mind" that St. Thomas "was not able to free himself from the intellectual climate of his time, and from the prejudices which reigned there."[107] Could this not be true, to some degree of which he was not conscious, in Maritain's own case? In the abstractive realm, the type of woman is pure and unchanging—and I should add—most often defined by male philosophers and theologians. But the condition of real women can and does change. And with that change we have seen what some thought belonged to the essence or subspecific modal-essential type of woman, "by right of nature," was simply the result of a centuries-old process of socialization to that male-defined role, a process through which the male-benefitting feminine gender role came to inform the very psyches of generations of women. If Maritain could have observed and read for another thirty or forty years, would he still have insisted on the two abstractive types?

In regard to difficulties presented in the practical order—the moral order!—by a theory of subspecific types of a modal-essential order, it is not inappropriate to ask who gains and who suffers from the definition and prescription of these types. The myth of the Eternal Feminine was touted in Catholic philosophical and theological anthropology from the 1930s through the 1950s. It was the idealization of certain traits which are supposedly natural—at least in a subspecific modal-essential way—to women, traits such as: silence, humility, modesty, tact, submission, self-effacement, passivity, and docility.

Those who propagated this myth included Gertrude von le Fort and Gerald Vann, O.P., among others. I have put into the notes several quotations from the writings of von le Fort and Vann and quotations giving the injunctions of A. D. Sertillanges, O.P., to the wife of an intellectual.[108]

106. Maritain, *Ransoming the Time*, 4.

107. Maritain, *Untrammeled Approaches*, 163.

108. "Wherever woman is most profoundly herself, she is not so as herself but as surrendered; and whenever she is surrendered, there is also bride and mother." Gertrude von le Fort,

These thinkers give the impression that certain virtues—silence, humility, submission, and self-sacrifice—were proper to women and really "above" poor aggressive men so that the latter, practically speaking, are effectively dispensed from the requirement of practicing them. The myth of the Eternal Feminine tended to identify women with life-forces, with the body, with nature, and to define the fulfillment of "their nature" as selfless service to others, primordially, to husband and children.[109] What this myth denied to women was the recognition in them of a rational center of mean-

---

The Eternal Woman, translated by Placid Jordan (Milwaukee, Wisconsin: Bruce, 1962), 6. The original German edition was published in 1934; "... the surrendering power of the Cosmos, which is the mystery of woman ..." Ibid., 16; "As woman primarily denotes not personality but its surrender, so also the endurance that she is able to give her descendants is not self-assertion, but something purchased at the expense of submerging herself into the universal stream of succeeding generations." Ibid., 18.

"Let the guardian spirit of the hearth be not its evil genius, but its muse. Having married a vocation let her have the vocation also. Whether she achieve something herself or through her husband, what does it matter? She must still achieve because she is but one flesh with him who achieves. Without needing herself to be an intellectual, still less a woman of letters or a bluestocking, she can produce much by helping her husband to produce, compelling him to keep watch on himself, to give of his best; helping him to recover after the inevitable lapses, buoying him up when he loses courage, consoling him for his disappointments without accentuating them through undue insistence, soothing his sorrows, being his sweet reward after his labors." A. D. Sertillanges, *The Intellectual Life*, translated by Mary Ryan (Westminster, Maryland: Newman Press, 1965), 44–45.

"Her part, in the last resort, is not to command and make decisions; otherwise he will never fulfill his stature as a man. But she herself will never reach her full stature as a woman unless she goes on to fulfill her destiny as a mother. Her life of labour in kitchen and nursery, with all the demands it puts on her of courage and patience and dogged endurance: it is this that can teach her, more than anything, her own deep wisdom. But only if she does it wholeheartedly." Gerald Vann, *Eve and Gryphon* (New York: Blackfriars, 1947), 35. This book is a collection of conferences Vann gave to a women's group in England on "The Vocation of Woman."

"And if you are a woman, then remember that this [pity] is your special vocation, the vocation of woman; and until you have fulfilled that vocation you will never be made whole. The male mind, the rational mind, has its schemes and ambitions; it tries to order the economy of the world, to marshal events and dictate policies and build up the outward structure of life; and it has great pride, the pride of the creator, in its achievements.... But reason without intuition, the male without the female mind, is often blind and often stupid; and one day its house of cards falls.... And then it is time for you to fulfill your vocation; to have pity on the rational stupidity of men.... [Y]ou have to have pity in order to heal and restore and re-create; and then in your pity you yourself are made whole.... [Y]ou have in Mary, the Mother of Mercy, the figure of what you have to be." Gerald Vann, *The Divine Pity* (New York: Sheed and Ward, 1946), 127–28.

And, of course, Mary, the figure and model of what women have to be, was "a woman wrapped in silence." In 1941 John W. Lynch published a beautiful book of blank verse telling the life story of Mary, the Mother of Jesus; the title Lynch gave his book was *A Woman Wrapped in Silence*. It was reprinted by Paulist Press in 1968.

109. See Mary Aquin O'Neill, "Current Theology: Toward a Renewed Anthropology," *Theo-*

ing, complete in itself, and of a personal *telos* and agency, surely essential aspects of human personhood.

I shall conclude by asking: could it be that those who raised what was the cultural norm imposed on women by patriarchy into the theory of an abstractive and eternal essence or of a subspecific modal-essential type were creating—through "an unconscious process, the origin of which lies in the obscure working of the will to power"[110]—the anthropological pseudo-science that would serve to justify the subordination of women?

logical Studies 36 (December 1975): 725–36, which offers a five-point critique of the myth of the Eternal Feminine (734–35), not all of which would be applicable to Maritain's subspecific modal-essential types.

110. Maritain, *Ransoming the Time*, 8.

NIKOLAJ ZUNIC

Philosophy and the Search for Peace

I. The Question of Peace

Peace is a most elusive phenomenon. Human beings universally desire it, yet it constantly evades our grasp. What peace exactly is mystifies the human mind since it belongs to the same order of vagueness as the timeless ideas of happiness, justice, and truth. According to our common linguistic usage, human beings are said to be "peaceful" or "at peace" and a particular people may be living "in a time of peace." The essence of peace, it may be asserted, is intimately related to concrete human life and is by no means an abstract reality with no bearing on how human beings fare in this temporal world. But the reason why human beings desire peace in the first place is due to its unfortunate absence in human affairs. It is plausible that peace would have no meaning for human beings if it were a permanent part of existence and if it were not identified in contrast to its absence or lack against which it is measured and prized. One may suspect that peace receives its very nature in relation to its opposite, an equally mysterious reality, but which at its core is manifested in conflict, be it internal or external, personal or social. However, it is worth noting that the absence of peace, as with peace itself, is known only in the context of human living which has been upset and traumatized in some fundamental aspect. In light of this initial hypothesis, therefore, it is worthwhile studying the state of life which is not peace in order to determine what peace truly is.

In *Totality and Infinity* Emmanuel Levinas wrote that "the state of war suspends morality."[1] These thought-provoking words serve as a meditation

1. Emmanuel Levinas, *Totality and Infinity: An Essay on Exteriority*, translated by Alphonso Lingis (Pittsburgh, Pennsylvania: Duquesne University Press, 1969), 21.

on the catastrophic impact that war inevitably has on the ethical dimension of human existence. As a Jew who lived through the terrors of the Second World War, Levinas was well aware of the chaos and irrationality that lie at the heart of hatred and violence, where the ethical categories and rules that normally govern our lives to promote peace no longer apply. The extreme examples of evil in recent human history, such as The Jewish Holocaust and the campaigns of genocide in Cambodia, Bosnia, Rwanda, and the Sudan, have led many a philosopher to wonder about the root cause of evil and human conflict, spurred on more by horror and shock than by a more placid motivation. In light of such horrendous events, philosophers have been forced to ask whether one can legitimately philosophize after Auschwitz, given that reason has been paralyzed in the utter incomprehension of unadulterated evil.[2]

Yet, historically, philosophers have always been concerned about the challenge that evil poses for philosophical reflection, dating back to antiquity in thinkers such as Plotinus and St. Augustine and continued in modern times with Leibniz, Kant, and Schelling. Indeed, there seems to be unanimous agreement among philosophers that evil belongs to an irrational or non-rational realm of being which escapes being intelligibly grasped. This is why it is more appropriate to speak of the *mystery* of evil instead of the *problem* of evil, as Gabriel Marcel has repeatedly stressed. Although the history of philosophy is replete with attempts by thinkers to understand the inscrutable reality of evil and the pernicious forces that destroy human lives, a project which usually leads one to the brink of despair and with few answers, seldom have we in philosophy come across the same passion for, and interest in, the topic of peace. How to contend with a fact of life that threatens the very foundation of philosophical reflection is a challenge that surely moves every serious thinker to search for solutions. However, in this paper I would like to argue that philosophy should not be overly burdened with trying to make sense of why evil and unhappiness exist, but should rather endeavor to establish the conditions for peace that positively counter the destructive tendencies inherent in the human soul. Instead of analyzing evil theoretically and then losing one's mind over its complete obscurity, philosophy should be rather oriented towards strengthening the sovereignty of wisdom, truth, reason, and morality in a much fractured and broken world.

2. See Richard J. Bernstein, *Radical Evil: A Philosophical Investigation* (Cambridge: Polity Press, 2002).

This is not done primarily by offering a philosophical theory or exposé of the essence of peace, as useful as this might be, but by developing a spirit of peacefulness and love that will influence the philosophical community, and the wider society, in a constructive manner. Philosophy does have a positive role to play in the building up and establishment of peace in our world, and I would like to outline here how exactly this can be done.

II. The Experience of Human Conflict

The starting-point for a philosophical investigation of peace has to be the consciousness of the raw fact of conflict in our human communities. Conflicts do differ in degree and type, from the more benign manifestations in sibling rivalries and interpersonal disputes to the more serious examples of violence, murder, and war. In each kind of human conflict, a tension is set up between individuals or groups which leads to an antagonistic exchange. This tension can be played out in three main ways: verbally, physically, or psycho-emotionally.

In a verbal conflict the two or more camps articulate their grievances and assail the opposing side through the use of words and ideas. For instance, schoolchildren are well-known to engage in name-calling if hostility erupts between them, and on a much grander scale, the Cold War was waged entirely by means of propaganda and on the front of diplomacy. This type of conflict can be viewed as a clash of ideologies where there is a dissonance or friction between two or more sets of rival ideas. It is important to recognize in this situation that the words and ideas are expressed and made public and that they are not simply thought and held privately. Put simply, only when one verbalizes the antagonism does it become an overt sign of conflict.

If the hostility is dire enough, then physical confrontation can ensue. The purpose of a physical conflict is to gain control of the other by dominating their physical body. Inflicting corporal punishment and torture, for instance, are means to achieving this kind of mastery of one's opponent. Moreover, war, the supreme example of physical conflict, is a form of violence that is waged proportionate to the physical and corporeal natures of individuals and states.

Finally, there is a psycho-emotional conflict that is carried out by the manipulation of feelings, moods, thoughts, and atmosphere. A particular environment, such as the workplace or the family home, can be poisoned by non-verbal and non-physical forms of violence. These include acts of ignoring or the "silent treatment" that aim to ostracize and demean the other as well as explicit forms of discrimination that can be experienced by what ought to occur but does not, for example, the denial of certain rights and privileges to a group of people on the basis of sex or race. Such actions create an environment that is saturated with self-destructive emotions, such as sadness, hatred, or anger, that envelop persons in a vortex of negativity. The specific effect of a psycho-emotional conflict is the disturbance of the other's psychological and emotional state.[3] This campaign is carried out to control and hence to injure the other through the manipulation of their minds and emotions. No doubt, an oppressive and debilitating atmosphere can in some cases lead to more harm than either verbal or physical abuse.

It is an irrefutable fact that we live in a world that is sadly beset by conflict. From our intimate family circles to the drama of international relations, conflict appears to be a widespread feature of life that crops up everywhere. Some philosophers have gone so far as to argue that conflict is a necessary and inescapable aspect of existence. The ancient thinker Heraclitus held that conflict and strife are the fundamental forces of the universe that give rise to the growth and decay of things.[4] The political thought of Thomas Hobbes depicts the state of nature as one in which there is "war of every man against every man."[5] And Friedrich Nietzsche has argued that the beginnings of human history gave witness to unimaginable brutality and violence as the Dionysian spirit exercised its will to power.[6] On a metaphysical plane, Nicholas of Cusa and his disciple Giordano Bruno developed the theory of the coincidence of opposites (*coincidentia oppositorum*) which was a source of inspiration for the systems of the dialectic in

3. An interesting discussion of this topic can be found in Richard Sorabji, *Emotion and Peace of Mind: From Stoic Agitation to Christian Temptation* (Oxford: Oxford University Press, 2000).

4. Heraclitus, *Fragments*, translated by T. M. Robinson (Toronto: University of Toronto Press, 1987). In fragment 53 (p. 37) Heraclitus writes: "War is the father of all, and king of all. He renders some gods, others men; he makes some slaves, others free"; and in fragment 80 (p. 49) he writes: "One must realize that war is common and justice strife, and that all things come to be through strife and are (so) ordained."

5. See *The Causes of Quarrel: Essays on Peace, War, and Thomas Hobbes*, edited by Peter Caws (Boston: Beacon Press, 1989).

6. See Walter Kaufmann, *Nietzsche: Philosopher, Psychologist, Antichrist* (Princeton: Princeton University Press, 1974), 178–207; Rüdiger Safranski, *Nietzsche: A Philosophical Biography*, translated by Shelley Frisch (New York: W. W. Norton and Company, 2002), 276–303.

the thought of Hegel and Marx, which regard history as a constant battle between opposites striving to achieve a state of unity and wholeness. To be sure, in the *Phenomenology of Spirit* Hegel holds that war is a necessary moment in the realization of freedom and unity:

> War is the Spirit and the form in which the essential moment of the ethical substance, the absolute freedom of the ethical *self* from every existential form, is present in its actual and authentic existence. While, on the one hand, war makes the individual *systems* of property and personal independence, as well as the *personality* of the individual himself, feel the power of the negative, on the other hand, this negativity is prominent in war as that which preserves the whole.[7]

Conflict has been traditionally viewed by thinkers to be somehow necessary to the development of human beings, and by extension, of a society into maturity, freedom and independence. Conflict has been interpreted by many as an acceptable means to achieving certain desirable ends, such as autonomy, that in the long run make for a prosperous and fulfilled life. The act of self-assertion certainly does form one's selfhood and individuality but it also creates the potentiality for interpersonal conflict. When I affirm my thoughts and wants against an other, insofar as I am distinct from an other, then I am simultaneously affirming my individuality, which is carved out from the unified community. Such an act has the effect of separating a person from others and thereby establishing a tension. This phenomenon of self-assertion is also evident in group dynamics on a larger scale. Entire communities and nations can assert their identity to such an extent that conflict with other communities and nations necessarily follows, as can be observed in the conflicts in Northern Ireland and Israel. The more we ponder the nature of conflict on the social and political level, the more it becomes clear that this situation has its roots in the souls of individuals who seek to oppose otherness and to defend self-interest. How are we to understand the inclination in human beings to create situations of conflict?

III. The Restlessness of the Human Soul

The view that conflict is a fundamental part of our humanity is not only a philosophical one, but also finds support in the theological tradition. The

7. G. W. F. Hegel, *Phenomenology of Spirit*, translated by A. V. Miller (Oxford: Oxford University Press, 1977), 288–89.

Old Testament recounts the story of Cain's murder of his brother Abel which sets the precedent for the rivalry and violence that have taken place between human beings throughout history. The disobedience of Adam and Eve led to their expulsion from the tranquil surroundings of the Garden of Eden, yet Cain's violence against Abel resulted in God's making him "a restless wanderer on the earth" (Genesis 4.12–14).[8] No longer could Cain enjoy the peace and serenity that comes with a well-ordered domestic life, for roaming the earth as a nomad, without home and land, became the punishment for his crime. It is precisely in this Biblical story that the connection is made between sin and restlessness that is humanity's inheritance. On one interpretation, restlessness can be viewed as the result of sin, as in the specific case of Cain, but with respect to our situation, as heirs of our first parents' transgressions, I believe that it is more appropriate to understand it the other way around, namely, as sin being caused by the human being's restlessness. Expressed differently, it is my contention that the ceaseless and insatiable movement within each human soul is the ground of sin and is, furthermore, the chief cause for human conflict.

In the Christian tradition, however, restlessness has always been regarded as a natural aspect of our human predicament that can lead to a positive end. This idea is best represented by St. Augustine at the beginning of his *Confessions* where he tells us that our heart is restless until it rests in God.[9] Ever since our separation from God in the Fall, human beings have been searching for a certain peace that can still our longing spirits, a peace that can only be found in God. Indubitably, nothing in this life can fully satisfy our deepest desires since we were made for union with God. So while we are alive on this earth, we all remain restless wanderers and pilgrims, constantly in search of our true resting place. The monastic tradition has described in detail the experience of acedia, a spiritual laziness, paralyzing apathy, and profound inner unhappiness, that afflicts contemplatives like a "midday demon" by diverting their attention from God and driving them to wander physically in an intoxicating stupor.[10] Acedia deprives the monk

8. *The New American Bible.*

9. Saint Augustine, *Confessions*, translated by Henry Chadwick (Oxford: Oxford University Press, 1991), 3.

10. Jean-Charles Nault, "Acedia: Enemy of Spiritual Joy," *Communio* 31, no. 2 (2004): 236–59. On this topic of mindless and aimless wandering see the interesting study on the phenomenon of the *fugueur* or "mad traveler," an inexplicable condition in which individuals spontaneously set off on long travels without knowing why they are doing so or where they are going. Ian Hack-

of joy and peace and besets him with an overpowering sadness. The incessant agitation and torpor that characterize the human soul impels one to find rest in God. This ceaseless striving is, of course, the impulse underpinning philosophy as the pursuit of wisdom, and more widely, it forms the basis for all human endeavors that are focused on achieving the treasured goals of happiness and goodness.

Despite these noble aims, a good portion of humanity responds to this inherent restlessness, not by attempting to seek a veritable rest for one's soul in truth, but by allowing this motion to continue unabated. Such individuals are in constant movement without any prospect for rest because, simply put, they are not actively seeking rest. What is lacking in this scenario is a vision for truth and wisdom, a focus on a final and higher goal in the divine that motivates individuals to overcome the plague of purposeless movement that afflicts their earthly existence. Bernard of Clairvaux, in his short treatise *On Loving God (De diligendo Deo)*, refers to such people as the impious who walk about endlessly in circles.[11] They have no attachment to a vision that can channel all their energies to a determinate goal which can bring them deep and lasting peace; hence, they simply move for the sake of moving, culminating in spiritual exhaustion. Peace is embedded in contemplation as the human being gazes upon the truth.[12] Contemplation focuses the soul on the meaning of human existence and enables the soul to discover rest. Not to foresee an end to the motion in life is, as Friedrich Schelling has pointed out, an utterly unbearable situation in which existence assumes the appearance of a meaningless and vain activity.[13] In

ing, *Mad Travelers: Reflections on the Reality of Transient Mental Illnesses* (Cambridge, Massachusetts: Harvard University Press, 2002).

11. "The wicked, therefore, walk around in circles, naturally wanting whatever will satisfy their desires, yet foolishly rejecting that which would lead them to their true end, which is not in consumption but in consummation. Hence they exhaust themselves in vain instead of perfecting their lives by a blessed end.... By the very law of man's desire which makes him want what he lacks in place of what he has and grow weary of what he has in preference to what he lacks, once he has obtained and despised all in heaven and on earth, he will hasten toward the only one who is missing, the God of all. There he will rest, for just as there is no rest this side of eternity, so there will be no restlessness to bother him on the other side." Bernard of Clairvaux, *On Loving God. An Analytical Commentary by Emero Stiegman* (Kalamazoo, Michigan: Cistercian Publications, 1995), 22.

12. "The problem of contemplation and the problem of peace are not merely of one substance with each other, they are really one and the same problem." Gabriel Marcel, *Men Against Humanity*, translated by G. S. Fraser (London: Harvill Press, 1952), 118.

13. Friedrich W. J. Schelling, *Philosophie der Offenbarung, 1841/42*, edited by Manfred Frank (Frankfurt am Main: Suhrkamp, 1977), 254–55.

this sense, then, rest as a realistic goal, as the *finis quaerendi et inveniendi*, becomes the meaning that gives life its ultimate purpose.

Yet some people prefer to indulge in this natural movement of life and even go so far as to present this tumult as rest. It is easy to recognize this type of individual in today's world with the frenetic pace and increased pressures of urban life. The contemporary image of the capitalistic producer and consumer, the workaholic who is constantly abuzz with busyness and worry and who rarely takes time off to relax, tends actually, against our better judgment, to coalesce with our vision of the successful individual. Shrewd observers of modern forms of life have noticed this general phenomenon of motion without rest as a distinctive characteristic of a certain segment of society that has become quite noticeable in modernity. In fact, there tends to be agreement that an epochal shift occurred in modernity that saw a transition from "the blissful repose of the *vita contemplativa* to that of laborious reconstruction in the *vita activa*."[14]

Graeme Hunter has shown how Pascal was aware of the onslaught on rest that was taking place at the beginning of the modern period by a peculiar group of individuals referred to as libertines.[15] Libertines were shallow, irreligious people who took pride in presenting themselves as independent thinkers, yet for Pascal their defining characteristic was that they sought rest through ceaseless activity.[16] By absorbing themselves in constant motion and vain pursuits, libertines tried to set up an artificial peace in which they could live contentedly in their ignorance and fancy. But this façade is not convincing in the least, certainly not for Pascal, who strongly criticized the prevailing trend to escape reality in *divertissement*, the countless distractions of modern pleasures that aim to amuse, rather than edify the soul. This critique was taken up more recently by Martin Heidegger in his examination of the everydayness of human existence in the persona of *das Man* (the They), the superficial citizen who flees an authentic life by succumbing to the temptations of idle curiosity and chatter.[17] No doubt, man

14. Elizabeth Brient, "From *Vita Contemplativa* to *Vita Activa*: Modern Instrumentalization of Theory and the Problem of Measure," *International Journal of Philosophical Studies* 9, no. 1 (2001): 24.

15. See Graeme Hunter, "Motion and rest in the Pensées—A note on Pascal's modernism," *International Journal for Philosophy of Religion* 47, no. 2 (2000): 87–99.

16. See ibid., 89–94.

17. See Martin Heidegger, *Being and Time*, translated by John Macquarrie and Edward Robinson (New York and Evanston: Harper and Row, 1962), 210–24.

has invented many ways to avoid assuming his responsibility to work for truth.

We live in a world where true rest and peace of mind are being constantly disturbed by the anxious agitation of people who feel compelled to persist in incessant motion. Increasingly, individuals find it difficult to be alone and still and quiet; instead, they are falsely comforted by the din of hectic activity. The main result of all this restlessness turns out to be the deprivation of thought and the flight from reality. Be this as it may, we have to ask ourselves how this form of restlessness can be the prime instigator of conflict which robs us of a genuine peace. Losing oneself in vain pursuits certainly does have the tinge of dissolute and reckless living, but can such a disposition lead to the misunderstandings and animosities that bar human beings from living in harmony with each other?

The state of agitation and restlessness gives rise to actions and behaviors that are the root cause of conflict. Without a calm and collected spirit, an individual can much more easily end up venting frustrations and forming damaging judgments that ultimately divide persons and communities instead of harmonize them. By unreflectively rushing to act and speak, the risk of provoking enmity is very high. Restlessness impels people to act without reflecting on the meaningfulness and purpose of their actions. As an illustration of this point, Pascal makes the intriguing claim in his *Pensées* that so much of the unhappiness in the world originates from people not being able to be content with their rest and solitude.[18] Pascal adds that man's condition is one of "inconstancy, weariness, unrest" and that "our nature consists in motion."[19] One could argue in this vein that leaders who wage wars do so largely to indulge their growing sense of restlessness and use this as an escape from their boredom. The truism that wars can be avoided if they are never started in the first place seems to escape the notice of the powers that be. If only people could sit still in their rooms and enjoy their rest!

18. "When I have occasionally set myself to consider the different distractions of men, the pains and perils to which they expose themselves at court or in war, whence arise so many quarrels, passions, bold and often bad ventures, etc., I have discovered that all the unhappiness of men arises from one single fact, that they cannot stay quietly in their own chamber. A man who has enough to live on, if he knew how to stay with pleasure at home, would not leave it to go to sea or to besiege a town. A commission in the army would not be bought so dearly, but that it is found insufferable not to budge from the town; and men only seek conversation and entering games, because they cannot remain with pleasure at home." Blaise Pascal, *Pascal's Pensées*, translated by W. F. Trotter (London: J. M. Dent and Sons, 1931), 39.

19. Ibid., 37.

IV. Inner Peace and Love as the Basis of Interpersonal Peace

The inability to be at peace with oneself, if left untreated, inevitably results in the inability to be at peace with others. All human conflicts ultimately stem from disordered and restless souls who have not yet found peace of mind, and conversely, a safe and peaceful society is created by people who emanate a peace within themselves. It is important to recognize that social or interpersonal peace has its roots in the structure of the individual human soul. How close one is to achieving an inner peace is determined by the individual person's desire to know absolute truth and, hence, to be comforted by it, which is traditionally understood to be God. The goals that we willfully pursue bestow on our souls their shape and direction, which make us either virtuous or vicious, depending on the types of goals pursued. The Augustinian notion of an order of loves (*ordo amoris*), which was adopted by Max Scheler in his phenomenological anthropology, underscores the relation of the state of the soul with the quality and thus morality of human acts.[20] To put it as succinctly as possible, "whoever has the *ordo amoris* of a man has the man himself."[21]

The point that I want to emphasize in this discussion is that the foundation of social and political peace, that is, interpersonal peace, lies in the souls of individual human beings who have achieved an inner peace by arriving at a state of rest in truth. Such a thesis opposes the view that peace is established by means of the rule of law or a social contract, in general, by an ordering of society on rational grounds. Many political theorists, the most notable recent example being John Rawls, have formulated a conception of peace and justice that is anchored in a social contract between citizens who have rationally chosen the principles that govern their interaction in society.[22] Moreover, my proposal also rejects the idea that genuine peace can be realized through physical means, such as by military force, a position famously stated in Carl von Clausewitz's classic study *On War*, which has been a tactic attempted throughout human history.[23] Recent examples

20. See Max Scheler, *Selected Philosophical Essays*, translated by David R. Lachterman (Evanston, Illinois: Northwestern University Press, 1973), 98–135.

21. Ibid., 100.

22. See John Rawls, *A Theory of Justice* (Cambridge, Massachusetts: Harvard University Press, 1999), 102–68.

23. See W. B. Gallie, *Philosophers of Peace and War: Kant, Clausewitz, Marx, Engels and Tolstoy* (Cambridge: Cambridge University Press, 1978), 37–65.

of a militarily imposed peace can be found in Cyprus, where the United Nations has been mediating a cease-fire between the Turkish and Greek inhabitants for the last forty years, and in Myanmar, where the unrest of the movement for democracy has been silenced by the military dictatorship. Both the rationalist and military conceptions of peace fail to achieve true peace because they ignore the actual source of peace in the inner reaches of the human soul.[24] How do such conceptions fail exactly?

It is one thing to bring about a situation which is free from conflict and it is another thing altogether to realize peace. The proposition that peace is identical with the absence of external signs of violence and war is severely misguided because it overlooks the fact that in a seemingly peaceful society the possibility for conflict can still be present in the hearts of many citizens. Although people can live side by side in a community without explicit conflict, animosity and hatred can lie dormant waiting to be brought to the surface. This powder-keg or time-bomb situation that can explode at the slightest provocation exposes the lie to the superficial peace of the moment. The racial tensions in the United States and the multiethnic rivalries of the former Yugoslavia and Rwanda, where one day neighbors live together in fraternal harmony and the next day are murdering each other, demonstrate the volatility of interpersonal relations, despite an official guise of peace. It is a very tenuous conception of peace that regards it in privative terms as merely the absence of war.

A more adequate notion of peace takes into consideration the potentiality for conflict, not just its actuality. As C. A. J. Coady and Jeff Ross indicate in their discussion of Augustine's ideal of peace, "a peace must have something in it that at least quiets the dispositions to violence, hostility, and aggression that are typical of war, even if it does not eliminate them entirely."[25] To fulfill this condition, they advocate a conception of peace that is defined as an "ordered harmony" and "tranquillity of order," in

24. This critique of a rationalist conception of peace also extends to Kant's Stoic cosmopolitanism in his short tract *Toward Perpetual Peace* (*Vom Ewigen Frieden*) where he develops the idea of a confederation of states joined together by a just constitution. Kant believes that international peace can only come about if all states become republics and then agree on the principles of justice that will bind them in a peaceful union. This "highest political good" of a just order of world peace rests on the conception of a process of rational deliberation that frames the conditions of peace, a conception that I take to task in this paper. See Immanuel Kant, "Toward Perpetual Peace," in *Practical Philosophy*, translated by Mary J. Gregor (Cambridge: Cambridge University Press, 1996), 311–51.

25. C. A. J. Coady and Jeff Ross, "St. Augustine and the Ideal of Peace," *American Catholic Philosophical Quarterly* 74, no. 1 (2000): 159.

which what is emphasized is a particular state of mind of individuals that is conducive to peace.[26] Removing the *disposition* to conflict and replacing it with a personal attitude of peace is the only viable path in the realization of social stability and prosperity. A revolution of thought has to occur, to borrow Kant's terminology, from a seething hostility to a warm sentiment of good will in the hearts and minds of all people if we ever hope to live amicably with one another.

Nonetheless, even if peace is achieved, this does not mean that differences between individuals and groups are abolished. On the contrary, peace does not efface difference and otherness, as if it could only exist in a cage of spiritless uniformity, but rather upholds it because of the realism that is the essence of peace. Respect and a love of others in their uniqueness and difference must be the disposition that forms our quest for peace. To be sure, this is not mere political correctness, an official policy of tolerance, or superficial politeness, but represents a genuine solicitude and concern for the well-being of others. The philosopher and social activist Jean Vanier echoes this same sentiment:

> Real peace implies something deeper than polite acceptance of those who are different. It means meeting those who are different, appreciating them and their culture, and creating bonds of friendship with them.... Coexistence is a foundation, and it is important, but peace is something much deeper. To create peace we have to go further than just saying hello. We have to discover who the other person is and reveal who we are. As we listen to and really meet one another, we begin to see the work of God in the beauty and value, in the deepest personhood, of those who are different.[27]

The problem with many of our societies today is that we all live together, but do not know each other; we coexist, but do so without any concern for our neighbor. It seems that the social peace that many of us enjoy in our countries, cities, and communities often comes at the huge price of ignoring the underlying tensions and injustices that feed feelings of resentment, anger, and hatred among people. What is needed is a spirit of openness

26. Ibid., 158. In this article the authors outline three distinct theories of peace in Augustine's thought. First, the thin conception of peace is simply the absence of war. Second, the rich or thick conception of peace is a heavenly peace that accompanies our salvation and joyful union with God. Finally, the medium conception of peace is a more earthly type of peace of an ordered harmony based on the two following rules: not to harm anybody and to help everybody to the best of each person's ability.

27. Jean Vanier, *Finding Peace* (Toronto: Anansi, 2003), 41.

and reconciliation rooted in love, for by embracing the other in his or her uniqueness, we sow the seeds for a real meeting of hearts. In this regard, Gabriel Marcel has argued that our modern democracies must reside on the foundation of fraternity, a hetero-centric love for our fellow citizen, which binds us together and upholds our human dignity.[28] The current craze in the Western world with rights and freedoms, especially the right to equality, has the deleterious effect of segregating human beings from each other and pitting human against human. The notion of equality is an abstract, rational principle which is incapable of establishing true and genuine peace, unlike fraternity, which penetrates deep into the core of the human heart and creates stable and life-giving relationships among people.

V. Philosophy's Responsibility for Peace

Everyone has the responsibility to work for peace and this is no less the case for philosophers. In fact, philosophy has a special vocation to nurture a mindfulness for peace that leads to its concrete realization in our communities. This essential project, however, does not demand a radical restructuring of philosophic activity towards a new and unfamiliar end, but only asks philosophy to live up to its traditional nature as the pursuit of wisdom and truth. It is my firm conviction that peace cannot be divorced from truth, a truth that embraces a human being in rest and love.[29] Truth emancipates human beings from pernicious ideologies, quiets the restless human soul, and brings us closer together in a spirit of friendship and reconciliation. Yet, since we live in a world of diversity and difference, this truth cannot be monological or univocal in character, but must preserve

28. See Gabriel Marcel, *Philosophical Fragments 1904–1914 and The Philosopher and Peace*, translated by Lionel A. Blain (Notre Dame, Indiana: The University of Notre Dame Press, 1965), 7–19; *The Existential Background of Human Dignity* (Cambridge, Massachusetts: Harvard University Press, 1963), 130–33.

29. It is inconceivable how peace can be achieved without truth or on the basis of lies and falsehoods. Truth is the necessary prerequisite for trust and a spirit of mutual openness that unites human beings in solid, caring relationships. From a moral perspective, truth resides in the domain of conscience which not only aids one to discriminate between good and evil acts, but also enables one to recognize one's own moral failures, shortcomings and guilt. Only if I can acknowledge that I have committed wrong is it possible for reconciliation with the other to happen. Forgiveness is a major component of the process of establishing peace in the world and this occurs through the voice of conscience which is the beacon of truth in the human soul. For a discussion of this issue, see Cardinal Joseph Ratzinger (Pope Benedict XVI), *Values in a Time of Upheaval*, translated by Brian McNeil (San Francisco: Ignatius Press, 2006), 75–99.

and incorporate difference within itself. In this sense, then, we can describe truth as a form of ecumenic wisdom, as Thomas Langan has argued, that is arrived at through respectful dialogue, a sharing of ideas, contemplation, and most importantly, hard work.[30] Indeed, truth is not offered to us on a silver platter, for it must be deliberately sought after and won through a focused and diligent will. This conscious awareness of the need to allow difference and otherness to flourish in philosophy has been a common theme in some philosophical circles over the last few decades, from the Derridean *différance* to the Levinasian Other, having grown out of an appreciation for the pluralistic and multicultural nature of our current societies, especially in the West.[31] It is practically impossible to ignore the stark reality of diversity in the world and philosophy has been doing an admirable job in paying careful attention to this undeniable fact.

Still, truth that respects otherness and difference must not degenerate into a vacuous relativism where every idea and doctrine deserves to be equally accepted. The task facing philosophers in their quest for peace is the elimination of a hostile antagonism through a resolute determination to know truth in the context of a fruitful exchange of ideas. Although a certain degree of conflict belongs essentially to the forum of dialogue and debate, this kind of disagreement should reap positive results in a cooperative endeavor to achieve true knowledge and understanding. An argument should never be considered an end in itself, but a means to the apprehension of truth and the attainment of ecumenic wisdom. Constructive disagreement and intellectual justice, in the spirit of Alasdair MacIntyre's vision of the university[32] and Jacques Maritain's view of philosophical cooperation,[33] that fundamentally aims at achieving genuine insight into truth, must be the standard by which interpersonal dialogue is executed. Resolving dis-

30. See Thomas Langan, *Tradition and Authenticity in the Search for Ecumenic Wisdom* (Columbia, Missouri: University of Missouri Press, 1992), 200–201.

31. "The unity of plurality is peace, and not the coherence of the elements that constitute plurality. Peace therefore cannot be identified with the end of combats that cease for want of combatants, by the defeat of some and the victory of the others, that is, with cemetaries [sic] or future universal empires. Peace must be my peace, in a relation that starts from an I and goes to the other, in desire and goodness, where the I both maintains itself and exists without egoism." Levinas, *Totality and Infinity*, 306.

32. See Alasdair MacIntyre, *Three Rival Versions of Moral Inquiry. Encyclopaedia, Genealogy, and Tradition, being Gifford Lectures delivered in the University of Edinburgh in 1988* (Notre Dame, Indiana: University of Notre Dame Press, 1990), 230–31.

33. See Jacques Maritain, "Philosophical Co-operation and Intellectual Justice," in *The Range of Reason* (New York: Charles Scribner's Sons, 1952), 30–50.

putes, instead of promoting them or allowing them to persist endlessly, is a fundamental attitude that philosophy can inculcate in others by example.

In relation to this pursuit of truth and wisdom, philosophy must continue to build up and strengthen the moral character of individuals. A person who is committed unswervingly to the ideals of reason, truth, wisdom, morality, and peace will stand firm in the world as a beacon of light and hope. When the political and social structures of human civilization begin to crumble all around and the moral fabric of cultures is untwined, the independence and fortitude of the philosopher will carry him or her forward through the uncertainty and darkness of such upheavals.[34] Peace can be established and maintained only if individual human beings place their trust in the highest ideals and virtues that are the foundation of happiness and joy. In a sense, we must become a law unto ourselves, as Aristotle describes the magnanimous human being,[35] and follow our conscience when external authority fails us. Even if we enter a state of serious conflict, such as war, morality need not be suspended, as Levinas suggested, because we still have the option and freedom to remain rooted in morality and peace against the current of the time. Put emphatically, peace need not be abandoned simply because the world on all sides is plunged into war and chaos.

The responsibility for peace strikes a powerful chord in the center of our humanity. There is no doubt that we all have to work together to create a world that is peaceful, yet in this essay I have been arguing that such a noble enterprise must begin in the soul of the individual human being. Each and every human being has the responsibility to make the personal choice for peace and orient his or her will towards truth; only then will the world become what we want it to become. In this task philosophy must endeavor to be a source of inspiration and leadership through the clarification of ideas and the resolute pursuit of truth. Emmanuel Levinas described peace as an eschatological reality, a phenomenon that beckons us from the uncharted, unknown future.[36] Peace, in a very real sense, is a reality which we desire for ourselves and for our world; it is not necessarily present, but it is

34. I would go so far as to describe the genuine philosopher, who is living up to his vocation, as a martyr, that is, a witness to truth. Being a martyr implies that some form of hardship and duress is placed on the individual as he or she testifies to the truth of conscience.

35. "The refined and well-bred man, therefore, will be as we have described, being as it were a law unto himself." See Aristotle, *Nicomachean Ethics*, in *The Complete Works of Aristotle*, edited by Jonathan Barnes (Princeton: Princeton University Press, 1984), vol. 2, p. 1780, 1128a32–33.

36. "Of peace there can be only an eschatology." Levinas, *Totality and Infinity*, 24.

dreamed about and hoped for. In a chapter entitled "The World as it Could be Made" from *Roads to Freedom* (1918), a book composed during the dark days of World War I, Bertrand Russell expresses his vision of the world free from totalitarianism and conflict and at peace with itself, which each of us has the responsibility to realize:

> The world that we must seek is a world in which the creative spirit is alive, in which life is an adventure full of joy and hope, based rather upon the impulse to construct than upon the desire to retain what we possess or to seize what is possessed by others. It must be a world in which affection has free play, in which love is purged of the instinct for domination, in which cruelty and envy have been dispelled by happiness and the unfettered development of all the instincts that build up life and fill it with mental delights. Such a world is possible; it waits only for men to wish to create it.[37]

37. See Bertrand Russell, *Roads to Freedom* (London: Unwin, 1977), 154.

THOMAS R. ROURKE

Moral Problems in Economic Organization in the Work of Yves R. Simon

Unequal Exchange and Man as the Principle of Integration

I. Introduction

Yves R. Simon's extensive work on the philosophy of democratic government is undoubtedly among the most significant contributions of the twentieth century. In the midst of this corpus, Simon addresses at length the issues of i. technology and democracy, and ii. socioeconomic equality and democracy. Although his work on the themes of liberty, authority, and democracy broadly considered has been increasingly recognized, his writing in these two areas remains relatively neglected. This is surprising, because no reader of Simon's corpus could emerge with any conclusion other than that they are crucial themes for the consideration of democratic development in our time. In Simon's most famous work, *Philosophy of Democratic Government*, he devotes close to 20 percent of the work to the theme of technology alone.[1] Concerning equality, Simon held that we could divide democracy's development into two phases. First, democracy struggled for equality in the sense of eliminating institutional forms of bondage and inequality: slavery, serfdom, and various forms of legalized

1. Yves R. Simon, *Philosophy of Democratic Government* (Notre Dame, Indiana: University of Notre Dame Press, 1993), 260–322.

inequality. Although a timeline is not easy to draw, Simon contends that at least after 1848, the central struggle of democracy shifted to a second phase, characterized by a conflict between propertied classes and workers, a struggle for economic equality against what he saw as institutionalized forms of unequal exchange. Simon insists that there is a culpable form of complacency in the belief that we can safely avoid the problem of dictatorship and totalitarianism without addressing the issue of alienation through unequal exchange.[2] His language could not be clearer or stronger. He writes, "Yet, alienation through unequal exchange is the thing that democracy, in the second phase of its revolutionary development, has to deal with, just as alienation through institutional bondage was the thing that democracy had to deal with in its first revolutionary phase."[3] Moreover, any economic system that would qualify as humanist must be one wherein man himself is the principle of integration. Yet, the development and use of technology threatens precisely this principle. Indeed, technology becomes an obstacle to democratic development to the extent that the technologically oriented society becomes oriented to the pursuit of power over happiness, reduces men's communion with nature and among themselves, and establishes predictability and regularity as the governing norms of social organization.

I have earlier attempted to underline the significance of Simon's writings on the subject of economic justice, in terms of both i. their centrality to Simon's work in political philosophy, and ii. their profound relevance for understanding political economy today.[4] In these earlier works, I focused predominantly on the themes of the common good and the role of political authority. In this essay, I will approach the theme of economic justice from a different angle. I will demonstrate that Simon underlines the significance of man as the center and principle of integration in economic organization and the threats technology poses to this principle and, hence, to democracy. Moreover, the market system, particularly under advanced technology, has a determinate tendency to heighten man's alienation through unequal exchange, illusory services, one-way exchanges in which wealth leaks out

2. See ibid., 248.

3. Ibid.

4. See Thomas R. Rourke, "The Common Good and Economic Justice: Reflections on the Thought of Yves R. Simon," *The Review of Politics* 54, no. 2 (1992): 231–52; Thomas R. Rourke, "Michael Novak and Yves R. Simon on the Common Good and Capitalism," *The Review of Politics* 58, no. 2 (1996): 229–58. Additionally, in the latter volume, see "A Response to a Catholic Whig," 265–67.

of society, and the exploitation of labor. Finally, in light of these arguments, we will revisit Simon's contention that production and distribution through market methods is insufficient and must be supplemented by mechanisms of distribution according to needs and free distribution. Throughout, my attempt is, in addition to bringing Simon's arguments to light, to show their heightened relevance for today. Twenty years ago, I contended that Simon's concerns about production and distribution in the market system were more valid than when he originally wrote them. Today, I can only repeat the same claim with multiplied emphasis.

II. Agriculture, Technology, and Man as the Principle of Integration

"The essence of humanism," according to Simon, is that man himself is the "principle of integration."[5] Here we find the central reason why Simon takes seriously the Jeffersonian ideal of democracy composed of landowning farmers, a theory rooted in the assumption that an agricultural society is most conducive to democratic government.[6] There is a wholeness and integration of economic activity on a small farm that makes of it a model not only for healthy economic organization, but also, as we shall see, an important contributor to democratic citizenship. On a small farm, production is tightly linked to the end of satisfying the real needs of the people who live on it. Two important principles are realized. First, production is entirely ordered to the service of indubitable human needs, such as food, clothing, and shelter for the inhabitants. Second, the amount of the various products produced tends to be determined by the proportion among the various human needs.[7] Small farmers tend to produce the amount of milk, meat, vegetables, and housing that corresponds to the needs of the family; they do not neglect to build a house so as to specialize in milk production. It is important to underline here that Simon's holding up family farming as a model of economic activity is grounded solely in a reasoned analysis of the relationship between production and needs, and has nothing whatsoever to do with any argument of an aesthetic nature. Nor is it an argument rooted in nostalgia for a world gone by. Yves Simon was far too much a proponent of practical wisdom and philosophical realism to lapse into views

5. Simon, *Democratic Government,* 300.
6. Ibid., 261.
7. Ibid., 300.

of this kind. His argument, rather, has a perennial philosophic, and, properly understood, political and economic validity.

In addition to the determinate tendency of family farming to guarantee the relationship between production and human needs, a society of independent farmers is conducive to promoting democratic tendencies and discouraging totalitarian ones. Simon sees this as central to the American ideal, best articulated by Jefferson, even to the point of saying that it "gives verisimilitude to the theory that a technological society does not admit of democratic government."[8] Simon contends further that the belief that a society of moderate landowners constitutes the ideal basis of a democratic regime is summarized in three propositions. First, rural life promotes a life ordered to happiness as opposed to the desire for power. This is based on the sound assumption that democracy is a form of government wherein power is employed in moderation, best realized by citizens who are not seeking power as an end in itself. Second, happiness is found interiorly; it cannot be found in anything external to man. Third, that which is conducive to happiness is enjoyed in peace, not through painful conflicts. Finally, human happiness is enjoyable in common with others.[9] Rural life, insofar as it is lived in accord with nature broadly conceived, respecting the processes of natural life, tends to discourage the pursuit of power as the end in life.

A second set of advantages of a society of small landowners is found in an insight that goes all the way back to Aristotle, reappropriated by Jefferson at the American founding. The moderate landowner has a lived experience of autonomy, of self-government, in his daily life, which suits him well when it comes to participation in the deliberative process at the core of democratic government. Moreover, he tends to seek moderate and limited government, with moderate laws. He wants a government that will help to preserve his family, his land, and his work. Moreover, a society of similarly minded people tends in the same direction. Additionally, Aristotle saw the obvious advantages for democracy in the relative economic equality of the people. The citizen of moderate wealth does not assume either that others should obey him or that he should be subservient to others. Therefore, he is the one most likely to be the democratic citizen, able to propose moderate and reasonable laws that he himself is willing to obey. Simon concludes that "farm work normally has ... a character of wholeness and integration

8. Ibid., 261.
9. See ibid., 265–66.

that industrial work cannot ... in most cases be expected to possess.... All other things being equal, the farm worker finds in the condition of his work an opportunity for training in self-government both in the technical order and in the human order, which industrial conditions do not furnish."[10] Moreover, in the rural world, the uniqueness of each person working in the family unit tends to be confirmed, reinforcing a healthy sense of personal autonomy.[11]

Third, rural life promotes communal feelings, the sense of life engaged in commonly. Because rural life strongly reinforces family, even extended family, and community among families, it provides a healthy antidote to the kind of individualistic loneliness that technological society is prone to. Life lived in accord with nature reinforces a community of human experience grounded in the permanent things: love, work, virtues, family, and continuity among past, present, and future.

So important is the role of rural life that Simon goes so far as to say that democracy in a given nation depends particularly on an intense democratic life in its rural communities. In its roots, democracy is rule by the people, and direct democracy is the archetype, that is, a regime wherein the people rule in the absence of direct governing personnel. Simon is, of course, aware that conditions generally no longer support direct democracy. Nonetheless, one of the distinct advantages of such a practice is that it avoids the frequent accidental feature of democracy in technological societies, namely, that government is turned over to experts. Whenever citizens characterized by their prudence turn over government to specialists, a certain violence is done to public life. In technological societies, it is becoming increasingly difficult to keep the technical experts from the governing functions. In addition to Simon's concerns, I would add the aggravating factor that, in areas as important as the economy, the so-called experts in fact do not have the kind of knowledge that warrants the influence they are given.[12] Hence, if democracy of this archetypal kind were to disappear,

10. Ibid., 301.

11. Ibid., 302.

12. The philosopher can only cringe at the role played by the speculations of economists in contemporary policymaking circles. Economists have been given an authority over a crucial dimension of the common good, the economy, that is unjustified by any historically demonstrated capacity to predict and thereby forestall disastrous economic results. Other areas of public policy, such as education and social welfare, are similarly given over to the disproportionate influence of experts who have not the competence to solve the problems they purport to know

then democracy could easily degenerate into an oligarchic or aristocratic government.[13] Consequently, "a society so industrialized as to leave no room for family-size farming would be devastated by unchecked lust for power."[14]

Consideration of the disadvantages posed to democracy by the unrestricted development of technological society can emphasize all of the points raised above. The following five considerations are here noteworthy. First, Simon contends that it cannot be doubted that technological society has contributed greatly to the weakening of family life. People lacking community and experiencing loneliness are material for antidemocratic movements, leadership by mobs.[15] Second, in technological organization, it is less likely that the uniqueness of the person will be emphasized, adding to the sense that one's labor is simply an impersonal factor of production. Under such conditions, one is less likely to become aware of one's irreplaceable identity as a person. On the other hand, the relative absence of the division of labor in rural life underlines the distinctly personal contribution to the work effort. Third, the division of labor leaves a great number of workers with no lived sense of self-government. Given the importance of and the time dedicated to work, lack of autonomy therein "is by itself a very grave privation." Such a person will not easily govern himself in moral or social life, either.[16] Fourth, technology stimulates the lust for power, the proliferation of which, as an attitude, is a permanent threat to democracy. Society relies on rural people to safeguard against this tendency by preserving "the sentiments of universal reverence, of mystery, of awe and unity, that result from communion with nature in daily life."[17] Fifth, technical power tends to centralization and concentration. This tendency is determinate, because technology is oriented to increasing rationalization and regularization of economic processes from production through sale. The cost-reducing motives that drive its development in the first place only encourage the tendency for technology to cut costs while increasing speed and output. Inevitably, the industries that are most efficient prevail over

the answers to. Would any honest observer truly wish to say that American education today is generally superior to what it was fifty years ago, or that American families and communities are happier and better off for the proliferation of psychologists?

13. See Simon, *Democratic Government*, 306–307.

14. Ibid., 296.

15. See ibid., 316.

16. See ibid., 399.

17. Ibid., 299.

those that are less so, increasing concentration of ownership and centralization of economic decision-making.[18]

Technology greatly increases the growth of, and hence the temptation to resort to, raw power. Over and above technology's inherent centralizing tendencies are the profound inclinations initiated within man by which he comes ever more to desire the kind of control increasingly exercised by technology over his environment, to acquire such power and be able to control the social order with it. As man becomes ever more submissive to technological requirements, he becomes less patient with problems caused by man in his freedom. Technology feeds the longing to control people. In a world increasingly dominated by the regularity of technological processes, man himself easily becomes the element that does not conform. Technology spawns a desire to remake society along technocratic lines in profoundly antidemocratic ways.[19] In such a demiurgical position, man is likely to lose his equilibrium and to erect himself into a sort of cosmic engineer strongly inclined to despise the mystery of nature and the greater mystery of human liberty."[20]

In light of all these considerations, we have reason to view with great alarm the tendencies concerning rural life in our own time. These trends are well discussed in the volume, *Hungry for Profit: The Agribusiness Threat to Farmers, Food and the Environment.*[21] Small-scale farming oriented to family subsistence and rural community has been subject to nothing less than an assault on multiple fronts. Increasingly, production of food has become big business; in fact, it is the second most profitable industry in the world. This, however, has not been good news for small farmers. The farmer's share of the food dollar is below ten cents. Technology itself has invaded agriculture in ways Simon could hardly have imagined. Low prices forced farmers to adopt new technologies and to increase the scale of production just to survive. An old New England jingle summarizes the situation well: "We grow more corn, to feed more cows, to make more milk, to buy more land, to grow more corn ..." Farmers have failed precipitously. No more than 1 to 2 percent of Americans today farm. If we look around the world, we see that

18. See ibid., 285.

19. See ibid., 290–92.

20. Ibid., 292.

21. See *Hungry for Profit: The Agribusiness Threat to Farmers, Food and the Environment,* edited by Fred Magdoff, Frederick H. Buttel, and John Bellamy Foster (New York: Monthly Review Press, 2001).

the tendency is accelerating. Every year, 20–30 million of the world's poor leave rural areas and head to urban ones. One scholar sums up the situation as follows:

> Over the past five decades, a massive number of the world's people have been dispossessed, uprooted, and displaced, the means whereby they have lived having been taken in the name of development, modernization, industrialization, growth, globalization, progress and profit. During this time, an enormous number of people who were involved in agriculture with direct access to the production of their means of subsistence were expropriated and displaced, creating huge masses of superfluous people. Between 1950 and 1990, the share of labor force in agriculture declined ... by 40 percent in the Third World.[22]

In light of the preceding discussion of Simon's insistence on the connection between democracy and a vibrant rural life of self-subsistent farmers and farming communities, it is clear that the industrialization of agriculture and the evacuation of rural populations, converting millions into the most marginalized urban dwellers, barely eking out an existence, hardly augurs well for the future of democracy.

II. The Problem of Unequal Exchange and Democracy

As we saw in the preceding section, small scale farming has the strong tendency to fulfill what we may call the natural teleology of economic activity, particularly insofar as production is oriented definitively to authentic human use, and there is a strict correlation between the profit of human work and the real service of work. Of course, in the context of a local community, the weakening of this natural teleology may be relatively insignificant, as in the case of the small businessman, say, the owner of a hardware store, who performs indubitable services to the community, in return for which he makes money, which he in turn uses to provide for his needs and those of his family. Yet, it is equally clear that, as the market system of exchange grows to become more all-encompassing, and economic relations largely cease to be of a personal nature, the distance between i. production and use, and ii. work and service, become substantial and troublesome. As

22. Farshad Araghi, "The Great Global Enclosure of Our Times: Peasants and the Agrarian Question at the End of the Twentieth Century," in *Hungry for Profit*, 145.

production for the purpose of exchange largely replaces production for use, the economic order suffers serious moral dislocations. Simon's concerns are summed up by the term, "unequal exchange," which includes what he refers to as "illusory services," "one-way exchanges," and the exploitation of workers. We will take up each of these. Again, it is clear that, for Simon, these problems are central to the success or failure of democracy. As stated at the outset, alienation through unequal exchange is the problem with which democracy in our time has to deal.

The first category of unequal exchange is that of illusory service. The concept is based on a principle not generally recognized by economists, yet very real and recognized by anyone who has not delivered himself of his common sense, that is, the difference between a want or desire, on the one hand, and a real human need, on the other. Everyone accepts the possibility of someone purchasing something he or she does not need, or, worse, that is downright harmful; this is a universally recognized truism. The market economy, particularly as its scale becomes national, then global, provides many examples of illusory services. Simon originally used the example of advertising and sales, in which salesmen convinced people to buy cars or homes they could not afford and which were largely beyond their needs. The service provided in such cases is clearly illusory. We can, moreover, consider the depth of the problem Thorstein Veblen originally dubbed "conspicuous consumption," which underlines the reality of production no longer ordered simply to service:

> The vital point of production with him [the businessman] is the rendibility of the output, its controvertibility into money values, not its serviceability for the needs of mankind. A modicum of serviceability, for some purpose or other, the output must have if it is to be saleable. But it does not follow that the highest serviceability gives the largest gain to the businessman in terms of money, nor does it follow that the output in all cases need in all cases have other than a fictitious serviceability.[23]

The larger point is that illusory services encompass more than what takes place under the categories of sale and advertising, but also the products themselves. For a striking contemporary example, we have been made aware that, prior to the 2008 financial meltdown, buyers who could not afford to pay for mortgages were purchasing them anyway. To make matters

23. Thorstein Veblen, quoted in Yves R. Simon, *Work, Society and Culture*, edited by Vukan Kuic (New York: Fordham University Press, 1971), 121.

worse, the mortgages themselves were sliced and diced and sold all around the world to institutional investors. These financial instruments, it turned out, were absolutely worthless, which occasioned a threat to the entire international financial system. In light of Simon's argument, we need to ask, in both cases, what kind of service was being provided by i. those who sold the mortgages to the insolvent buyers, and ii. those who sold the repackaged failed mortgages to investors. In return for the large profits made, clearly no service was being provided at all. Beyond such obvious and extreme examples, Simon is of the opinion that, under contemporary circumstances, illusory services are prevalent throughout the economy. We have automobiles with far more power than can be safely used, tempting many to use them unsafely, resulting in deaths every day. We have piles of superfluous clothing piled up in stores, expensive cosmetics and ornaments for body and home. In the midst of an obesity epidemic, food stores sell tons of food with unhealthful levels of sugar and salt that no one needs. Now we have the further spectacle of drinks spiked with high doses of caffeine. Finally, we have industries purportedly devoted to serving unmet psychological and spiritual needs. All of this, of course, is supported by millions of dollars in advertising. The flip side of this coin, of course, is all of the genuine unmet human needs. Millions are hungry, lack affordable health care, potable water, arable land, and much-needed public transportation. At the time of the height of the housing boom in South Florida, and, I am sure, other areas, there was a boom in expensive condominiums. Yet, one of the unsung factors in the crisis was the lack of more affordable homes for working class people, which contributed to the tendency for people to buy beyond their means. In a market of rapidly increasing prices, the prevalent feeling was that the failure to buy now condemned one to future incapacity to purchase a home. In short, the market tended to overproduce high-end condos and neglect lower-income housing. Simon speaks in very strong language of the imbalances created by the proliferation of illusory services in words that are strikingly relevant today. Illusory services, he contends, "may annul the genuine service of work ... by crippling the system of distribution." He cites examples from the 1930s when some farmers were paid more to destroy produce than they could get for actually selling it as a service, and this while people were hungry. The products of genuine service could not be sold at viable prices and were left to rot, or used in extraneous ways, as in the case of using coffee to stoke locomotives. The results were the worst imbalances of appalling poverty in the midst of plenty. Simon does not think that these results were incidental, writing, "And I have strong suspicions that there was a cause/effect relationship between the plenty of wealth and the extremes of poverty."[24]

Another phenomenon of concern to Simon is what he terms, "one-way exchanges," "wherein wealth leaks out of society."[25] In its pure form, what Simon has in mind here are operations in which one makes a profit simply by buying a product at one price and selling it at a higher one, without producing anything useful in the meantime. This corresponds to what Aristotle refers to as "commerce," or what is more commonly termed speculation. Following the treatments of Aristotle and Aquinas, Simon does not characterize the one who profits through speculation as immoral. However, there is a species of unequal exchange involved, which results in a moral problem in the system of distribution. Some make enormous profits while producing nothing, while others cannot find work or make ends meet. No just person can be indifferent to such results. Simon makes the clarification that a profit need not be completely speculative in order for it to cause concern. In our time, it must be noted that Simon's concerns apply with a multiplied force. Speculative financial activity occurs at a level in our society that no one in Simon's time could even imagine. Speculation has grown in many areas, and social and political philosophy has failed to reflect sufficiently upon these developments. Speculative finance has in our time become a kind of entire secondary economy of its own, the result of a search for profitable sources of investment.[26] The sheer magnitude is staggering. As Foster and Magdoff put it, "stock markets and currency trading have become little more than giant casinos where the number and value of transactions have increased far out of proportion to the underlying economy."[27] World currency markets trade up to 1.8 trillion dollars a day. Every twenty-four days, the dollar volume of currency trading equals the entire world's GDP.[28] This means that 90 percent or more of this market has nothing to do with the underlying economy of buying and selling goods. It approximates pure

24. Simon, *Work*, 127.

25. Ibid., 34–39; Simon, *Democratic Government*, 237–41.

26. See Fred Magdoff, Frederick H. Buttel, and John Bellamy Foster, "An Overview," in *Hungry for Profit*, 18.

27. John Bellamy Foster and Fred Magdoff, "Liebig, Marx, and the Depletion of Soil Fertility: Relevance for Today's Agriculture," *Hunger for Profit*, 56.

28. See ibid.

speculation. Money drifts away from expansion in production to financial speculation, with the generation of more and more types of financial products and speculative games that only a specialist can keep up with. One can bet on the future value of almost anything. Although many people are familiar with futures markets, wherein one speculates on the future value of a commodity, few are aware that today 90 percent of this activity is in the financial sector of the economy, betting on the prices of currencies, municipal bonds, treasury bonds, stocks, interest rates, and various indices. In 2003, the Department of Defense created one in conjunction with a private company betting on the likelihood of assassinations and terrorist attacks. In 2007, a hedge fund, Amaranth Advisors, lost six billion dollars in one week betting incorrectly on natural gas prices.[29] It is precisely the search for the "one-way exchange," the motivation to earn profit merely by a hoped for change in the price, that was behind the speculative mania that took hold of the U.S. housing market.

> Speculative mania is characterized by a rapid increase in the quantity of debt and equally rapid decrease in its quality. Heavy borrowing is used to buy up financial assets, not based on the income streams they will generate but merely on the assumption of increasing prices for these assets. This is what economist Hyman Minsky famously called "Ponzi finance" or hyperspeculation. CDOs,[30] with their exposure to subprime mortgages or financial "toxic waste," increasingly took this classic form. Not just mortgage lenders and subprime borrowers were caught up in the frenzy. A growing crowd of real estate speculators got into the business of buying houses in order to sell them at higher prices. [31]

It often seemed to be an entire system of money begetting money with no relation to production and humanly useful services.

Despite the generation of new forms of speculation, still among the worst and most socially damaging forms of unequal exchange remains the exploitation of labor. Simon identified exploitation with a situation wherein unequal exchange is forced upon workers by circumstances. These may be institutional, as in the case of forced labor or slavery. However, they also

29. John Bellamy Foster and Fred Magdoff, *The Great Financial Crisis: Causes and Consequences* (New York: Monthly Review Press, 2009), 56–58.

30. A CDO is a collaterized debt obligation, a financial instrument developed in the 1990's, which mixed together a variety of mortgages at different levels of risk.

31. Foster and Magdoff, *The Great Financial Crisis,* 96–97. A fine example of a very pure form of speculation was the case of realtors who would purchase a home and sell it at a profit prior to having made even one payment.

exist in conditions of modern labor markets, particularly when workers are not unionized. When workers must simply accept the wage offered, there is generally exploitation, because the wage is unequal to the service rendered. It is tribute exacted from the workers, and Simon does not hesitate to call it servitude.[32] The problem, moreover, is not simply found among the employers, but pervades the society. Iniquity enters in whenever someone overvalues one's own contribution and undervalues his neighbor's.[33] Such attitudes support the exploitation of certain kind of work. Many demand $100,000 for their own work, but want to buy their vegetables at low prices only possible if the workers are paid well below minimum wages. Such dispositions support the exploitation of farm workers who cannot bargain fairly. Labor in this case becomes a commodity, and exploitation will prevail in many labor markets so long as labor is such. These workers do not feel that they are part of the democratic community, and they will have a tendency toward secession. Despite the positive trends Simon saw in his own lifetime reversing such trends, he also believed that he had witnessed "the worst counterattack of oligarchic exploitation in modern history."[34]

The struggle against unequal exchange in recent decades has been greatly complicated by the increasing domination of the market ideology. Allegedly, Adam Smith's invisible hand delivers the ideal social result. The implication is either that i. the market wage is the functional equivalent of the just wage, or ii. we should abandon discussion of just wages altogether as impractical. Simon clearly accepts neither presupposition, and for good reasons. The classical economists revealed their ideological bias when they denied to those who sell their labor what they granted to all other sellers. Producers and sellers were permitted a profit over and above their costs of operation. The price of labor, on the other hand, is not calculated with an increment for profit. This is why the struggle for fair wages has always been a political struggle against the market wage.[35] Theory aside, Adam Smith's entire portrayal of work and workers was from the beginning ahistorical. He excluded exploitation from the narrative arbitrarily when he interpreted work as a purely voluntary transaction. He misrepresented the actual world of labor, referring to a largely fanciful world of many em-

32. Simon, *Work*, 130.

33. Simon, *Democratic Government*, 249.

34. Ibid., 136.

35. See Vukan Kuic, *Yves R. Simon: Real Democracy* (Lanham, Maryland: Roman and Littlefield, 1999), 113.

ployers and few workers, wherein workers routinely became employers. There is in Smith's world no exploitation or domination, no working class struggling for its rights. The worker-merchants he referenced were historically few.[36] Simon's views, on the other hand, seem far more justified by a glimpse at contemporary labor. Unionization has declined considerably, while the globalization of the labor market has brought results resembling the abuses of the nineteenth century. In the United States alone, we have in the neighborhood of 200,000 children working 10–12 hours per day in the fields. Not surprisingly, such children drop out of school far more frequently. Far from a movement for social justice, the global labor market today presents distressing levels of exploitation, and not only in market relations. We have today new forms of slavery growing alongside the global economy. According to Kevin Bales, who has studied slavery globally, there are approximately 27,000,000 slaves in the world today, a figure larger than all the people taken from Africa during the transatlantic slave trade. Most of these modern slaves live under one of two forms of servitude. The most common is debt bondage. This is when a person pledges himself against a loan of money, but neither the length nor the nature of the service is clearly defined, and the labor done does not actually reduce the debt. The second form is contract slavery, wherein workers are tricked, often into leaving their own country, to go to work in jobs where they are fenced in and effectively enslaved. The contract is a mere cover for the servitude, and serves to legitimize it should questions arise. Lest anyone miss the point, we are not talking here of developments independent of the market system. As Bales underlines it:

> Slaves touch your life indirectly as well. They made the bricks for the factory that made the TV you watch. In Brazil slaves made the charcoal that tempered the steel that made the springs in your car and the blade on your lawnmower. Slaves grew the rice that fed the woman that wove the lovely cloth you've put up as curtains. Your investment portfolio and your mutual fund pension own stock in companies using slave labor in the developing world. Slaves keep your costs low and the returns on your investments high.[37]

36. See Michael Perelman, *The Invisible Handcuffs of Capitalism* (New York: Monthly Review Press, 2011), 72–79; 169–72.

37. Kevin Bales, *Disposable People: New Slavery in the Global Economy* (Berkeley and Los Angeles: University of California Press, 1999), 19–20.

Simon also believed that advances in social conscience would lead to upward limits on compensation as well. Beyond a certain point, Simon contended, compensation becomes another one-way traffic in wealth. He writes:

> A day will come when the conscience of the just will realize that the recompense of human labor ... is comprised between a lower limit, which cannot be very low—for it takes a terrific amount of money to prevent children from dying and to bring them up decently—and an upper limit, which cannot be very high—for no aspect of the common good demands that any person should enjoy an income many times greater than his avowable needs.[38]

Simon is denying the contemporary tendency to claim that inequality is irrelevant to democracy, an attitude that he condemns as democratic complacency.[39] The reasons are clear. Take, for example, the case of the CEO, who, having been unsuccessful in his work, is fired, yet on his last day of work, receives in compensation a figure greater than that received by any number of other workers in an entire lifetime of work. It is shallow to classify such transactions as simply private, because they clearly have profound implications for the sense of community upon which democracy also depends. It is hard to see in what sense this CEO and an employee of the same firm would experience community, and how the workers would not perceive themselves as victims of injustice sanctioned by society, encouraging the tendency of working people simply to withdraw from society. In truth, as Vukan Kuic summarizes Simon's attitude, liberty and equality must be held together to the greatest extent possible. When there are equal exchanges, liberty and equality are joined. When there is unequal exchange, they are divided with profoundly negative consequences for democratic community.[40]

III. Challenging the Sovereignty of Market Theory and Practice

Simon does not hesitate to challenge modern economic theory in its roots, particularly in its claims to be scientific, value neutral, and to support exchange through the market as the sovereign principle. We will deal with

38. Simon, *Democratic Government,* 250. 39. See ibid., 248.
40. See Kuic, *Real Democracy,* 112.

these in order. As discussed earlier, Simon considers the existence of illusory services plainly demonstrable to anyone with common rational sense. Of course, the concept hinges on a distinction between authentic human use and its counterfeits, which leads us precisely to the point. Ultimately, economic theory needs a clear concept of wealth, but wealth in turn is contingent on the concepts of use and service, which cannot be defined without reference to what is good for people, what corresponds to human nature. Ultimately, economics cannot be independent of the sovereignty of morality and the philosophy of human nature. To deny the existence of illusory services, or the distinction between profit and the fulfillment of human needs, is in the final analysis to equate all human desires with needs, something that no one ever really does anyway. We all really know people who desire all kind of things that they do not really need, and that modern advertising is designed precisely to foment an unrealistic sense of human need corresponding to desire. Economic theory becomes illusory to the extent that it prescinds from realities such as one-way exchanges, illusory services, and exploitation, all of which occur with a distressing frequency that has increased geometrically since Simon's time. To make matters worse, economists will turn right around and promote what they call free market economics, at the same time claiming they make no value judgments. Simon rejects out of hand the postulate of value neutrality for good reasons, as it does not in fact describe the actual functioning of the economy, nor would it qualify as the ideal even if it did. Economics is clearly part of the social organization of human communities, and is hence a necessary component of the common good, the overarching ethical goal. There is no basis for the postulate of ethical neutrality in any discipline dealing with human societies.

Simon rejects the whole project of attempting to make market exchanges the predominant means of distributing wealth. His concerns originate in his suspicions as to the extent today to which production is actually oriented to use instead of mere financial gain, leading to a distribution system in which human needs remain unmet, while many have wealth and incomes hundreds of times greater than any rationally defensible notion of human needs. For this reason, distribution by exchange must be supplemented by mechanisms of distribution according to need. Take the obvious instance of a married man with young children who are not self-supporting, and compare him to a bachelor. (Obviously, in our own time, one must equally consider the case of the working woman with children.) If one were to say today that the salary of the man with a family to support should be higher than that of the bachelor, the catcalls will be deafening. One is paid, they say, for one's work; the work being equal, both men should be paid the same. Simon sees in this, however, nothing but the old laissez-faire liberal notion that labor is nothing but a commodity. In a variety of ways outside labor markets, the principle is recognized. One is permitted to pay less taxes according to the number of one's dependents. Simon writes approvingly of family allowances, which he experienced in France. Employers paid into a fund according to the number of employees they had, and out of this fund came supplements to salaries based on the number of the employee's children. Simon does not think, however, that such programs would be likely to work without law and public authority to support them.[41]

Inextricably related to the principle of distribution according to needs is a reconsideration of the pricing of all products made with human labor. Simon challenges us to accept the conclusion that if we reject the notion that human labor is a commodity, then we must reject the practice of treating the products of human labor as though they were merely commodities. A low market price occasioned by oversupply can also be the occasion of unequal exchange. Simon gives the example of an oversupply of herring that means very low prices for fishermen. If human labor cannot be reduced to a mere commodity, then neither should the herring, since the price thereof is compensation owed in strict justice to the fishermen.[42]

Finally, there is the element of free distribution. So foreign is this notion that Simon even in his own time had to endure ridicule for even mentioning it. Simon makes it quite clear that he is not talking about people of means handing out dollars on street corners, but of more institutionalized methods. Simon finds it puzzling that the notion meets with so much hostility, because wealth has been freely distributed in every society and it is inconceivable that a society could really survive without it. No society ever existed simply by distributing goods according to the market. The perennial imbalances of market exchange systems, in which there is abundance in the midst of need, necessitate mechanisms of free distribution. We have the undercompensated, the involuntarily unemployed, the old, the sick, the mentally ill, victims of accidents, widows and orphans to take care of.

41. See Simon, *Work,* 133–38.
42. See ibid., 136–37.

Simon has no doubt that in the face of unmet human needs, society has only really two choices: leave them to chance or take responsibility for them. Simon does not doubt that the common good demands that society not only seek to assist the needy, but to organize the distribution institutionally. Simon is equally aware of the dangers of having the state do the organizing. There is more freedom and autonomy of life if the mechanisms are organized privately, and this is clearly Simon's preference.[43] However, it must be added that there is a big difference between, on the one hand, stating a preference for private organization as opposed to organization by the state, and, on the other, simply to oppose distribution by the state. In the latter case, if there is no real provision to meet the needs, we in effect leave the needy to chance. If private mechanisms are unequal to the task, a role for the state is not excluded, the state being the final authority responsible for the realization of the common good considered materially. Nonetheless, Simon remains concerned that state action does indeed tend to stifle private initiative.[44]

The timeliness of Simon's remarks on the limitations of market exchange as a mechanism of meeting human needs is perhaps no more poignant than when we consider the global food market in recent decades. Due to pressures by the World Bank and the IMF—public agencies that represent large financial and corporate interests—Third World nations in particular have moved away from subsistence agriculture. Yet, subsistence agriculture is truly a model of production for use, and is an excellent example of the importance of distribution by means other than the market. Nevertheless, due to the pressure to produce for profit rather than use, there is a global restructuring of agriculture to make it more and more exclusively based on market distribution. There are the examples of the promotion of agricultural exports, deregulation of land markets, cutting farm subsidies and price supports, and, in general, forcing small producers to compete with the transnational food companies. Hundreds of millions of people have lost their land and nonmarket access to food. Araghi sums it up well:

> With the rapid, massive and global incorporation of formerly self-sufficient agricultural peoples into market relations, and with millions of people having lost their nonmarket access to the production of their means of subsistence, hunger

43. See ibid., 141.
44. Simon, *Democratic Government*, 48.

has assumed a uniquely global character. Hunger amidst scarcity has given way to hunger amidst abundance. The contemporary food problem is rooted in the increasing global commodification of food.... Currently there is a global surplus of food, and we can safely assume that people who are hungry are willing to eat; it is therefore people's inability to purchase food as a market commodity and the loss of their direct access to the production of their means of subsistence that explains the global character of hunger today.[45]

IV. Simon and the Recovery of Natural Teleology in Economic Thinking

Decades ago, Yves R. Simon underlined the importance of some moral fundamentals for economic reasoning in a just, democratic society. We might better call these fundamentals the "natural teleology" in the economic order. Three principles seem to stand out. First, production of goods should be oriented to the fulfillment of human needs. Second, human work should be ordered as well to the service of human needs. Third, there should be a correspondence between financial remuneration, whether of work or investment, and legitimate human service. Under the mechanisms of the market society, however, there is increasingly a tendency for these bonds to be weakened, and increasingly in serious ways. Production for profit weakens these natural connections. Production at times has only a weak or dubious relationship with the actual hierarchy of human needs. The bond between work and genuine service is often tenuous. There is a troubling separation between financial reward and human service. What proliferates in place of the fulfillment of the economy's natural teleology are what Simon terms illusory services, one-way exchanges, and the exploitation of labor. Imbalances frequently develop in the system of production and distribution whereby many human needs go unmet. "The proletarian revolutions of our time," Simon writes, "revealed to the world that modern democracy had remained, to an unsuspected degree, the concern of the happy few."[46] At the root of all of these are processes of unequal exchange, which most assuredly impair the formation of democratic community. Simon sees no hope in the remedy of these ills simply by increasing reliance on market mechanisms of production and exchange. In fact, in our time, the expansion of the market

45. Farshad Araghi, "The Great Global Enclosure of Our Times," 155.
46. Simon, *Democratic Government*, 217.

globally, in tandem with increasing economic liberalism on the part of governments (often imposed on developing nations via International Monetary Fund mandates), grants ever-greater sovereignty to exchange by the market alone. There is nothing in Simon's thinking that would lead us to conclude that these developments are likely to enhance democratic equality. What is needed is a resurgence of effort to distribute goods according to human needs, which means at times distributing them freely. If methods of state distribution have not worn well, methods which Simon himself saw more as last resorts than as intrinsically desirable, then what we need today is the courage and creativity to develop new institutions. We must insure that the billion people who remain largely outside the system of adequate human compensation and distribution do not stay there.

On one final note, as I said at the outset, it is puzzling that contemporary Thomists have largely ignored Simon's writings on economic justice. At the same time, they are very much aware that the withering away of the sense of natural teleology in the sexual order has caused profound human pain and social chaos; no Thomist would deny the natural relationship among sexual activity, marriage, and family, and hence the moral necessity to keep them together. Yet, the economy today is just another example of what happens when natural teleology is discarded in favor of technocratic developments combined with theories that seek to justify self-seeking behavior. It is indeed the same misguided understanding of human freedom, promoting the same vacuous sense of subjective, material, or sensual fulfillments, with the same rejection of any appeals to natural teleology as outdated, which is undermining the economic order, just as surely as it undermines the sexual.

ABOUT THE AUTHORS

SAMANTHA BERTRAND received her M.A. in Philosophy from the Franciscan University of Steubenville in 2012. She is currently working in religious education in the Archdiocese of Washington, doing rogue philosophy in contemporary phenomenological thought, on the side.

JAMES CAPEHART is a doctoral student of philosophy at the Center for Thomistic Studies at the University of St. Thomas in Houston. He is currently working on his dissertation under the direction of R. E. Houser on the topic of Étienne Gilson and the Problem of Christian Philosophy.

JOHN J. CONLEY, S.J. holds the Francis J. Knott Chair in Philosophy and Theology at Loyola University Maryland in Baltimore. He specializes in ethics, aesthetics, and French philosophy. Recent monographs include *Adoration and Annihilation: The Convent Philosophy of Port-Royal* (University of Notre Dame Press, 2009).

DANIEL D. DE HAAN is a doctoral student in philosophy at the University of St. Thomas in Houston and the Katholieke Universiteit Leuven in Belgium. His research interests include philosophical anthropology and metaphysics, especially within the thought of Avicenna and Thomas Aquinas. He is the recipient of the American Catholic Philosophical Association's Young Scholar Award, the Metaphysical Society of America's Aristotle Prize, and the American Maritain Association's Yves R. Simon Institute Graduate Student Award. Starting in 2014, he will be a postdoctoral research associate in the Theology, Philosophy of Religion, and the Sciences Project: Neuroscience Strand, directed by Sarah Coakley, Faculty of Divinity and the Translational Cognitive Neuroscience Lab at Cambridge University.

BERNARD DOERING is Professor Emeritus of French at the University of Notre Dame. His main research interest is Jacques Maritain, his thought and his influence. He recently published his English translation of *Simone Weil: Attention to the Real* (University of Notre Dame Press, 2012).

JOHN MARSON DUNAWAY is Professor of French and Interdisciplinary Studies at Mercer University in Macon, Georgia. His publications have centered on French religious writers, notably Jacques Maritain, Simone Weil, and the Catholic novelists. His translation of Vladimir Volkoff's novel *L'Hôte du Pape/The Pope's Guest* was recently published by Mercer University Press.

HEATHER MCADAM ERB is Assistant Professor of Philosophy at Lock Haven University of Pennsylvania. Her area of research lies in the nexus between metaphysics and mysticism in the thought of Aquinas, as well as medieval philosophy and issues in Catholic culture. She recently published "The Varieties of Wisdom and *The Consolation of Philosophy*" in *Logos: A Journal of Catholic Thought and Culture.*

JOSUHA HREN is Assistant Professor of English and Catholic Studies at the University of Mary, and Editor-in-Chief of Wiseblood Books, a publisher rooted in the Catholic literary tradition. He is currently translating Charles Péguy's play *The Mystery of the Charity of Joan of Arc.* He recently published "Love of Mankind: The Genealogy of *Ressentiment* and the Achilles' Heel of Amour-Propre" in *Logos: A Journal of Catholic Thought and Culture.*

JAMES F. KEATING is Associate Professor of Theology at Providence College. His writing focuses on the intersection between historical research and Christology, the theology of Wolfhart Pannenberg, and contemporary moral theology. He recently published (with Thomas Joseph White) "Divine Impassibility in Contemporary Moral Theology" in *Divine Impassibility and the Mystery of Human Suffering* (Eerdmans, 2009).

JOHN F. X. KNASAS is Professor of Philosophy at the Center for Thomistic Studies at the University of St. Thomas in Houston. His most recent publication is *Aquinas and the Cry of Rachel: Thomistic Reflections on the Problem of Evil* (Catholic University of America Press, 2013).

MICHAEL NOVAK is currently Distinguished Visiting Professor at Ave Maria University in Naples, Florida. He was the recipient of the Templeton

Prize and on three occasions served as a U.S. ambassador under President Ronald Reagan. His latest book is a personal memoir, *Writing from Left to Right: My Journey from Liberal to Conservative* (Image, 2013).

ROGER W. NUTT is Associate Professor of Theology and Director of the Master of Arts in Theology at Ave Maria University in Naples, Florida. His research focuses on medieval Christology and sacramental theology. He recently published "Faith, Metaphysics, and the Contemplation of Christ's Corporeal Presence in the Eucharist" in *Antiphon: A Journal of Liturgical Renewal.*

BERNADETTE E. O'CONNOR is Professor of Philosophy at the University of the Incarnate Word in San Antonio. Her research interests include Thomistic metaphysics, Heideggerian *Seinsdenken,* and the philosophy of Jacques Maritain. Her most recent publication is "The Freudian and Maritainian Theories of Sublimation and Their Ontological Bases" in the American Maritain Association volume on *Scholasticism and Politics.*

THOMAS R. ROURKE is Professor of Politics at Clarion University in Clarion, Pennsylvania. His research interests are religion and politics, with an emphasis on Catholic Social Thought. He recently published *The Social and Political Thought of Benedict XVI* (Rowman and Littlefield, 2011).

RANDALL B. SMITH is Professor of Theology at the University of St. Thomas, Houston, where he holds the Scanlan Chair in Theology. He teaches primarily in the area of moral theology and publishes regularly in *Crisis* and *The Catholic Thing.* Two forthcoming books treat divine order and justice in Homer's *Iliad* and *Odyssey* and the sermons of Thomas Aquinas.

C. A. TSAKIRIDOU is Associate Professor of Philosophy at La Salle University. She specializes in aesthetics and metaphysics. She recently published *Icons in Time, Persons in Eternity: Orthodox Theology and the Aesthetics of the Christian Image* (Ashgate, 2013).

ANNE M. WILES is Professor of Philosophy at James Madison University in Harrisonburg, Virginia. She is the author of several articles on the epistemology and metaphysics of Plato and Aristotle as well as articles on Wittgenstein, Dante, and Tagore.

NIKOLAJ ZUNIC is Associate Professor of Philosophy at St. Jerome's University in Waterloo, Ontario. His research interests include philosophical anthropology, particularly the tradition of Christian personalism, the philosophy of religion, and metaphysics. He has published articles in *Maritain Studies, American Catholic Philosophical Quarterly,* and *The Heythrop Journal.*

INDEX

Abe, Masao, 48n95, 49–50, 52
Action française, 223
Adam and Eve, 107, 302
Addleson, Kathryn Pyne, 287n66
Ad Tuendam fidem, 160
Aertsen, Jan, 78n54
aesthetics, x–xi, 203–25, 226–34, 235–50
Albert the Great, 126–29
Alexander of Hales, 126, 141
Allen, Prudence, 292
American Maritain Association, xi, 82, 229, 234
anthropology, philosophical, 23–98
Anscombe, Elizabeth, 273, 346
anti-Semitism, x, 166, 203–25
Araghi, Farshad, 320n22, 330–31
Arianism, 52
Aristotle, viii, xi, 6, 11, 20n24, 99, 105, 226, 228, 311; and economics, 316, 323; and gender, 288–89; and history, 176–78; and theology, 138–39; on education, 256, 263–79
Aristotelianism, 60, 66, 84n4, 163, 228
Arnold, Matthew, x, 181–83
Art and Scholasticism, 216, 226–33
Asals, Frederick, 233
Aubert, Roger, 134n8, 139n21
Augustine of Hippo, 24n4, 136, 298, 302, 307
Augustinianism, 34, 48, 306
Auric, Georges, 212
Averroes, 66, 138
Ayer, A. J., 103

Bainville, J. V., 144–46
Bales, Kevin, 326n37
Barnes, Corey, 127–29
Bars, Henry, 24n4
Bauman, Zygmut, 204
Bellah, Robert, 28
Benedict XVI, 137, 161, 184, 208, 309n29
Benelli, Giovanni, 155
Bergson, Henri, vii, 100
Bernanos, Georges, 156, 231
Bernard of Clairvaux, 303
Bernstein, Richard J., 298n2
Berrigan, Daniel, 229
Bertrand, Samantha, xi, 263–79, 333
Billot, Louis, 144–46
birth control, ix, 150–62
Birth Control Commission, 150–53
Blondel, Maruice, 146–47
Bloy, Léon, x, 156, 203–25
Bodéüs, Richard, 278n65
Bonaventure, 126–28
Bouyer, Louis, 290n86
Brady, Mary Rosalie, 214
Brient, Elizabeth, 304n14
Brooks, Cleanth, 234
Brown, Stephen, 117
Bruno, Giordano, 300
Buddhism, 27–33, 40n58, 50–51, 101–106
Burnyeat, Miles, 55n2, 73n41, 267n22, 277n59

Cajetan, Thomas de Vio, 66, 67–69, 73n41, 118–26
Caldecott, Stratford, 43n71
Camus, Albert, ix, 100, 111
Capehart, James, viii–ix, 83–98, 333
Cartesianism, 28, 84n4
Cashdollar, Standford, 164
Catechism of the Catholic Church, 163–69
Casti connubii, 150, 151
Catholicism, 39, 131, 134–35, 142, 145–49, 210
Chagall, Marc, 221
Chalcedon, 50, 116
Chenu, Marie-Dominique, 45n84, 46n87, 47n91

Chesterton, G. K., 196–97
Christology, ix, 45–52, 115–29
Church, 38
Claudel, Paul, 156, 217
Clement of Alexandra, 137–38, 290
Clerrisac, Humbert, 209
Coady, C. A. J., 307
Cocteau, Jean, x, 159, 212–14, 217
Code of Canon Law, 160, 161
cognition, 54–82
Cohen, Sheldon, 55n2
Colberg, Shawn, 119, 123–24
Collins, Susan, 269n32, 270n36
Colombo, Carlo, 152
Communism, 285, 287
Conley, John J., vii–xii, 163–69, 333
connaturality, vii, 99
Cottier, Georges, 42n66, 157
Courthion, Pierre, 221
Crane, Richard Francis, 204, 207
Crittenden, Jack, 278n69
Credo of the People of God, 155
Curren, Randall, 267n21

Dante Alighieri, 103, 110,
Darwinism, 284
David of Dinant, 16
Dawson, Christopher, 21
De anima, 7, 56; and epistemology, 60, 61, 63, 74
De Anna, Gabriele, 55n2, 65n20
Decaen, Christopher, 64n20, 68n28
Declaration of Human Rights, xi
De ente et essentia, 83–98
Degrees of Knowledge, 6, 8, 24, 120–21; and epistemology 54–82; and mysticism, 33, 39–45
De Haan, Daniel D., viii, 54–82, 333
Deloffre, Helen-Marie, 124, 126
De Lubac, Henri, 45n79, 132, 147, 148
De potentia, 45, 54, 60, 67
Derrida, Jacques, 239
De Trinitate, 7, 45
De Vaux, Roland, 289–90
De veritate, 34, 37
Dewan, Larence, 43–44, 78n54
Dickey, James, 229
Diepen, Herman, 117, 121, 124–29
DiNoia, Joseph, 36n39
Disputed Questions on Truth, 4, 7, 46

Doering, Bernard, ix, 150–162, 333–34
Dostoevsky, Fyodor, 108, 276n54
"Dover Beach," 181–83
Dowling, Christine, 248
Drumont, Edouard, 206
Dulles, Avery, 134n8, 135n9, 136n11, 141n32, 145n39, 161
Dunaway, John Marson, x, 226–34, 334

Ebberl, Jason, 93–94
Eberstadt, Mary, 107–108
Education at the Crossroads, 253–62
economics, xi, 313–31
education, xi–xii, 253–62, 263–79
Eiten, Robert, 33
Eliot, George, 173
Eliot, T. S., 175, 187n26, 194, 199, 228
Emmerich, Anne Catherine, 221
Epistle to the Ephesians, 48–49
Epistle to the Hebrews, 198
Epistle to the Philippians, 49–52
epistemology, 54–82
equality, xi–xii, 280–96, 313–32
Erb, Heather M., viii, 23–53, 334
Eucharist, 167–69, 247
Exodus, 17, 166, 168
expressionism, 203–25

Fabro, Cornelio, 74n43
feminism, xi, 280–96
Fergusson, Francis, 228
Feuerbach, Ludwig, 173, 178
Fitzgerald, Sally, 229, 233
First Epistle of Peter, 186
Foster, John Bellamy, 323, 324
Fowler, Wallace, 226
Foucault, Michel, 239
Franciscans, 126, 141
Francis Xavier, 5
Frankl, Victor, 174–80, 185, 187
Fredericks, James L., 50n101
Frost, Robert, 195
Fukuyama, Francis, 275n52

Gallie, W. B., 306n23
Gardeil, Ambroise, 38n51, 39n54, 39, 146n49
Gardet, Louis, 38n51
Garver, Eugene, 269, 276
Garrigou-Lagrange, Reginald, 23–26, 32–38, 52, 118, 131, 209

Getz, Lorine, 233
Ghéon, Henri, x,
Gibson, James J., 58n5, 74, 75n45
Gillam, Alice, 239n27
Gilligan, Carol, 286
Gilson, Étienne, 70n34, 72n38, 79n56, 97, 293
Gioia, Dana, 234
Giroux, Robert, 233
God, 15–20, 29–30, 34, 35, 48–49, 53, 101, 186–87
Gordon, Caroline, x, 227–34
Grant, Sara, 43n71
Green, Julien, 231, 232
Gregory, Brad, 149
Griffin, John Howard, 203, 228
Griffiths, Bede, 42n68

Hacker, Peter M. S., 58n5, 59n6, 75n45
Haldane, John, 55n2
Hamlyn, David W., 55n2
Hancock, Curtis, 43n69
Harnack, Adolf, 137
Hastings, Adrian, 118
Haught, John, 189, 194–95
Hegel, G. W. F., 301
Heidegger, Martin, 3, 12, 19, 304
Hellman, John, 205–206
Heppenstall, Rayner, 215, 220
Heraclitus, 300
Hervaeus Natalis, 5
Hesse, Herman, 102
Hinduism, 27, 33, 38, 39, 40n58, 101, 102, 104, 106
Hitler, Adolf, 110, 111
history, x, 173–99
Hobbes, Thomas, 66
Hoffman, Paul, 55n2, 73n41, 271n38
Howells, Edward, 27, 30
Hren, Joshua, x, 235–50, 334
Humanae Vitae, ix, 150–62
Hunter, Graeme, 304n15
Hütter, Reinhard, 132
hylomorphism, viii, 83–98

Inge, Dean, 32
Introduction to Philosophy of Knowledge, 54–82
Irwin, Terence, 269n28
Islam, 38, 39, 40
Israel, x, 164, 203–25

Jaffa, Henry V., 270n35
James, William, 25, 27, 30
Jansenism, 33
Janz, Denis, 45n81, 46n87, 47n91
Jarrell, Randall, 229
Jazz Age Catholicism: Mystic Modernism in Postwar Paris 1919–1933, 209–13
Jefferson, Thomas, 315–16
John XXIII, 150
John of the Cross, 32, 101, 103–105
John Paul II, 42n66, 160, 177, 266
John the Evangelist, 105, 246
Journet, Charles, ix, 23, 150–62, 207
Judaism, x, 40, 164, 203–25, 298
Julian of Norwich, 24

Kabbalism, 30
Kaelin, Father, 153–54
Kant, Immanuel, 65, 103, 298, 307n25
Kantianism, 28
Katz, Steven A., 30, 31,
Keating, James F., ix, 130–49, 334
Keller, Helen, 236–39, 241, 244–45
Kenny, John Peter, 25
Kernan, Julie, 209n29
Keyt, David, 269n30
Kierkegaard, Søren 12, 249
Klenicki, Leon, 207
Klubertanz, George, 5n3, 54n2, 55n2, 66n25, 67n27, 74n43
Knasas, John F.X., viii, 3–22, 70n34, 334
Knowles, David, 32
Kohlberg, Lawrence, 278n67
Kuic, Vukan, 325n35, 327
Küng, Hans, 133

Lacombe, Olivier, 54
La Douceur, Emile, 213n48
Lamont, John, 130, 136n11, 138
Langan, Thomas, 310
language, 235–50
La Salette, 211–12
Lash, Nicholas, 161
Lawlor, Peter Augustine, 236–37, 245
Lazare, Bernard, 206
Lehrberger, James, 84–98
Leibniz, Gottfried Wilhelm, 19, 298
Lemonnyer, Antoine, 33
Levinas, Emmanuel, 297, 311
Leo XIII, 143

Lewis, C. S., 264n4, 279n71
Lindbeck, George, 28, 29
literature, 203–225, 226–34
Little Brothers of Jesus, 152, 157, 158
Locke, John, 66, 130
Lonergan, Berrnard, 3, 65n20, 105, 132
Long, Steven A., 30
Lost in the Cosmos, 237–50
Louth, Andrew, 23
Lowell, Robert, 229
Lucey, Frances, 181
Lynch, John W., 295n108

Macchi, Pasquale, 157, 158
MacDonald, Paul, Jr., 55n2
MacIntyre, Alasdair, 310
Magdoff, Fred, 323n27, 324
Man's Search for Meaning, 175–79
Marcel, Gabriel, 12, 100, 298, 303, 309
Maréchal, Joseph 101
Maritain, Jacques, and American literature, 226–34; and birth control, 150–62; and Christology, 115–29; and nihilism, 99–111; and Judaism, 203–25; and ontology, 3–23; and redemption, vii–xii; epistemology of, 54–82; on education, 253–62; on equality, 280–96; on mysticism, 23–53; semiotics of, 163–72, 235–50
Maritain, Raïssa, x, 100, 152, 203–25
Marr, David, 75n45,
Marx, Karl, 173, 178, 301
Marshall, Bruce, 131n2
Martin, Christopher, 192
McEvoy, James, 11
McGinn, Bernard, 26, 30, 31
McInerny, Ralph, 139n19, 223–24
Merton, Thomas, 228
metaphysics, viii–ix, 23–53, 54–82, 83–98, 99–111, 115–29
Metaphysics, 7
Moore, Brenna, 232
Moses, 17
mysticism, 23–53

National Socialism, 284, 290
naturalism, 33
Nault, Jean-Charles, 302n10
Neoplatonism, 33, 38
Neo-scholasticism, ix, 132
New Criticism, 234
Neuhaus, Richard John, 188
New Age, 193
Nicgorski, Walter, 224
Nicholas of Cusa, 300
Nichols, Aidan, 24n5, 32, 131n3
Nicomachean Ethics, 20n24, 177–78, 263–78, 311
Nieto, Jose, 27
Nietzsche, Friedrich, 102, 106, 242–43, 300
nihilism, 99–111
Noë, Alva, 58n5, 65n20
Novak, Michael, ix, 99–111, 314n4, 334–35
Nuremberg, 282
Nutt, Roger W., ix, 115–29, 335

Obenauer, Klaus, 118
O'Callaghan, Casey, 58n4, 65n20
O'Callaghan, John, 55n2
O'Connor, Bernadette E., xi, 280–96, 335
O'Connor, Flannery, x, 227–34
Oedipus, 189–90
Ogino method, 151, 152, 158
O'Meara, Thomas, 36n39, 162
O'Neill, Mary Aquin, 295n109
On the Church of Christ, 39, 40, 162
ontology, 54–82, 115–29
Origen, 138
O'Rourke, Kevin, 161
Osborne, 37, 38
Owens, Joseph, 46n86, 70n34, 72n38, 78n54
Oxenhandler, Neal, 234

Pannenberg, Wolfhart, 137n13
Pascal, Blaise, vii, 304–305
Pascendi Dominici Gregis, 130
Pasnau, Robert, 55n2, 95n33
Passion of Christ, 223
patristics, 137–38
Paul VI, ix, 150–62
Paul of Tarsus, 38, 47–52, 106–107, 135, 187, 257
peace, 297–312
Peddicrod, Richard, 131n2
Pegis, Anton C., 12n15, 35n37, 83–84, 91–97
Péguy, Charles, 203
Peirce, Charles S., 237
Pelagianism, 32, 33
Pelikan, Jaroslav, 137n13
Percy, Walker, xi, 180, 229, 235–50
Perelman, Michael, 326n36
Phillipe, Paul, 155
Philosophy of Democratic Government, 313–31

Pieper, Josef, 179–80, 184, 194
Pilgrim of the Absolute, 213–16
Pimlico, 196–99
Pindar, 254
Pinker, Steven, 191–92
Pius IX, 142, 289n78, 289–90
Pius XII, 153
Plato, 99, 228, 257, 284
Plotinus, 40, 43, 298
Poe, Edgar Allan, 228
Polimeni, Emmanuela, 211
Politics, 263–79
Price, Reynolds, 229
Princeton, 227–28
Protestantism, 130, 141–42
Pseudo-Dionysius, 39
Psichari, Ernest, 100

Rabanus, 51
Rahner, Karl, 12, 132, 147, 148
Range of Reason, 233, 310n33
Ransom, John Crowe, 234
Ransoming the Time, 33, 73n40; and anti-Semitism, 203–25; and feminism, 280–96; and nihilism, 99–111; and semiotics, 163–69, 235–50
Rawls, John, 306
redemption, vii–xii
Reno, R. R., 131
Rocca, Gregory, 46n86
Rosen, Stanley, 235, 239
Ross, Jeff, 307
Rouault, Georges, x, 219–25
Roulet, Anne-Marie, 217–18
Rourke, Thomas R., xi, 313–32, 335
Rousseau, Jean-Jacques, 277
Rousseau, Mary F., 293n101
Rousselot, Pierre, 146–47
Rouveyre, Andre, 220
Royal, Robert, 205
Russell, Bertrand, 312

sacraments, 163–69
Salas, Victor, 128–29
Sartre, Jean-Paul, ix, 3, 100,
Saussure, Ferdinand de, 239
Schaef, Anne Wilson, 287n66
Scheeben, Matthias, 131
Scheler, Max, 306
Schelling, Friedrich W. J., 298, 303
Schleiermacher, Friedrich, 29, 130
Schloesser, Stephen, 209n30, 213, 222
Schklovsky, Victor, 243–44
Scotus, Duns, 5, 119–20, 123, 133, 141
semiotics, x–xi, 163–69, 235–50
Sertillanges, A.D., 294–95
Short, Larry, 27
Simon, Yves: viii, xi, 203, 205, 224; economic theory of, 313–32; epistemology of, 54–82
Simpson, Peter, 264n2, 265n6
Smith, Quentin, 183n21
Smith, Randall B., x, 173–99, 335
Socrates, 89, 100, 177
Sokolowski, Robert, 56n5, 65n22, 70n34, 74
Song of Songs, 30
Sophocles, 189–90
Sorabji, Richard, 300n3
Stace, Walter, 27
Strauss, Leo, 264
Stolz, Anselm, 26
Styron, William, 229
Sufism, 27
Sullivan, Francis A., 34
Summa contra Gentiles, 30, 62, 116; and faith, 138–41; and metaphysics, 7, 13, 15, 16, 17
Summa theologiae, 9, 10, 13, 16, 25, 107; and Christology, 115–129; and epistemology, 63n14, 78, 80; and faith, 140–41; and mysticism, 32–46; anthropology of, 94–97

Tamisiea, David, 117
Tate, Allen, 228, 234
Taylor, Peter, 229
Tellkamp, Jörg Alejandro, 55n2, 66n25, 73n41
Teresa of Avila, 5, 101,
theology, ix–x, 130–49
Thomas Aquinas: viii, ix, 105, 176, 216, 226, 228, 254; and economics, 323; and gender: 288–90, 293–94; and mysticism, 23–24, 32–53; and ontology, 4–22,
Thomas of Sutton, 5
Thomas, Dylan, 192
Thomism, vii–xii, 8, 13–14, 26, 53–54, 71, 84n4, 131, 163, 228, 332; Neo-, 3–4, 70, 133, 209; Transcendental, 3, 13, 133
Tillich, Paul, 29
Torrell, Jean Pierre, 24n5, 45n84, 46n87, 47n91, 121
Totality and Infinity, 297–98, 311

Trapnell, Judson P., 42n68,
Tsakiridou, C. A., x, 203–25, 335

Underhill, Evelyn, 24n4, 27

Vanier, Jean, 308
Vann, Gerald, 294–95
Vargas Llosa, Mario, 187
Vatican Council I, 142–44
Vatican Council II, 130, 132, 150
Veblen, Thorstein, 321n23
Veritatis splendor, 177
virtue, 263–79
Vischer, Friedrich Theodor, 240
Von Balthasaar, Hans Urs, 132
Von Clausewitz, Carl, 306
Von Hügel, Friedrich, 23
Von Le Fort, Gertrude, 294–95

Wallace, William, 65n20, 65n21
Warren, Robert Penn, 229, 234
We Have Been Friends Together, 210–25
Weil, Simone, 249–50
White, Morton V., 103
Wilken, Robert Louis, 136
Wiles, Anne M., xi, 253–62, 335
Wilson, Nelly, 206
Wippel, John F., 78n54
work, 325–31
Work, Society, and Culture, 325–31

Yale, 253, 260

Zunic, Nikolaj, xi, 297–312, 336

PUBLICATIONS OF THE AMERICAN MARITAIN ASSOCIATION

GENERAL EDITORS

Anthony O. Simon (1990–2004)
Michael D. Torre (2009–2013)
Giuseppe Butera (2013–)

Jacques Maritain: The Man and His Metaphysics
Edited by John F. X. Knasas, 1988
ISBN 978-0-268-01205-2, (out of print)
Distributed by the University of Notre Dame Press

Freedom in the Modern World: Jacques Maritain, Yves R. Simon, Mortimer J. Adler
Edited by Michael D. Torre, 1989, Second Printing, 1990
ISBN 978-0-268-00978-6
Distributed by the University of Notre Dame Press

From Twilight to Dawn: The Cultural Vision of Jacques Maritain
Edited by Peter A. Redpath, 1990
ISBN 978-0-268-00979-3
Distributed by the University of Notre Dame Press

The Future of Thomism
Edited by Deal W. Hudson and Dennis Wm. Moran, 1992
ISBN 978-0-268-00986-1
Distributed by the University of Notre Dame Press

Jacques Maritain and the Jews
Edited by Robert Royal, 1994
ISBN 978-0-268-01193-2
Distributed by the University of Notre Dame Press

Freedom, Virtue, and the Common Good
Edited by Curtis L. Hancock and Anthony O. Simon, 1995
ISBN 978-0-268-00991-0
Distributed by the University of Notre Dame Press

Postmodernism and Christian Philosophy
Edited by Roman T. Ciapolo, 1997
ISBN 978-0-8132-0881-7
Distributed by the Catholic University of America Press

The Common Things: Essays on Thomism and Education
Edited by Daniel McInerny, 1999
ISBN 978-0-9669226-0-8
Distributed by the Catholic University of America Press

The Failure of Modernism:
The Cartesian Legacy and Contemporary Pluralism
Edited by Brendan Sweetman, 1999
ISBN 978-0-9669226-1-5
Distributed by the Catholic University of America Press

Beauty, Art, and the Polis
Edited by Alice Ramos, 2000
ISBN 978-0-9669226-2-2
Distributed by the Catholic University of America Press

Reassessing the Liberal State:
Reading Maritain's Man and the State
Edited by Timothy Fuller and John P. Hittinger, 2001
ISBN 978-0-9669226-3-9
Distributed by the Catholic University of America Press

Faith, Scholarship, and Culture in the 21st Century
Edited by Alice Ramos and Marie I. George, 2002
ISBN 978-0-9669226-5-3
Distributed by the Catholic University of America Press

Jacques Maritain and the Many Ways of Knowing
Edited by Douglas A. Ollivant, 2002
ISBN 978-0-9669226-4-6
Distributed by the Catholic University of America Press

Truth Matters: Essays in Honor of Jacques Maritain
Edited by John G. Trapani, Jr., 2004
ISBN 978-0-9669226-6-0
Distributed by the Catholic University of America Press

The Human Person and a Culture of Freedom
Edited by Peter A. Pagan Aguiar and Terese Auer, O.P., 2009
ISBN 978-0-9669226-7-7
Distributed by the Catholic University of America Press

Maritain and America
Edited by Christopher M. Cullen, S.J. and
Joseph Allan Clair, 2009
ISBN 978-0-9669226-8-4
Distributed by the Catholic University of America Press

The Renewal of Civilization:
Essays in Honor of Jacques Maritain
Edited by Gavin T. Colvert, 2010
ISBN 978-0-9669226-9-1
Distributed by the Catholic University of America Press

The Vocation of the Catholic Philosopher:
From Maritain to John Paul II
Edited by John P. Hittinger, 2010
ISBN 978-0-9827119-0-3
Distributed by the Catholic University of America Press

Reading the Cosmos: Nature, Science, and Wisdom
Edited by Giuseppe Butera, 2011
ISBN 978-0-9827119-1-0
Distributed by the Catholic University of America Press

Distinctions of Being: Philosophical Approaches to Reality
Edited by Nikolaj Zunic, 2013
ISBN 978-0-9827119-2-7
Distributed by the Catholic University of America Press

Love and Friendship: Maritain and the Tradition
Edited by Montague Brown, 2013
ISBN 978-0-9827119-3-4
Distributed by the Catholic University of America Press

Aquinas and Maritain on Evil: Mystery and Metaphysics
Edited by James G. Hanink, 2013
ISBN 978-0-9827119-4-1
Distributed by the Catholic University of America Press

Human Nature, Contemplation, and the Political Order: Essays Inspired by Jacques Maritain's Scholasticism and Politics
Edited by Peter Karl Koritansky, 2014
ISBN 978-0-9827119-5-8
Distributed by the Catholic University of America Press